Bernard St Jett

LANGUAGE AND ECONOMY

Voor Judith, voor de verandering

LANGUAGE AND ECONOMY

Florian Coulmas

BLACKWELL
Oxford UK & Cambridge USA

First Published 1992

Blackwell Publishers
108 Cowley Road
Oxford   OX4 1JF
UK

238 Main Street, Suite 501
Cambridge, Massachusetts 02142
USA

British Library Cataloguing in Publication Data
A CIP catalogue record for this book is available from
the British Library.

Library of Congress Cataloging-in-Publication Data

Coulmas, Florian.
    Language and economy / by Florian Coulmas.
        p.   cm.
    Includes bibliographical references and index.
    ISBN 0-631-18524-0
    1. Language and languages—Economic aspects.   2. Sociolinguistics.
I. Title.
P120.E27C6   1992
306.4'4—dc20   92-13158
                                                                              CIP

Typeset in 11 on 13 pt Garamond
by Best-set Typesetter Ltd., Hong Kong
Printed in Great Britain by T. J. Press Ltd, Padstow, Cornwall!

In like manner are languages gradually establish'd by human conventions without any promise. In like manner do gold and silver become the common measures of exchange.

> David Hume, *A Treatise of Human Nature*

The language barrier was for a long time forbidding. And great economic ideas were not expected to come from small countries.

> John Kenneth Galbraith, *A History of Economics: The Past as the Present*

CONTENTS

ANALYTIC TABLE OF CONTENTS

stitutes and maintains itself by means of it, as does business which needs communication competence in order to function. Under certain conditions, language-related expenditures can be subjected to cost-benefit analysis.

Chapter 5   Language Careers: *Economic Determinants of Language Evolution*

Which examines the socioeconomic conditions of the birth and death of languages and how they compete with each other. The role of writing is also discussed. It is demonstrated that the extension of language in space and time depends in an essential way on economic conditions.

Chapter 6   Economy in Language: *Economic Aspects of the Language System*

Linguistic subsystems such as lexicon and phonology have properties which can be described in terms of economic categories. This is taken as an indication of the fundamental relatedness of function and structure of language and languages, which can be grasped analytically, on one hand, by means of the notion of value familiar in linguistics and, on the other hand, by the principle of least effort. It is shown why languages can behave like economic systems and why the metaphor of exchange points the way to basic insights into the social functions and properties of language.

Chapter 7   Language Adaptation: *Differentiation and Integration*

Which deals with the relationship between language adaptation, a micro-sociolinguistic process of progressive systematic differentiation and integration, and language spread, a macro-sociolinguistic process of social change. Along the way, a dogma of mainstream linguistics is called into question, namely that value judgments about languages cannot be justified because all languages must be assumed to be equally good as regards their expressive potential. Against this position it is argued that it is well-adapted languages which have a better chance to spread and that well-adaptedness is one of the forces underlying language spread.

1

At Face Value: *The Metaphor of Exchange*

What we accept, or refuse to accept, at its face value is usually some-body's word or promise. By and of themselves metaphors cannot explain anything, but they often embody the linguistic distillate of a con-nection, intuitively felt or consciously grasped, which may warrant our attention and scrutiny. An analogy that is sedimented in language testifies to the comparability of two phenomena belonging to different realms of experience and discourse, and thus invites us to examine whether the regularities governing one of them are also valid for the other.

We speak of the stock of words, of linguistic loans, and the wealth of language, which many of us employ, confident or at least hopeful, that we can thus increase our own wealth. Already Solomon found that "the tongue of the just is *as* choice silver,"[1] and ever since it has been popular wisdom that speech, if not golden, is at least silver, which is why some weigh their every word or are careful not to spend too many.

Like coins words are minted and are in circulation as long as they are valid. They are the currency of the mind. We have liquid assets and are fluent in a language. When we come to terms, we agree on a price to be paid, and when we are insincere, we pay only lip service. By calling both language and money assets, we draw attention to their function for the unfolding of the individual. They are a potential which makes individuality possible by extending their possessors' range of action and thus socializing them.

A bill of exchange is something linguistic, and words are like bills standing, as they are, for something they are not. The childlike assumption that a word has a meaning inherent to it is like the naïve idea that money is valuable as such. Both can only be, however, what they are, because this is not so. They are essentially conventional in character and can fulfill their functions thanks to their abstractness – as a means of exchange of spiritual goods the one, and as one of material goods the other.

Word and Coin

The analogy of money and language which is so conspicuously encoded in language itself has often been regarded as mere stylistic decoration. For instance, in the early seventeenth century, Stefano Guazzo used it in his rhetorical teachings in order to point out that in public speech the valuable and useful must be separated from the futile and worthless.

> Just as all sorts of coins – golden, silver and copper – issue from a purse, expressions and other words of greater and lesser value come out of the speaker's mouth.[2]

In his critical account of the English language Thomas Nashe makes use of the same simile, somewhat coquettishly remarking that

> our English tongue of all languages most swarmeth with the single money of monasillables which are the onely scandall of it. Bookes written in them and no other, seeme like Shopkeepres boxes, that containe nothing else, saue halfepence, three-farthings and two pences.[3]

However, the analogy of word and coin has also a long tradition of being taken as an indication of a genuine connection between them. In his *Essay Concerning Human Understanding* John Locke, near the end of the seventeenth century, characterized words as "the common measure of commerce and communication," which is "no man's private possession" and the stamp they are current in "is not for any one at pleasure to change" (Locke 1959: 154). Without explicating this point, Locke describes the essence of language in terms which can be applied, with like cogency, to that of money. At about the same time, the metaphor of exchange that connects money and language appears in Leibniz's writings. In his essay "Concerning the use and improvement of the German language" he compares calculating with mental operations relying on, and making use of, language:

> By way of proceeding to the conclusion, instead of images and things, we often use words like ciphers or counters and thus eventually arrive at

the heart of the matter. From this it appears how important it is that words, as models of the mind and, as it were, bills of exchange, are well conceived, distinct, accessible, plentiful, current, and pleasing.[4]

To Leibniz language was "a mirror of the mind" (1983: 5), in the sense that a highly cultivated language reflects and reinforces the intellectual achievements of its speakers. As a language critic his concern was with the improvement of German so that it would become an instrument of precise reasoning.[5] His interest in the analogy thus was in comparing counters as an aid of calculating with words as an aid of thinking. Only a clear determination of the value of the former makes possible the reliable functioning of the latter. The surrogate character, which is peculiar to both words and counters, is what makes them comparable. Just as a less than fully developed numerical system "makes calculating slow and cumbersome," "the mind is held up too long" where an undifferentiated vocabulary necessitates roundabout expressions (p. 26). A monetary system comprising only coins of great denomination works after a fashion, but it is awkward, because it will often compel its users to put up with more than they bargained for. This process of purchase in excess of wants is comparable to the surplus of meaning generated where a specific concept is intended, but only a general term is available for expressing it, which, therefore, needs to be qualified by additional epithets and circumlocutions. A universalist at heart, Leibniz did not believe that, as a matter of principle, the expressive power of one language was greater than that of another. Nevertheless, he realized the advantage of precision. The smaller the unit, the greater the exactitude of the transactions that can be carried out in a system that uses it.

It was only a few decades later that David Hume in his *Treatise of Human Nature* made it clear that the analogy of word and coin was more than a matter of metaphorically elucidating one domain of human experience by the conceptual means of another. To him the analogy was founded in the parallel development and functions of language and money in society:

> In like manner are languages gradually establish'd by human conventions without any promise. In like manner do gold and silver become the common measures of exchange, and are esteem'd sufficient payment for what is of a hundred times their value. (Hume 1964: 263)

Both language and money were conceived by Hume as a convention without any promise, that is, without compulsion or constraint. To be

provided with one or the other implies no obligation for others to
accept, at face value or otherwise, what the possessor has to give.
Nothing can force the owner of a certain object to give it up even
if offered as much (or more) money as it is worth. And nobody is
compelled to take somebody else's word for what it means. Yet the
possession of money, by virtue of social contract, entails the possibility
of purchasing an object of like value, which in effect simply means that
the value of all things can be measured in money. The currency of a
country, according to Adam Smith, "is the exact measure of the real
exchangeable value of all commodities. It is so, however, at the same
time and place only" (Smith 1904: 39).[6] Correspondingly the value of
words is contingent upon temporarily and locally limited common
practice. A German contemporary of Smith, the philosopher Johann
Georg Hamann, addresses this connection in one of his essays in 1761:

> Money and language are two objects whose investigation is as profound
> and abstract as their use is common. Both are more closely related to each
> other than should be conjectured. The theory of the one explains that of
> the other; they seem to issue from common grounds. The wealth of all
> human knowledge is based on the exchange of words. . . . All treasures of
> civic and social life, on the other hand, are related to money as their
> universal measure.[7]

Hamann does not elaborate on this idea and, without trying to demonstrate exactly how "the theory of the one explains that of the other,"
confines himself to the observation that "in antiquity, eloquence was as
important for the affairs of state as financial matters" were in his time
(Hamann 1761/1967: 97).[8]

Words do not derive their meaning from their material substance – a
sequence of sounds, for example – but from the purposes they serve in
transmitting nonmaterial content, and likewise the value of money is
not based on its material embodiment, but on the function it fulfills as a
common means for the exchange of goods. Where the economic system
is little developed, the division of labor is at a low level, and moneymediated trade has replaced barter only in the form of a minted currency
of precious metal, the purely functional nature of money is not yet
clearly manifest. In the perception of the public the utility value of the
precious metal is still dominant: this obscures the function of money as a
universal measure of all values, which is quite independent of the value
of the metal in the form of which it appears. To this day this two-fold

function as a substitute and a value by virtue of its material substance, is embodied in coins worn as jewelry.

Attempts at explaining the meaning of words in terms of onomatopoeia point in the same direction.[9] They too start out from the assumption that rather than function, material form is the source from which meaning flows, that is, basic words allegedly echo sounds of nature. By believing in the identity of, or an essential link between, a word and its referent, word magic[10] too misjudges the true nature of linguistic meaning as a relationship between form and content based in social convention which has as its precondition the possibility of being different. *Nomen est conventio* rather than *nomen est omen*.

Commodity Value vs Functional Value

Money and language are among the most important social institutions. As the complexity of the social system increases and the relations between individual and society and the individuals among one another become ever more indirect, the purely functional character of the institutions which govern social intercourse comes more strongly to the fore. The magical aspects, or properties, of language are lost, and money is debunked of the nimbus of being of and by itself valuable. Words like coins or banknotes derive their value and meaning only from the use to which they are put by those whose intercourse they serve to mediate. At a time when most societal activities were already mediated through money, a few years before the French Revolution, Antoine de Rivarol was, therefore, able to declare with some justification:

> Words are like monies: they have a precise value before they express all the kinds of value.[11]

In de Rivarol's time, the commodity theory of value still had many adherents, yet, from the point of view of the economic layman, he put into words the basic insight of the functional theory of value which, he realized, could explain the intuitively grasped likeness of money and language. Both lack value in use but have value in exchange, which is called "purchasing power" by economists and "meaning" by linguists. In order to accomplish their purpose, these values must be indifferent to, and independent of, the individual. When I make a payment with money, my solvency is not called into question; on the contrary, the fact that I have money at my disposal is taken as proof of that, for which the whole of society is accountable. By the same token, a unique thought can be communicated only when the individual is prepared to this end to step back into the ranks of society by using current words deemed fit by the society at large. Thus, as de Rivarol saw it, "to change the meaning of the words of a language, is to alter the value of the moneys in an empire."[12]

This analogy cannot be accepted by those who deny that the roots of meaning are to be found outside the body of the linguistic sign in the interactional conventions governing its use. Marx is one prominent example. The mind, he suggests, is irrevocably under the curse of being afflicted with the material (Marx and Engels 1969: 30). Mind is an epiphenomenon producing reflections of matter in consciousness, with language being the embodiment of ideas. Hence his criticism of the comparison of language and money as means of exchange. Rather than being merely a means of making ideas communicable, language is the materialization of ideas and, as a matter of fact, their only form of existence. This notion is obviously commensurate with his notion of money which is basically related to the commodity theory of value, as it puts the commodity value of the precious metal at its center, rather than its function as mediating the exchange of goods. Thus, it is not surprising that, at one of the rare places where Marx explicitly comments on the nature of language, he criticizes as inadequate the idea that form and content in the linguistic sign should be related in a way similar to that of money and commodities.

> Language does not transform ideas, so that the singularity of ideas disappears and their social character runs alongside them as a separate entity, like prices alongside commodities. *Ideas do not exist separately from language.* Ideas which must be translated out of their mother tongue into a foreign language in order to circulate, in order to become exchangeable, offer more analogy; but the analogy then lies not in language, but in the foreign quality of it.[13]

The sentence I have emphasized is crucial for Marx's argument. Both in the analysis of money and of language, he insists, the material sign vehicle cannot be separated from its denotatum.[14] Since this claim is not so much based on a sound monetary theory or on the results of psychological research on the possibility of language-independent thought – which at the time was not in hand – but on philosophical conviction, it cannot seriously undermine the usefulness of our analogy. In the end, the philosophical question of how mental objects exist is for psychologists and perhaps neurologists to answer. Quite apart from this, however, Marx's account of language in the above quote suggests that he greatly overrates the difference between mother tongue and foreign language. This overemphasis which, given his commitment to the insoluble link between language and consciousness, he can hardly avoid, suggests that by language he does not mean an abstract universal system whose units serve as catalysts for concept formation, but a particular language. He fails to explain how, on the basis of this assumption, translation could be feasible. And from this point of view it is quite impossible to admit that translation is the basic form of all linguistic communication rather than the special case of conveying a message phrased in one language by means of another. The assumption that in the mental interaction of two individuals there is no threshold of foreignness to overcome only because they share the same mother tongue leads to extreme linguistic determinism. The mother tongue is attributed so strong an influence on thinking that the possibility of individuality would be severely curtailed, if not extinguished altogether. While members of the same speech community naturally communicate on the basis of the mutual assumption that they speak the same language, the actual identity of the code they use needs to be reaffirmed anew with every speech act. The foreignness that has to be surmounted in translation is thus only different in degree, but not in kind, from that inherent in forms of mental exchange using the same language.[15]

Change

A more obvious analogy of translation than the exchange of goods that is alienated through the intervening medium of money, as proposed by Marx, is currency exchange by means of which the moneychanger enacts the potential of expressing a certain value represented in one medium in terms of another. For the translator, too, the medial aspect is crucial. The translator's basic working hypothesis is that the ideas expressed in one language can be reproduced in another, and are hence independent of individual languages. Since no two languages can be mapped onto each other in a homologous manner, translation is generally thought to be an art rather than purely mechanical transposition. Consequently, the translator is proverbially suspected of being not only the honest broker, but a not entirely reliable artiste as well: "Translator, traitor." As illustrated in many dramas and novels, moneychangers do not fare much better in the opinion of the public. Translators and moneychangers have long shared this dubious repute. To recall but one piece of prominent testimony, the former, if we count them among the scribes, were expelled from the temple by the biblical Jesus together with the latter.

To look at money changing and translation as analogous processes is a direct consequence of the metaphor of exchange. Its fundamental significance for the human condition in both its social and individual aspects is that the possibilities of direct cooperative action without any intervening means are subject to very narrow limitations, and that, moreover, the individual's action becomes human to the extent that it is not immediate but mediated. This is the general insight embodied in Simmel's *Philosophy of Money*. In this massive work Simmel puts money at the center of an elaborate sociology of culture, emphasizing "the tremendous importance of money for understanding the basic motives of life." Money, he argues, is "the clearest expression and demonstration of the fact that man is a 'tool-making' animal" (Simmel 1978: 211). He finds the essence of human existence in the necessity of intermediate steps between ourselves and our ends. "Man is an indirect being" (Simmel 1978: 211). Human beings are not bound to the immediacy of natural drives and instincts, but lead a life aware of past and future. The capacity of consciously transcending the limitations of the here and now are at the heart of Simmel's view of humanity: "The concept of means characterizes the position of man in the world" (1978: 211). What he has in mind here, above all, is money which, because of its purely functional nature, he describes as "the ultimate means" (*das absolute Medium* (1977: 219)). Simmel's thoughts provide the most profound philosophical foundation of the functional value-theory of money. The notion that, in this regard, money shares essential features with language was, however, not alien to him, as evidenced by a number of explicit comments.

> Just as my thoughts must take the form of a universally understood language so that I can attain my practical ends in this roundabout way, so must my activities and possessions take the form of money value in order to serve my more remote purposes.[16]

At the same time Simmel realizes the social nature of the medium whose creation presupposes cooperative interaction in a community. The means which, he maintains, is entirely a social institution and quite meaningless if restricted to one individual, can bring about a change in general conditions only by changing the relations between individuals.[17]

At this point Simmel again refers to money which he also characterizes as "entirely a sociological phenomenon, a form of human interaction" (1978: 172). It would not be farfetched or inappropriate, however, to interpret his words as referring to language. It is more than a chronological coincidence that we find the following description of the social nature of language in Saussure's *Cours de linguistique générale* which, as is well-known, was conceived under the influence of Durkheim's sociology at about the same time as Simmel's book. Saussure explains

> . . . the social fact alone can create a linguistic system. The community is necessary if values that owe their existence solely to usage and general acceptance are to be set up; by himself the individual is incapable of fixing a single value.[18]

In Saussure's view of language the notion of value occupies a central position,[19] providing its characterization as a social fact, where, at the same time, "everything is basically psychological" (1974: 6), with more than trivial content; since, as conceived by Saussure, the notion of value encompasses both the social contract aspect and that of systematicity. Values, inasmuch as they have a bearing on human society, are relational rather than absolute entities. In Saussure's view this means more specifically that objects whose value is to be determined can, on the one hand, be substituted by objects of essential incompatability and, on the other hand, be compared with objects of essential likeness. Saussure explains this double relational structure in the midst of which the linguistic sign unfolds by means of the by now familiar analogy:

> To determine what a five-franc piece is worth one must therefore know: (1) that it can be exchanged for a fixed quantity of a different thing, e.g. bread; and (2) that it can be compared with a similar value of the same system, e.g. a one-franc piece, or with coins of another system (a dollar, etc.). In the same way a word can be exchanged for something dissimilar, an idea; besides, it can be compared with something of the same nature, another word. Its value is therefore not fixed so long as one simply states that it can be "exchanged" for a given concept, i.e. that it has this or that significance: one must also compare it with similar values, with other words that stand in opposition to it. Its content is really fixed only by the occurrence of everything that exists outside it.[20]

That the meaning of the linguistic sign is thus determined by things outside itself, that is, other signs belonging to the same system and ideas belonging to a different class of things, is a corollary of Saussure's conviction that in its essence language is form, not substance. It is "a convention, and the nature of the sign that is agreed upon does not matter" (1972: 10). It is a worthwhile exercise, I believe, once again to compare this characterization of language as a system of values based on contract with one of Simmel's analytical attempts to get to the bottom of money. A proper understanding of money is, according to him, hampered because "it is rarely appreciated how incredibly small is the quantity of material with which money renders its services" (Simmel 1978: 194). To the extent that money historically developed from a tangible into an abstract means of exchange it comes to realize its function proper:

> The form in which money exists for us is that of mediating exchanges and measuring values. . . . It is true that the functional value of money still needs to be represented. The decisive point, however, is that its value no longer arises from what represents it; on the contrary, the latter is quite secondary, and its nature has no importance except on technical grounds which have nothing to do with the sense of value.[21]

Like money, language manifests itself in material form, but in the former as in the latter the manifestation is external to the nature of the means and does not really matter. The important difference between sign and sign vehicle, between the sense and that which represents it, becomes apparent here. "Five francs" is an abstract unit of a certain monetary system as an element of which it has a value. The unit itself has no material existence, even though it presents itself to the users of the system in the form of tangible instances only. None of these instances can, however, be said to embody "the real five francs". Likewise a word is not a perceptible entity, but an abstract model instantiated more or less accurately in various audible and visible manifestations. This relationship that connects every instance with its model is decisive; without it money and language could not fulfill their functions as media of exchange; for, in order to mediate the exchange, every sign instance must be replaceable without qualification. If it was the individual sign instance which counted, there would be no substantial difference between the exchange of goods with and without the mediation of money.[22] The primary feature of money to act as a means rather than an object could then not unfold. Linguistic communication could obviously never be accomplished if the same word instance had to be reproduced whenever we want to say what another said earlier or repeat ourselves; for, as a matter of principle, it is physically impossible to reproduce the same phonetic instance. This is what Bühler (1976: 29) called the "principle of abstractive relevance."

Phlogiston and Bogus Money

In commenting on Marx's definition of language as the embodiment, or "reification," of consciousness we touched upon the question of whether or to what extent language and money are independent of their material manifestations, a point to which we now return for more detailed discussion. Bühler can be quoted here as another witness supporting our claim that a careful comparison of language and money will shed light on the social functions of both. In his original and authoritative work *Sprachtheorie* he addresses himself to this connection.

> The counterpart of the sign process is the *exchange of goods*. Let us clarify how trademark products, coins, and words, the three objects of circulation, can be formalized by means of a schematic comparison.[23]

We shall restrict our attention here to the latter two, coins and words. The indifference vis-à-vis the individual coin, its essential substitutability, finds expression, Bühler argues, in that "the partners engaging in the traffic rely, by and large, on the agreement that 'dollar is dollar'" (Bühler 1934: 60). The qualification "by and large" is of some consequence for Bühler's further line of argumentation, for "in certain respects words in linguistic intercourse work even more independently of matter (in a desubstantiated, abstract way) than dollars" (Bühler 1934: 60). Exactly what he means by this, he explains as follows.

> The coin has an imprint put on it by the die. When we engage in an unsuspecting sales act, we do not examine it at length but rely on recognizing it at a glance. However, where doubts arise as to whether it is genuine, it may be more prudent to inspect the piece or refuse to accept it. Unsuspecting linguistic interaction does not usually bear the risk of a later loss. As long as we know what a phonematically badly

minted coin is supposed to be, according to the speaker's intention, we
can accept it; where necessary we can re-coin it in order to avert mis-
understanding or to advise the speaker.[24]

Clearly, Bühler here thinks of the form of words only and fails to
recognize that the analogy with the minted coin also applies to its
content. But the metaphor as it is frozen in the language refers to the
relation between form and content, rather than to form alone. To take
something at face value has to do with the meaning that is supposedly
associated with the form of an utterance. Some of the implications of
taking words at face value are best sorted out by reviewing an old
problem. It has to do with how combustion occurs and what happens
when things are consumed by fire. Until modern times, there was no
satisfactory answer. Not long ago, around the turn of the eighteenth
century, the most influential theory centered about the notion of phlogiston. Combustability, went the idea, was the property of a certain
substance which made it possible for physical objects to burn and then
be set free during combustion. This substance was called "phlogiston."
It was only through the discovery of oxygen that this theory was
rendered obsolete and phlogiston proven to be a chimera. Thus "phlogiston," quite literally, turned out to be an empty word, a word without
content, that is, without a referent in the material world.

   In this regard, one might want to argue, "phlogiston" is hardly
uncommon, belonging, as it does, to the same group of words as
"unicorn," "centaur," "cyclops" and many others. Yet, there are important differences here. A centaur has certain properties, for example, a
human-like upper part of the body on a horse-like torso. Some centaurs
even have names, Chiron, for instance, who was said to be gifted with
great wisdom. However, when talking about centaurs, we leave the level
of discourse which is grounded in the world of facts and enter a fictitious
world where words are not expected to derive their meanings from
referring to reality. But "phlogiston" is not part of a fictional discourse.
Rather, its use implied the claim that it referred to a natural phenomenon which was its denotatum, namely the substance phlogiston. Intuitively it is clear that the realization that men with hipparchic rumps do
not really exist has implications for the future of the race of centaurs
which are quite different from the implications of the realization that
there is no substance that has the property of combustibility for the
continued "existence" of phlogiston and phlogiston theory. "Centaur" is
like play-money, "phlogiston" like bogus money. Not too fine a point

should be put on this aspect of the analogy, however, since "phlogiston" was not brought into circulation with the intent to deceive and harm others. The tertium quid is that both words like "phlogiston" and counterfeit money do not stand the test of genuineness and, therefore, on the level of exchange to which they seemingly belong, fail to fulfill the promise they profess to embody.

Materialization of Language and Dematerialization of Money

Let us return to Bühler. By comparing only the *"phonematic imprint* on the *sound pattern* of words" (1934: 61) with stamped coins while ignoring the contents of monetary and linguistic signs, he confines his thoughts to the material aspects of the sign process. He states a word is

> a sign-thing, while a dollar will always be rooted in the realm of goods, however much, in the form of paper, it approximates the sign-things. For, although you cannot eat it, you can obtain something for it through a purchasing act, which cannot usually be said of "linguistic coins." (1934: 61)

Is this, hence, where the analogy of money and language is exhausted, because the former but not the latter is essentially a material thing? This would be, I believe, a premature conclusion. Certain technological innovations allow us to realize that the difference stressed by Bühler is rather problematic and must not be overemphasized. These innovations concern the dematerialization of money and the materialization of language. Some banks nowadays work without cash. American banks spearheaded this development in order to reduce the losses afflicted on them by forms of robbery which are rapidly becoming outmoded.[25] A steadily growing part of money transfer is carried out electronically, without a coin or a banknote ever changing their position, indeed in the absence of coins or banknotes. To be sure, the ultimate trace – an electronic recording of credits and debts; its representation on paper – must remain. But is this fundamentally different from language?

We can conceive of a word as an abstract model which can be manifested in indefinitely many different instantiations. This concept is no less valid, however, for money than for the linguistic sign. Bühler points out that every dollar bill is stamped with an individual mark of identification, a serial number which is different from all others. But when I have $10,000 in my bank account, the particular bills and serial numbers do not matter. As a matter of fact, such a bank deposit does not even mean that there are certain dollar bills at a certain place which is my account. Only in the event that I want to convert my deposit into cash will every one of the bills have its unmistakable imprint and number.

A similar relation obtains between a word as the common property of all who know it and its concrete realizations, for example, printed on this page or verbalized by an individual speaker. Under the microscope every printed realization of the word differs, however minutely, from every other, just as every spoken realization bears the unique mark of the individual speaker's voice quality at a given time and place. This uniqueness of the human voice can be exploited for certain practical purposes. Sophisticated speech recognition techniques make it possible to use passwords as keys for opening doors. To this end the word in question, pronounced by a certain speaker, is recorded and serves as the pattern against which all other instances are matched. Electronic speech recognition programs are now accurate enough to guarantee that only the same speaker can reproduce other instances of the password sufficiently similar to be accepted as a trigger for the door-opening mechanism. And the word must be pronounced carefully, for even a slight cold or a piece of chewing gum may be enough to cause a mismatch and frustrate the speaker. It might seem, then, that a material object, a door key, which heretofore one had to carry in order to open the door, has been replaced by something immaterial, namely the remembrance, or should we say: the memory, of a word.

However, the realization of the password as a key is no less physical than the realization of the dollar credited to my account. The door-opening mechanism is not triggered by the abstract model of the word,[26] but by its material realization in an actual utterance. Whether or not the password has a meaning is irrelevant, and its use is thus not typical of how language works. Of course, this kind of oblique use of words can also be encountered, on occasion, in human communication, but, as a general rule, the identification of a form is not dissociated from the understanding of its meaning. The "re-coining" of a word referred to by Bühler involves both. To map "a phonematically badly minted coin" onto a model may be quite difficult out of context, but where clues as to the possibly intended meaning are available, such a task is easily accomplished.

This does not mean, however, that we know exactly how it is

accomplished in every normal act of verbal communication, because two fundamental questions concerning the performance of the linguistic sign are still waiting to be answered. They have to do with the linguistic aspects of the old mind–body problem.

Saussure thought of the linguistic sign as an entirely psychological entity. The linguistic sign, according to him, is the relation between a sound-*image*, acting as the "signifier," and a concept, acting as the "signified." Both the signifier and the signified are psychological entities, the association between them being sanctioned in the language. As pointed out above, every sign can be realized only as a physical event. How this physical event, which can be described in its various phases as consisting in muscle movements, sound waves, and neuro-electronic impulses, is mapped onto the non-physical, abstract model is still largely a mystery. We are quite ignorant both of how concrete auditory events are identified with an abstract sound-image, and how this is then matched with a concept. The dispute about the reality of Popper's "world 3" has not been concluded. There are those who assume that mental states exist independently of the universe of physical entities and can, indeed, exercise an influence on matter,[27] and there are others who believe that the Cartesian dualism of the psychophysical is no more than a cultural commonplace which must be replaced by the insight that the conscious mind is a biological phenomenon.[28] It is far from clear yet which party will eventually prevail. We do not know whether, in order to explain the relationships obtaining between sign-event and sign-model and between sound-image and concept, it is really necessary to postulate the existence of mental entities not reducible to physical states. As long as this is an open question, Bühler's claim that money, but not the linguistic sign, is bound to matter, must be taken for what it is, a conjecture. It should be taken seriously, but not as an established fact.

Banknotes and words incorporate the interesting relationship between the uniqueness of a material object and the universality of an abstract object. It is only on account of it that they can fulfill their function as means of exchange. Although, as has become evident by now, money and language have often enough been metaphorically linked to each other, this particular parallel is frequently overlooked. For example, Eco identifies words and coins as signs "which have an abstract prototype which no one has ever seen" (Eco 1979: 58), but at the same time emphasizes the difference between the two, which, he maintains, rests in the fact that coins, but not words, have a commodity value. Clearly, he ignores both the material side of words and the spiritual side of coins.

As regards their functions, the difference between coin and banknote is one of degree rather than kind. Paper too has a commodity value, however small. Decisive, however, is the fact that as means of exchange and measure of value coins and banknotes fulfill exactly the same function, and that there is no difference in principle in the relation between nominal value and commodity value of coin and note.

Eco derives the value of coins from the commodity value of metal, while assigning words no value at all. He argues that "the only difference between a coin and a word is that the word can be reproduced without economic effort while a coin is an irreproducible item" (Eco 1979: 25). To this notion we must take exception, because, unwittingly perhaps, Eco seems to compare the individual concrete coin with the abstract word model. For, of words he claims that they can be spent indefinitely without ever exhausting the total amount of available words. This is untenable when we think of words as individual instances. To utter or in whichever way produce words consumes time and energy.[29] The stock of utterable words is hence finite in exactly the same sense as the raw material of which coins are struck.

But there is another difference between dispensing words and money which cannot be denied. Retaining the memory of a $100 bill is clearly not the same as retaining the memory of a word. As long as I retain a word in my memory, I can spend it again and again, but retaining dollars in my memory does not help me pay next month's bills. An analysis of this distinction between the two means was proposed by Luhmann. In his system-theoretic approach, money is "an instance of symbolically generalized representation" (Luhmann 1988: 232) which must be understood as a means of communication serving the purpose of regulating social relationships. Communication of this kind differs characteristically from what he calls "normal communication," that is, verbal transfer of information. Like Eco, he insists that "by making a payment the payer loses what the beneficiary obtains" (1988: 247), whereas "by making an utterance the speaker loses nothing, but retains what he gives away" (p. 246). The paradoxical phrase should not lure us away from the real problem; for that which the speaker gives away is not the same as that which he retains. What he retains is the sense of what he said and the capability of repeating it – not infinitely often, however. What he gives away is a concrete utterance item which, assuming, for instance, that it is insulting, can cost him dearly.

The material side of words is no less important than that of money, be it as a coin or bill. Words can have a commodity value. If that were

not the case, the entire guild of phrase-mongers (not just the unfortu-
nate majority) could not make a living. Although it is not the unique
instance of a word that is being paid for whenever words are being paid
for – herein lies the fundamental difference between verbal and fine art –
words cannot realize their commodity value unless they are presented in
material form. While Saussure claims "that language is only a system of
pure values" (1974: 111), something entirely abstract, he also points out
that it

> is at every moment everybody's concern; spread throughout society and
> manipulated by it, language is something used daily by all. Here we are
> unable to set up any comparison between it and other institutions.[30]

Individuals can use language daily only as utterance events. This duality
of being an abstract system of values which becomes tangible only in the
concrete event, is not unique to language. It is also characteristic of
money. This is why Simmel would surely have contradicted the last
sentence in the above quote from Saussure. As a social institution he
sees language stand side by side with religion, moral custom, law, and
money, whose essential significance he identifies as mediating the unique
subjective mind with the general objective mind of society:

> In some respects, money may be compared to language, which also lends
> itself to the most divergent directions of thought and feeling. Money
> belongs to those forces whose peculiarity lies in a lack of peculiarity.[31]

Inflation of Ideas

The value of money and language as means of exchange rests not in
their singular employment, but in the fact that society recognizes the
relationship obtaining between the general concept and the particular
instance. The fundamental prerequisite for upholding this symbolic
relationship, which is valid once and for all and reaffirmed in every
instance, is mutual trust. The potential lack of trust proves it to be a
social rather than a natural fact and thus relativizes its general validity
and justification. Distrust in money or language is more than just a
theoretical possibility. Where it is nourished, society is rocked to its
very foundations.

The advent of paper money was accompanied with suspicion. Because of incompetence, lack of control, and abuse of the new instrument for the cancellation of public debts, this was understandable. But these defects as well as the mistrust also result from the failure to grasp the abstract nature of money as such, both on the part of those using it and those having the right to issue it. That a scrap of intrinsically worthless paper should be accepted as payment, is hardly less in need of explanation than the fact that a sequence of intrinsically meaningless sounds is accepted as an expression of ideas. Good faith is even more necessary here than the insight that money, rather than being a value, only measures values, and that words derive their meaning from that which they are not, namely their relationships to objects, mental experiences and all other words.

Goethe, as we know from his secretary, Eckermann, adopted a very skeptical attitude towards paper money, to which, in the second part of *Faust*, he gave expression by presenting it as a piece of devilry. Eckermann (1955: 356f.) makes it clear that Goethe had in mind the disastrous monetary experiments which for most of his contemporaries had resulted in paper money being discredited. The most famous case during Goethe's lifetime was the assignats of the French Revolution, but he was also aware of the peculiar designs of John Law, the Scottish financier who went down in history as the inventor of the land bank that would issue notes against the security of the land of the country.[32] Adam Smith described his plan as follows:

> That the industry of Scotland languished for want of money to employ it, was the opinion of the famous Mr. Law. By establishing a bank of a particular kind, which he seems to have imagined might issue paper to the amount of the whole value of all the lands in the country, he proposed to remedy this want of money. . . . The splendid, but visionary ideas still continue to make an impression upon many people, and have, perhaps, in part, contributed to that excess of banking, which has of late been complained of both in Scotland and in other places. (Smith 1904: 300f.)

The "excess of banking" and the idea to use land as the supporting asset of notes show up in *Faust* as part of a diabolic plot. To the Emperor's impatient command, "Our need is gold;[33] then get it, here and now," Mephistopheles mockingly replies: "Your want I'll solve, and make still greater levy." He then persuades the Emperor to replenish his empty coffers by issuing treasury certificates on the gold still hidden in the ground. Later, the Emperor is surprised to find out that the scheme actually seemed to work, asking his treasurer:

> And do my people value this as gold,
> Do court and army think these payments hold?
> However much amazed, my will submits.[34]

Whereupon the Lord Seneschal explains how rapidly the new money has come into circulation:

> None now has power to stay the flying chits,
> They ran as quick as lightning on their way,
> And money-booths kept open night and day,
> Where every single note is honoured duly
> With gold and silver – though with discount, truly.[35]

The seemingly harmless qualification, "though with discount," indicates the reason why the introduction of paper money was regarded with alarm and suspected of satanic origin. Like elusive words it could not be seized and was threatened by devaluation. A "convention without promise," it can dissolve into thin air, as soon as those who established it cease to adhere to it. Money is as elusive as words, whose deceptive character nobody exploits more shrewdly than Mephistopheles himself.[36]

The users of a currency and the participants in a language are a community of mutually dependent creditors. Only the belief that the others will uphold it lets me do so, and thus makes the convention hold good. It is an expression of more than just piety that the Americans turn to Him, whose importance for their society supposedly surpasses everything else, to get a blessing for what the uninitiated observer might tend to think they actually value most. *In God we trust* is stamped on every coin and every dollar bill, a maxim which also betrays the vague anxiety that trust in the social institution, which depends on the support of all individuals, cannot be unlimited. That such anxiety is not without reason has been proven time and again in a way sparing no one and thus understandable to all, inflation. The most celebrated example to date is the German inflation of 1921–3. Galbraith (1976: 166) gives us a sense of what it was like.

> At the middle of 1921, domestic prices were 35 times the 1913 level. . . .
> The increase continued in 1922; at the end of that year they were 1475 times higher than before the war. Then in 1923, things became serious. By 27 November 1923 domestic prices stood at 1,422,900,000,000 times the pre-war level. Prices of imported items were up a bit more.

The social contract had been broken and turned out to be an empty phrase, quite literally not worth the paper it was printed on. The affinity of hollow word and worthless banknote was, in the course of events, demonstrated in a way that was both most ironic and provided the Germans an opportunity to live up to their reputation as a nation of philosophers and poets. On various occasions the press was employed not only to add more zeros, but also to adorn the inflation bills with quotations from Goethe's *Faust*. A note with a face value of one trillion marks shows Gretchen exclaiming in despair: "The lure of gold has power to hold the hearts of all: alas for all us poor."[37] Another note of the same year with a face value of 500 billion marks epitomizes the actual equivalence of worthless monies and meaningless words by quoting the pettifogging linguistics by which Mephistopheles confuses Faust's student. Since words and concepts are linked only by convention, they can also be dissociated, and the former can be used in the absence of the latter. The credulous student suggests "that words must have some meaning underlying," but Mephistopheles instructs him otherwise.

> Why yes, agreed,
> But never fear to find that mortifying,
> For if your meaning's threatened with stagnation,
> The words come in to save the situation:
> They'll fight your battles well if you enlist 'em,
> Or furnish you a universal system.
> Thus words will serve us grandly for a creed,
> Where every syllable is guaranteed.[38]

Those who trust these words in the sense intended by Mephistopheles, however, destroy the foundations of trustworthiness. To use words devoid of conceptual content, pretending that they had one, is like increasing the amount of money in circulation in the absence of any increase in the gross societal product, that is, the totality of collectively created values. Both involve abuse, endangering the utility of the entire system.

The inflation at the beginning of the 1920s and the stock exchange crash at the end demonstrated the vulnerability of a system that for the exchange of goods depended on a means founded solely on convention. The shock of this experience had thoroughgoing sociopsychological consequences which are yet to be fully appreciated. One of the questions to be pursued in this connection is whether the preoccupation of this century's philosophy with the means of the exchange of spiritual goods is not one of them. The old philosophical question, "What is truth?" has been reduced, or sharpened – depending on how one evaluates this turning away from metaphysics, ontology, and ethics – to linguistic criticism. What logical positivism, analytic philosophy, phenomenology, existentialism, hermeneutics, and structuralism have in common is an interest in language. Language reform was promoted as a remedy of faulty reasoning (Russell 1918); the formulation of truth conditions of sentences was put at the center of the only proper explication of truth (Carnap 1934); the philosopher's task was described as advancing beyond language to the phenomena as such (Husserl 1913); language was claimed as "the home and foundation of being" (Heidegger 1951); it was understood as "the horizon of a hermeneutic ontology" (Gadamer 1960); its double articulation was taken as the universal paradigm of the structures underlying human society (Lévi-Strauss 1958); the problem of translation was seen to hold the key to an understanding of the world and ourselves (Quine 1960); discourse was contemplated philosophically as a reality in itself (Habermas 1976); and a "post-structuralist" approach to understanding the world by way of deconstruction presents itself as "grammatology" (Derrida 1967). In all of these cases, philosophy appears as the critique of the means that makes possible the exchange of ideas, rather than of the ideas themselves. In a form which is a part rather than a reflection of the language of advertising, the philosophical aporia presents itself in the 1960s by the "insight" that "the medium is the message" (McLuhan 1964).

Balance

Summarizing the deliberations of this chapter, we are compelled to recognize that there is more to the conceptual comparison of language and money than a capricious metaphor.[39] It is grounded in the fact that the essence of both is to act as means of exchange, which, however, does not mean that this homology can exhaustively explain them. Exploring its details can, nevertheless, be instructive when we are interested in the social nature of language and money and in their utility for society. Language must be regarded as valuable not only in ideal, but also in material terms, and the value of money transcends by far its function as a means of exchange of economic goods. Both owe their existence to the mutual dependence of people, although they distance them from each other by socially mediating their interactions. There are, moreover, relationships between them which are important for the constitution of society: money also fulfills communicative functions and language economic ones.

It is the objective of the following chapters to explore these relationships. The assumption for which metaphorical evidence has been provided here is that, unless we understand the economics of language and languages, we cannot understand the development of the linguistic map of the world. On the other hand, a proper understanding of certain economic developments (and mismanagement) is dependent upon taking words at face value, that is, recognizing language as an economic factor in its own right.

2

"Language is an Asset":
Language and Money in the Development of National Economies

Multilingualism as an Indicator of Social Wealth

"Language is an asset." This well-known adage has flown out of many a writer's pen on various occasions. How is it to be understood, and in what sense, if any, is it justified? These are the questions addressed in this chapter.

In 1988, Britain's 57 million inhabitants had a per capita income of US $12,810, an achievement in which speakers of seven languages had a part. The 59 million Filipinos call a total of 164 languages their own. Their per capita income in the same year was $630.

The 14.5 million residents of the Netherlands are composed of five language groups. The per capita income there was $14,520 in 1987. $480 was the per capita income of the 23 million Sudanese in that year. 135 languages are spoken in Sudan.

Japan with a population of 122 million boasted a per capita income of $21,020 in 1988, as compared to the $440 per capita income of Indonesia's 174 million in that year. Five different languages are spoken in Japan, 659 in Indonesia.

The 8 million Swedes had a per capita income of $19,300 in 1988 in which, counting generously, five language groups had a share. Papua New Guinea's 3.7 million inhabitants had a per capita income of $810, but as many as 849 languages.[1]

What do these figures mean? They are summarized together with some others in Table 2.1. On the pages that follow we will attempt to find out whether they can be related to each other in a meaningful way.

Objections against using per capita income or per capita GNP as a

Table 2.1 Comparison of per capita income and number of languages in some industrial and developing countries.

Country	Population (millions)	Per capita income ($)	Number of languages
Ethiopia	50	120 (1987)	120
France	56	16,090 (1988)	10
Vietnam	64	180 (1985)	77
Germany (FRG)	60	18,480 (1988)	7
Philippines	59	630 (1988)	164
UK	57	12,810 (1988)	7
Chad	5	160 (1987)	117
Denmark	5	18,450 (1988)	4
Benin	4.5	390 (1987)	52
Iceland	0.25	21,660 (1987)*	1
Bolivia	6	570 (1988)	38
Uruguay	3	2,470 (1988)	1
Indonesia	174	440 (1988)	659
Japan	122	21,020 (1988)	5
Sudan	23	480 (1988)	135
Netherlands	14.5	14,520 (1987)	5
Sweden	8	19,300 (1988)	5
Papua New Guinea	3.7	810 (1988)	849

* Per capita GNP.

comparative indicator of economic development are well-known and to some extent justified,[2] but for our considerations they are irrelevant. Our concern is not with an accurate comparison of the wealth of individual societies, but with revealing certain tendencies. However crude a measure for detailed economic assessment, per capita income can serve a useful purpose here. For the same reason it is of no importance that the above table includes figures from different years.

A similar point must be made regarding the number of languages given for a country. Counting languages is difficult, on one hand, for theoretical reasons,[3] and, on the other, there is the practical question of how many speakers a language should be spoken by in order to be taken into consideration in such a count. Turkish is spoken by some 1.5 million people in Germany, Japanese only by a few thousand. The Turkish language group has, moreover, become much more acclimatized in the former Federal Republic of Germany (FRG) than the Japanese, for, although the latter are as conspicuous in Düsseldorf as the former are in Berlin and many other cities, most of the individuals of the Japanese colony stay for a few years only, while many of the Turks are second generation residents. Clearly it makes more sense to count Turkish among the languages of Germany than Japanese. Another aspect is the question of autochthonous versus migrant groups. Scots Gaelic is an autochthonous language of the British Isles, but since its native speaker community is rapidly dwindling away, it has only a sentimental claim to be counted among the languages of the UK. By contrast, Chinese arrived in the UK quite recently, but with some 150,000 speakers it is an undeniable presence.[4] Exactly how many languages are spoken in the UK or in Germany may thus be a controversial question which cannot be settled here. The point at issue is the order of magnitude: one-digit numbers for the industrialized countries and two- to three-digit numbers for the developing countries.

These observations indicate that the contention that language is an asset must not be taken to mean that a multiplicity of languages is conducive to social wealth. Rather, the inverse connection seems to suggest itself and has, indeed, been interpreted as a causal rather than merely an accidental correlation. Pool (1972: 222) reduced it to the short formula that "linguistically highly fragmented countries are always poor." If a causal relationship exists, there is, however, still the question as to the directionality of the causality. We will have to come back to this point later. Pool's formulation of the relationship between multilingualism and social wealth allows for the possibility that linguistically highly homogeneous countries are also poor, for which it is not difficult to find examples. (With only two languages, the 6 million population of Rwanda is highly homogeneous, not only for African standards. The per capita income there was $320 in 1988.) However, it is ruled out that a high level of socioeconomic development is compatible with linguistic fragmentation. This view reflects an opinion popular with many language planners which is based on the high degree of coincidence of virtual and, more importantly, perceived monolingualism and economic development observed in the industrialized world.

The fact that in most industrial economies, population and speech community are highly congruent means that, even in countries where several languages enjoy official status, the configuration of the nation state makes one language altogether dominant,[5] while the others are reduced, to a greater or lesser degree, to the function of folkloristic accessories of symbolic rather than practical significance. Government, in particular, functions by and large in one language, and where such is not the case, this is generally seen as a defect which finds expression, as witnessed time and again in Belgium or Yugoslavia, in a weak state. Linguistic homogeneity is a peculiar feature of the states of Europe where it is perceived as natural and advantageous.[6] Switzerland is the only conspicuous exception which proves the rule. Participation in three major neighboring culture languages has become a positive component of national identity, while the shadowy existence of the fourth official language, Rhaeto-Romance, underscores the special character of Switzerland's multilingual identity. Multilingualism appears in many different forms. It co-exists with prosperity only where very particular languages are involved. Especially in countries lacking an overarching common language which is known not only to a thin elite, but serves as the most important vehicle of regulating political and commercial relations, as in many African states, multilingualism usually coincides with a low level of economic development.

Common Language and "Protestant Ethic"

What are the underlying reasons for this correlation of linguistic multiplicity and economic poverty? We can only hope to find a satis-factory answer to this question if we keep two important things in mind. First, the virtual monolingualism of most European states is not a condition that is naturally given, but the result of a process which took centuries to complete. Second, with regard to languages, the industrial countries and the developing countries differ not only in that the former have few and the latter many; there are also qualitative differences between their respective languages. The most important of these is a feature usually played down by linguists,[7] but appreciated as highly important by sociologists, namely literacy. Social scientists have traditionally recognized writing as the key criterion distinguishing "civilized" from "primitive" societies. The justification of this view has been called into doubt, especially in connection with the blows that the optimistic belief in the continuous progress and elevation of humanity suffered on account of the atrocities committed in this century by the most "civilized" of societies. However, one need not conceive of devel-opment as moral progress in order to acknowledge the difference between the two kinds of societies.[8] Most social scientists continue to rely on this criterion, including those who have taken exception to the notion of "primitive society." Some have even attached more importance to it, for example Goody (1977) who, instead of posing primitive against civilized societies, prefers to speak of literal and oral societies.

The European culture languages which play such an important role nowadays, not only in the framework of the European state system, but on a worldwide scale, made their appearance gradually from the tenth century. How could they succeed in being established as the authoritative vehicles of literature, as the media of interchange in government and culture? An investigation of this question can reveal how far the development of language reflects and, perhaps, influences socioeconomic development. That the development or 'Ausbau' (Kloss 1967) of these languages coincided with the transition from the middle ages to modernity and thus with the emergence of a capitalist economic order is only a general observation calling for closer examination. The point at issue is to find out whether and in what sense this coincidence was a necessary one, and if so, what it implies for the assessment of language as a spiritual and material phenomenon. As pointed out in the previous chapter, language, from a Marxist point of view, is seen as the reification of consciousness and thus belongs to the sphere of material phenomena. Without denying that language does have certain important material aspects, we now turn to the greatest critic of Marx's philosophical imagination, Max Weber, whose works on economic history represent a countermodel to dialectical materialism.

Weber's concern was to demonstrate that

> the question of the motive forces in the expansion of modern capitalism is not in the first instance a question of the origin of the capital sums which were available for capitalistic uses, but, above all, of the development of the spirit of capitalism.[9]

This approach was directed against Marx's one-sided materialistic view of history, but it was not, as has sometimes been suggested, a design for replacing it with an equally one-sided spiritualistic interpretation of history and culture. Rather, he was intent to show that economic history cannot be explained on the basis of economic factors alone, but, in addition to a proper consideration of economic, geographical, and political facts, what he termed *Wirtschaftsethik*, the spirit of economic life, also had to be taken into account as a major influence on the development of the capitalist system of economy. Central to his con-

siderations is the idea that the rational conduct of business is a consequence of Christian ascetism, which especially the Reformation had
elevated to an all-pervasive guiding principle of everyday life. For, in
his account, rather than being a liberation of ecclesiastical coercion,
the Reformation

> meant the repudiation of a control which was very lax, at that time
> scarcely perceptible in practice, and hardly more than formal, in favor
> of a regulation of the whole of conduct which, penetrating to all de-
> partments of private and public life, was infinitely burdensome and
> earnestly enforced.[10]

"Protestant ethic" in this view was the identification of the fulfillment of duty in worldly affairs with a pious way of living acceptably to
God. This 'spirit of capitalism" is epitomized in Luther's conception of
a calling (*Beruf*) which Weber perceived as the "central dogma of all
Protestant denominations" (1920: 80). The reinterpretation of Christian
ascetism, from a command whose violation could be repaired through
confession and penance to an uncompromising principle of domesti-
cating everyday life, turned the efficient and dutiful conduct of worldly
labor into an expression of morality and piety. The pursuit of material
riches was thus freed from moral stigma. Prosperity and salvation were
no longer mutually exclusive aims in life, but were seen as virtually
the same endeavor. However, the possibilities of taking pleasure in
one's possessions were at the same time severely restricted by ascetic
regulations. Prodigality was incompatible with a God-fearing life.
Taken together, these two factors, the acquisition of wealth through
deliberate work and the forced renunciation of its idle enjoyment,
formed the foundation of capitalist ethics, which was more conducive to
the accumulation of capital and its use for investment than any other
religiously sanctioned system of moral conduct for all.

Weber's analysis of the link between the Reformation and the rise of
capitalism in Europe is based on the study of numerous theological and
other religious documents, which, in his interpretation, must be seen as
having a bearing not only on the formation of a new conception of
religious creed, but on socially sanctioned ways of livelihood as well.
His view of cult and social institutions as different expressions of a
common psychological attitude has been criticized as one-sided in that
it attributes too much weight to spiritual as opposed to material factors,
but it is still absorbing and warranting of careful deliberation.

One of the most obvious and hence least conspicuous features of the texts Weber examines is that most of them were written in German, Dutch, or English, not in Latin. Weber paid surprisingly little attention to this most important fact which, far from being an accidental concomitant of the Reformation, was both a precondition of its success and one of its most consequential results. Without phrasing the gospel in the common language, the regimentation of everyday life, as achieved by the Protestant ethic, would have been quite impossible. Baxter's *Christian Directory*, the religious diary as God's book-keeping, where "the relation of a sinner to his God [is compared] with that of customer and shopkeeper" (Weber 1920: 124), and other Puritan texts Weber analyzed, could have produced no effect had theological discourse continued to be conducted in the language of learning, Latin. The same can be said of the institution of lay priests, so important to many Protestant sects, and of the *Entzauberung der Welt*, "the rationalization of the world" (p. 117). Scientific insights could only be communicated to a wider audience with a language that was closer to their speech than the Catholic language of the time, Latin.

The controversy between the Reformers and their opponents was fought out to a great extent in writing. Throughout Europe the Protestant clergy promoted the use of vernacular languages with the hope of facilitating the conversion of the native population. In many languages religious texts are, therefore, the earliest written documents. The evangelical principle that everyone had the right to read the scriptures in his or her mother tongue became one of the principal weapons for wresting the monopoly of exegesis from the Catholic church. By translating the Bible into the profane languages of the common people, access to religious wisdom was made independent of knowledge of the sacred languages. These Bible translations were major achievements because, rather than pouring the conceptual contents from one linguistic container into another which was equally suitable, they contributed to making the vernaculars more suitable for higher communicative functions than they previously were. Of course, the works of individual writers must not be overrated, and the Reformation must not be seen as opening up entirely new dimensions of linguistic usage. But the intellectual upheaval that came with it helped to focus developments which originated in earlier times and continued after the Reformation. In the wake of Luther's translation of the Bible, the German language was also increasingly used on the pulpit. Latin was gradually displaced from cult by the language of the people (Vossler 1925: 34).

Spreading the Word, Mechanically

Had the Reformation been limited to theological dispute, it could never have had the revolutionary consequences that are now commonly associated with it. It was crucially important that the polemic was carried to the common people by means of pamphlets directed at everyone who was able to read them. This was made possible by the introduction of the printing press with movable type, the most important technological innovation of the time (Eisenstein 1979). What is more, the Humanists had prepared the ground for attempts at spreading education beyond the walls of the traditional Latin schools. For them as well as for the Reformers the printing press was the proper technology for disseminating their ideas by means of the vernacular language.

The new market for printed material[11] developed its own dynamics quite independently of these ideals. In the sixteenth century the bulk of all books were still printed in Latin.[12] Printing in the vernaculars was not welcomed by all echelons of society, because it was seen as degrading the sacred languages – Greek, Latin, and Hebrew – and depriving the scriptures of their exclusiveness.

However, the objectives of the Reformers and the owners of the new technology coincided in important respects. Both had a vital interest in expanding the market. To reach more people with a pamphlet was both an advantage in the ideological struggle and a more profitable use of the machinery. It is no coincidence, therefore, that the Reformation brought with it the publication of many primers and spelling books[13] pressing for the unification of the written language; both measures suited to increase sales. In this way demands of the market led to a gradual enlargement of the range of the languages used in print. On the basis of what came to be known as the "printers' language" a grammar could be formed which was valid, for instance, for *the* German language, making it learnable and teachable with the help of verifiable rules.[14] The spreading of the emerging common standard languages which were superimposed on vernacular varieties thus appears as a result of coinciding ideological and economic interests. At the same time it created ever more favorable conditions for the realization of these interests.[15] The market itself expanded, especially the domestic market, where forms of trade came into existence unknown in medieval times (Weber 1924: 252).

The Common Language as an Asset

The driving force behind language standardization and the advance of literacy was the educated bourgeoisie (Große 1980). Likewise it was the bourgeoisie that developed new forms of trade, especially standard trade using specimens as well as wholesale links connecting domestic and foreign commerce. The newly emerging standard vernacular languages thus were the languages of the economic and in due course the social elites.

It is somewhat of a mystery that Weber did not pay more attention to the parallel developments from the sixteenth to the nineteenth century of Europe's modern standard languages and the capitalist system of economy. He asserts that a sufficiently elaborate network of communication and traffic links was an indispensable precondition of the development of wholesale trade (Weber 1924: 252). In this connection he finds the noble family von Thurn und Taxis, the owners of the postal regalia, important enough to mention, while remaining silent on Luther's contribution to the development of a supra-regional German standard language.[16] The inability of most Chinese mandarins to understand the dialects of the provinces they administered was, he explains, one of the reasons why, in spite of the early introduction of a non-hereditary civil service, no "rational state" could develop in China (1924: 289). The rational state curtails the power of arbitrary rule and thus makes economic action more calculable. It is, therefore, again in Weber's view, a prerequisite of the unfolding of capitalism. Yet, he does not comment on the fact that in Europe the formation of the rational state and the standard common languages advanced in close association with each other.

This is all the more surprising, as he recognizes that "language facilitates mutual understanding and thus the formation of all types of social relationships, in the highest degree."[17] It is, therefore, of great importance for society, he argues, "since the intelligibility of the behavior of others is the most fundamental presupposition of group formation (*Vergemeinschaftung*)" (Weber 1978: 390). It is, furthermore, "the bearer of a specific 'cultural possession of the masses' and makes mutual understanding possible or easier" (1978: 390). Nevertheless, Weber did not assign language a central position in his theory of society, probably because he considered "orientation to the rules of a common language . . . primarily important as a means of communication, not as the content of social relationship."[18] It is for this reason that he fails to take account of the qualitative changes that languages undergo by being developed into standard common languages on the basis of a fixed written norm. However, Protestantism created a novel kind of language community, precisely in the sense of raising to a higher level "the intelligibility of the behavior of others." For the translation of the Bible had disclosed to all the rationality of the ethical regimentation of everyday life, thereby depriving the magician-priest of his most efficient means of social control, his privileged access to God's word through the secret and sacred code of the "Biblical" languages. Just as trade in the rational bureaucratic state became calculable, in contradistinction to the arbitrary rule of the feudalistic state, religious conduct also became calculable, since the basis of assessing it was no longer the authority of monarch or priest, but the gospel objectified in the common language.

Obviously, what we are dealing with here is a lengthy historical process. Latin survived in certain social domains through the nineteenth century, especially in the Catholic church, but also in some chanceries,[19] while business, science and literature took to the vernaculars much sooner. It must also be noted that language standardization itself was not an achievement of post-medieval times. But it could unfold its social impact only in modern times, when the emphasis shifted from horizontal to vertical communication. In the form of canonical texts and dictionaries the tools lay ready, but they were still waiting to be fully exploited. Recalling that at the time of the French Revolution standard French was spoken by only an estimated 30 percent of the French population,[20] it is evident that the triumph of the standard vernaculars was then still far from complete. This remained a task for the nineteenth, the national, century when the European standard languages conquered the territories and populations of the states which by then had come to claim them as their own. In the nineteenth century, the written norm of Europe's vernacular languages at last reached the majority of the increasingly literate population, simultaneously, that is, with the advance of industrialization and the full unfolding of the capitalist economic system, bringing about the autonomy of economic life as distinct from political, cultural, and religious affairs.

The "principle of autonomy" which, with Parsons (1964) we view as characterizing modern society, finds its most noticeable expression in the establishment of money as a general means of exchange on the market. The custom of using money is, of course, much older. It was familiar in medieval and even in ancient times. However, as a universal means of evaluating not only commodities, but services too, it became institutionalized only in the twilight of the middle ages, and only in Europe. As discussed in the first chapter, it could realize its universal role as a means of relating all goods and services to each other, and penetrating all domains of society, to the extent that its factual and conceptually perceived essence shifted from the material to the functional. This became possible in full measure only when money was all but stripped of its tangible, material properties, and precious metal was replaced by paper. Paper money as a universal means of exchange prevailed only in the nineteenth century, and it is only in modern society, characterized by an advanced degree of division of labor, that money exhibits its purely intermediary function.

Likewise, the virtual identity of language, state, and nation was approximated only in nineteenth-century Europe. The establishment of the European common languages and new forms of monetary interaction were not two unrelated developments which just happened to take place at roughly the same time. Both had received major impulses from the Reformation, language as the means of spreading new ethical guidelines, and money as the means of using funds for capitalistic purposes in accordance with these guidelines. The standardization and cultivation of the European vernaculars was not only influenced by economic development, but in its turn had an effect on it by widening the range of communication. That "language is an asset," we can thus reinterpret somewhat more accurately in the sense that the common language is an asset.

Common Language and National Language

In Europe, the common language also became the national language. In his essay on nationalism, which he explains as an economic necessity, reflecting the objective need for homogeneity, rather than primarily an ideological phenomenon, Gellner highlights the role of communication. In modern industrial society, he maintains, "for the first time in human history, explicit and reasonably precise communication becomes generally, pervasively used and important" (Gellner 1983: 33). Industrial production requires standardized and orderly ways, as well as a mobile, homogeneous and more highly educated population. These requirements imply the need for using a single standard language by means of which all members of society who are drawn into the economic process can be reached.[21] Commenting on the intellectual aspect of the linguistic unification thus necessitated, Gellner (1983: 21) speaks of "a single conceptual currency" which describes the world. That "all referential uses of language ultimately refer to one coherent world" (1983: 21); that, thanks to the lexicographic codification of hundreds of thousands of words, the standard common languages can be relied on as precise and highly differentiated, intertranslatable conceptual tools, available, in principle at least, through general education to the entire population, is an expression of the rationalization of the world, in the Weberian sense, which is bound together in a rationally organized market. The more this market becomes a national market, and the more the capitalist order of economic affairs and industrialization come to dominate social life, the more people will learn to handle and actually use this tool.

The New Quality of the European Culture Languages

This is not to deny that cultural and political developments also left their marks on the European culture languages. The language academies of the Renaissance in Italy and France; the emergence of the Netherlands as an independent state; the cultural achievements of the German classical period in the eighteenth century; the French Revolution and the romantic nationalism it inspired in the nineteenth century; to name but some of the more important landmarks. All of them have often been mentioned, and sometimes overemphasized, in recounting the histories of the various languages. This cannot be said of the interaction of language and the spirit of economic life in the sense under discussion here.

The Florentine Accademia della Crusca preceded the Prussian Akademie der Wissenschaften (1700) by 120 years. Yet, the distance between the written and the spoken language is to this day much more pronounced in Italian than in German. Should the fact that the Reformation never reached Italy and that the effects of the Protestant ethic and the spirit of capitalism on economic developments were hence much watered down there have no part in this? In Spain, in spite of strong political backing, Castilian could never be established as the sole common language, and at present Catalan is experiencing a more than symbolic revival. In Protestant northern Europe, by contrast, national linguistic uniformity is predominant. In Eastern Europe, several new literary languages emerged in the wake of the Reformation, for instance, Finnish, Lithuanian, Latvian, and Slovenian.[22] In England, as in other European countries, the triumph of the standard language went along with urbanization and the rise of capitalism, as well as the establishment of the national Anglican church and the ensuing retreat of Catholicism.[23] Only in Catholic Ireland, the poorest country of western Europe, did the replacement of Latin not result in the establishment of the vernacular as a viable national language. Instead, Irish was reduced to a minority language without any functional significance, while Latin was superseded by English, the language of the powerful Protestant neighbor.[24]

In the given connection small-scale comparisons within a single language area also come to mind. The language of Catholic Flanders, until World War II the poorer part of Belgium, is characterized by high dialectal heterogeneity. The only standard of Flemish-Dutch is that of the Protestant north, Algemeen Beschaafd Nederlands.[25]

On a global scale, we may notice that the only non-white country which was able to close the development gap and join the most advanced industrial countries, Japan, is linguistically highly homogeneous.[26] Above all, the contrast with China is instructive: after the forced opening of Japan to the West, far-reaching language reforms during the last decades of the nineteenth century led, within a generation, to the nationwide spread of the standard language based on a new written norm,[27] while the general spread of the Chinese standard language, Putonghua, is yet to be accomplished.[28]

That in Canada Catholic French can only stand its ground thanks to legal measures protecting it against the onslaught of Protestant English, shall be mentioned only in passing, because the relationship between these two languages throws some light on the competition among the economic elite of the world's languages, on which we will have occasion to comment in more detail below.[29]

The general point at issue here is that, from a sociological point of view, the European common languages that have emerged since the sixteenth century were a qualitatively new means of social integration, commensurate with, and conducive to, economic development. Highly cultivated languages, of course, existed much earlier, but in Renaissance Europe both the size of the speech community and its social composition made for a qualitative difference. The Greek Koine was the language of a city-state elite. Classical Chinese was used throughout the country, but only by a small class of mandarin administrators. In India, the cultivation of literary Sanskrit was the sole responsibility of the Brahmin caste. The new quality of the modern common languages is that they extend over large areas, while at the same time ranging across social strata. By virtue of their capacity to meet all of the communicative needs of society, they reflect a more closely woven social fabric than existed in antiquity or the middle ages, facilitating social mobility and participation in the political process. For the societies possessing them, these languages, which rendered function-specific societal multilingualism superfluous by replacing it with polystylism, constituted an evolutionary advantage relative to those societies which continued to depend on using several different languages. This advantage had important economic consequences.

Integration and Differentiation

After the problem of social evolution had long been avoided, Parsons re-established it on the sociological agenda. His concern was to identify organizational developments "sufficiently important to further evolution" and, therefore, "likely to be 'hit upon' by various systems operating under different conditions" (Parsons 1964: 339). Such developments he called "evolutionary universals" of which religion, linguistic communication, the organization of social groups on the basis of kinship relations, and technology he considered basic. On a higher level, an administrative bureaucracy in the Weberian sense, money, and markets also become important (1964: 347). For Parsons, money is the primary model of what he called "generalized symbolic media of interchange," that is, the components that hold a social system together and make it work. Money, in his definition, is

> both a "language" and a medium of communication, and the relation
> between language, medium, and physical consequences, is essentially
> the same here as in other cases of communication. . . . The essential
> phenomenon is the *generalization* of commitments and the expectations
> associated with them. (Parsons 1960: 272f.)

"The generalization of commitments and the expectations associated with them" is not a bad summary of the crucial features that make a standard common language. And, as will have become apparent by now, the autonomy of language was no less a necessary aspect of modern society than the autonomy of the economic sphere, which is much emphasized by Parsons.

It should be noted that Parsons (1964: 343) also considered written language as an evolutionary advantage, since literacy increases the adaptive capacity of social systems by advancing differentiation and specialization. However, to his considerations it must be added that the acquisition of writing by a society can affect languages and their use in different ways. Three developmental paths can be distinguished: (1) the co-existence of a written language with (an) unrelated vernacular(s), which precludes large-scale influences on the latter by the former, for instance, the use of literary Chinese in Vietnam prior to the development of a Vietnamese writing system; (2) the consolidation of a wide rift between written language and vernacular in spite of their genetic relationship, a situation typical of restricted literacy resulting in diglossia where the vernacular develops, by and large, unaffected by the literary variety, as, for instance, in Arabic; (3) the establishment of a written norm followed relatively quickly by the promotion of mass literacy which enables the written language to exercise an influence on the vernacular, while at the same time fostering the ideal that the written language should be a faithful mapping of it. The promotion of general literacy in the wake of Reformation and Enlightenment made it possible for the first time for written language to have extensive effects on the vernacular and was thus instrumental in establishing supra-regional norms of linguistic usage. Such norms then could give rise to a speech community in which language, instead of, or in addition to, serving the purpose of social differentiation, can begin to create more integration and cohesion. In this sense, the establishment of the European common languages can be said to represent a new level of social evolution.

In Parsons' framework, as it has been elaborated by Eisenstadt (1964) among others, the interaction of integration and differentiation occupies a prominent position in explaining social evolution. Written language, we have just argued, is to be regarded, from this point of view, as an integrating innovation, but we must not lose sight of the fact that it also opens up new possibilities of social differentiation – not least in the sense of the three types of relationships between spoken and written language distinguished above. If the availability of writing is one evolutionary step, its close association with the vernacular is another, which does not coincide with, or necessarily follow, the introduction of writing into a society. The common language, based on a written standard, must be seen as an organizational development in its own right. What it achieves is this: more integration and more differentiation. More integration, since it reduces the distance between spoken and written language and between those making use of these means; more differentiation, since it encompasses the expressive potential of various registers and functional styles. The common language thus presents itself in different guises: on one hand, the citizens bound together by other social institutions, such as money and market, now speak the same language or, at least, have easy access to it; on the other hand, it perpetuates residues of the linguistic stratification of feudal society. On one hand, the citizens of the rational state are united by the same language; on the other hand, professionals (*Berufsmenschen* in Weber's sense) develop languages for specific purposes, which, on the new level of integration, once again create more differentiation.[30]

This, however, is not a prolongation of the linguistic delimitation of social domains in feudal society such as cult, scholarship, and government, but rather the formation of functional varieties on a common basis. Notwithstanding their highly specialized nature, which is an immediate result of the high degree of division of labor, mutual accessibility across languages for specific purposes is greater than was that between regionally bound languages of the crafts and the supra-regional language of learning in feudal society. The important aspect here is that the increasing differentiation of the common language in terms of languages for specific purposes is due to the growing needs of conceptual discrimination, while the function of social discrimination recedes into the background. Languages for specific purposes grow out of the common language, which is one reason why it is more highly differentiated than earlier states of the language. The common language is both a presupposition and an expression of a new evolutionary level of social systems characterized by a network of communicative interrelations cutting across regional affiliations and social ranks. For this to be achieved, it was necessary, if not to supplant, at least to supplement the individual's coordinates of identification in feudal society – region and station in life – by another, the nation, which, if we follow Gellner's reasoning, is above all the sociopolitical structure of the market required by industrial economies.

Market and Language

In the previous section, the formation of the common language has been described as a necessary part of social evolution, bringing with it, in the process of adapting to novel communicative needs, more differentiation and more integration. One of the crucial features of the common language turned out to be its range. This section takes up the question how language and market interact.

Market and language have been viewed as homologous systems. The nature of this homology has been investigated in greatest depth, so far, by Rossi-Landi (1968, 1974). His basic idea is to conceive of language as the product of collective labor, as accumulated social wealth (Rossi-Landi 1974: 146). Utterances he compares with commodities circulating on the market:

> Barter would correspond to the communicative exchange of one or more meanings in an immediate manner. (1974: 151f.)

Certain words, for example, function words, take on the functions of privileged commodities which can be exchanged for all other commodities, precious stones, for instance.

It is not altogether clear what Rossi-Landi means by "communicative exchange of meanings in an immediate manner." Perhaps he thinks of very concrete words; perhaps he thinks of highly context-dependent expressions. In any event, he contrasts this simple form of "linguistic barter," as he calls it, with a more complicated level of exchange carried out by means of linguistic capital, which "lies in the memory rather like money in a coffer" (Rossi-Landi 1974: 152). This analogy of elementary, direct communication with barter and more involved, indirect communication with monetary trade appears to be somewhat contrived. It is easiest to accept if we take gestures and interjections, where the expressive and referential functions are not yet dissociated from each other, as the linguistic counterpart of barter; though this comparison, too, is rather clumsy. While barter must be recognized as an accomplishment of higher-level civilization, pre-linguistic communication can only be associated with an early stage of phylogeny or ontogeny. One might want to think, instead, of the (primitive) gesture which accompanies the (complex) speech act, where the correspondence would then be with barter which continues to exist alongside monetary trade. In this manner, the homology of language and market could be applied to various forms of commercial interchange. It shall not be overtaxed here, however. Instead, we turn to another aspect of the relation of language and market which commands our attention, that is, the influence the market has on language.

The market is a place of encounter for the exchange of goods where communication and agreement are achieved.[31] Inasmuch as it replaced robbery as the common form of transfer of possessions, it embodies an organizational breakthrough of civilization. The market presupposes the conventional regulation of the participants' interaction. However, this does not necessarily imply use of a shared language adapted to the needs of trade. Such necessity only arises with the transition from the exchange for consumption to the exchange of goods produced for the market. Calvet has pointed out that barter is often carried out silently, without the mediation of language or money.[32] While those involved in barter many, in many cases, have lacked a common language, this is not why this kind of exchange is carried out silently; rather, the participants of the transaction are silent in order to barter. The commodity of bartering is a more or less accidental surplus product not needed for one's own consumption. Object is held against object. The equivalence thus achieved is entirely subjective and momentary. Silent bartering is a primitive form of exchange on a market with a narrow scope.

Where commodities are produced for the market and a generalized equivalent of values is introduced to relate all commodities to each other thereby objectifying the determination of values, and the scope of the market expands, bargaining is no longer done in silence. The loquacious vendor is the very symbolization of monetarized trade. He raises his voice in order to reach the ears of those visiting the market, doing his utmost to make himself not only heard but also understood by potential buyers.[33] The modern equivalent to the loud-mouthed merchant, advertising, makes the connection at issue even more obvious. To the extent that language in advertising is used in referential rather than decorative function, its reach extends at least as far as the market on which the product in question is offered. Nowadays, this is often a national market. Trade relates people from different walks of life and origins to each other. They need to have the assurance that what is said is understood as intended, an assurance which is enormously enhanced by a common reference system. Following Simmel, Parsons explained that money and language are such reference systems, inasmuch as they constitute a "shared basis of normative order" (Parsons 1977: 168). The necessary abstractness of such reference systems was already succinctly analyzed by Simmel:

> The more people develop relationships with one another, the more abstract and generally acceptable must be their medium of exchange; conversely, if such a medium exists, then it permits agreements over otherwise

inaccessible distances, an inclusion of the most diverse persons in the same project, an interaction and thereby unification of people who, because of their spatial, social, personal and other discrepancies in interests, could not possibly be integrated into any other group formation.[34]

This aptly characterizes the change in the social functions of language which takes place in conjunction with the expansion of the market, although Simmel actually deals with the social function of money, which once again highlights the similarity of language and money as factors of the evolution of social systems. The great significance of linguistic homogeneity for the unfolding of economic activity was also recognized by another influential thinker, Lenin. What he had to say about language and trade is like a mirror image of Simmel's above statement:

> The uniformity of language and its unimpeded development is one of the most important presuppositions of a truly free and all-encompassing trade commensurate with modern capitalism . . . and eventually a presupposition of the close relation of the market with every entrepreneur, even the pettiest, with every seller and buyer. (Lenin 1961: 398f.)

In its formation the social reality thus described had received important impulses from the Reformation which had provided the ideological legitimization for including everyone in the social system. It finds expression in the expanded, more abstract, depersonalized market which is freed through money from the immediacy of bartering, and in the common language which for the first time incorporates society in its entirety. Both money economy and common language constitute a qualitative step in social evolution, since they create new kinds of interindividual relations and open up new possibilities of participating in economic, social, and cultural life.

The historical parallelism of expanding trade spheres and language standardization at the threshold of modernity was no coincidence.[35] In pre-industrial stages of economic development ordinary persons were dependent on a small number of individuals, with most of whom they were personally acquainted. High division of labor and specialization in a monetary economy, however, "require an infinitely extended range of other producers with whom we exchange products" (Simmel 1978: 297f.). The range of the language is as narrow or as wide as the circle of its users; for, since every language evolves by being used for fulfilling everyday communicative needs, it is the common product of those employing it and thus valid only for them. For the human species, to associate is an existential need, primarily an economic necessity. In the final analysis, how who relates to whom is, therefore, however indirectly, economically determined.

In the initial difficulties facing the European precursors of colonialism in their attempts at establishing trans-oceanic trade relations, again both money and language were involved. In the absence of an accepted currency, they were forced to barter, which was not only cumbersome and inflexible, but also left the problem of an objective value equivalent unresolved. For lack of a shared language, intricate negotiations were precluded from the outset. These difficulties were resolved gradually, in a way reflecting the sporadic nature of these trade contacts. The European traders exported their currencies, whose acceptability outside the territories where they functioned as legal tender was, however, inevitably very limited and restricted to species minted of precious metal. In some ports only certain coins were used. Simmel (1978: 186) reported that as late as the 1880s only the Maria Theresa Taler of 1780 was accepted in Abyssinia. Since smaller coins were practically non-existent, trade was considerably hampered, because traders were often obliged to take more or other goods for the balance of their payment. The linguistic counterpart of restricted monetary systems of this sort are the trade or pidgin languages which sprang up wherever the European seafarers came into contact with trade partners on other continents. In keeping with the communicative needs of their users, which were limited to a particular domain of interaction, the expressive power of these languages in the beginning was severely restricted.

Not only the flag follows trade but idiom and money as well. As an expression of the economic power relations, both the languages and the currencies of the countries of origin of the European merchants were brought into circulation wherever they established their trading stations, and typically for higher communicative and commercial functions at that. In the long run, this meant a competitive disadvantage of major proportions for the native means of exchange. The linguistic heritage of colonialism testifies to the one-sidedness of the economic relations: while the Europeans exported their languages wholesale, they only took a few words from their trading partners, colonial goods, as it were. Besides, we can recognize a principle of mercantilist thinking here. Johan Joachim Becher, a German exponent of this doctrine, put it this way:

It is always better to sell goods to others than to buy goods from others, for the former brings a certain advantage and the latter inevitable damage.[36]

The European language export was prosecuted only partly following the conscious application of this principle, but in practice the effects were in keeping with it, although coercion or elaborate sales strategies were often quite unnecessary. For the co-opted elites in the colonies were easily convinced of the superiority of the European products and, therefore, readily and in their own best interest adopted their masters' languages. This turned out to be a lasting economic advantage for the colonial powers, as they were in this way afforded easy access to the overseas markets, which they still enjoy today, long after their flags have ceased to fly there.

The American Precedent

It is hence not surprising that the drive for political independence has always been accompanied by the desire for a national currency and language. The precedent was set by the Americans. In 1789 the Continental Congress discussed the currency problem: pounds and pennies were to be replaced by coins peculiar to the young republic. The names of most of the coins eventually approved in 1792 were minted by Thomas Jefferson who proposed the words *mill*, *cent*, *disme*, *dollar*, and *eagle*.[37] At the same time Noah Webster propagated the linguistic independence of the nation. Until that time Samuel Johnson had been the undisputed mint-master of the language, but this authority, embodied in his massive dictionary of 1755, was now to be contested.

In keeping with the conservative currents of the politics of his country, Johnson leaned on the literary elite as the providers of the linguistic norm. He was ill-disposed towards every usage deviating from theirs. In particular, he feared the evil influence of trade as a threat to the constitution of the language:

Commerce, however necessary, however lucrative, as it depraves the manners, corrupts the language; they that have frequent intercourse with strangers, to whom they endeavour to accommodate themselves, must in time learn a mingled dialect, like the jargon which serves the traffickers on the Mediterranean and Indian coasts. This will not always be confined to the exchange, the warehouse, or the port, but will be communicated by degrees to other ranks of the people, and be at last incorporated with the current speech. (Johnson 1964: 25)

Since Johnson's dictionary was long without competition, he did more for the standardization of English than perhaps anyone else. Somewhat ironically, more extended trade on a more highly integrated market, so much despised by him, was not the least of the forces which helped to establish the norm he had codified.

Noah Webster was Johnson's declared enemy and his first successful challenger. True to the European spirit of the time, the American nationalist declared that "as an independent nation, our honor requires us to have a system of our own, in language as well as government."[38] To break with Johnson was no less important, therefore, than with George III. Thus Webster could not accept the British elites as the trustees of a norm to be established against Johnson. Instead he argued that "the general practise of the nation" should determine the American standard, a politically skillful move, because the nation was yet to become one, and of "the general practise" nobody could have a very clear picture. In contradistinction to Johnson, Webster placed much confidence in the driving force and beneficial effects of trade in this regard.

Commerce is the parent of civilization. . . . Every where we see the mildness of manners, and the humanity of laws and institutions, are in direct proportion to the extent of commerce. (Webster 1802: 214f.)

It is part of the American dream that differences between social classes are leveled in American society. The linguistic aspect of this myth, which is not quite as unfounded as the social one, is that American English exhibits no very pronounced social differentiation. On the basis of this belief, Webster built in his *Dissertations on the English Language* of 1789 and various other writings a political doctrine of linguistic democracy, designed not only to dispute the predominance of the English class language, but also to establish American English as the leading language of the future. In his first dictionary of 1806 (p. xxiif.) he declared:

In fifty years from this time, the *American-English* will be spoken by more people, than all the other dialects of the language, and in one hundred and thirty years, by more people than any other language on the globe, not excepting the Chinese.

A society of such heterogeneous composition as the American colonies was united by nothing more forcefully than by the common striving after profit, which was generally accepted in the sense of the Protestant ethic even more readily than in the old world. The social conditions obtaining in America were better suited for allowing the leveling influence of commerce to take effect in language, rather than loathing them as a contamination of established usage. Joel Barlow, a contemporary of Webster's, gave poetic expression to this sentiment in a way that reads like a plea for free trade.

> That every distant land the wealth might share,
> Exchange their fruits and fill their treasures there;
> Their speech assimilate, their empires blend,
> A mutual interest fix the mutual friend
> (Barlow 1970, 2: 344)

Less Successful Colonies

Taken together, political, monetary, and linguistic efforts resulted in the complete independence of the United States. Other parts of the world, which only came under colonial sway proper at the time of the American revolution and emerged from it during the present century, were less successful. Although political sovereignty was achieved, continuing economic dependency became an almost universal characteristic of the newly created states, especially those which came into existence as the result of the last wave of decolonization during the 1950s and 60s. The monetary and linguistic indications of this state of affairs are unmistakable. A stable currency of an economically flourishing postcolonial state is just as rare as a language native to such a country which is fit to assume all of the functions of the colonial language.[39] Both of these phenomena witness the fact that the structures externally imposed onto these societies did not further, and to some extent hindered, the development of those they superseded.

To mention but one example, despite the declared intent of the leaders of the Indian independence movement, Hindi could not replace English as India's most important language of wider communication, and the Indian rupee is still traded under its nominal value. Herein we can detect a late but unquestionable echo of Lord Macaulay's well-known proposition for the promotion of English in India, because "English is better worth knowing than Sanskrit or Arabic,"[40] the traditional languages of learning in India. The standards according to which a language is better worth knowing than another, or can reasonably be evaluated as such, warrant special attention. At this point, it can only be noted that the subjective endorsement Macaulay's assessment received on the part of many Indians, did not turn out as quite the objective advantage which they and he must have anticipated. Rather, the asymmetric relationship between Great Britain and India, which finds expression in the fact that English is an accepted means of communication in India, but not Hindi – or any other Indian language – in Britain, and that likewise Sterling is widely accepted as a means of payment in India, but not rupees in Britain, is a historical legacy which, far from being a mere epiphenomenon, is an essential part of the economic conditions. However, much like the foreign language, the foreign currency remained just that, foreign. Both could not, therefore, fulfill the important function of creating identity and homogeneity, not in the same manner, anyway, as in an indigenous environment. Not that social contrasts in traditional India could have been eliminated effortlessly without external influence; and nobody would describe the linguistic landscape there prior to the arrival of the Europeans as anything but patchy. However, the possibility for this heterogeneity to be eliminated from within was once and for all blocked up by the colonial intervention. If, as the language of political and economic power, English had not arisen as a superior rival, Hindi most likely would have had a better chance to grow into the role of the pan-Indian language. But, though English did play this role for a considerable while, it was adopted only by a small elite and thus helped to solidify the social hierarchy. It is no coincidence that command of English and possession of foreign exchange are distributed rather similarly in the Indian population.

The debt crisis has made it painfully clear that it is a euphemism at best to describe as a double-edged sword the introduction of foreign money into the national economies of post-colonial countries. For those who argued that industrialization could not be accomplished there without external capital, overlooked the fact that debt servicing, even at modest rates, would be too much of a burden for underdeveloped national economies where industries were locally introduced into environments quite unprepared for the ensuing social changes. Likewise it would be naïve to assume that the European languages left behind in the former colonies have only beneficial effects there. If we recall that some 30 percent of all physicians in Britain are of Indian and Pakistani extraction, it becomes immediately obvious how language facilitates the drain of intellectual capital. Although all speakers of a language seem to gain equally when the realm where it is serviceable expands, the economic consequences of linguistic expansion are far from transparent. Rather, language is yet to be appreciated as a factor of economic development, both in national and international contexts.

Economic Development and Language Development

"Development" is a protean notion. It is here used to refer to countries whose social, political, and economic structures were jolted by their encounters with Western institutions and which, at present, are undergoing far-reaching changes which, inasmuch as they move in the direction of Western models, are usually understood as modernization. The great majority of these countries are multilingual. This does not mean that by reducing their multilingualism these countries could also reduce their underdevelopment. In this regard we can only agree with Lieberson's (1980: 12) conclusion that "essentially no *substantial causal linkage* exists in either direction between changes in a nation's development and its level of linguistic homogeneity" (emphasis added). Statistical correlations holding between these features – for instance that most industrialized countries are linguistically relatively homogeneous – must be carefully distinguished from long-term changes in one or the other. Such a correlation, as it was observed, for instance, by Pool,[41] does not support the conclusion that the features in question co-vary historically.

Since economic organization and the standard of living in the West are the yardstick against which development and underdevelopment are measured, economic theories of development and modernization are almost inevitably Eurocentric. Approaches differ to some extent in the assessment of measures which are thought necessary in order to transform traditional societies and thus make them susceptible to economic development.[42] However, there is general agreement, tacitly or explicitly, that development is essentially tantamount to Westernization. This is so in spite of increasing sensibilities for the destruction of social structures and cultural systems caused by the impact of Western technology and economy on traditional societies. Of those concerned with development in theory or practice, virtually nobody believes that effective development is possible in the absence of capital accumulation, industrialization, a work force, institutionalized relations between capital and labor, and a more or less free market. Man as an economic animal is of European descent. To emulate his success without taking on some of his characteristic features has proven difficult, if not, as some believe, impossible.

The identification of development with Westernization has, of course, often been challenged, but a convincing criticism which does not rest on or imply a sweeping renunciation of modernity is yet to be put forth. Gandhi's powerfully presented and intriguing but ultimately helpless criticism of modern civilization illustrates this point. "If I could," he wrote (Gandhi 1960: 54), "I would certainly destroy or radically alter a large part of what is called 'modern civilization'." High on the list of the things he would like to dispense with were socioeconomic mechanisms such as division of labor and capital accumulation which already Adam Smith had described as essential for a modern capitalist economy. Gandhi accused Adam Smith of postulating as universal an economic order which is based mainly on the calculation of costs and benefits (Gandhi 1959: 205f.). Individual competition and striving for profit could only destroy the traditional village economy of the Khadi which, Gandhi held, should be revitalized in the spirit of freedom and equality for all. He regarded "industrialism as a curse for mankind" (1954: 39) and argued for the elimination of money currency in the villages (1954: 164) as a precondition for achieving self-sufficiency.

In the West, too, voices have occasionally been raised, deploring the subversion of traditional social orders, the erosion of the values of tribal loyalties, and the destruction of non-western cultures.[43] Yet, all theories of modernization share the conviction that Third World countries will not be able to pursue an effective course of development without in the process adopting Western ways and values. Some argue that this must be so for lack of an alternative model which provides both for the preservation of traditional structures and the eradication of hunger, poverty, illiteracy, and low productivity. Others hold that through financial assistance, technology transfer, and trade the developing countries have come to depend on the West to such an extent that it is now infeasible for them to deviate from the model of industrialized technological society which relies on a monetary economy and the legal institution of private property, as well as on a relatively open political system allowing for the participation of a large part of the population.

What is more, the level of international integration has reached such an intensity that it has become virtually impossible for a country to look for its own path and its own pace of development in "splendid isolation."

In retrospect this means that the development of Europe's national economies disturbed and sometimes obstructed piecemeal social evolution in other parts of the world and, indeed, that the phenomenal expansion and acquisition of wealth and global power of Europe between the sixteenth and nineteenth centuries was possible only through the economic exploitation of Asia, Africa, and South America. This connection, epitomized as "the development of underdevelopment," has been worked out most pointedly in Marx's analysis of colonialism.[44]

Against this background it becomes obvious that economic development cannot be pursued independently of sociopolitical and cultural change. This may seem paradoxical in view of the fact that modern society, as analyzed by Weber and Parsons, is characterized by the emergence of economy, society, government, and culture as increasingly autonomous spheres. However, at the time of mercantilism and colonialist expansion, the Europeans encountered social systems which did not exhibit this differentiation. Hence, these contacts had economic, as well as social and cultural consequences, and it is for the same reason that in our days modernization also has a bearing on all of these spheres. This implies, what for our considerations is especially important, that modernization affects language and not only as a cultural asset at that, but as a social fact which has economic and political utility as well. For the liberation movements of the period of decolonization prior to and during World War II, language was an important topic which remained on the agenda of the newly independent countries. It was part of the political discourse concerning the potential of language as an instrument, symbol, and catalyst of, but sometimes also obstacle to, nationalism.[45] On the other hand, this discourse had an economic dimension from the very beginning. Once again we can quote Gandhi here for illustration. Although he attributed great importance to the question of a national language above all because of its political symbolism, he repeatedly pointed out the economic aspects of this question. As early as 1920 he declared that "the nation has very materially suffered by reason of the proceedings of the Congress having been conducted almost entirely in English" (Gandhi 1965: 19). A few years before independence he was more specific:

Think of the time and energy of our youth expended on learning the English language, as if it was our mother tongue, and calculate by simple multiplication the number of years and the volume of precious energy that are lost to the nation. (1965: 60)

He regarded Japan as a model to be emulated, because as opposed to India no foreign language was used there as the medium of education, but rather everything the West had to offer was translated into the language of the country. In this way the Japanese "economize their energy."

> Those who need to learn [foreign languages] do so for enriching the Japanese culture with thought and knowledge which the West alone can give. They take care to turn into Japanese all that is worth taking from the West. . . . The knowledge gained thus has become national property. (1965: 601)

However, this model can be emulated only if there is a language suitable for absorbing and giving expression to Western knowledge. That most of the languages of developing countries are in this respect deficient is the real economic dimension of the language problems of these nations. For in most of them multilingualism is not coupled with an overarching language which is fully adapted and understood throughout the nation. Rather, they usually lack an autochthonous common language in this sense. Even in languages with old literary traditions, such as Bengali, Tamil, or Arabic, the critical properties of the common language are wanting, because, as Kandiah (1978: 60) points out with respect to Tamil, "the question of a standard language is not raised in any genuine way until the socio-historical conditions create the need for such a language." While the European common languages were formed during a period spanning several centuries coinciding and interacting with the formation of the capitalist economic system and the modern bureaucratic state, this development never took place in other parts of the world. This was due in large measure to the fact that the countries now constituting the Third World first came into contact with modern science, technology, economy, and administration through the medium of European languages which, moreover, for a long time remained the only languages in which the respective communicative functions were carried out there. "The introduction of the colonial languages into African societies," professes Spencer (1985: 394), "froze the opportunities for functional development of almost all the African languages." The autochthonous languages are, therefore, underdeveloped in precisely the same sense and for largely the same reasons as the societies using them.

The underdevelopment of the languages of Third World countries is an indication and part of their economic underdevelopment, since these languages cannot, on a level comparable to the Western common languages, enhance national unity, nor do they exhibit the differentiation necessary for a modern society. To this point we shall return below in chapter 5. In the present context our concern is with the parallelism of economic and linguistic development and with measures suitable for combating underdevelopment in both areas. Just as there are designs for socioeconomic development, there are also designs for linguistic development; and like the former, the latter imply, to a greater or lesser extent, Westernization.

Language Development — Linguistic Westernization

Much as societal modernization is impractical without Westernization, at least in some measure, certain modern forms of communication cannot be enacted without Westernization in the domain of language. There are, of course, differing ideas as to the specific measures to be espoused. While some advocate the adoption of Western institutions part and parcel as they are, others call for the transformation of local institutions or the adaptation of Western institutions to local conditions. Similarly divergent approaches exist regarding linguistic modernization. The indispensability of a common language for a modern society is taken by some to imply the necessity of adopting a European language. Léopold Senghor, for example, is a well-known proponent of Francophonie in Africa. The advantages of French he portrays as follows.

> We express ourselves in French since French has a universal vocation and since our message is also directed to French people and others. . . . In our [i.e. African] languages the halo that surrounds the words is by nature merely that of sap and blood; French words send out thousands of rays like diamonds.[46]

Another prominent example for the promotion of European languages is furnished by King Hassan II of Morocco. In an address concerning the educational system of Morocco he made the following statement.

> We must organize our culture and our instruction as seems necessary, and reform what must be reformed, in order to turn into an instrument capable of shaping our children, who hope thanks to it, to become citizens of their country, and of their continent which does not speak

Arabic. We live in a continent which speaks English and French. (Quoted in Ibrahim 1989: 48)

We shall not dwell here on the fact that Africa speaks English and French to about the same extent as medieval Europe spoke Latin. The Moroccan king's statement is interesting as it testifies to the hope that linguistic underdevelopment can be overcome by means of spreading the said European common languages. It thus is in sharp contrast with another notion of language modernization which in the Arabic speaking world is known as "Arabicization" (Ibrahim 1989) and involves the *Ausbau* of non-Western languages and their adaptation to Western patterns.

This process has been variously called "language modernization" (Alisjahbana 1967), "language reform" (Heyd 1954), "language development" (Ferguson 1968), and "language adaptation" (Coulmas 1989c). While highlighting somewhat different aspects, these terms have a common nucleus which focusses on the normative manipulation of linguistic change pertaining to properties of the language system, functions of language for the speech community, and attitudes of the speech community towards the language(s) in question. Ferguson (1968) concentrates on aspects concerning the language system, pointing out three dimensions which are relevant for language development and its assessment. These are (1) graphization – reduction to writing; (2) standardization – the creation and establishment of a supra-regional norm which overrides social varieties; (3) the development of intertranslatability with the modern languages which give expression to the technical and scientific discourse of industrial societies. These three dimensions which are meant to serve as criteria of orientation for the deliberate management of linguistic change can evidently also be read as an abbreviated account of the critical phases of the formation of the European common languages. Thus, in this connection too, everything points in the direction of Westernization as an inevitable consequence of modernization.

An important question, left open by Ferguson and usually ignored where language development is discussed as part of socioeconomic development, is whether the leveling of dialects and the repression of patois and minority languages which accompanied the rise of the European common languages must also be seen as inevitable components of contemporary language modernization processes. At least some language planners in the countries concerned prefer to deny this. Daswani who has been involved in various language planning programmes in India summarizes the difference in analysis and perspective.

> While the Western viewpoint of language planning is generally accepted, linguists in the developing countries are now raising questions about the validity of this viewpoint in a stable grassroots multilingual society. The issue that is being raised is whether a political and economic model can be found to sustain multilingualism without sacrificing national development. (Daswani 1989: 81)[47]

Is it possible, then, to invalidate the correlation discussed at the beginning of this chapter of social poverty and linguistic fragmentation by coordinating development and language planning measures to create a modern *and* multilingual society, or is this merely wishful thinking? It is not the purpose of this chapter to make predictions. What can be said here without indulging in unwarranted speculation is this. Multilingualism in Third World countries has many different faces, and perspectives for future developments are, therefore, highly diverse. That India will maintain at least the 15 officially recognized languages while pressing for socioeconomic modernization, is more likely, simply on account of the size and the literary traditions of these languages, than that the multilingualism of many African countries, which rely mainly on European languages for written communication, can survive the leap into modernity. Rather, it is to be expected that many of the minor languages there will remain restricted or be further reduced in their functions, as industrialization, urbanization, and other developments characteristic of modern societies progress.

Overcoming Linguistic Underdevelopment – Summary

Development will have different consequences for the linguistic situations of different countries. Nevertheless, Westernization will in no case be completely absent, although it will manifest itself in different degrees. Two models of Westernization can be distinguished. The design represented by Senghor and Hassan II mentioned above involves uncompromising linguistic Westernization by adopting a Western language at the expense of autochthonous languages. The counter model is that of language adaptation which in turn comprises two basic subtypes corresponding to different linguistic and cultural conditions. The Chinese language has been modelled and standardized over millennia by its literary tradition. This tradition blocks certain remodelling measures in accordance with Western patterns. The modernization of Chinese, therefore, consists by and large in creating a great many loan translations, making use, for the representation of Western concepts, of morphological material already present in the language (Pasierbsky 1989). Malay, by contrast, has a history characterized by adaptability and flexibility and thus offered itself for deliberate modernization in accordance with Western patterns and the adoption of Western loan words on a large scale in order to be turned into the common language of Indonesia, Bahasa Indonesia (Alisjahbana 1984).

In sum, deliberate attempts at overcoming linguistic underdevelopment in order to turn a language into a suitable medium of modern communication take the form of one of the following three approaches: (1) adopting a Western language, as in Mali where French is the only official language; (2) adapting an autochthonous language to the model of the common language by way of incorporating words, structures, and norms of Western languages, as in the case of the modernization of Indonesian; (3) adapting Western concepts by providing them with native expressions, especially loan translations, as in the case of Chinese. On the basis of these considerations, the statement heading this chapter, that language is an asset, gains a sharper outline and a more precise meaning. The utility of a language for a society increases inasmuch as it takes on the structural, functional, and attitudinal features of a common language in the sense suggested above. The European common languages are the result of centuries of differentiation and normalization. They evolved in conjunction with the communicative needs of modern societies and are thus adapted to them. Wherever such communicative needs have emerged, often rather suddenly, in non-Western societies, linguistic Westernization follows; because the linguistic means for meeting these needs cannot but adopt or develop some of the crucial properties of the European common languages.

3

The Value of a Language:
Factors of an Economic Profile of Languages

Language Evaluation in Linguistics

Being above all a means, language is not a value, but it has value. Like the possession of money, the possession of a language implies a potential for unfolding individuals' range of action and hence their enrichment. Yet, it is no easy task to ascertain the criteria which determine the value of a language.

Linguists have very little to offer in this regard. Nowadays many indeed deny the rationale or the desirability of value judgments about their objects of investigation. This was not always so. Rather, this attitude reflects the positivist orientation of present mainstream linguistics. In the nineteenth century, it was quite common to appraise languages as inferior or superior. Humboldt's candid remark gives expression to the spirit of his time: "That nations more happily endowed and under more favorable conditions should possess more excellent languages than others is grounded in the very nature of things."[1] The notions that nations are both more or less "happily endowed" and subject to the influence of more or less "favorable conditions" testify to two important aspects of Humboldt's philosophy of language. Language is a natural, organic endowment, but it is also culturally shaped. The interaction of these two factors provides every language with its own characteristic world outlook. Humboldt viewed languages as products of the mind, formed by it and giving expression to it. Languages differ in their ability to represent the basic categories of thought, which is due both to their grammatical structure and lexicon. From this it follows that not all languages are equally suitable for all purposes; for example, one language may be more fitting for poetry and another for rational discourse (Humboldt 1963b: 78).

Humboldt's evaluation of languages was teleological rather than ethnocentric. Sanskrit was to him the supreme example of linguistic perfection.[2] However, in twentieth-century mainstream linguistics, such value judgments were thrown overboard, chiefly in order to rid the discipline of its Eurocentric heritage, which among the social sciences distinguished, above all, early cultural anthropology but had been communicated to linguistics as well. The description of a great diversity of unwritten languages, especially in North America, had shown that languages could not reasonably be distinguished in terms of their total complexity, and, moreover, that there was no connection between the complexity of a language and their speakers' socioeconomic development as measured by Western standards. It was important, therefore, to denounce such terms as "primitive language," which at the beginning of this century were still in common use, even among linguists.

The insight that in structural terms there are no primitive languages was a necessary and important step in the theoretical development of linguistics. The philosophical shift to cultural relativism that followed, which in effect amounted to an equal opportunity act for the universe of languages, all of which were suddenly to be regarded as equal, in the long run obscured the view on questions such as the one we are interested in here. This is the question of language valuation. We nevertheless want to pursue it, without wishing to call into doubt that all human languages are entities of the same kind and do not, therefore, warrant classification as structurally more or less primitive.

In his influential book of 1921, Edward Sapir gave expression to and helped to shape the common view of linguistics regarding the evaluation of languages. "We must disabuse our minds of preferred 'values'," he wrote. "We are not in the least concerned with whether or not a language is of great practical value or is the medium of a great culture" (Sapir 1921: 124). The delimitation of the realm of linguistics which was thus achieved was undoubtedly conducive to its systematic development. Yet, in this way certain kinds of questions were dismissed which require the methodological tools of linguistics. That these questions, nevertheless, fall outside the realm of linguistics proper is a defendable position, but inasmuch as linguists also have an interest in the social nature of languages and their employment by socially organized groups of people, they can hardly evade these questions. It cannot be ruled out *a priori* that among the factors determining the value of a language are some which do fall into the realm of linguistics in a narrow sense. Whether or not the differing valuations of the languages of the world, which are in evidence in many societies, can be explained, partly at least, on linguistic rather than sociopsychological or cultural grounds, is a question which, obviously, also concerns linguistics, but which so far has been raised in some peripheral areas at best, and only quite recently. Attempts at identifying factors which determine the value of a language cannot, therefore, start out from linguistics, but we must also not dismiss its potential contributions.[3]

Value in Use and Value in Exchange

Different people mean different things when talking about the value of a language, just as the concept of value itself is used in different ways, for example, in economics, politics, ethics and aesthetics.[4] In other words, languages can be deemed valuable for a variety of reasons. In the present context the main question is how to represent the economic value of a language and how to compare languages in terms of their economic value. It is quite possible that values of other kinds may have an influence on their economic value, or vice versa. Let us begin, then, by considering in what sense languages behave as valuable entities and hence factors of economic life.

Whoever deliberates the question of the value of goods is confronted with the twofold economic sense of this notion, that is, the value of an object in use and the value of an object in exchange. Economists have long been intrigued by the fact that there is a peculiar difference between the two, inasmuch as things with great value in use, water, for instance, may have a very small exchange value, while things of little practical value, such as precious stones, may have a high value in exchange. For this relationship makes it quite impossible simply to derive the exchange value from the utility value. Attempts to relate these apparently altogether different values with each other have, moreover, long obscured the fact that they do not really constitute clear-cut categories. Food products, for instance, primarily serve to satisfy basic needs, but in some societies they have the characteristics of exotic valuables. A sushi bar in my neighborhood has recently enriched its menu with seasoned rice balls wrapped in gold leaf, testifying not only to the luxury that of late has become a fairly common feature of life in Japan, but also to the fact that there are various shades between utility value and exchange value. A house is useful because it provides shelter and derives its utility value thereof. But it can at the same time be recognized as a work of art because of its architecture and, therefore, have an exchange value much higher than that of another which is similar, or even superior, in terms of satisfying practical needs. The variable relationship of utility and exchange value cannot be explained without more sophisticated conceptual tools. Here we can draw on one of the basic notions of micro-economics, that of marginal utility. It says that the value of a commodity is determined by its minimal usefulness to rational consumers, that is, that those to whom a certain commodity is of great value need not pay more for it than those to whom it is of only little value. This explains why the prices of basic foodstuffs are usually so low that they are bought even by those to whom they are of little value, while very valuable objects may be given in exchange for them at times of shortage.

Additional factors influencing the value of commodities are the cost of producing them and the relationship of demand and supply. Before it is clear whether or in what sense it can be said that languages have utility and exchange values, it may suffice for the moment to mention these two kinds of value without any further discussion. The necessity to answer this question affirmatively is, however, rather compelling. We can thus direct our attention to examining, in more detail, how the utility value and exchange value of languages are determined and how they vary.

The Communicative Range

To communicate with one's fellows is a question of survival, both for the human species and the individual. Language, and here we can safely refer to it in the generic sense, is by far the most efficient system of communication that human beings have at their disposal, from which fact immediately follows its eminent utility value. This is indeed so critical that speechless people are usually thought of as deficient or deviant.[5] Human language is, therefore, commonly referred to as "natural," especially by linguists. It is a natural possession of every normal human being. From this one could be lead to the conclusion that it makes little sense or is even misleading to attribute a utility value to the faculty of language, because, much like the grasping hand, it is a defining feature of the species *homo sapiens*. Yet, if we think, for example, of pianists who take out insurance for their hands, it appears that even essential parts of our physical or mental equipment can be regarded as embodying a utility value.

Advancing from the generic to the specific, from language to languages, a variable feature that is immediately striking is the range of different languages. More specifically, this is a difference between speech communities rather than their languages, which is why sociologists tend to pay more attention to it than linguists. Every language serves those using it to communicate with others, but obviously languages differ greatly in the number of others with whom they enable their speakers to communicate. A simple, yet plausible hypothesis which this observation suggests is that the value of a language correlates with the number of its speakers. The more numerous the group of those with whom I can interact by means of a language, the greater is its utility to me in a very practical sense, as every speaker increases the total of potentially useful interactions. Testing the applicability of this hypothesis within the framework of the nation state, it is not difficult to find examples supporting it.

That the utility of German in Switzerland is greater than that of French or Italian is surely not because it is culturally more valuable, but because the German-speaking population outnumbers the French- and Italian-speaking population, and German is, therefore, more frequently used in the domains of political and economic life. Rhaeto-Romance, Switzerland's fourth national language, is economically insignificant.[6] At only about 50,000 its speech community is the smallest which, moreover, unlike the other three, has no links to an important neighbor, but only relates to Friulian and Ladin in Italy. Notwithstanding the liberal climate of the Netherlands, Frisian has a much smaller utility value there than Dutch, simply for numerical reasons. It allows for not only fewer, but also less varied opportunities to communicate. This holds true to an even greater extent of the much smaller community of Northern Frisians in Germany.[7]

On an international scale too, examples are easily found that corroborate the assumption of a causal correlation between the size of a speech community and the utility value of its language. In this sense German which is spoken by almost 100 million speakers is more valuable than, say, Dutch with a speech community of roughly one fifth that size; English is more valuable than Spanish, and French more valuable than Italian. Between neighboring speech communities the economic predominance of the bigger one usually finds expression in the inverse proportion of speakers proficient in the neighboring language. Thus,

Table 3.1   The 15 most populour speech communities

Language		Primary speakers (millions)	Speech community including secondary speakers (millions)
1	Chinese	(?) 800	
2	English	403	800
3	Spanish	266	
4	Hindi	180	300
5	Russian	154	270
6	Bengali	152	
7	Portuguese	150	
8	Japanese	117	119
9	French	109	250
10	German	100	130
11	Arabic	(?) 100	
12	Javanese	70	
13	Marathi	50	
14	Tamil	45	
15	Italian	40	

(Figures from Grimes 1988)

Frisians usually speak Frisian as well as Dutch, while only few native speakers of Dutch also speak Frisian. On the other hand, German is more widely spoken in the Netherlands than Dutch in Germany. Such disproportions can have other than economic reasons, but they are a reflection of economic conditions. The Dutch economy depends on Germany much more than vice versa. Since Frisland is a Dutch province, its economy is tightly interwoven with the other provinces.

To what extent does this obvious relationship between the size of a speech community and the economic value of its language allow for generalization? When we examine the 15 most populous speech communities of the world, thereby necessarily transcending the European context, the simple equation "the bigger the better" proves faulty.

Let us ignore for the moment the special problems of Chinese and Arabic. The numbers for their speech communities are here given with a question mark, because it is doubtful in both cases whether it can be reasonably claimed of so many speakers that they speak anything recognizable as one and the same language. However, the other figures, too, force us to rethink the significance of the number of speakers as a factor of the economic value of a language. Portuguese, for instance, has more speakers than French, but is it, therefore, more valuable? Is Italian less valuable than Japanese? Further, if number of speakers is a factor at all, does this mean that there is a proportional relationship between the two dimensions such that, for example, the utility value of German is twice that of Marathi and that of Russian one and a half times that of French? Is the intuitively felt difference between the utility values of English and German adequately represented as a ratio of $4:1$?

Such detailed comparisons seem rather disputable, if not absurd. Yet, it is even more improbable that the number of speakers should be altogether insignificant. This is quite obvious when we reduce our considerations, by way of a thought experiment, to minimal speech communities. A speech community with two members allows each of them linguistic exchanges with exactly one other speaker. A speech community of three enables each member to make a choice between two other speakers or to communicate with both of them. A speech community consisting of ten speakers means nine potential interlocutors for each of them, and so on. Linguistic communication serves a variety of purposes, among others the establishment of economically beneficial relationships. The opportunities in this regard a member of a speech community of ten are undoubtedly better than those of the members of a two-member speech community; the deca-language is more useful and hence more valuable than the dia-language. The evident objection to this line of approach is that this kind of reckoning cannot be carried on at will. Let us ignore non-reciprocal forms of communication by speakers who can reach millions through the mass media and assume that on average a speaker communicates with ten others per day. Even if these ten were never the same, the communicative history of a lifetime of 75 years would allow one to speak with only a little more than 270,000 people. This rather peculiar calculation invites the important conclusion that there is a threshold for the size of speech communities beyond which it makes little difference whether a language has a few speakers more or less or even a few million speakers more or less.

Yet, this assumption too seems rather simplistic. A non-specialized general library should contain as many volumes as possible, although the limits in terms of what can be read in a lifetime are rather narrow. But this is not the issue. The important point is to increase the chances for all possible users to find what they are looking for, even the most abstruse book. Similarly, a large speech community offers a wide spectrum of communicative opportunities and allows its members to realize these opportunities at many different places, entailing not only differentiation but also mobility.[8] After all, then, "the bigger, the better" is not altogether wrong. However, it does not necessarily follow that this correlation is equally significant in speech communities of all sizes. It seems more likely that the economic weight of the size of the speech community diminishes with size such that the difference between a speech community of 100,000 and one of a million speakers is economically more significant than that between a million and ten million speakers. On the basis of these considerations it is tempting to postulate a law of the diminishing returns of additional speakers, although at the present state of our knowledge it is not clear whether the value increase of a language indeed steadily diminishes as the speech community grows or whether there are, maybe, several quantitative thresholds.

That the importance of size has more weight for smaller speech communities than for relatively large ones is evident when we take into consideration the functional requirements and differentiation of modern communication. The social relationships that give rise to modern forms of communication, especially in science, technology, administration, commerce, and legislation, presuppose a minimal community of inter-actants, if all of these functions are to be carried out by means of the same language. Is there a critical order of magnitude below which number of speakers is economically significant, but above which the economic correlates of the size of the speech community are negligible? Where is the threshold? What is the minimal size of a speech community that can enact all modern functions of communication?

With some 230,000 speakers, Icelandic is surely at the lower margin in this regard. It should be difficult to find many other languages that are equally small and fit for all purposes of modern life. Many other languages, by contrast, are numerically stronger but much more restricted in their expressive resources and hence threatened by regression or extinction. Breton, for instance, counts almost three times as many speakers as Icelandic, but in contradistinction to the latter it suffers from progressive degeneration (Dressler and Wodak-Leodolter 1977, Durkacz 1983). However, except for the fact that both are small European languages, the ecological and topographical conditions of Icelandic and Breton are so different that they can hardly be compared with each other. Because of its geographic isolation on an island, Icelandic is exceptional as a highly developed culture language which, moreover, is a national language.[9] Breton is spoken within the borders of the French state only, which, at least since the French Revolution, are claimed as the realm of the French language. It co-exists in contact with and under the pressure of French. Breton is a minority language, but Icelandic is not.

In addition to the absolute size of its speech community, the functional differentiation of a language thus also depends on its geopolitical position and its size relative to politically rather than linguistically defined groups. These additional factors make it very difficult to assess the size of a speech community as a factor of the economic value of its language. The proper question to be asked is how, *ceteris paribus*, the number of speakers affects the economic evaluation of languages; but the problem is that this *ceteris paribus* is hardly ever given and that, therefore, the number of speakers is hard to isolate as an economic factor. Since languages are historically grown objects, they differ from each other in many respects. At least the following factors potentially interact with the size of the speech community as parameters of the socio-economic profile of a language: geographic position, sociopolitical status, association with a religion, literary and cultural tradition. It is well-known that these factors also have a bearing on how attractive a language is as a foreign language. Accordingly, Kloss (1974: 11) has singled out as the strongest indicator of the international status of a language the number of speakers studying and/or speaking it as a foreign language. The criterion of the size of a speech community hence needs to be amended to include both primary and secondary proficiency in the language.

For two reasons this makes the assessment even more difficult. First, although for some select languages widely used proficiency tests exist, there is no clear and uniform definition of what proficiency in a foreign language means; and secondly, there are hardly any census data about foreign language proficiency. The few figures given in table 3.1 are based on very rough estimates. What makes matters yet more complicated is that the difference between mother tongue and second or foreign language is not as distinct everywhere as it generally appears to be in the European context. In traditionally multilingual societies it usually makes more sense to distinguish various domains of language use (Fishman 1964). For instance, in view of the instable patterns of language allegiance and mother tongue identification in India's Hindi-speaking region, it is probably not only difficult but outright impossible to make any reliable statements about how many people speak it as their native language and how many as a second or foreign language (Khubchandani 1983: 45f.). Nevertheless, even very rough estimates indicate that the ranking of languages will be different when, instead of primary proficiency, secondary proficiency is taken into account. The outstanding position of English then becomes immediately apparent (Conrad and Fishman 1977). Russian, German, and French also appear in a different light. In this connection it must be noted that the overwhelming majority of all languages are never systematically studied or taught as foreign languages. Rather, foreign language education on a significant scale is limited to a few European culture languages, which both is a reflection of and reinforces their economic strength. It is for a variety of reasons that certain languages rather than others are studied as foreign languages (see below, p. 79). One of them is their relative development, that is, a property pertaining to contents rather than numerical strength. Hence, in addition to the size of the speech community, including those using a language proficiently as a foreign or second language, we need to take into account other parameters determining its economic value.

Languages as Means of Production

Apart from the question of how many others a language enables its speakers to communicate with, about what it enables them to communicate with each other is of great importance. Our experience with translation and the assumption that everything can be translated into any language, which implies that it is possible, in principle, to talk about everything in all languages, do not render this question meaningless or superfluous; for in many cases intertranslatability is just a potentiality which can only with great difficulty be turned into an actuality. The fact is that there is not a single scholarly journal on semiconductor technology in Bengali actually, almost nothing is published about semiconductors in Bengali. Obviously, Bengali is not in itself unsuitable for semiconductor technology or any other science; however, because science first emerged in India in the guise of the English language, the necessary terminologies were never developed in most Indian languages, which is why it is difficult to communicate in Bengali about semiconductors and other such matters. In more general terms this means, as already observed in chapter 2, that only a very small fraction of the languages of the world is suitable at all for the exchange of scientific ideas. It is quite telling in this connection, for instance, that Nobel Prize winning physicists have so far had only nine different mother tongues. Similar observations can be made for technology, administration, the juridical professions, and other domains of highly developed modern communication. Evidently, this greatly enhances the economic value of the fully adapted standardized common languages as opposed to those which cannot, or not without great difficulty, serve these communicative functions. For by virtue of their serviceability in the said domains, these languages provide access to knowledge which is useful to both the individual and the society at large.

From this point of view languages are readily recognized as a means of production, although one which, within the context of the speech community in question, is quasi-latent because it is the common property of all. Inter-group comparison, however, reveals the specific economic weight of different languages. Even in traditionally multilingual societies the utility value of languages makes itself felt on the labor market. With reference to West African cities such as Dakar, Bambara, and Lagos, Hodgkin, for example, notes that

> the difficulty of organising unskilled African workers is increased by the fact that most of them are illiterate and that most industrial towns . . . are polyglot. (Hodgkin 1957: 121)

In the industrial countries every migrant worker has first-hand experience of the importance of language as a means of production.[10] It is a result, among other things, of the fact that the labor market is integrated into a national economy and of the ensuing necessity to communicate with government departments, insurance companies, etc. The linguistic deficit of labor migrants often becomes the livelihood of their more senior bilingual colleagues. For instance, in many Parisian cafés French-speaking and writing North Africans have set up shop handling on a commercial basis the correspondence of less educated newcomers. Such mediators whose business is a byproduct of massive labor migration across linguistic boundaries have been labeled "language brokers" by Gumperz and Cook-Gumperz (1981). Opportunities in the labor market are affected by language skills even where purely manual jobs are concerned. In their study of Southeast Asian immigrants in Canada, Starr and Roberts (1982) discovered a positive correlation between income and proficiency in English (and, to a lesser extent, French). Insufficient knowledge of the language of the country, or, more precisely, the labor market where one wishes to earn a living drastically reduces one's competitiveness.[11] And conversely, control of ample linguistic resources may yield a profit.

Linguistic resources are unequally distributed in many societies. This is Bourdieu's (1982) motivation for introducing the notion that language skills must be recognized as a form of capital, linguistic capital, as he calls it. Since a distinction can be made between language skills that are naturally acquired and those that are commercially acquired, we prefer the notion of language as means of production to that of linguistic capital, but there is no significant difference in substance here.

Two aspects need to be carefully distinguished when languages are regarded as a means of production, first, the nature of the means of production, and secondly, the circumstances of its employment. The first aspect has to do with the functional potential of a language as compared to others in the sense of the degree of its adaptedness to the requirements of modern communication discussed above. The second aspect concerns the potential a language has in a certain setting, that is, more particularly, on a certain market. An example: both English and German are fully adapted common languages; they hardly differ in their functional potential, certainly not with respect to the critical communicative domains of science, technology, etc. Nevertheless, the exploitable potential of German is much greater in a German-speaking environment than in an English-speaking environment. A German lawyer or pharmacist who wants to settle down in Zurich brings his linguistic means of production with him, whereas the same means of production is only of limited utility only when he wants to set up shop in Nottingham where he cannot get by without acquiring an additional one. As with other means of production, the acquisition of an additional language is only a prerequisite but no guarantee of economic success.

Thus every language has a general functional potential which can be described in terms of the communicative functions that can be carried out with it: is it a suitable means for juridical, technical, scientific, commercial, religious discourse, etc.? But this general potential can be exploited in a particular setting and context only. Therefore, it must be determined for every individual case whether and how far a language is serviceable and hence economically useful in a given market.

Today Japanese is a fully adapted common language with a functional potential fit for all requirements of modern communication, just like English and German. Yet, no Japanese businessman ever tries to operate on the American market without a sufficient command of English, whereas the reverse case, of American businesspeople who expect to be able to do business in Japan without being proficient in Japanese, is not at all rare. On one hand, this is a reflection of the arrogance of power, but on the other hand, it testifies to the fact that the opportunities for realizing the functional potential of English on the Japanese market are far better than those of realizing the functional potential of Japanese on the American market.

The actual opportunities for realizing the functional potential of a language in a certain market are not determined by economic factors alone. Other interfering factors of a political or sociopsychological nature have to be taken into account when analyzing particular cases. In this connection we can turn to the Hispanic population of the US for illustration. Although English is a virtually indispensable prerequisite of social and economic success, even survival, in the US, and although the economic utility of English has been emphasized time and again by conservative groups lobbying against bilingual education in that country, the Spanish-speaking population in the US has not been able to realize this utility for itself. Some 25 percent of this group lives below the official poverty level, a proportion which, as Fishman (1988: 131f.) has demonstrated, is two to three times higher than the non-English-speaking part of the Hispanic population. In a study of one of the Hispanic sub-groups, Zentella (1988) has established that English proficiency is higher by 14 percent above the average of all Hispanics among New York's Puerto Ricans, but their income is $4,200 lower than the annual average of US Hispanics. Thus, for this group, as for Hispanics in general, there is no positive correlation between command of English and prosperity. Rather, there is a negative correlation between their extraction and their socioeconomic status which does not seem to be strongly related with language.

The general functional potential of a language has at all times an upper limit. This does not imply, however, that command of a language with a greater functional potential in all settings provides a competitive advantage over that of one with a lesser functional potential. In many cases, parts of the greater functional potential of a language are not in demand, as evidenced by the report of the Linguistic Minorities Project which deals with linguistic minorities in the UK. For historical, political, and social reasons, several of these minorities live in compact communities. Relative to the society at large, these geographical concentrations allow for partly extended opportunities of use for some of the minority languages, although their functional potential is inferior to that of English. In certain areas like the East End of London, where minorities are highly over-represented, and in certain sectors of the economy such as the clothing or food industry, minority language skills may even "have a positive economic value" (Linguistic Minorities Project 1985: 201).

It follows from these observations that the general functional potential of a language and the opportunities for its application are partially independent factors. If the functional potential of a language is limited, its use for certain purposes is hampered or ruled out altogether, but an optimal functional potential does not imply the economic superiority of the language in question for all purposes and in all settings. The Indian restaurant trade, for example, is an economic niche where certain Indian languages such as Hindi, Bengali, and Panjabi predominate (Linguistic Minorities Project 1985: 271). Only some of those working in this industry have direct contact with English-speaking customers and thus need English for their jobs. For other communicative domains of this trade, for example dealing with wholesalers and internal communication, command of one of the Indian languages is often more important. The Indian languages enjoy as it were a monopoly position, which explains why in this industry speakers with only limited or no proficiency in English are more numerous than speakers who know none of the Indian languages. In order to run a restaurant or a tailor's business it is not essential to have command of a language which is also suitable for cognitive science or biotechnology. Thus, owing to the specific demographic circumstances, the potential advantages of a language which is serviceable in these domains do not come into play.

At the beginning of this section we made a distinction between the nature of a means of production and the circumstances of its employment. As appears from the above observations, another distinction follows from it, namely that between the utility value of a language to society at large and its individual or group-specific utility value. The economic advantage which under certain conditions is tied for some individuals to a functionally restricted minority language does not affect the global superiority of the dominant language.

Investment into Language

The functional potential of a language is always the result of historical processes concerning both the language itself and the socioeconomic and cultural circumstances of its speech community. For language is a means of production not just for individuals professionally dealing with language, but also for society at large. This is particularly clearly evidenced by the important role that language plays in modern society. To a much greater extent than ever before it is crucial in the information society to have rapid access to information of every conceivable kind. In order to make sure that language is instrumental rather than obstructive to this end, it is necessary to work on the language and refine it, just as material implements need to be improved in the interest of enhancing productivity. Accordingly, languages are capital investment projects, in a literal rather than a metaphorical sense. The most important investments contributing to an improved utility of a language are the following: (1) the compilation of dictionaries for common use as well as terminologies for specific purposes; (2) word processing equipment; (3) automatic translation; (4) artificial intelligence, specifically the creation of knowledge systems and data banks; (5) the improvement of man—machine communication, that is, the adjustment of computer languages to human languages.

Inasmuch as such activities bring on costs, promoting and maintaining a cultivated norm can also be considered an investment. The pertinence of this view to language is obvious where industries are immediately involved. The speech community of Gujarati, for instance, is about six times the size of that of Hebrew. That, this notwithstanding, there are more word processing programs for the latter than for the former is plain evidence of this connection. To make a language electronically processible requires substantial investments which can be expected to be made by the private sector only when they promise to yield a return and which, in the absence of profitability, only affluent countries can afford. Moreover, such an investment is economically reasonable only if the language in question is highly enough developed to meet the requirements of technical and scientific discourse.

The production of non-fiction literature and textbooks for the Israeli market clearly demonstrates that Hebrew fulfills these requirements. Of the 1,147 titles published in 1986/87 84 percent were originally written in Hebrew and only 16 percent were translations.[12] In this sense, Gujarati is not as highly developed. What is more, its speakers mostly live in rural areas, and about 70 percent of them are illiterate, both reasons why, in spite of its relatively numerous speech community, Gujarati is not an attractive investment. Inevitably, the Government of India has other priorities than pumping a significant amount of money into the Gujarati language. This again is in sharp contrast with the situation of Hebrew with its small speech community whose members, because of their high level of education, make it an economically profitable investment, and which, in addition, benefits from government subsidies.[13] Economically speaking it is a platitude that a low capacity for investment is likely to be followed by a reduction in the capacity for innovation and competitiveness. These considerations help to explain why Hebrew, unlike Gujarati, is today a means of production which meets all of the requirements of modern communication and has a fair chance to sustain this capability. For potential investors as well as for its users, Hebrew has a high linguistic capital value.

This example of a small language which is more attractive as an investment than others with more numerous speech communities must not obscure the fact that, especially in this respect, the size of a speech community is an important factor which can be decisive for the economic viability of capital investments in language related industries. What counts, however, is not the total numerical strength of a speech community, but only the strength of that part which is a potential target group for the product in question. The clientele varies from one product to another and from one speech community to another. To keep to the example, many speakers of Gujarati are potential consumers of primers and other literacy materials, whereas there is less demand for such material in Hebrew. The book market is similarly indicative. Not only are books in languages that were only recently given a written form, or which are used in writing by a small minority of the speech community only, printed in small numbers of copies; the variety of printed material in such languages is also limited. A divers assortment of titles is possible in large highly literate speech communities because the mass circulation of some titles supports the production of those for a more restricted readership.

Dictionaries

Dictionaries are a special case. They require more substantial investments than most books, but they also promise greater and more lasting revenues. Nowadays dictionary making is a considerable industry which bears little similarity with the one-man enterprises of the pioneers of monolingual lexicography. As Harris (1980) has pointed out, the monolingual dictionary, at least in the Occident, was a Renaissance invention which became one of the most important innovations of the Enlightenment.[14] Dictionaries of this type play a major role for the self-perception and esteem of speech communities of cultivated standard languages, simply because they have greatly contributed to language standardization. The monolingual dictionary objectifies and reifies the vocabulary of a language, thus turning it into a potential material possession of each and every member of the speech community. Samuel Johnson undertook the work on his monumental dictionary which first appeared in 1755, almost incredibly, all by himself. It took him about ten years to compile 40,000 entries exemplified by 114,000 quotes. Evidently exhausted from his work, he made no secret of the hardship he endured in the process:

> The world is little solicitous to know whence proceeded the faults of that which it condemns; yet it may gratify curiosity to inform it, that the *English Dictionary* was written with little assistance of the learned, and without any patronage of the great; not in the soft obscurities of retirement, or under the shelter of academick bowers, but amidst inconvenience and distraction, in sickness and in sorrow. (Johnson 1964: 28)

About the great dictionary of the French academy he wrote:

> When fifty years had been spent upon their work, [the French academicians] were obliged to change its economy, and give their second edition another form. (1964: 29)

In the preface to his 1807 work, Campe, the editor of one of the major German dictionaries with 50,000 entries, records on several pages the almost insurmountable difficulties accompanying his work and complains about its meager proceeds. He could realize his project only if he succeeded "by means of various economizing measures in reducing the length of the dictionary, at least to the extent that its retail price would not be higher than that of Adelung's [1793] dictionary" (Campe 1807: v). Campe promised his readers more and better language than they could buy from Adelung and his publisher at the same price.

Commercial competition was also at the center of a dispute between Noah Webster and Joseph Emerson Worcester, the so-called "dictionary war" of the late 1820s and 30s in the United States. With his first dictionary of 1806 and its second revised edition of 1828, which had 70,000 entries and bore the ostentatious title *An American Dictionary of the English Language*, Webster had not only given expression to his claim of linguistic independence from England for the young republic, but also created a new market by introducing new spelling conventions. For acceptance of these conventions in America would make it more difficult for British publishers to supply and dominate the American market. Worcester's dictionary was also published in the United States in the same year with the explicit intention to foil Webster's attempt of keeping the proceeds of marketing the language in the country rather than letting them drain off to England. Its awkward title, *Johnson's Dictionary as Improved by Todd, and abridged by Chalmers; with Walker's Pronounciation Dictionary, combined*, indicates that it was designed to defend the southern English norm codified by Johnson and thus Great Britain's econolinguistic hegemony. As is well known, Webster and his publisher eliminated the competitor and prevailed in the USA. It was a stiff competition, though, because the market was small and the expenses were considerable. During the two decades or more that he devoted to the dictionary, Webster never stopped soliciting financial support from friends and acquaintances who he hoped were sympathetic to his project (Rollins 1980: 125). Initially, big profits were not in store. A mere 2,500 copies were printed of the 1828 edition. However, "the" *Webster* whose name, like *Robert* in France and *Duden* in Germany, became synonymous with "dictionary," still competes for control on the English language market today. The title of the third edition of 1971 is very telling indeed: *Webster's Third New International Dictionary of the English Language*. America, which at the beginning of the nineteenth century was yet to be established as an independent market, has disappeared from the title. Instead international currency is proclaimed and with it a claim on the world market.

It would doubtless be wrong to assume that the great lexicographers began their work in the expectation of material gains. On the contrary, they toiled under constant threat of personal financial ruin. An entire chapter of Elisabeth Murray's biography of her grandfather James Murray, the editor of the *Oxford English Dictionary*, deals with the perennial financial troubles that accompanied his travail of 35 years (Murray 1977). For the publisher, too, this project was a sacrifice and tribute to scholarship rather than a remunerative investment. In his preface to Murray's biography, R. W. Burchfield, the editor of the supplementary volumes to the *OED*, the last one of which was published in 1985, remarks:

> Faced with the exasperatingly lengthening forecasts of the date of completion and of the size of the Dictionary, and confronted with a des-

perately inadequate financial return from their heavy investment, the Delegates of the O.U.P. would have been justified, one feels, in abandoning the project altogether.

Yet, being as it is a unique historical dictionary of the English language, the *OED* will, in spite of the massive costs it brought about, not be a losing business for the publisher in the long run. Even if its sales will never yield a profit, it greatly enhances the prestige of Oxford University Press. What is of much greater importance, however, is that the *OED* is a tremendous enrichment of the English language, a lasting increase of its value, which throws open its many-layered differentiation refining it as a means of production. The public have acknowledged and appreciated this achievement, if not materially, at least symbolically: James Murray was knighted even before bringing his work to a conclusion and other honors were bestowed upon him. The publisher, too, paid tribute to the importance of the project by upholding its commitment to the *OED*'s continuation and supplementation.

Dictionaries are the cornerstone of language cultivation, and in this sense they are an investment, since they provide languages with the property that Kloss (1969: 77) summarily described as "the functional force of modern culture languages." Languages belonging to this class are the subject of an often closely braid network of dictionaries of various kinds: pronunciation, spelling, meaning, rhyme, style, etymology, frequency, idiomaticity, terminology, names, homonyms, synonyms, basic vocabulary, to name but some of the most important types. Languages differ greatly in the density of lexicographic recording. For Luxembourgish, which has been taught as a subject in school only since 1912 and became Luxembourg's official national language only in 1939 when proficiency in the language was made a precondition of citizenship, there are just a handful of dictionaries (Hoffmann 1979). For German, by contrast, 2,703 monolingual dictionaries of various types are quoted in one source (Kühn 1978). Kühn's bibliography covers a time span of just over 200 years which means, on average, some ten new dictionaries every year, although most of the recorded titles are from this century.[15]

With the great historical dictionary of the brothers Grimm and the various editions of the Duden, which is brought up-to-date every seven years, this is certainly more than most languages can boast in terms of dictionaries. Yet, the argument has been made that this is still not enough to stand the comparison with French and English lexicography. Weinrich (1985: 69) fears for the competitiveness of German which he sees threatened by its failure to adapt to future communicative requirements, the main problem being the drifting apart of the common language and the many languages for specific purposes. To counter this trend, Weinrich advocates the creation of a comprehensive interdisciplinary dictionary of the German language. For, he argues, "we must accommodate ourselves to the fact that the common language must be the shared basis for a variety of languages for scientific and other specific purposes, which is so essential for life under conditions of a highly industrialized civilization" (Weinrich 1985: 73). To uphold this function of the common language is no small order for a dictionary, and, as Weinrich admits, the quality requirements on such a work would be extremely high, if not "utopian." He does not comment on the enormous investment needed for such a project, but it is implied in his argument that in the interest of preserving the value of the German language such costs can be no object.

Johnson, Campe, Webster, Murray, and some of the other pioneers of modern lexicography worked alone or assisted by only a few aides. Such a solitary way of dealing with words would be altogether impossible for such ambitious projects as the interdisciplinary dictionary envisaged by Weinrich. Even traditional dictionaries are medium-scale operations nowadays. *The Random House Dictionary of the English Language*, for example, employs a full-time editorial staff of 130 who are assisted by more than 200 consultants.

To calculate the real expenses of compiling a dictionary for one of the great standard common languages is very difficult, because dictionary publishers typically market a variety of products composed by the same employees and on the basis of the same or partly identical material. But it is clear that considerable resources are necessary for financing the nascent phase of new dictionary projects. That eventually such projects usually generate substantial and steady revenues is a characteristic of modern society which relies so much on reference works.

Monolingual dictionaries are perhaps the most conspicuous area of the reification of a language requiring financial expenditures, and thus can be considered both a part and an indication of their value. Bilingual and multilingual dictionaries are another such indicator. With respect to any pair of languages A and B, a distinction must be made as to whether the typical user of the dictionary relating these languages to one another is a primary speaker of the one or the other, because the internal structure of the dictionary entries will differ accordingly.[16] Hence there are potentially four different dictionaries for every language pair, one each for the primary speakers of A and B for each direction, from A to B and from B to A. Lexicographers sometimes refer to "In-translation dictionaries" and "Out-translation dictionaries:" The former treat the respective foreign language as the target language, whereas in the latter it is the users' primary language.[17] Accordingly, there are two markets for the dictionaries of every language pair. That these markets are typically different in size has nothing or very little to do with the numerical strength of the respective speech communities. For instance, there is a wealth of English–Japanese dictionaries for Japanese users, but the supply and quality of English–Japanese dictionaries for primary speakers of English is much poorer. This is a reflection of the fact that the sales outlet for such a work has been very limited so far, which is why publishers have been hesitant to defray the necessary investments.[18]

The costs of compiling bilingual dictionaries are to be regarded as language-related investments not only because the finished product can be sold, potentially with profit, as a commodity on the market. The creation of such dictionaries is also an investment into the language itself, for every dictionary which relates a language to another is a potential source of its enrichment. Although dictionaries are often intended by their compilers to be purely descriptive, they are inevitably based on normative decisions. Of bilingual dictionaries this is even more true than of monolingual ones.[19] On one hand, the dictionary compilers just provide equivalents, but on the other hand, they also make suggestions how a word or expression of A for which there is no obvious equivalent could be rendered in B. Moreover, dictionaries exemplify the authority of the printed letter more forcefully than almost all other print products. By virtue of its sheer existence the descriptive dictionary, too, therefore acquires a normative quality.

There is great variation in the density and quality of the lexicographic recording of the languages of the world. For some languages there are many dictionaries, for others none at all, which means that language investments are distributed very unevenly across languages.[20] Claes (1980) lists 3,092 dictionaries for Dutch of which as many as 1,163 are monolingual. Of the remainder two-thirds (1,270) are bilingual and the rest (695) are multilingual dictionaries. An index of Japanese dictionaries in print in 1989 contains 1,224 entries of which about half are monolingual dictionaries.[21] Evidently, then, both Dutch and Japanese are languages in which heavy investments have been made.

As these examples illustrate, there are good reasons to look at the available dictionaries of a language as a value indicator in a literal and not just in a vague metaphorical sense. This perspective is instructive in two different ways. First, the total of all bilingual dictionaries for a language is indicative of the mental and financial efforts that have been, and are being, made in order to relate a language to others. Above all, bilingual dictionaries are auxiliary means for translators. From this follows the second point. The total of all in-translation dictionaries of all languages is indicative of the relative value of these languages for other speech communities. That is, an in-translation dictionary of language B for primary speakers of language A is evidence of the interest in translations from B by at least some speakers of A. In this way, a rank order of languages could be constructed where the language that occupies the top rank is the source language of the greatest number of in-translation dictionaries. This would be the language from which translation into others is in greatest demand. Conversely, a great number of in-translation dictionaries for the same target language is indicative of the fact that the respective speech community is willing and able to translate from a great variety of other languages into its own and thereby to enrich it.

While not being an absolute value indicator, the density of the lexicographic network that describes a language and relates it to others is a useful criterion. It makes languages comparable, at least in one objectifiable point; and it reveals the hidden value of lesser-used languages. This is very apparent in the case of classical languages which, while no longer used in everyday life, have nevertheless not lost all of their value. Rather, the lexical relationships between classical and modern languages, as documented in dictionaries, demonstrates that languages with minimal speech communities can yet be valuable. Moreover, such languages, especially Latin, Greek, Sanskrit, and Chinese, continue to serve as sources of lexical innovation and enrichment for modern languages, which in the absence of dictionaries would not in the same way be possible.

Translations

What was said about dictionaries also applies in a wider sense to translations. Where languages are considered as social resources, translation is to be understood as a long-term investment in the interest of maintaining or increasing their value. Since every translation into a language adds value to it, the totality of all translations into a language can be viewed as another indicator of its value. Furthermore, the translation activity into a language demonstrates how much qualified labor a society can afford to devote to this kind of occupation. Japan's potential in this regard is forcefully evidenced by the few available statistical data. During a period of just over three years from 1984 to 1988 more than 22,000 titles were translated into Japanese (Nichigai Associates 1988). These roughly 7,000 titles per year are books. The volume of translations into Japanese would be much more extensive yet, if articles in scientific and other journals were taken into account. The Japanese, it follows from these figures, are both willing and able to apply considerable expenditures in order to make scientific insights and literary works first published in other languages accessible in their own language, and in this way continuously adapt their language to the most recent functional requirements.[22]

The volume of translated literature is related to the size of the literate speech community of the language in question. Japanese publishers supply a huge market, and so do their German colleagues, who in 1987 produced 65,680 new titles of which 9,325 were translations (6,329 from the English and 1,108 from the French). That these were matched by only 2,391 licenses granted to foreign publishers for the translation of German books is a reflection not so much of the low esteem of German literature as of the fact that many German scientists nowadays choose to publish in English[23] which indirectly weakens the strength of the German language on the world market.

As mentioned above, intertranslatability is, on one level, a universal potential: it can be achieved, by means of appropriate language planning measures, even for languages into which nothing is ever translated. On another level intertranslatability is a graded quality which every language at every moment in its history possesses to a greater or lesser extent. To guarantee unrestricted intertranslatability for a language by means of standardization and continuous terminology innovation is in the best interest of the national economy which relies on it. For, to once again return to our analogy, a language which does not offer itself easily for translations from the most highly developed languages, enjoys as little esteem as inconvertible currencies.

Language as a Commodity

It follows from the above considerations concerning dictionaries and translations that the value of a language is determined in relation to that of others. In other words, languages have a market value. That is the exchange value a certain language has as a commodity, or the index of

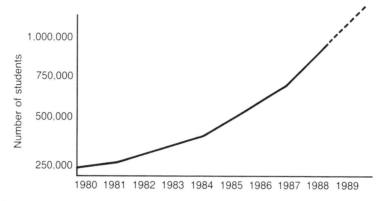

Figure 3.1 Increase of JFL students worldwide between 1980 and 1988; on the basis of surveys by the Japanese Foreign Ministry and the Japan Foundation, adapted from (Coulmas 1989b: 124).

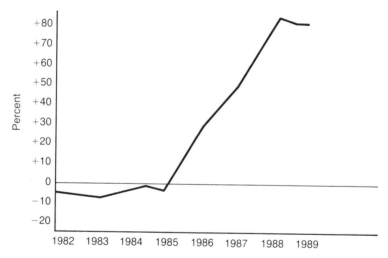

Figure 3.2 Movement of the Yen-rate with respect to the U.S. Dollar in percent, 1982–1989.
Source: IMF, International Financial Statistics.

its appreciation by a relevant group as compared to other languages. The commodity nature of languages manifests itself most clearly in the domain of foreign language learning and teaching which can be described as a market. Local, regional, and national markets as well as the world market, can be distinguished here. As in other markets, such as those for branded goods, securities, or currencies, there are fluctuations in the language market. The factors determining the market value of a language at a given point in time are of various kinds, political, cultural, but above all economic. Chinese, for instance, is the language of a huge speech community with a profound cultural tradition and a country which is of considerable political importance in the world of today. Moreover, it enjoys official status in a number of other countries and dependent territories. Yet, in spite of these qualities, there is no great demand worldwide for Chinese as a foreign language, because the potential for its economic exploitation is limited. Japanese, by contrast, advanced across the board on the world market of foreign languages during the past decade, a development which was almost as conspicuous as the upturn of the Japanese yen on the currency market (see figures 3.1 and 3.2).[24] Clearly, the cultural value of Japanese cannot have changed much during this period. Rather, the four-fold growth of the number of students of Japanese as a foreign language (JFL) during the 1980s reflects the fact that Japan has become an important trading partner for many countries on all continents.

To look at languages as commodities is warranted inasmuch as acquiring them as foreign languages usually causes costs, both on the individual and on the social level. As already mentioned, this is the economic basis of an entire industry: publishers, printing shops, language schools, recording studios for audiovisual materials, language-education software producers, etc. Evidently, only a few select languages can support such an industry, namely those for which there is a large-scale demand, the economically valuable languages (Cooper and Seckbach 1977). From this we can derive yet another indicator of the economic value of a language: the number of professionals it affords a living. The fact that of the many thousands of languages in the world only a few furnish the basis of a language industry reflects a general feature of the language market: it is oligopolistic and rather narrow in nature, being dominated as it is by a small number of big producers. As in many other industries the completely free market is only fiction.

Nevertheless, languages behave much like other commodities on the market, since growing demand results in increased sales and/or a rise in market price. Like other intangible goods, the commodity language has the peculiar property that by selling it the sellers do not diminish their own stock, since, obviously, the language teacher does not lose what the student acquires. Although the buyer pays in order to acquire a language, it is not this that the seller can supply, but only his or her services or products into which these services have entered and which in this sense transform intangible into tangible goods (for example: textbooks). Yet, it can be said with some justification that the supplier has something that the customer wants to obtain. The transaction between them thus involves a commodity, on one hand, and a service, on the other.

The Snowball Effect

Another characteristic of the commodity language is that its value increases by every speaker who acquires it, or, whom it acquires. This is much like the snowball effect with popular stocks which are appreciated because they gain value, which they do because they are being appreciated. The more people learn a language, the more useful it becomes, and the more useful it is, the more people want to learn it. The outstanding position that English has attained in this century as the most commonly taught foreign language, the dominant language of scientific publication, the main language of international organizations, media and tourism (Conrad and Fishman 1977, Strevens 1982, McCallen 1989, Truchot 1990) illustrates this connection most graphically. It is not primarily inherent properties of the language which are responsible for its spread throughout the world, but its great utility value which has been increasing steadily through its advances on the foreign language market. This is not to suggest that English has arrived at its predominant position quasi-naturally, simply as a result of unimpeded market forces. This would be like assuming that multinational group companies emerge spontaneously. The general conditions for the spread of a language in relation to others are aptly characterized, also for English, by Toynbee's remark that "a language which wins this kind of victory over its rivals usually owes its success to the social advantage of having served . . . as the tool of some community that has been potent either in war or in commerce" (Toynbee 1965: 534). Taken together, the English-speaking countries are today by far the largest import market in the world. 70 percent of the world's mail is estimated to be written in English, and 80 percent of all information stored in data banks is in English. Its is, therefore, only economic common sense that export-oriented countries in the non-English-speaking world prefer English to all other foreign languages. The demand for English language training thus engendered is satisfied by an industry operating

Table 3.2 Share of national currencies in total identified official holdings of foreign exchange, end of year 1979–87 (in percent)

Currency	1979	1980	1981	1982	1983	1984	1985	1986	1987
US dollar	73.2	68.6	71.5	70.5	71.2	69.4	64.2	66.0	67.1
German mark	12.0	14.9	12.8	12.3	11.6	12.3	14.9	14.9	14.7
Sterling	1.8	2.9	2.1	2.5	2.6	3.0	3.1	2.8	2.6
French franc	1.3	1.7	1.4	1.2	1.0	1.1	1.3	1.2	1.2
Swiss franc	2.4	3.2	2.7	2.8	2.4	2.1	2.3	1.9	1.6
Dutch florin	1.0	1.3	1.1	1.1	0.8	0.8	1.0	1.1	1.1
Japanese yen	3.6	4.3	4.0	4.7	4.9	5.7	7.8	7.6	7.0
others	4.8	3.1	4.4	5.0	5.5	5.8	5.4	4.5	4.7

(Source: International Monetary Fund 1988: 68)[26]

on a worldwide scale with an estimated annual turnover of some £6bn (McCallen 1989: 116).

English, this transpires from such an order of magnitude, has risen to become the tabular standard of the world's languages. Although this analogy is by now somewhat worn-out and can hardly stimulate the reader's imagination anymore, it is instructive to exert it once again. Looking at the reserve currencies, that is, those currencies which are held as reserves outside the countries in which they function as legal tender, it comes as no surprise that we find a close parallel with the international ranking of the languages of the countries concerned. According to the International Monetary Fund,[25] only the following currencies are used for reserves: US dollar, German mark, pound sterling, French franc, Swiss franc, Dutch florin and Japanese yen. Except for the absence of the Spanish peseta, there is an almost perfect match with the great foreign languages of the world. It is also conspicuous that among the reserve currencies the yen is the only non-Western one. Moreover, the increasing volume of yen held as reserves exhibits a tendency which is quite parallel to the spread of Japanese as a foreign language (cf. fig. 3.1). The development of the yen and the other currencies is summarized in table 3.2. The difference between the reserves held in the identified currencies and the total of all known currency reserves is listed in the table as "others," that is to say, currencies such as the Swedish crown which is held in small amounts in various countries.

The changes in the composition of foreign exchange reserves documented in table 3.2 reflect developments of the currency market and market interventions by some major industrial countries. On the whole, the decade covered in table 3.2 saw a diversification of the currency composition of foreign exchange reserves accompanying the depreciation of the dollar. That from 1986 the proportion of reserves denominated in dollars rose again is a result of massive support buying by central banks of industrial countries intended to arrest the decline of the dollar. Once again a parallel interaction of intervention and market mechanisms can be observed in the domain of the foreign language market.

The Imperfect Market

Since foreign language school curricula are virtually everywhere a matter of political decisions, there is no free market of foreign languages which is regulated by demand and supply only. Nevertheless, the language industry operates under the general premise of economic rationality. In the field of foreign language education, the notion of language needs is well-established and commonly used in planning the supply, packaging, and marketing of the commodity language.[27] Christ (1987: 213) has pointed out that a distinction must be made between the actual need, the demand, and the subjective desire to learn a foreign language. The demand for a given language may not concur with the determinable need for it in a community or the inclination of individuals to learn it. What we have here are the characteristics of a split market. As for example, on the market for agricultural products, production is determined only partly by potential sales according to real demand; to a large part sales are guaranteed by market intervention mechanisms. The inherent risk is that the consumers' wishes and interest as well as the objective demand for a commodity/language have next to no influence on production.

Examples for such disregard of actual language needs are not hard to find. Kutsuwada et al. (1987) have diagnosed the teaching of German as a foreign language at Japanese universities as a case in point. That some 300,000 students annually are enrolled in German classes does not reflect, they maintain, the students' wishes or the society's language needs. Those familiar with the situation of foreign language instruction at Japanese universities can hardly disagree with this assessment. The reasons for this over-production of German language skills are to be sought both in the tradition of Japanese academe where, since the Meiji period, German was regarded as the language of humanistic education, and in the lobby of more than 2,500 scholars anxiously defending their turf. Since as yet they have never depended on the market, only few of them take an active interest in analyzing existing demands and needs, which explains why in spite of the present over-supply actual needs are not satisfied: those who want or have to learn German because they want to work in a German-speaking country or co-operate with German companies usually have to rely on professional language schools, because the German courses in most universities fail to equip their students with the necessary practical language skills.

Another example, which highlights the risks of a guided demand on the language market, is found in China. During the 1950s and early 60s the most important foreign language there was Russian. After harmony turned into rivalry between the two socialist neighbors, however, the expenditures for training translators, interpreters, and university professors of Russian quickly proved a massive misinvestment with long-lasting consequences. Many fully qualified professionals have never worked in their proper field. Within the university, Russian teachers were transferred to administrative jobs or other departments. As late as 1980, many Russian departments of Chinese universities had more teachers than students (Coulmas, Thümmel, and Wunderlich 1981). In the meantime, foreign language curricula have been adjusted to actual language needs, allowing English to become the most widely studied foreign language (Pride and Liu 1988). But since the educational system is by no means able to satisfy the demand for English, a niche for private language entrepreneurs is opening up in China (Zhu and Chen 1991). Private language teachers cater mostly to individuals who want to improve their professional opportunities. As Hildebrandt and Liu (1991) have demonstrated, English is by far the most important foreign language used by Chinese enterprises.

It happens everywhere, of course, that individuals choose the wrong subject to study. However, the danger that financial and intellectual resources are wasted on a large scale is especially great where university curricula are by necessity strongly oriented to practical needs, as is the case in China and other developing countries where marketing research for language needs is often made subservient to political preferences.

It can be infered from examples of this sort that the number of students learning a language as a foreign language is no perfect criterion of its evaluation either. Yet, it does serve a certain indicative function. The fact that every year 300,000 Japanese students study German indicates, among other things, that Japanese society is able and willing to afford what to some appears to be a luxury with little utility. Moreover, the foreign language market is often subject to political influences. The Chinese example is not really exceptional, although it is rather drastic, for where financial resources are scarce and curriculum planning is strongly motivated by economic considerations, misguided decisions weigh particularly heavy. However, a certain part of the national expenses for foreign language training are almost everywhere allocated regardless of the demands of the market. It must be determined, therefore, on a case by case basis whether the market situation is stable or whether shifts in the demand or supply of a certain language are to be expected.

Turning to another aspect of language as a commodity, it is instructive to inspect the trade relationship between language pairs and their speech communities. For instance, the relationship between Germany and France is more or less balanced, that is, in both countries roughly the same percentage of students are enrolled in courses of the other's language. The relationship between Germany and its northern neighbor, Denmark, is quite different: relatively speaking and even in absolute numbers many more Danes learn and speak German than Germans learn and speak Danish. Obviously, in comparisons of this sort speech communities rather than languages are to be matched. But this does not alter the general picture: typically the relationship between any two speech communities with respect to their mutual linguistic proficiency is unbalanced, and thus speech communities typically have a surplus or a deficit on the international language market. A surplus is only found in some Western industrial countries, to be specific, in the Anglophone countries and in France. In economic terms this means that in these countries revenues of exporting language-related goods and services surpass the necessary expenditures for imports. This can be seen as an indication of the fact that, in spite of all non-economic forces acting on the foreign language market, those languages which are systematically studied as foreign languages at all and thus available on the market are unevenly evaluated. The general pattern is one of an inverse relation of import and export: the less a speech community is able to export its language, the more it is forced to import other languages.

However, this general tendency is partially counterbalanced, or, depending on one's view about such market interventions, distorted, by educational and cultural policies. Affluent countries, in particular, can afford for political or cultural reasons to maintain foreign language curricula withstanding market developments. In the long run, however, as witnessed by many examples, market control of this sort cannot be sustained. The decline of Latin discussed in the previous chapter is a case in point. The rapid depreciation of Dutch in Japan during the second half of the nineteenth century after the country's forced opening to the West is another. The most dramatic contemporary example is the replacement of French by English as the preferred language of diplomacy after World War II and the advance of English in foreign language curricula almost everywhere. In Dutch schools, for instance, as in those of many other countries, French was replaced by English as the first foreign language.[28] Hence, in spite of the fact that, because of partially controlled demand, the foreign language market is an imperfect market, the extent to which a language is studied as a foreign language is an expression of its international appreciation. To put it differently, the proportion of GNPs worldwide spent for teaching a language as a foreign language and the balance of payments for language goods and services of its speech community, its linguistic current account, are to be regarded as further indicators of its economic value.

Since English is acquired as a foreign language by more individuals and institutions than any other language, it occupies a special position on the world market of languages. Its balance on current account is much better than that of any of its competitors. Since its primary speakers are now outnumbered by a factor of two by its secondary speakers, the question can be asked with some justification of who owns English,[29] or who should benefit from the profits generated by its spread. That this is not merely an academic question is evidenced by McCallen's (1989: 117) assessment:

> A market valued in the billions of pounds a year is obviously attractive to a wide number of suppliers of the service – not only organisations and companies from the English speaking countries but, perhaps more significantly, those from the non-English speaking countries also.

As McCallen (1989: 117) further relates, the fact that some countries of the non-English-speaking world, especially in Scandinavia and western Europe, have begun to export as well as import English is considered by the director general of the British Council as a threat to British domi-nance on this market which will be intensified by the removal of trade barriers within the EC after 1992.[30] In order to fend off foreign com-petition by non-English-speaking countries, he has therefore proposed to coordinate the promotion of goods and services offered by British EFL suppliers.

Value for Whom?

Our considerations so far have made it clear that, if the economic value of a language can be determined at all, it depends on a cluster of factors rather than being linked to a single criterion. Although the factors discussed above which come into play here are difficult to operationalize in a precise manner, their examination lends support to the general premise underlying this chapter, which is that the value of a language can reasonably and justifiedly be contemplated in a material sense. It must not be forgotten, however, that values are not inherent properties of objects, but indexes of their appreciation by a relevant community of people in whose lives these objects fulfill a function. This discussion of the value of languages would hence be incomplete without addressing the question, "value for whom?"

An obvious and important distinction here is that between a primary and a secondary language. The criteria for evaluating one's first language are probably different from those to be applied to any of a number of foreign languages. Once again this distinction has a monetary counterpart: it is reminiscent of that between using money on the domestic market and as foreign exchange. The factors determining the domestic value and the trade-weighted exchange rate of a currency are not the same. The relationship between the exchange rate and the domestic purchasing power of a currency, therefore, is a highly complicated matter; the former is not simply a derivate of the latter. To quote a specific example: the international depreciation of the dollar relative to other currencies during the 1980s did not entail domestic inflation on the American domestic market to the same extent. Conversely, a higher international evaluation of the Japanese yen did not entail deflationary developments in Japan. Further, even currencies which are not traded on the exchange market do not therefore lack any domestic value; for on the domestic market they are the accepted means of payment for most goods. By the same token, for those acquiring it as their first language, every language is highly valuable, even indispensable, no matter whether or not it is studied as a foreign language by others, because it initiates them not only into the speech community in question but into human society, allowing them to give expression to their impressions of the world.

In a generic sense, the first language is equally important and valuable for every individual. Typically, this is the language of the environment into which one is born. Regardless of how the functions of the first language are assessed in this connection, its vital importance for the individual's mental development and socialization are beyond all doubt. However, from this it can be concluded in a very abstract sense at best that all languages are equally valuable, because "mother tongue is mother tongue." It is a delusion to assume that as mother tongues languages are of equal value, and that value differences become apparent on the foreign language market only. Language shift, that is, the social and individual behavior of parents who under certain circumstances fail to make their native language that of their offspring, attests to the fact that some languages are not thought valuable enough in a given socio-historical setting to be transmitted to the next generation, and that others are objectively of greater economic utility (see chapter 5 below). This holds true not only of immigrants and speech communities under occupation that assimilate and adopt the dominant language of their environment, but very generally. For, although the acquisition of a first language is a basic part of the human condition, it is not achieved without effort. This effort is generally assumed to be about the same for all languages.[31] But the payoff to an inhabitant of this planet is clearly not the same if that effort is directed at the acquisition of Maltese or at that of, say, Spanish, because as a first language Spanish opens up a much wider horizon of economic opportunities than Maltese. The relaxation during this century of foreign language requirements at all levels of the American educational system is also an immediate result of this general fact; for, thanks to the present politico-economic constellation of the world, the range of action of those learning English as their first language is so wide that the economic necessity and other incentives of foreign-language study are generally perceived as unimportant. For similar reasons, former British prime minister Thatcher tried to torpedo the LINGUA program of the European Community which calls for an expansion and diversification of foreign-language education in the Member States. From her point of view, Britain was asked to pay for a program which, because of the enormous imbalance on current accounts of the major European languages in favor of English, benefited her country least.

For the individual speaker the unequal balances on current accounts of languages imply that the first language is an economically exploitable qualification for some, but not for others. British university graduates, for example, can make a living in many places around the globe without any further professional training, simply by marketing their mother tongue skills. For their Danish or Greek counterparts such opportunities are much more limited. Conversely, for those anticipating to take up occupations in international business, politics, or cooperation of other kinds, English has been for some time, and will continue to be in the foreseeable future, the safest investment. Yet, it must not be overlooked that, although their numbers are rising, on the whole only relatively few people work in jobs which require foreign-language skills, although many of these jobs are in the medium or higher income brackets.

The analogy of the market for languages and foreign exchange which has guided the considerations of this chapter must not be pushed too far. Fluctuations in the language market are not as rapid as those in the foreign exchange market, because changes in the valuation of languages do not happen as abruptly as can sometimes be observed in the case of currencies; although shifting patterns in the valuation of languages are of a more lasting and effective nature than the appreciation or depreciation of currencies. However, there are some surprising similarities in the dynamics of the two markets. Changes are not always brought about by rationally calculable factors only. Languages are subject to sociopsychological attitudes interacting with other sociocultural features. The more a language is perceived by the members of a culture or ethnic group as being associated with their identity, the greater the emotional attachment to it. This nexus usually counteracts economic forces and ensures the survival of languages under economically and politically adverse conditions. Furthermore, languages have a cultural value which is not causally related to their economic value. For individuals the cultural value of their mother tongue may be more important than its economic potential. And finally, knowledge of a rare and economically insignificant language can still be economically valuable for the proficient individual (who in that case controls a scarce resource). Under the bottom line, however, such "exotic" individual valuations of languages do not carry much weight with respect to the value of a language on the world market.

Interim Results: Factors of an Economic Profile of Languages

From the observations in this chapter it follows that the value of a language is determined by a number of factors, all of which contribute to make language not only a medium but also an element of economic processes. By recapitulating the most important ones we can now approximate a more detailed specification of what is to be understood by the term "value of a language," although the weighing of the factors is a difficult problem yet to be resolved. At the present state of our knowledge it seems impossible to me to offer a solution which is not only well-argued but also free of arbitrary decisions. This is due to a deficit in theoretical and empirical research which can only be amended gradually by collecting more information on how economic processes are affected by linguistic conditions. To this end it should be helpful more rigorously to compare and scrutinize the factors discussed in this chapter. They are, therefore, presented here without weighing their importance. Instead they may serve as categories of an economic profile of languages, on the basis of which a first comparison of the economic value of any two languages is possible which must then be subjected to a more detailed analysis geared to the individual case. The economic profile of a language encompasses (1) the communicative range of a language as expressed in the demographic strength of the community using it as (a) a first and (b) a second/foreign language; (2) the level of development of the functional potential of a language as a societal means of production and the opportunities for its employment; (3) the total amount of investment that has been made in a language, where lexical recording, the density of the network of bilingual dictionaries relating it to other languages, the translation flow into and out of it, and the level of electronic processibility can serve as partial indicators; (4) the demand for a language as a commodity on the international market of foreign languages and the size of the industry it supports, as well as the shares of national GNPs which are spent worldwide for its acquisition; (5) the balance on the current account of a language for its speech community.

This profile is obviously heuristic and preliminary in nature. Moreover, it fails to take into account an important economic aspect of the social reality of individual languages, namely the expenditures brought about for a community by language and languages. They are the subject of the next chapter.

4

The Costliness of the Polyglot World: *Language-related Expenditures of Government and Business*

The dubious renown of having created the first historically attested construction ruin belongs to Nebuchadnezzar II, the builder of the Babylonian tower, which was never completed because of communication barriers among the work force. In the original account of this economic débâcle (Genesis 11), the people are said to have spoken the same language until that time, when it was confounded by divine intervention for fear that things were getting out of control. Yet, a more realistic scenario, perhaps, is that domestic labor shortage had forced the builders to bring in foreign craftsmen from too many different places with no common language. Linguistic chaos at the construction site followed, eventually leading to the break-up of the ambitious project.

Ever since, it has been common knowledge that we not only value language as a dear possession, but that it can also cost us dearly. Or is it the other way around, that it is the costs inevitably transpiring from a diversity of languages which are at the bottom of our esteem of language? The inescapable contradiction between rationale and rationalization which complicates an answer to this question cannot be resolved here; but an analysis of language in terms of calculable costs is possible to some extent. This should not be taken to mean, however, that on the following pages an itemized calculation shall be made of that part of the gross global product consumed by this planet's multiplicity of languages. This would be much too aspiring a design. What we can do is point out the most important areas in which language-related costs arise, and discuss the question of whether such expenses are always justified and cost-efficient.

The following considerations proceed on the assumptions that language costs are brought about both in the public and private sectors, that some of these costs are inevitable, while others are not, and that some of them can be related to a prospective return.

Budgeting Language Costs: The Public Sector

The contemporary world of nation states is at the same time the world of national languages, which means that virtually everywhere language is considered a matter of government responsibility. Only very few things for which political responsibility is claimed do not generate costs for the public sector; likewise with languages. Of course, there is variation on a wide scale as regards the political and sociolinguistic conditions of the countries of the world and the dominant ideas and necessities concerning language policies as well as the resources allocated to their implementation. Moreover, not all language-caused expenditures are recognized and accounted for as such. There are overt and hidden language costs. If, for example, a telephone conversation takes twice as long than it should because of a civil servant's insufficient proficiency in a language he can be expected to know, the avoidable additional costs thus engendered are very hard to relate to language where they show up, namely on the telephone bill. On the other hand, there are many budget items which are explicitly set out as relating to language. Among them are official multilingualism, bilingual education, foreign language teaching, mother tongue education, language planning and language cultivation, language export, and communication in international organizations. That language engenders costs is particularly evident in officially multilingual countries which pursue an institutionalized language policy. Such a policy has economic aspects with regard both to costs and benefits. Referring to Africa, Djité (1990: 96) therefore points out:

> The formulation of a rational language policy in a multilingual nation is in itself an economic issue and should have as high a priority as other economic issues.

Expenditures brought about by national multilingualism are dealt with at the beginning of this chapter. In the impoverished countries of the Third World, the ensuing problems are especially urgent and serious.

However, not many data are available for these countries to allow for detailed analysis. Instead, Canada offers itself as an exemplary case, since the Canadian government has more extensive experience in this regard, which is recorded in more comprehensive documents than exist in any other country. What is more, economic aspects of multilingualism have received a great deal of attention in scientific and public discussions in Canada.

Official Multilingualism

Multilingualism, although not equally valued by all Canadians, has always been a feature of Canada's national identity. In the early days of the European colonization of the North American continent, the British and the French competed with each other, initially with equal chances of success. But the Seven Years' War in effect thwarted all plans for establishing a self-sufficient French colony. In 1759 British troops took Quebec, and four years later Canada became British. Nevertheless, the Franco-Canadians maintained their cultural identity, for the most part under the leadership of the Church of Rome which the British, in an act of 1774, tolerated together with French laws and the land-tenure system. From the very beginning, language was recognized as the most important means of maintaining cultural identity, and as a central component of it. Indeed, the church declared language loyalty a matter of faith, trying to keep control over its congregation with the help of the famous slogan, *Qui perd sa langue, perd sa foi*, "to lose your language is to lose your faith." In view of the fact that, to this day, Quebec is a French-speaking enclave surrounded by a continent of English speakers, these efforts must be considered successful, if judged against the self-set goal.

Canada is a bilingual federal state whose two official languages, English and French, enjoy certain rights and privileges. It was found necessary to provide legal instruments for regulating the relationship of the two languages and their use, because, in spite of undiminished Franco-Canadian linguistic nationalism, French slipped into a defensive position vis-à-vis English, chiefly for economic reasons.

In an excellent paper, Breton (1978) has analyzed the historical background of this development as follows. In order to uphold its authority and maintain control over its clientele, the church used the school system to discourage francophones from entering the domains of big industry, commerce, finance, and corporate law, urging them to limit themselves to agriculture and smaller enterprises instead.[1] The rationale of this policy was that knowledge of North America's lingua franca was indispensable for engaging in the said areas of activity, that is, the higher levels of business and industry. Bilingualism, the church realized, was to be avoided, because it was as likely as not to be the first step towards language shift and thus posed a real threat to the church, provided, that is, the association between faith and language was more than demagogy. According to Breton, the church supported by francophone nationalists allowed the anglophone elite to dominate the more lucrative domains of the economy in order to accomplish the goals of their language policy. This vantage point can explain the economic imbalance between the two Canadian population groups which disfavors the francophones,[2] as well as the fact that French increasingly comes under pressure, since it lacks an economic base appropriate to the cultural aspirations associated with it. English has thus become the unchallenged language of Canada's economic elite (Daoust 1987).

Since the early 1950s French has been losing ground in Canada. For more than a century about 30 percent of the Canadian population were French-speaking. In 1951, 29 percent of all Canadians reported French as their mother tongue; but 20 years later, only 26.9 percent did so, and by 1981, the proportion of French speakers had further slipped to 25.7 percent (Ridler and Pons-Ridler 1986: 52). A precipitous decline in the fertility rate of French-Canadians, the increasing willingness of the socially upward mobile to learn and use English, and the strong preference for English by immigrants of language backgrounds other than French or English have led to such a precarious situation that it was felt necessary to support French in the unequal competition with English by means of a number of language laws. The declared objective of these measures, however, was to improve the French-Canadians' chances of participating in economic life, rather than to protect the French language for its own sake. The Charter of the French Language of 1977 (Bill 101) makes French the 'official language of Québec' (article 1). The purpose of the Charter as stated in the preamble is

> to make French the language of the State and the Law, as well as the normal and usual language of work, teaching, communications, commerce and business.[3]

For professional life this means that job applicants have to be able to speak French.[4]

The implementation of this legally based policy brought about considerable costs.[5] According to Esman (1985: 52) the costs of official bilingualism reached 1 percent of the federal budget or C$503 million for the fiscal year 1978/79. How can these expenditures be measured? The most important cost engendering components of Canada's policy of official bilingualism on the basis of the legal provisions that came into existence in the 1970s, particularly the francization of Quebec, are as follows.

1   *Agencies* established for the implementation of language policy objectives; for Quebec:
   a   French Language Office;
   b   Commission for the Protection of the French Language;
   c   Council on the French Language.[6]
   Vaillancourt (1987) estimates the running costs of these agencies for the period from 1974 through 1984 at between C$172 million (minimum expenses) and C$232 million (maximum expenses), using 1984 C$ as a standard. Other expenses for francization activities include costs of federal agencies which are obliged to offer bilingual services.

2   *Language training* for civil servants. Pons-Ridler and Ridler (1987: 103) estimate C$10,000 for a minimum of a six months language course per person, a figure which does not include the civil servants' salaries during training.

3   *Bilingualism bonuses* to some 48,000 civil servants. In the fiscal year 1982/83, some C$38 million were spent for this purpose (Pons-Ridler and Ridler 1987).

4   *Translation of official documents.* Translating a French text of 5,000 words into English costs about C$1,500. The civil service produces some 25 million words of text each year. Only some of the expenses for the necessary translations are covered by the expenses mentioned under (1) above. Landry (1987: 50) provides the following figures for the Translation Bureau: in 1986/87 it had a staff of 1,492 and a budget of C$87 million.

5   Changes in *public signs and billboards.* The language law requires that in Quebec signs be written exclusively in French.

6   Grants for programs in support of *linguistic minorities.* More than C$250 million are spent each year (Pons-Ridler and Ridler 1987).

7   Grants for French language training to *immigrants* in the Centres

d'orientation et de formation des immigrants. Such programs are not strictly mandated by the language laws or other provisions of Quebec's language policies, but they can be considered supplementary measures. Vaillancourt (1987: 83) reports the figure of C$20 million annually for the period 1976–1981.

The expenditures listed under (1) to (7) are calculable, but these are hardly the only public expenditures of official bilingualism. Other more or less hidden costs must be added. The Canadian situation nevertheless offers itself for illustration, for although in many countries official bi- or multilingualism swallows up tax monies, language itself is only rarely the object of a budgeted policy. In the absence of a clearly defined policy designed to bring about, or prevent, certain changes in patterns of social language choice and use, the statement that multilingualism engenders public expenditures is bound to remain general and vague.

To take but one example, it can hardly be doubted that Belgium's official multilingualism which, as in the Canadian case, is territorial and occupies a prominent position on the political agenda,[7] causes considerable costs. Yet, these costs are much harder to estimate than those of Canada's language policy since 1977. After prime minister Martens' government was brought down in 1987 over the language issue, it was decided after five months of negotiations that the constitution be reformed in such a way as to transform the Kingdom of Belgium into a federal state on the basis of linguistically defined territorial boundaries (Schaling 1988, Couttenier 1989). Fundamental administrative changes of this sort are expensive. New government departments and agencies are created, others are broken up or scaled down. A regional financing law was enacted, providing for the transfer of budget allocations from the central government to the regions and communities. During the negotiations and the Parliamentary debate about the law, language repeatedly played an important role. For financing mother tongue education, the experts had calculated that by the end of 1998, Dutch language education would receive BF 14 billion less than it had received in 1988, and that a proportionally similar reduction would occur for French language education. Although equal and just, such a shortfall in receipts is more difficult to bear for the poor Walloon communities than for the affluent Flemish. Thus, although the constitutional reform aims at decentralization and regionalization, a provision had to be included in the regional financing law for a "national solidarity allocation," that

Table 4.1 Official languages at the highest government level of some multilingual countries

Country	Official languages	Simultaneous interpretation	Documentation
Belgium	Dutch, French	yes	both languages
Finland	Finnish, Swedish	no	both languages
India	Hindi, co-official English; 15 regional languages admitted for deputies who do not speak Hindi or English	yes, Hindi and English; 7 regional languages are interpreted into English and Hindi	Hindi, English
Ireland	Irish, English	House of Representatives: yes; Senate: no	both languages
Israel	Hebrew, Arabic	yes	Hebrew (subsequent translation into Arabic)
Yugoslavia	Serbian, Croatian Slovenian, Macedonian	yes	in the four official languages; federal laws also in the languages of national minorities
Pakistan	Urdu, co-official English	yes	both languages
Switzerland	German, French, Italian, Rhaeto-Roman	National Council: yes; Council of States: no	German, French, Italian
South Africa	Afrikaans, English	yes	both languages
Sri Lanka	Sinhalese, Tamil, English	yes	Sinhalese with subsequent translation into Tamil and English
USSR	no official language for the Supreme Soviet; 61 languages admitted	yes	documents of Supreme Soviet in languages of all Union Republics

(Sources: *Fischer Weltalmanach* (1990), European Parliament Working Documents 1982/83, no. 1-306/82)

is, financial compensation between affluent and less affluent regions, allowing for the actual needs of Wallonia rather forcing it to cut expenditures and reduce public services.

In Belgium, as evidenced by this example, language is a social feature which causes costs to the government and plays an important role in the allocation of funds. However, it is so integral a part of the overall political process rather than the object of specific policies designed to influence social language use that, as opposed to the case of Canada, it is quite impossible even to offer an estimate of the costs of official multilingualism in Belgium.

The tax payers of many countries have to foot the bill of official multilingualism. Interpretation and translation services for government and administration have to be budgeted on a regular basis, although such costs vary on a wide scale. As in Canada, two languages are used in official documents and publications and to some extent in official meetings in Finland (Finnish and Swedish), Ireland (English and Irish), Israel (Hebrew and Arabic), and South Africa (Afrikaans and English). Yugoslavia, as long as its central government functioned, had to deal with four languages of state: Serbian (in Cyrillic letters), Croatian (in Roman letters), Slovenian, and Macedonian, as well as Magyar and Albanian as additional official languages and Slovak, Rumanian, Turkish, and Italian as recognized languages of education. And a large multi-ethnic state such as the former Soviet Union admitted as many as 61 languages on the highest level of government, in the Supreme Soviet, which means that these languages were used for documentation and in sessions where interpretation was provided on the basis of actual demand. Table 4.1 provides a synopsis of the provisions of official multilingualism at the highest government level in a number of select countries.

Multilingual proceedings are part of the regular functioning of many countries. The necessary staff of language services are institutionally provided for. Their salaries are current expenditures like those for other government services. To be sure, the language services must work cost-effectively in the sense that the personnel ought to be employed to capacity in accordance with socially common standards. But these expenditures are running costs rather than service investments which are expected to yield a return that can be estimated on the basis of a profitability calculation. This is only the case where a certain policy is adopted and funded in order to change existing conditions, as in the case of Canada's language policy discussed above where tax monies are spent for the implementation of a language policy intended, among other things, to improve the economic opportunities of a clearly defined part of the population. In many cases bilingual education is part of such a policy.

Bilingual Education

In the narrow sense bilingual education concerns certain population groups who are afforded the opportunity to use, in school education, their mother tongue in addition to the language of the country or region where they form a minority in such a way that, on one hand, the students' academic achievements are not adversely affected by insufficient language proficiency and, on the other hand, they acquire equal competence in both languages. Such groups can be allochthonous minorities such as labor migrants in Britain, Germany, and other northern European countries, or autochthonous minorities living within the domain of a national or official language as the Welsh in Britain or the Frisians in the Netherlands. Establishing bilingual schools or bilingual tracks is inevitably a financial burden for the educational system. Inasmuch as public educational institutions are concerned, tax monies have to be defrayed for this purpose, which implies political accountability and the weighing of conflicting interests. A substantial and relevant case of such conflicts is the heated discussion that bilingual education has sparked in the United States.

The Bilingual Education Act passed in 1968 first created the possibility to sponsor, at the federal level, bilingual education programs for students of non-English-speaking homes.[8] For the development of bilingual education curricula and teaching materials $15 million were earmarked in 1968 and twice that sum in the following year. Ten years later the budget allocation for bilingual education under Title VII had been raised to $200 million with possible increases up to $400 million in 1983 (Weinstein 1983: 110f.). These figures reflect the growing readiness of the federal government during the 1970s to recognize and promote languages other than English, especially Spanish, as medium and subject of school education. This tendency came to a halt under the Reagan administration. Bilingual education was found too expensive, and the respective budget titles were accordingly drastically reduced. In 1982, still $200 million were appropriated to bilingual education in the federal budget, but by 1985 the title had been cut down to $130 million. Moreover, the definition and contents of bilingual education was changed. Bilingual education was combined with minority affairs, mainly concerning recent immigrants and refugees. The 1982 budget explains the bilingual education program as follows:

> This program supports the development of bilingual education programs in local schools to help children of limited English proficiency learn English while they develop subject matter skills. (Appendix to the US budget for fiscal year 1982, I-I34)

However, the 1985 budget made explicit what was really at issue, assimilation, not pluralism:

> This program supports the development of programs in local schools to prepare children of limited English proficiency to enter an all-English-language education program. (Appendix to the US budget for fiscal year 1985, I-I4)

Thus, public funds were not to be spent for bilingual education programs designed to produce graduates fully proficient in two languages, but only for providing immigrants with survival English language skills, that is, for transitional bilingualism.[9] In the 1990 budget just $173 million were appropriated for bilingual education, including programs for immigrants and refugees. This is the logical result of President Reagan's attempt to reverse the policy that had been initiated in the 1970s. He held very clear views on bilingualism. Mixing up ideological and economic arguments, he branded as un-American the desire to cultivate, in addition to English, another tongue linking individuals and groups to pre- or extra-American cultures and traditions.

> It is absolutely wrong and against the American concept to have a bilingual program that is now openly, admittedly dedicated to preserving their [the immigrants'] language and never getting them adequate in English so they can go out into the job market and participate. (Reagan 1981: 181).

Reagan's hostility toward bilingual education lent support to a political movement called 'US English' which opposes bilingual education as well as bilingual services in the public and private sector, and which has as its ultimate goal a constitutional amendment that would make English the official language of the United States.[10] Although, in its many publications, US English often refers to new immigrant groups with their various languages, the chief target of its campaign are the Hispanics who, according to their view, which is widely shared by members of the anglo-oriented middle class, pose a threat to social cohesion in the United States. This is not only because at about 13.6 million in 1990 the Hispanics are by far the largest ethnic minority, but also because, unlike most other groups, they maintain their language for practical rather than only symbolic use. The anti-Hispanic thrust of US English transpires from a comment by its executive director:

> By insisting on bilingual/bicultural education, by stretching the time children spend in these classes from months to years, by extracting concessions such as bilingual voting ballots and a bilingual social service delivery system, by demanding – and obtaining – federal funds to operate a National Hispanic University, the unwritten compact between immigrants and the host society has been violated. (Bikales 1986: 84)[11]

The dispute between the opponents and the supporters of bilingual education is political, but economic arguments are often invoked on both sides, playing a somewhat unexpected role in the debate. As in President Reagan's criticism cited above, it is often implicitly or explicitly assumed that lack of English proficiency is to blame for the economic misery of the Hispanics as a group, and that this in turn is a result of bilingual education. This is a convenient line of argument, as it makes the Hispanics responsible for their own plight and, moreover, promises to cut apparently futile public expenditures.[12] It does not, however, take into consideration the facts. For a high level of English language proficiency does not really have an impact on the socio-economically marginal situation of the US Hispanics. As already mentioned (p. 67), some 25 percent of them live below the poverty level, a proportion which is three times as high as the percentage of non-English-speaking Hispanics.

As these figures suggest, language is not the real issue but only a pretext for making access to economically attractive positions more difficult for a marginalized group. This anyway is the reproach voiced by many Hispanics in response to allegations such as those by US English, former President Reagan, and other conservative politicians. The root of the problem, Zentella (1988: 50) says, "lies in an inability to accept an expanded definition of an American," one which includes the Hispanics. Thus, the arguments of the opponents of bilingual education which allegedly aim at economic equality of opportunity, appear to be grounded in the underlying political motivation of established groups who feel the need to defend their privileges against upstarts and late comers to the land of no longer unlimited opportunities.

Conversely, proponents of bilingual education often employ economic arguments which they expect to be more likely to be taken seriously than, for example, arguments drawing on cultural or sentimental values. Fishman (1985a), for instance, emphasizes the greater cost-effectiveness of multilingual experts in the civil service, industry and business, and the military who, he maintains, have a greater potential than their monolingual colleagues to succeed and do their jobs efficiently. They can communicate better and with more people, they can serve more people, they can "sell" more people. To recognize that multilingual civil servants are a great asset, Fishman insists, has nothing to do with one's preferences or political point of view, but is simply a matter of accounting. There is, after all, a calculable demand for multilingual executives in industry, business, and administration.[13]

Advocates of bilingual education believe that multilingualism is part of the American tradition and a value in itself which, therefore, is worth supporting, but its opponents do not agree. This is why the former say "economy" and mean "language and culture," while the latter say "language and culture" and mean "economy." There are no unequivocal economic indicators vindicating either one by showing that cultivating multilingualism has a positive effect on the GNP, or, conversely, that it leads to the fragmentation of the labor and commodities market which impedes growth. Therefore, it is to be expected that budget titles for bilingual education in the United States as well as in western European countries such as the UK, Germany, the Netherlands, the Scandinavian countries, and also in North Africa or South Asia will remain an object of political controversy.[14] This also holds true for other publicly funded language-related responsibilities such as foreign language training, language planning, and language export.

Foreign Language Training

In most countries foreign language training is, in some measure, a government responsibility for which public funds have to be spent. Teachers' salaries account for the largest share of such expenditures. Since financial resources as well as time of school attendance are limited quantities, it is necessary to make a selection from the available potential supply of foreign languages. What are the factors determining the selection? To be sure, existing institutional and curricular structures, traditions, and political considerations come into play here, but in the long run the weightiest factor of all is the economic utility of a language in the sense discussed in chapter 3. Even if attempts are made to determine foreign language curricula on the basis of a cultural policy alone and to counterbalance economically motivated trends, no national economy can afford to finance long-term mass education which fails to yield a return. Promoting or censuring the instruction of certain languages is not the issue, but rather what public outlays a government is able to justify for what languages. For this reason it has become almost impossible in most western European countries to fund Latin and classical Greek as regular subjects of high school instruction.

Important factors influencing the kind and contents of publicly funded foreign language education include the size of a country, its geopolitical location, its level of industrialization, and economic relations with other countries. As a relatively small country whose economy has for centuries relied to a very high degree on foreign trade, but whose language is not widely spoken outside its borders, the Netherlands is strongly motivated to acquire the languages of its most important trading partners. These are English, German, and French. For the Netherlands it is a matter of economic necessity that all of these languages are actually compulsory subjects of higher education.

Most politicians concerned with educational and cultural affairs nowadays consider English the most important foreign language, thereby reducing themselves to executors of economic policy. In Germany some 80 percent of all high school students learn English as their first foreign language, 18 percent French, and 2 percent Latin or other languages. In France as many as 85 percent of secondary students learn English as their first foreign language. In Denmark English is the first foreign language for all students. 75 percent of all Turkish high school students learning a foreign language study English. McCallen (1989: 21) estimates the number of students of 36 countries learning English at 68 million. This demand is satisfied almost entirely through public funding.

From the point of view of those countries that need not teach this language for which there is such a massive demand, its wide international spread can lead to the conclusion that heavy financial commitments for foreign language education are unnecessary. Such an attitude is, indeed, reflected by the thriftiness of the big English-speaking countries in the field of obligatory foreign language education.[15] In

1989, the British government issued Statutory Orders for the National Curriculum, in which, for the first time, learning a modern foreign language became compulsory for all secondary school pupils, "whereas previously a foreign language has been seen as a subject for the academic elite" (Stubbs 1991: 223). In the United States it is not uncommon that students graduate from college without having received any foreign language education at all.

That the LINGUA Program for the promotion of foreign language education in the countries of the European Community met with resistance on the side of the British government testifies to the same attitude. The EC Commission had originally earmarked 250 million ECU for the program, which is designed especially to promote the 'smaller' languages of EC member states, for a period of five years beginning 1990. But as a result of England's opposition, the program was cut by 50 million ECU, taking out the parts intended for high schools. LINGUA is thus confined to college and university education. The underlying reasons for the attitude adopted by the British government – the anti-European posture of then prime minister Thatcher, or the view that foreign language education in the EC countries is quite sufficient – are none of our concern here. The point at issue is that the government of a country whose language occupies the leading position on the international foreign language market refuses to subsidize the spread of other languages for which it believes it has no need. The question whether such a policy is really economically sensible is quite a different matter, to which we will return. In the present connection it shall only be noted that political decisions about the appropriation of public funds for foreign language education are influenced by economic considerations. That such decisions not only guide consumer behavior, that is, the actual extent of foreign language study in a given society, but also reflect existing demand, is illustrated by a survey carried out in 1984 in Switzerland, where it was found that, in spite of this country's very special multilingualism, English had become the most popular first foreign language. The most important reasons for learning the language advanced by the students indicate a clear dominance of economic motivations. They are summarized in table 4.2.

To some extent public budgets are also charged with costs for extra-scholar foreign language training, including programs for teaching the country's or region's dominant language as a foreign language. This applies in particular to countries where immigrants and refugees are entitled to grants for tuition fees, tax reliefs or other forms of public

Table 4.2   Motivations of Swiss high school students for learning English 1984

Rank	Motivation	Percent
1	English can be used all over the world	97.4
2	English is the language of business	65.4
3	English is the language of tourism	60.2
4	Knowledge of English increases job opportunities	55.1
5	English is the language of science	51.3
6	English is the language of entertainment	25.6
7	Want to learn about USA	17.9
8	Want to read Anglo-American literature	12.9
9	Want to learn about England	10.3

(Source: *Bulletin Celia*, 1984, no. 44, adapted from McCallen 1989: 25)

support. With the influx of citizens from their former colonies as well as labor migrants from the Mediterranean periphery, the Netherlands, for example, has reacted with a decisively integrationist policy. One of its priorities is the funding of Dutch classes and literacy programs. The government, moreover, sustains six translation centers which offer services to the various minority groups, especially assisting them in their dealings with government agencies.[16] Similarly, in Japan, where the needs of unskilled foreign workers (many of them illegal) are just beginning to be acknowledged, many cities and wards have started Japanese classes free of charge.

Finally, foreign language education is a cost factor to the public sector as regards training for civil servants such as customs and immigration inspectors, diplomats, and others who need foreign language skills for professional purposes.

Mother Tongue Education

Mother tongue education is the chief instrument for the cultivation and upkeep of a standard culture language. It transmits to the oncoming generation of speakers the norms whose maintenance and guided adaptation to the changing communicative needs of the speech community eventually guarantee the continuance of a common language suitable for all purposes. Only a small fraction of all languages is subject to institutionalized mother tongue education, but those languages which are systematically taught in this way usually occupy a prominent position in the overall school curriculum. It is not uncommon that pupils are taught their own mother tongue from the first grade of elementary school through the last grade of secondary school, so that more time is spent on this subject than on any other. The Federal Republic of Germany provides a good example of the substantial expenses involved in mother tongue education. The school system is publicly funded and run. Teachers are civil servants. In 1989 an estimated 120,000 German teachers taught in Germany's schools,[17] and 2,400 German philologists were in charge of teaching and research at the university level[18]. Since all of these teachers are on the public pay-roll, mother tongue schooling is by far the highest cost-factor of language-related public expenditures.

Admittedly, it is not the only purpose of mother tongue education to impart to the pupils knowledge of linguistic and metalinguistic facts, but grammar, orthography, and style typically remain part of the syllabus until graduation. In addition, the history of the language in question and the literature written in it are vital elements of the syllabus which are indispensable for the formation or maintenance of an individual language competence which is both norm-adhering and creative.[19] Anyway, dealing with language in the strict sense as well as literary topics, mother tongue schooling is the most significant public investment in language.

Since the notion "mother tongue" is theoretically problematic and often used in a misguided or improper way,[20] it may not be unnecessary to recall that its meaning is properly to be determined with reference to the speaking individual. In the present connection this implies two things. First, not every individual has one, that is, only one mother tongue. Questions intended to ascertain the respondents' mother tongue force upon some individuals a decision which they are not really able to make, unless an answer in the plural is admissible.[21] Secondly, for a part of the resident population of virtually all countries, receiving mother tongue education is not the same as schooling in the country's dominant language. Indeed, mother tongue education in some contexts appears to be a shorthand for minority language teaching provisions. All major industrial countries have increasing migrant populations which have, to a greater or lesser degree, changed the monolingual assumptions that used to be typical of these countries' educational policies. Of course, attitudes and policies toward minorities differ greatly across countries, but the general tendency is for more recognition of minority education rights. The EC Council Directive on the Education of Children of Migrant Workers (EC 1977), for example, obliges all EC member states to provide mother tongue education for these children.[22]

Claiming a language as one's mother tongue is not tantamount to fluent proficiency in it. This is clearly evidenced by the Soviet and other eastern European citizens of German extraction who have come in increasing numbers to settle in the former Federal Republic of Germany during the 1980s. For many of these German mother tongue claimants, and especially for their children, German can be said to be their mother tongue in a symbolic sense at best, because, prior to their emigration from Poland, Rumania or the former Soviet Union, their dominant language was another. They are in need of compensatory "mother tongue" teaching, which is another language-related task largely depending on public funding. In 1983, some DM194 million were spent by the West German government for language training programs directed at migrants of this sort, refugees, and other immigrants.[23]

Language Planning

In a wider sense, language planning encompasses all "government inter-ventions in the communication market place," to borrow a phrase from Weinstein (1990: 18), including provisions such as those identified in the preceding sections as language-related public cost-factors, that is, the legal regimentation of language use in situations of official multi-lingualism, bilingual education, and formal language schooling, especially mother tongue education in the country's dominant language. In this section we are, therefore, only concerned with language planning in the narrow sense which is limited to publicly funded measures for the resolution of language problems as well as the supervision and guidance of language adaptation processes. This is accomplished by means of (1) institutionalized language academies and other supervisory bodies; (2) temporary language reform or modernization projects; (3) specific research projects; and (4) information about, and promotion of, desired solutions to language problems.[24]

Language Academies   World-wide there are more than 150 language planning institutions[25] charged with observing the systematic evolution and social functioning of languages in order to develop, recommend, or implement measures suitable to influence their development where such is found desirable. Most important among these various institutions are language academies such as the Académie française, the Aqademiyah la-lashon ha-Ivrit (Hebrew Language Academy), the Arabic academies in Damascus and Amman, or the Yäityoppeya qwanqwanwocc for Ethiopian languages. In addition, there are other government agencies such as the Kenya Education Commission or the Svenska Spraknämnden (Office for the Cultivation of Swedish), as well as consulting bodies advising governments on language questions such as Japan's Kokugo shingikai (Council on the National Language) or the Nederlandse Taalunie (Dutch Language Union) which is financed jointly by the Netherlands and Belgium (at a rate of 2:1). Finally, independent or university affiliated research institutes are to be counted among the numbers of language planning institutions, such as the Institute of Kiswahili Research of the University of Dar es Salaam, the Institute of Applied Linguistics of the Academy of Social Sciences in Beijing, or the Institut für Deutsche Sprache (Institute of the German Language) in Mannheim, Germany.

The funding of these institutions varies on a wide scale, reflecting, on one hand, the financial constraints of their sponsors and, on the other, the magnitude of the problems to be dealt with as well as the varying importance assigned to language cultivation in different countries. Little Ireland, one of the poorest countries of Europe, for example, goes to relatively great expenses for language planning. The superordinate aim of Ireland's language policy is the maintenance and strengthening of the Irish language, which by many Irish, although they do not speak it anymore, is considered a symbol of Irish identity. The society at large is, therefore, prepared to meet the financial requirements of a language policy pursuing this aim. The Bord na Gaeilge, a statutory agency charged with language planning for Ireland, alone has a permanent staff of 26 officials.[26] In addition there is the Instituid Teangeolaiochta Eireann (Linguistics Institute of Ireland) which is also entrusted with language planning tasks, as well as some other government agencies indirectly concerned with language planning. Ó Riagáin estimates the annual expenses for language planning in Ireland at IR£8.5 million.[27]

In contradistinction to Ireland, Israel pursues a language policy which is not only symbolically significant, but of vital importance for the modern state, particularly because of the terminology work which is indispensable for science, technology, and industry. Yet, the Hebrew Academy has only six permanent officials who are supported by a varying number of part-timers. Assuming that salaries account for between 70 and 80 percent of the running costs of the academy, its total expenses can be estimated as about \$150,000 per annum.[28] By comparison, the Académie française is a large-scale enterprise which, moreover, is not the only official organ for the guarding the French language and its use.[29] Other government bodies in this domain are the Haut Comité pour la défense de la langue française and the Commissariat général de la langue française which is under the direct control of the office of the prime minister. They are entrusted with spreading and defending the French language.[30]

Language Reform Projects   Publicly funded language reform projects are carried out in many countries. Script reforms such as the introduction of a roman orthography for Turkish and the subsequent abolition of Arabic letters, or the simplification of Chinese characters and the development and implementation of a roman orthography for Chinese are costly and sometimes lengthy projects. This is also true of less drastic orthography reforms such as the Dutch spelling reform of 1946/47 and that of Denmark in 1948. Even the preparations of a spelling reform are connected with considerable expenditures. The Dutch Language Union has been working on new spelling reform proposals ever since it was established in 1980. In the German-speaking countries, various spelling reform proposals have been discussed at various international meetings over the past 15 years. In 1987, the Institut für Deutsche Sprache was requested by the West German government to produce suggestions for reforming the German spelling conventions.[31] The implementation of script and spelling reforms brings about non-recurring expenses for changing signs and various official print materials, and, in cases of very far-reaching modifications, for retraining.

Even minor regimentation of linguistic usage such as the avoidance of androcentric forms in order to purify public documents of sexist bias can be quite costly if it is decided, for example, to change the language of existing laws accordingly, as is currently debated in various countries inspired by the American example.

Another area of language reform projects has to do with desired status changes of a language in a society. When Morocco became independent in 1956, the government used French almost exclusively in carrying out its functions, especially in administration and education. Converting the French-run domains of the state into Arabic ones as required by the Moroccan constitution of 1962 was a monumental task, because there was not only a severe shortage of skilled personnel, but the Arabic language itself posed serious problems, as it was to be employed, all of a sudden, for functions for which it had never been used before.[32] In 1960 the Institute of Studies and Research on Arabization was established as part of the University of Rabat. Its main task was to advance the modernization and standardization of Arabic so as to make it intertranslatable with the European standard languages and accessible to processing by electronic media.[33] The state was furthermore burdened with enormous costs for retraining and continued education of officials and teachers.

Terminology formation is an important aspect of language modernization, for without standardized terminologies, communication in science and technology is no longer possible nowadays. Since the early 1970s many international organizations have taken an active interest in terminology and nomenclature. In 1971, Unesco established the International Information Centre for Terminology (Infoterm) in Vienna which is affiliated to the Austrian Standards Institute. Both organizations are publicly funded. The terminological upgrading of a language can be accomplished only by highly educated professionals and is both time-consuming and costly. The Commission for Scientific and Technical Terminology set up by the government of India, for example, has coined more than 200,000 technical terms for Hindi alone.[34]

Research Projects Many countries fund research projects on lexicon and terminology which have no immediate application, but which eventually provide important foundations for the development of languages for specific purposes, terminologies, and other knowledge systems.

In addition to surveys which are directly related to language reform projects or to an adopted language policy, there are also numerous publicly funded research projects which are only indirectly related to a concrete policy. The British Department of Education and Science, for example, funded the Linguistic Minorities Project (1985) which investigated patterns of bilingualism in Britain's various language minority groups. The European Science Foundation sponsored a project on second language acquisition (with a total budget of 1.5 million), which can be considered an expression of increasing public awareness of the language problems of migrant workers, although it was not intended as a preparatory measure of a specific policy. Similarly, the Commission of the European Communities has commissioned the Instituto della Enciclopedia Italiana to carry out a survey of the linguistic minorities of EC member states without any recognizable intention of taking political action in this connection.[35]

Yet another important research field in the language planning domain concerns literacy campaigns, especially where new writing systems are to be created and speakers of hitherto unwritten languages are concerned.

Public Relations   The success of language planning depends critically on the acceptance by those directly concerned, that is, the people whose language behavior the specific measures are designed to influence. In many cases, especially where language planning is not, or not primarily, implemented through the school system, this implies that it is necessary to actively promote the approved objectives. The respective promotion campaigns are commonly executed by commercial advertising agencies, at considerable expense. The Bord na Gaeilge committed "substantial resources to manipulate attitudes" (Tovey 1988: 60) toward Irish by means of an advertising campaign launched in October 1978 in newspapers, radio, television, cinema, and on billboards. It was organized by an advertising agency around the theme "Our language – It's part of what we are." In Indonesia, October has been declared the month of the national language. During this month, various publications, television broadcasts and posters promote the Bahasa Indonesia calling attention to its importance for society. During the 1980s, the government of Singapore carried out a lengthy campaign promoting Mandarin as the common language of the various Chinese groups speaking different dialects. Events such as the second Euskara Congress, which took place under the auspices of the government of Spanish Basque country and to which scientists from various countries (with no relation whatsoever to Basqology) were invited at government expense, must also be counted among languagerelated promotion activities.[36] Finally, mention should be made of the cost of market research which is sometimes commissioned after the completion of an advertising campaign, for instance, after the Irish campaign mentioned above.

Subsidizing Language Export

A handful of languages are being exported from the country or territory where they are natively spoken to other parts of the world. In chapter 3 (pp. 81–4) we had occasion to comment on this fact at some length. The export of certain languages is subject to massive subsidies by state grants. The German Foreign Ministry, for example, has a division for "the promotion of the German language" which appropriates up to 50 percent of the cultural budget of the Foreign Ministry, about DM500 million per annum,[37] to language export subsidies, using to this end intermediary agencies such as the Goethe Institut, the German Academic Exchange Service (DAAD) and the central office for German schools abroad. This is not the sum total of government expenditures for the promotion of German abroad, for some of the said intermediary agencies also receive funds from other departments.

More expensive than the German language spread policy is its French counterpart which is without a doubt the most generously funded policy of its kind. Already in 1977 total government expenditures for the promotion of French were estimated as amounting to between 25 and 30 billion francs.[38] These monies were spent for operating 1,200 offices of the Alliance Française in more than 100 countries, for the Haut Conseil pour la francophonie created by President Mitterand in 1984, as well as some other institutions such as the Office de la langue française established in 1937 and the Comité d'étude des termes technique français set up in 1954. French politicians like to stress the spiritual significance of French as the universal language of *clarté*, *beauté*, and *perfection*, in short, of European civilization. However, that their intellectual esteem is accompanied, if not determined, by not so lofty economic motives is also occasionally made explicit. In 1985 the French minister of national education, Jean-Pierre Chevènement, declared that "the Anglo-American linguistic monopoly was an unacceptable cultural impoverishment," and that a policy of diversifying foreign language teaching was *"an essential component of the economic striking force* of France."[39] The then minister of external trade, Michel Jobert, was similarly candid when he identified the 'sale' of French as one of his priorities.[40]

The Francophonie movement, which was inaugurated in 1986 under the leadership of President Mitterand, is at present in the process of becoming an important instrument for the spread of French and its defence against the preponderance of English in the world market, since with it France has succeeded to win the support of other countries for the pursuit of its own objectives. As of the first summit in Paris, Francophonie was given a political and economic orientation (Djité 1987). This has become most obvious in a recent report on the economic value of the French language by the Conseil Economique et Social, an official body which advises the French government on economic and social problems (Renouvin 1989). The presence of French abroad, the report points out, is more than a matter of tradition and prestige. Directly or indirectly it elicits the desire to get to know France, to use her commercial services, to consume her goods and enter into an exchange. The French government is therefore advised to anticipate the demands for French and 'to balance the cultural and economic presence of France in other countries (Renouvin 1989: 10). Language is portrayed as playing a particularly important role in modern society because "the 'communication society' has immediate repercussions for economy and commerce" (1989: 11). Since language has become a commodity, "the separation of language and commerce should be abolished" (1989: 12). However, the report concludes,

> a permanent link between language and commerce cannot be established unless a number of prejudices are given up in the process: vulgar materialist preconceptions about economic activity, outdated ideas about culture, and the radical separation of cultural exchange and commercial exchange. This means that there is still immense work to be done to demonstrate the economic and commercial value of the French language.[41]

The Francophonie movement must be seen, among others, as an instrument, maybe not initially designed but of late employed, towards achieving this end. France and the other two industrial countries participating in the movement, Belgium and Canada, share the cost of its operations, while the poor member countries, most of them African, are the beneficiaries, as evidenced by President Mitterand's spectacular announcement at the Francophonie summit of Dakar (May 24–28, 1989) that France would write off the public debt of the 35 poorest African countries, 16 billion francs in all. In exchange, they are expected to continue to secure the preeminent role of French in government and education.

French is certainly the language which is officially promoted most vigorously and at greatest expense. However, English has not achieved its superior position in the world without government subsidies either. The United States employs at least five different agencies for promoting English: the Agency for International Development (AID), the United States Information Agency (USIA), the Peace Corps, the State Department, and the Department of Defence. With the British Council (annual budget about £200 million) Britain has established an extremely effective institution for the execution of its language spread policy, which is supported in an equally impressive way by the publicly subsidized language learning programs of the BBC. The programs of the "English by Radio and Television" series reach more people than any other language programs in the world.

The Russian language, too, is subject to export subsidies. Its spread from the Russian Republic to the other Soviet Republics and, before its disintegration, to the member states of the Warsaw Pact was heavily supported by the Soviet government.[42]

In 1990, Spain decided to increase to 70 the number of its cultural institutes, which primarily serve to further knowledge of Spanish in other countries. In fiscal 1990/91, the government appropriated some $75 million to the implementation of the "Cervantes Plan." The cultural institutes are subordinate to the Foreign Ministry and considered an instrument of Spain's foreign policy.[43]

There are thus both economic and political reasons why certain countries find it worthwhile to fund export promotion measures for their languages. There are essentially three methods of boosting exports: (1) increasing supply, (2) stimulating demand, and (3) price reduction.

(1) The supply of a language can be increased by creating possibilities for learning it in places where such have not previously existed or existed on a minor or insufficient scale only. In the wake of the collapse of communism, the big language suppliers were faced with new possibilities of increasing their supply in the former Eastern Bloc countries where an enormous demand for foreign language training in English, French, and German manifested itself. Under such conditions, prudent exporters must carefully weigh their options and possibilities and determine which countries are willing and able to satisfy the growing demand by themselves and which ones need support by financial grants, teachers, textbooks, teacher training scholarships, etc.

Another way of increasing the supply is to diversify and extend the range of products. The past two decades have seen the introduction of a whole set of new language products. Although languages for specific purposes have long been recognized as an important area of linguistic research, they have been systematically marketed by foreign language suppliers only relatively recently. Whereas in former times typical foreign language learners would attend introductory, intermediate, and advanced courses, making use of them to the best of their needs, language courses are much more specific nowadays, allowing the consumer to study a language selectively and with particular objectives in mind, business English, technical writing, *le français scientifique*, *Wirtschaftsdeutsch*, etc. Courses of this sort have been developed both by the language industry and by publicly funded language spread agencies.[44] Such courses open up new, specialized markets.

Also of a very specific nature is the demand for certain languages at the southern periphery of Europe. In Turkey, for instance, math and science are taught in German in certain high schools. These so-called Anadolu-Liseler are attended by a high proportion of returnees, that is, children of former *Gastarbeiter* in Germany. The idea of teaching certain subjects in German is to facilitate the pupils' (re)integration and to help them maintain their knowledge of German (Emmert 1987). Eleven percent of all Turkish secondary students study German, a relatively high proportion, which is recognized by the Turkish and German governments as a matter of mutual interest, because the graduates of these schools can be expected to take an active part in the bilateral relations of the two countries. Some 80 German teachers and consultants work in Turkish schools at the expense of the German government, thus increasing the supply of German in Turkey.

(2) Just increasing the supply does not always have the desired effect. It is, therefore, sometimes found necessary to also stimulate demand. For example, in a report on the state of the German language in the world, the German government declared:

> The Federal Government will promote German not only where German language teaching is in demand. It will make efforts also to generate an active interest in important partner countries.[45]

While on the government level it is mainly political means which are used to stimulate demand, that is, diplomatic attempts at influencing the education policy of other countries, advertising plays an important, though controversial, role on the individual level. For example, Harald Weinrich, who was called as an expert to comment at the hearing about the said government report, criticized the government's intention to promote German by means of publicity campaigns.

> Publicity for the German language as marketing, maybe even through an advertising agency, is to be rejected. The best advertising agencies for the German language are the literature and science of the German-speaking countries.[46]

The active creation of demand for German abroad has also been criticized as "economic and unrelated to foreign cultural policy" by some politicians.[47] What these critics apparently fail to realize, however, is that any foreign cultural policy has both economic preconditions and consequences.

It is often impossible to draw a sharp line between information and advertisement, which makes it very difficult to assess the financial means applied by the various agencies for stimulating demand. Most agencies regularly set aside funds for public relations work, but only some have a budget title for advertising. In the 1989 budget of the Goethe-Institut, for instance, DM2.5 million (roughly 1 percent of its entire budget) was appropriated for this purpose.

(3) The third method of boosting language export, price reduction, is applied in a number of different ways. On one hand, the big language exporters support other countries by reducing their necessary acquisition cost in the form of library donations, textbooks and other educational materials, teacher training grants, and by dispatching teaching personnel. On the other hand, individuals also benefit from export subsidies, for instance when language promotion agencies offer language courses at cost price or below, undercutting commercial language schools.

Language export promotion is pursued by very rich countries only, which testifies both to the fact that they dispose of the necessary resources and that their languages are traded most in the international market place.

Communication in International Organizations

Finally, language matters as a cost factor in public budgets in connection with communication in international organizations. Various regulations exist for communicating in such bodies. The United Nations Organization has six official languages, Arabic, Chinese, English, French, Russian and Spanish, of which two, English and French, are used as working languages. The procedural rules of the UN determine that speeches in one of the two working languages are translated into the other, and that speeches in any of the other official languages are translated into both working languages. The language service, which provides for simultaneous and consecutive interpretation as well as for the translation of official documents, is financed out of the UN budget which is defrayed after a quota system by its members. It employs a permanent staff of 120 interpreters and, on a regular basis, a great number of free-lance conference interpreters paid by the day.[48] Countries requiring documentation of UN proceedings in languages other than the six official languages have to provide for translation out of their own coffers. For example, Germany and Austria jointly pay for a German translation service. Participants of UN sessions are free to use languages other than the six official languages, but the thus generated additional interpretation costs are borne by those who make use of this possibility.

Some international organizations have cost-minimizing rules for language use. For instance, the member states of both ASEAN and EFTA use English as their sole working language which allows them to convene their sessions without interpreting. Only documentation is provided for in the respective national languages. The Council of Europe, which had 23 members in 1991, uses English and French as official languages and, in addition, German and Italian as working languages. The working languages of the Organization of American States, OAS, with 31 members are English, French, Portuguese, and Spanish. And the 50 members of the Organization of African Unity, OAU, use Arabic, English, and French as official languages.

With its nine official languages, the EC is a rather special case: Danish, Dutch, English, French, German, Greek, Italian, Portuguese, and Spanish all enjoy equal status. This multiplicity of languages forces the EC to maintain for its various institutions an array of conference and translation services which are quite unique. All documentation is published in all nine official languages, because many acts and decisions of EC institutions have immediate legal force in the member states. Furthermore, sessions of the Commission, the Council of Ministers, and the European Parliament are to be interpreted into the nine languages, which implies that the language services have to deal with 72 language pairs. The European Parliament especially cannot do without interpretation, because the adoption of a single working language would be tantamount to a social selection of potential members in some countries but not in others. The prestige factor must not be underrated either. In formal sessions, deputies and other politicians of smaller countries, although fully proficient in one or both of the de facto working languages French and English, often use their own language, in order, as it were, not to renounce their identity.

To calculate the cost of the multilingualism of the EC is not easy, because it cannot easily be determined how many of the roughly 11,000 Eurocrats devote how many working hours to language-related tasks. Language-related work cannot always be neatly distinguished from other work, and not all language costs can be itemized. Also, it is hardly possible to calculate how many working hours are spent throughout the various EC institutions not for translation and interpretation, but simply because they produce documents in nine different languages and to some extent conduct their internal business in several languages. The proportion of language-related work varies across the EC institutions,[49] but it is a realistic estimate that some 40 percent or more of the EC's administrative budget is spent on its official multilingualism. This seems to be exorbitant, but it must not be overlooked that the EC's administrative expenses are low if compared with national civil services. Every 100,000 European citizens are served by an average of 4,000 national civil servants as compared to only six Eurocrats. Administrative expenditure accounts for just 4.8 percent of the EC's total budget. Yet, the actual amount, which comes close to 700 million ECU, is a clear indication of the value the EC members attach to their languages.

By granting, say, Greek and Danish, theoretically at least, if not in actual practice, equal status with English and French, the Europeans pay tribute to the national language principle by sharing the ensuing costs. As compared to these expenditures, the means appropriated by the EC on behalf of other languages spoken in EC member states are very modest. In some cases this is quite implausible. Catalan in particular must be mentioned in this connection. Its speech community is comparable in size with that of Danish or Greek, but it does not enjoy the privileged status of a national language.[50] The nine languages mentioned above are the exclusive official languages of the EC. All other languages spoken in EC countries are recognized only as minority languages which are in some measure financially supported by EC programs. Ironically, they benefit from the defense of the national language ideology on account of which the EC has developed an ethos of multilingualism, because its members (with the exception of Luxembourg) insist on the recognition of equal rights for their respective languages.[51] In the final analysis, it is hence the ideological heritage of the national language idea which is responsible for the EC's willingness to spend so much more for its official multilingualism than any other international organization.

Public Expenditures for Language – Summary

Languages are a cost factor for national and local governments. They are assets in need of proper care which are recognized in many parts of the world as an object of government responsibility. For properly executing their functions, in order to perpetuate themselves and to reinforce their stability, states depend in large measure on language. Many of their functions manifest themselves verbally. Communication of the various organs of the state with each other and with the citizens is largely by means of language. Language costs vary on a wide scale across countries. Multilingual countries, which in their structure and operations take into account the multilingualism of the population, are often forced to bear higher language-related expenditures than are incurred by monolingual countries, but the latter do not use language free of charge either. As a matter of fact, some monolingual countries go to extraordinary extents for language-related tasks, be it in order to make a large part of their population proficient in other languages, as in the case of the Netherlands, or in order to promote their own national language in other countries, as in the case of France.

To the extent that the importance of information processing and communication increases, language too becomes ever more important, because it is the fundamental means of communication in human society. Given the complexities of life in modern society, it is hardly surprising that language has become a matter of state responsibility whose upkeep generates financial burdens. In the previous sections, a number of areas have been pointed out where the costliness of language for national and community budgets is apparent: official bi- or multi-lingualism in national administrations, school education of mother tongue and foreign languages, language planning, language export promotion, and communication in international organizations. These are not the only language-related cost factors, but the most important ones. Costs which are related to language in incalculable ways were left out, for instance, damages by terrorist strikes which are motivated mainly or partly by a state's repression of a language,[52] damages caused by imprecise wording in public inscriptions, instruction manuals, etc., or losses incurred by mistranslation or other communication obstacles. Notwithstanding the failure to account for such costs (which can be considerable), and notwithstanding the fact that the said factors play varying roles in different countries, it is evident that language is a cost factor in every public budget which cannot be neglected. The same holds true for the private sector.

Budgeting Language Costs: The Private Sector

In January 1990, the Bundestag, the German parliament, asked the government to make efforts for German to become the third official language of the Council of Europe, in addition to English and French. The government was also advised to make sure that German does not fall further behind in the various institutions of the European Community where French and English, although on an equal footing with German and the other six official EC languages in terms of recognized status, are the preferred working languages. The political and demographic setting of this request is obvious enough: in Europe, it was pointed out, German is spoken as a mother tongue by more speakers than any other language except Russian. However, the rationale of the parliamentary initiative is economic rather than political. It was criticized that, in spite of the nominal equity in status of official languages of the EC, negotiations were frequently carried out, and documents drafted, in French and English, before the other versions were made available. According to the Parliamentary Secretary of State of the ministry of economics, this practice constitutes a disadvantage for German industry. Middle-sized companies in particular, the secretary indicated, have no translation services at their disposal to enable them quickly to process relevant information that comes out of EC organs or to correspond about such matters as bidding offers and contests.[53] That this initiative in support of the German language was championed by the ministry of economics shows that it does not just reflect Germany's regained self-confidence after unification, and, maybe, a relapse into linguistic nationalism as can be witnessed elsewhere in Europe. There is more behind this campaign than national pride; for today language has greater economic significance than ever before.

This is so because of the enormous expansion since World War II of the global economy, and because certain language-sensitive industries have seen spectacular growth rates, among them information technology and tourism. At the present time, moreover, the world economy is characterized by an unprecedented degree of international interdependence and cooperation which has not only resulted in the existence of powerful multinational companies, but has also made middle-sized and small companies engage ever more in import–export business. The most successful economies are export-oriented. Thus, more people with different linguistic and cultural backgrounds come into contact with each other. Furthermore, during the 1970s and 80s, language has become an important component of an increasing number of products. This is one aspect of these fast-moving times, which are now routinely referred to as the information age; that is, the fact that to a much greater extent than under conditions of slower cycles of innovation and adaptation, information itself has become a commodity. More companies than ever before work for improving techniques of storing, processing, and transmitting data. Although most of the machinery is just as language-independent as the products of, say, heavy industry, their main function is to facilitate access to information and make it easier for people to deal with. And for people, natural languages are still unqualifiedly the most important means of communication.

For some industries, the multiplicity of natural language is profitable, even the very basis of their existence, but for others it is a cost-factor. Were the creators or recorders of the story of the construction of the inglorious tower not right to portray the Babylonian events as a catastrophe? It is hard to disagree with O'Brien (1979: 83) who remarked that "multiplicity of languages are an obstacle to trade and the mobility of labor, technology and information generally." Linguistic boundaries impede economic integration and the improvement of the standard of living it is expected to bring about. Especially in many Third World countries multilingualism slows down modernization. The dissemination of basic knowledge is not made altogether impossible by it, but certainly delayed. O'Brien argues against the linguistic unification of the world as a solution and calls for a change of the economic rather than the linguistic conditions which make the multiplicity of languages appear as a disadvantage and burden. However, in the present context, his plea is of less importance than the premise on which his argument is based, namely that the polyglot structure of the world actually *is* a cost factor for the economy. For, to quote another student of the economically detrimental effects of multilingualism, "an 'ideal' economy presupposes a single language for the whole world."[54] Since such an economy is only an ideal one and ideal from a certain point of view only, active players on the stage of the world economy have to reckon with linguistically fragmented markets. This is exactly what they do.

As a cost-factor language plays a role in several areas of the economy, the most important ones being marketing, company internal communications, and the development of new products. In addition, there are language costs imposed on industry and business by virtue of language policy decisions.

Marketing

Trading in goods and services inevitably involves a seller and a buyer who establish a relationship with each other. The entire sales process is a complex form of interactive behavior with linguistic communication fulfilling multifarious and important functions. The product has to reach the customer, who, to this end, needs to be addressed, informed, and persuaded. His or her needs and desires must be investigated and stimulated, and changes in this regard anticipated or, at least, recognized. Marketing experts agree that all of this is more difficult where seller and buyer do not speak the same language.[55] Unless one of them is fully proficient in the other's language or both are equally proficient in a third language, the language barrier acts as an additional trade barrier, since the exchange of information between the potential business partners is made more difficult.

While this insight comes as no surprise to the economic layman, the ways in which companies have translated it into corporate behavior vary greatly. A survey of 200 executives of British export companies revealed that no more than 60 percent of them considered knowledge of foreign languages a significant advantage.[56] In contrast, Dutch managers and sales agents consistently said when interviewed that good command of foreign languages was an important prerequisite of success in international trade.[57] According to their own testimony, 34 percent of the managers of Dutch companies often use German, and 17 percent French, for professional purposes. The corresponding figures for Britain are 4 percent and 9 percent for German and French respectively, and this in spite of the fact that, just like the Netherlands, Britain has its most important export markets in the European Community. Rather than reflecting the different economic weight of these two trading nations,[58] this contrast is indicative of a difference in linguistic culture and the economic strength of the two respective languages.

It would seem, however, that British business people have a tendency to rely too much on that of English. 60 percent of Britain's export sales agents and 40 percent of the sales managers have no knowledge of a foreign language, and as many as 80 percent of all companies involved in import–export trade rarely have any correspondence with their business partners in a language other than English (Lowe 1982). Since colonial times, British business people have been used to carrying out overseas trade exclusively in English, and nowadays there is less reason than ever to change this habit, since English is generally perceived as the international language of business. In many respects this is undoubtedly true, but at the same time the insight that English only is not enough is also gaining ground in the international business community.

For establishing more than only superficial contacts, it is essential for foreign company representatives in many markets to have a good command of the local language. In order to communicate this message to the British business community, the Berlitz School in the 1980s used just one sentence in their advertisements: "The only language of business in France is French." In Latin America, Beneke (1981: 39) observes, the new economic and political elites "have developed a sense of cultural identity that does not favour the use of English in trade and other contacts." That English, while serving an important auxiliary function as a vehicular language, does not suffice to thoroughly penetrate non-English-speaking markets transpires from a survey of 5,814 leading executives in ten European countries. Only 31 percent of them reported regular use of English for professional purposes. On the basis of this and a number of other observations, Lowe arrives at the conclusion "that English can not be relied on as 'the language of international business'" (1982: 25), and that, therefore, there is "a real need for the British to learn a second language" (1982: 24). Similarly, Beneke (1981) recommends more diversified foreign language education for the business community which is adjusted to the real needs of the economy.

These needs cannot be satisfied without considerable expense, which raises the question by whom this should be defrayed. As regards the western European languages belonging to the traditional set of foreign languages, business and industry can largely rely on government which, in most countries, provides for the ensuing costs through curricular foreign language education. With other languages this is so to a much smaller extent. Japanese is a good example.

Japan's reputation of being an exceptionally lucrative but very difficult market is usually explained as resulting from Japanese protectionism, on one hand, and the great cultural distance between Japan and its most important trading partners, the industrialized countries of the West, on the other. Many American and British companies, in particular, have failed in Japan, because it was taken for granted by their managers that their representatives could get by in the Japanese business community with their mother tongue only.[59] Thanks to innumerable stories of cultural and linguistic misunderstandings, students of Japan know better.[60] If foreign companies want to succeed in Japan, Erlinghagen (1975: 117) remarks, the staff of their branch offices must include executives on the managerial level whose Japanese is good enough not to be an impediment to the regular conduct of business. In order to meet this requirement, foreign companies in Japan have to provide for the language training of their personnel largely by themselves, since not enough people are available on the labor market who have acquired the necessary professional and linguistic qualifications at school or university. Bringing an employee with no prior knowledge of Japanese up to a level of proficiency where he or she can use the language in speech and writing for professional purposes without difficulties, costs a minimum of between £10,000 and £15,000 for language classes alone.[61] In addition, there is the employee's regular salary which the company continues to pay. The length of time assumed for language training in this calculation implies a minimum of six months full pay for no work. For small companies this is a considerable burden.

There are some government subsidies of which corporate enterprise can take advantage, such as tax rebates for the expenses of continuing education and also, on a small scale, direct cash subsidies. For instance, in order to promote business activities in Japan, the EC has created the Executive Training Programme in Tokyo which sponsors up to 60 executives of EC companies per year with allowances for language training and living expenses. The program, which has an annual budget of 6 to 7 million ECU, comprises a one-year intensive language course with six lessons per day. Its purpose is to help European companies become as successful in Japan as their Japanese counterparts are in Europe.

Although the cultural distance between Japan and its Western trading partners is not greater than that in the opposite direction, the Japanese are in a somewhat advantageous position, because Western languages have been taught in Japan on a large scale for more than a century. Since Japanese business leaders are keenly aware of the importance of language, overseas branch offices of Japanese companies are usually staffed with personnel proficient in the local language. Thus, economist Ohta (1979: 84) writes about the necessity of English language proficiency for Japanese business people:

> Like it or not, even the most convinced ultra-nationalist, intent upon making Japan a beacon for world culture, cannot ignore the economic need for the general vehicle of verbal exchange that happens to be the English language, unless he wishes to see Japan close its frontiers again and try to feed 100 million people under miserable conditions of autarky.

English is not the only language for which a demand is generally recognized.[62] For, as a member of the board of the Bank of Tokyo put it, the Japanese economy is so deeply intertwined with the world economy that it can no longer exist by itself (Watanabe 1989). Rather than being a single huge market, the world economy is a multiplicity of markets, all with their peculiarities and specific conditions to which the exporter has to adjust. With respect to the more than 650 branch offices of Japanese companies in Germany, Watanabe (1989) remarks that misunderstandings which are harmful to business can only be avoided if the Japanese staff have a good command of German. To Japanese business people it is self-evident that, in spite of the foundations laid in high school and university, this implies expenditures which in the best interest of business are to be shouldered by the companies concerned.

That Western business leaders have been slow in reaching the corresponding conclusion with respect to Japan, is often deplored in the Japanese business world as one of the factors responsible for the trade imbalance between Japan and its Western partners and the difficulties many Western companies experience in their attempts at penetrating the Japanese market. As a matter of fact, Japanese business leaders consider the success of Western companies in Japan as too modest and thus potentially harmful to their own future development, because they are worried that the trade imbalance in their favor will get out of hand and incite protectionism. They have therefore made the promotion of Japanese in Western countries their own concern. Especially in Britain, which is a relatively underdeveloped country as far as foreign language education is concerned, Japanese industry since the 1970s has made strong commitments in this regard. Between 1975 and 1988, about 13 billion yen were channeled to England in order to promote knowledge of Japanese language and culture. Most of these monies were provided by the private sector. In 1978, the University of London received a stipend of £2 million from Toyota and Suntory, Nissan financed a Centre for Japanese Studies in Oxford in 1981, and the University of Cambridge was given a grant of some £500,000 by Keidanren, the Federation of Economic Organizations.[63] The real significance of these measures is obvious: if there is a language barrier between two trading partners, both sides must make efforts to bridge it, because it is in their mutual interest to learn to understand the other's culture and society and to speak their potential customers' language.

Language training for industry and commerce can be a considerable burden for a company, but those who hesitate to make the necessary financial outlays have to ask themselves which is more costly, language training or losses and forgone gains brought about by lack of language proficiency. In larger companies foreign language schooling for company personnel is not a new fad, but has a relatively long tradition. For example, Schering AG of Germany, a big company of the chemical industry, offered its staff courses in English, Spanish, French, and Portuguese as long ago as the 1930s. Lindner (1984) has described how these language courses became more varied and sophisticated in conjunction with the company's development, how they were dismantled during World War II and reestablished after the war (cf. also Kocks 1989: 24ff.). The rationale of language courses such as those initiated by Schering as well as many others is that foreign language proficiency is an indispensable component of cross-border business. The inability of a company to communicate with its customers in their language can have far-reaching disadvantages which have been described in some detail by two marketing specialists, Turnbull and Cunningham (1981). Deficient language competence

considerably reduces the ability to communicate effectively and offer the product to the customer;
interferes with the ability of the seller to understand the needs of the customer (both in a commercial and technical respect);
stands in the way of close personal interaction, which can do so much for mutual understanding and cooperation;
can create negative, indeed hostile, attitudes among buyers.

Such undesirable side-effects of export business can be anticipated and avoided by proficient marketing. Holden (1987) has developed the concept of "communication competence" in order to assign the foreign language needs of import–export companies a place in their marketing strategies. This notion is to be clearly distinguished from that of "communicative competence" familiar from the Ethnography of Speaking which refers to an individual's ability to communicate. As opposed to this, communication competence refers to the ability of companies or other organizations to communicate with their environment. Holden defines communication competence as

the capacity of an organization, using the various channels of communication at its disposal, to interpret, and *anticipate* changes in, overseas

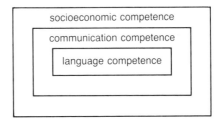

Figure 4.1   Socioeconomic competence. (Adapted from Neustupný 1989: 50).

business environments where the language of decision-making, consultation and referral is not the same as that of the organization. (Holden 1987: 124)

Language is the central factor of communication competence, although it is not the only one. It is also that which can be most easily assessed in terms of financial cost and thus can be acquired by means of deliberate investment. In addition to the linguistic code in the narrow sense, it is necessary to learn how correctly to use it, that is, how to use it in accordance with the communicative and sociolinguistic norms of the speech community in question, which in turn must be embedded into the rules of socioeconomic behavior. On the basis of similar considerations, Neustupný has integrated the above components in the model shown in figure 4.1.

Competence in the sense of the capacity to act on the basis of rational choices, assessing and anticipating the actions of others, is not an alien notion in the discipline of economics. For instance, Pelikan (1989: 218) defines economic competence as "the competence to receive and use information for solving economic problems and taking economic decisions." Decisions of this kind refer to the hiring of personnel, job assignments, the execution of transactions, cooperation between a company's head office and its branches, negotiations, and client counseling, all of the activities in other words that are dealt with in business administration and management with the purpose of optimizing company organization and performance. All of these activities are highly language-dependent. The ability to process information which is of crucial importance both to Pelikan's definition of economic competence and Holden's definition of communication competence presupposes language as the most important vehicle of information, more particularly, of information relevant for economic decision making. Under conditions of a linguistically homogeneous market as assumed in the above model, it is a regular component of economic competence, since it can be assumed to be a non-discriminatory asset of everyone. But with regard to economic transactions across linguistic borders, this is not the case. Rather, here language competence becomes an element of economic competence which is discriminatory and not self-evident.

Carriers of economic competence are corporate agents rather than individual agents, which implies that a company can, and typically does, possess language competence by way of division of labor. This is true especially of foreign branch offices. Personnel sent abroad by the company head office are not always proficient in the local language. They cooperate with locally hired personnel speaking their language or with whom they share a vehicular language. Such a pattern of linguistic cooperation is certainly practicable for short-term engagements, but in the long run it is questionable whether it allows another, recursive component of economic competence to be fully operative, namely the ability to augment and reinforce one's economic competence. For the long-term prospects of a company's foreign operations it is crucially important that its management can unrestrictedly participate in this ability. Even an excellent translation and interpretation service is no substitute for a manager's unrestrained direct access to the information offered in the local daily press, technical journals, radio and TV broadcasts, conversations with customers, business partners, and other company members. To be sure, there are differences in this regard between industrial branches, countries, and languages. For a German businessman it is easier to get by without knowledge of the local language in Denmark than, say, in the USA; and the seller of grain is less dependent on a good command of his client's language than the wine merchant or the agent of a company that sells complicated machines. The correspondingly variable requirements of actual communication competence in a certain market can usually be assessed more accurately by business people who work there than by their colleagues of the head office, because they are more knowledgeable with regard to the disadvantage of limited communication competence in competing with local companies, and with regard to the expenditures that are necessary and justifiable for compensating the linguistic deficit. Some comments by employees of foreign companies based in Japan who participated in the above-mentioned one year Executive Training Programme in Tokyo may be quoted here for illustration.

The investment in Japan and its language through the ETP programme became rewarding for my company's business and my personal functioning in Japan.

The ability to tap the vast resources of written information is a sweet reward for twelve months of endeavour.

My Japanese helps me a lot in the daily relations with the company staff and even more in the relations with our customers.[64]

Economic transactions are always communicative in nature. Not only do economic agents receive information, they also release information, especially for the consumption of potential and actual clients. This is done largely anonymously in the form of written and audio-visual advertising and information material, product labels and names, instruction manuals, handbooks, etc. Export-oriented companies thus have to elaborate their communication competence in such a way that they can provide these materials in the languages of the markets in which they operate, or else they have to pay subcontractors for producing them. In any event, the production of information, advertising, and packing materials suitable for the targeted markets generates additional costs. Once again, it must be noted that it is not only knowledge of the respective language(s) that must be provided for, but also knowledge of appropriate contextualization, that is, the ability, in formulating messages addressed to potential buyers, to take into account the local expectations as they are determined by culture, social hierarchy, fashion, and existing prejudices.[65]

Company Internal Communication

In the present context, company internal communication refers to communication both between the employees of a company working in the same location and between the head office of a company and its divisions and branch offices. Throughout the world, company internal communication is characterized by various patterns of multilingualism reflecting the multilingual environment of the company's location, a significant presence of migrant labor in the workforce, or the company's multinational relationships and the diverse locations of its branches. For every job there is an optimal configuration of language competencies. At the present level of automation of industrial production, there are only very few jobs with no explicit or implicit language requirements attached, because more or less continuous skill transfer has become a vital element of the ever faster moving cycle of innovation and adaptation. In order to optimize internal communication, many companies have their own language policy regulating language use between its divisions and branches, or designating a particular language as the company language. For example, the German tyre company Continental, the Dutch electronics concern Philips, and the Swedish car maker Volvo use English as company language.

A number of studies have investigated corporate language needs in various industries. Kocks (1988) found that 75 percent of the companies of the steel industry in Duisburg, Germany, have foreign language needs. Not unexpectedly, English plays a dominant role here, but most companies need language competence in two to four foreign languages, always including English and French; the importance of Spanish and Dutch is also conspicuous. An exploratory study of the language needs of industry and business in three economic centers of Germany revealed that about 80 percent of all companies need two foreign languages and 45 percent need three or more. Virtually all companies have a need for English, but French, Spanish, Italian, Dutch, Portuguese, and Russian must also be considered economically important foreign languages (Finkenstaedt and Schröder 1990: 26f.).[66] To a large extent such language needs are fulfilled by the companies themselves.

Language instruction Language instruction has an institutionalized place in many companies, be it in the form of in-house training facilities or external language courses which are designed largely, if not exclusively, to improve company internal communication. In a study of 15 Hong Kong based companies of various industries where the staff is offered foreign language training, Cheng and Zi (1987) determined that these courses were intended to improve (1) the company's overall communication competence, (2) communication between staff and management, and (3) communication between staff members and customers. The companies surveyed were banks, hotels, and firms of the telecommunications and energy industries. While most of them had been offering mainly English language classes for many years, they reported that, in view of the approaching transfer of Hong Kong's sovereignty from Britain to China in 1997, they were also increasingly offering courses in Chinese (Mandarin). The majority of the companies were using teaching materials designed by their own language teaching staff for their specific purposes. These language courses, teachers, teaching materials, technical equipment such as tape recorders, VCRs and, in a few cases, language labs, etc. were always paid for by the company. Participation during or after working hours was optional, recommended, or, in some companies and for some staff members, obligatory.

In-house language training is a common practice, especially in large multinational companies. Although foreign language needs do not correlate with company size (Finkenstaedt and Schröder 1990: 27), large companies can more easily afford to set up their own training facilities. A well-documented case is that of Ford of Europe. Its founding in 1967 brought with it increased language needs for Ford Cologne which through its industrial relations office developed a modern language teaching system designed to cover the language needs of approximately 2,000 employees per year. From the point of view of the company language training is necessarily performance-oriented like other matters with economic consequences. Since it is intended to improve the company's overall performance, the educational requirements must fit into a controllable economic framework. This implies, among other things, fixed time allowances for achieving function-specific proficiency levels; minimum class-attendance requirements, and maximum ceiling of training costs per hour and per course. Industrial language training programs cannot dispense with control mechanisms of this kind. Thelen and Reinhold's account of language training at Ford Cologne makes the reasons for this explicit: "In any case language training costs money and Ford is prepared to take over the costs as long as the training is necessary to improve job performance" (Thelen and Reinhold 1981: 144). This statement reflects the fact that generally industry is more sensitive to the cost-effectiveness of language training than public educational institutions.

The frequency of in-house language training is revealed by McCallen's (1989: 88f.) survey of 29 big companies in Germany, France, Italy, the Netherlands, Norway, Austria, Sweden, and Switzerland. At the time of the investigation, 24 of them sustained language courses on a regular basis, two reported on earlier training programs, and the remaining three supported staff members' foreign language education on a case by case basis in response to actual demand. McCallen's attention is focussed on English, but he also reports on French and Spanish courses in some companies. As suggested by the above example of Ford Cologne, big companies have in-house foreign language training programs on a scale unimagined by outsiders. The German chemical concern BASF provides regular language training for 1,000 employees during working hours and for another 1,000 in evening classes (Finkenstaedt and Schröder 1990: 26). The largest of the companies McCallen surveyed, a multinational oil company, offered English lessons to between 6,000 and 7,000 of its staff members every year, at a cost of some £2.5 million. McCallen estimates the total annual expenditures of the 24 companies for English lessons alone as £9 million. Some companies have designated budget titles for language training, whereas in the case of others the necessary funds are part of company expenses for continuing education or general overhead expenses.

Rationalization Language courses for employees are investments into a company's human capital.[67] In order to optimize company internal communication as well as their communication competence in general, companies also make investments for rationalization, that is, the substitution of human labor power by machines and operation systems, especially in the domains of telecommunication and electronic data processing. Some of these, such as word processing and data management programs as well as machine(-assisted) translation programs, are directly language-related.

Automatic Translation Although the first translator has yet to lose his job to machine translation programs, because they are still not quite reliable and serviceable without limitations, such programs are commercially marketed and employed by many companies. In 1988, the German electronics giant Siemens introduced the English–German translation program Metal (Machine Evaluation and Translation of Natural Language)[68] which works with a basic vocabulary of 10,000 words and a set of 550 grammar rules at a speed of one word per second. This adds up to some 200 pages of text per day, more than ten times as much as the average performance of a translator. Other systems that are applicable to different degrees and commercially marketed include STS (Saarbrücker Translationssystem), the LOGOS system of the American company of that name, and the systems SYSTRAN and ALPS. Technical texts of clearly delimited fields can be translated in a comprehensible, if not always stylistically satisfactory, manner with a rather low error rate. Many companies have use for raw translations of this sort, especially for internal purposes. The machine output is informative enough to decide whether a more polished version is needed. The need for technical translation is enormous already and growing steadily. The documentation of a simple personal computer, for instance, comprises some 10,000 pages. In western Europe alone an estimated 100 million pages of technical material are translated every year.[69]

Co-ordination and Harmonization of Terms and Labels   Language is an economically significant factor for corporate business not only as the most important means of company internal communication, but also with respect to its referential function as a means of designating objects. The general requirement on language in this regard has been characterized as follows:

> Good quality at a low price, in other words: rationalization of the working process – this is the overall goal to which everything that happens in a company must be subordinated. Language, too, must serve this purpose wherever it is used in the company.[70]

This means, above all, that it is necessary to harmonize designations of products and their parts. Seemingly straightforward and simple though this requirement may seem, it is not easily met by big companies with several production plants and decentralized management. Yet, the harmonization of terms is a very important aspect of rationalizing production. Every company engaged in industrial production must have an interest in using as many existing parts as possible when designing and producing new commodities. This is very difficult in the absence of referential unequivocality, that is, unless every part has one and only one designation under which it is registered in all warehouses and production plants. Designations of parts should furthermore avoid ambiguities and be self-explanatory, simple, and as short as possible. An additional requirement is that many of the parts to be designated have to be recorded in cross-border trade statistics, which implies that their designations must conform to the Standard International Trade Classification.

The larger the company and the more numerous the products and parts it produces or processes, the more consequential the harmonization of designations. For big companies, such as car makers, which handle, if not produce, tens of thousands of different parts, systematic terminology work is a necessity. Industry has a strong interest, therefore, in the creation of international standards as promoted by the International Information Centre for Terminology ("Infoterm"). Even middle-sized companies have made enormous investments during the last decade in data banks and other software programs designed to facilitate the standardization of terms and labels, stock-keeping, the compilation of ledgers and inventories, and the harmonization with international standards.

Word Processing   While the computerization of language in certain areas, for example, automatic translation, is useful for some companies of some industrial branches only, other less complicated devices have met with almost universal acceptance during the last decade. In the industrialized countries of the West, offices without word processors, FAX, electronic mail, etc., are a rarity already. The pressure of competition makes the rationalization of company internal communication virtually indispensable. The social and sociolinguistic implications of the new media of office automation have not yet been thoroughly investigated. It would seem, however, that the view that they have nothing to do with language and are no more than a prolongation of pencil and typewriter fails to do justice to their far-reaching effects. For they exercise an influence on both quantity and quality of language use. Handwriting loses some of its traditional functions of generating, communicating, and storing knowledge. Access to electronic dictionaries, multilingual thesauri, data and terminology banks accelerates the production of texts, while at the same time necessitating new skills of information processing. What is more, the new media wield an influence, however subtly, on the writer's relationship to, and conception of, language which he or she now experiences as partly controlled by the computer. Certain functions such as the correct spelling of words are largely taken over by the machine.

Office automation on a large scale is a very recent phenomenon. Its general consequences and the specific effects of language processing products on language behavior are yet to be fully understood. But whatever these effects will be, they can be expected to be perpetuated if not intensified, since business and industry are evidently ready to make significant financial commitments in order to further advance electronic control over language in this domain.

Costs Incurred by Language Policy

As has become evident in the two previous sections, the demands on a company's communication competence are primarily determined by the economic fundamentals, first of all its location, the ethnolinguistic composition of its staff, the nature of the contact it has with its customers, and the structure of company internal communication. These conditions can be translated into criteria for optimizing communication competence, which is directly related to a company's competitiveness. However, the above conditions are not the only requirements on communication competence. Companies must also meet certain political and legal conditions, no matter whether or not these are considered economically reasonable.

For example, in Germany no one can become branch director of a bank without being accepted by the Federal Office of the Supervision of the Banking Business in Berlin. Although its examination focusses on contents rather than language, it forces non-German-speaking applicants to be proficient in German, since no allowances are made for limited German proficiency. Hence, even though the management of a foreign bank may not share the conviction that German language proficiency is indispensable for heading a branch office in Germany, it cannot but comply with this requirement.

Indirect language requirements of this sort are quite common, but there are also more explicit political regulations which have a bearing on the communication competence of private enterprise. Quebec's francization policy, the costs of which for the private sector have been estimated by an economic research institute as amounting to some C$100 million per year (Hanley 1981), is an outstanding example. These costs comprise only expenses caused by the implementation of the language laws, rather than measures to get around them, for instance by moving the company's head office from Quebec to another province.

Most language reform policies, such as the deliberate expansion of the functional domains of a language, the creation of bilingual institutions, or the adoption of new spelling conventions or a new script bring on short-term costs both for government and the private sector, even though they may be intended to simplify language use and thus help reduce expenses. However, the effects of such projects on the economy are usually negligible, because they affect all economic agents in a like manner.

A very special kind of language-related costs are those caused by violations of language laws. In February 1984, the police of Pantin fined the restaurant chain France-Quick 3,500 francs, because its menus included items such as *Hamburger, Big cheese, soft drinks*, and *Irish coffee*, instead of offering these dishes and beverages under French labels, as required by the French language law of 1975. Reference to *20 filter cigarettes* in an ad cost another company 7,500 francs. By reversing the last two letters of *filter*, the company could have saved this money. Abuses of the French language like these are usually brought to the public prosecutor's attention by l'Agulf, "The general association of the users of the French language", which works like a consumer protection organization and is the main beneficiary of the collected fines.[71] Although the actual sums are quite insignificant, the individual cases in which penalties were handed down have attracted a great deal of media attention. Truchot (1990: 328) mentions the figure of 704 infringements of French language laws between 1982 and 1984 of which 216 were penalized with fines.

To use not only public relations measures but also police surveillance in order to guard the purity and usage of a language is not a common practice in many countries. During the early years of Quebec's francization policy, Canadian companies, too, were threatened with fines (between C$25 and C$1,000) and, after repeated warnings and orders to comply, actually penalized. Other than that, companies are usually free to decide how to regulate their internal language use as well as the company's linguistic presentation of itself and its products to the outside world. This notwithstanding, it can well be imperative for a company to regiment certain aspects of its language use, for instance by making sure that customers receive sales contracts drafted in a language that they understand. In the single market of the European community as of 1993, requirements of this sort will become increasingly important. In the interest of consumer protection, legal provisions are called for in this connection.[72] It is interesting that with regard to the above-mentioned case of France-Quick the Commission of the European Communities has reprimanded the French government, arguing that the descriptions on the menu are appropriately informative for the consumer. The obligatory requirement of using French terms was considered an additional economic cost for importers equivalent to a quantitative trade restriction and hence a violation of the treaty of Rome.[73] The case, however, was not tried before the European Court of Justice.

New Products

Products can be said to be language-sensitive if language is a composite part of them, for instance, electronic calculators that can be programmed. There are more language-sensitive products today than ever. The "Mama"-crying doll has undergone remarkable metamorphoses and evolutionary jumps, presenting itself nowadays not just in the guise of artificial doormen that salute customers when entering or leaving a shop. The lip-reading robot of Stanley Kubrick's *Clockwork Orange* is still science fiction, but cash registers whose synthetic voices express gratitude for our purchase and announce the price of the merchandise and the change we are due, have become inconspicuous gadgets of everyday life in many parts of the world. Those who feel the need for some vocal encouragement can have their microwave grill tell them about the appropriate cooking time and other aspects of their recipes, or listen to an almost human voice in their car that informs them about the distance from their destination, the speed, and the traffic jams to be expected along the way. To announce the continuously changing altitudes of landing airplanes used to be one of the tasks of the flight engineer of passenger planes. In the most modern airplanes, these announcements are made automatically by voice synthesizers, thus turning a three-person cockpit into one for a crew of only two. Synthetic voices are also used for telephone directory information services. Voices are scanned for criminological and other purposes by voice detectors, much like fingerprints. Telephones for the deaf, reading machines and transcoding machines which transform printed texts into auditory or Braille signals, electronic dictionaries, machine translation programs and translation support programs, telephones with integrated translation components, automatic transliteration programs which transform Latin into Cyrillic letters or Chinese characters, software for computer-assisted language learning are only some of the recent innovations by means of which ever more mechanical and electronic elements become integral parts of human communication behavior. The industries involved in the production of these devices are booming. Unremitting investments are made in order to make human language more efficiently, and for ever more purposes, electronically processible.

The most profitable products so far are word processing systems and other software programs which can be implemented on personal computers which have become household articles almost overnight. Newspapers have their "computer corners" or entire pages. The technical literature for computer users is so voluminous that regular bookstores are quite unable to keep an up-to-date stock. Innovations are being made at such a speed that improved programs, manuals, and comments are marketed continuously, thus creating a market with its own dynamics and growth. In the industrialized world, the personal computer has become a standard accessory of most white-collar jobs. For those performing these jobs the pressure of competition makes it imperative to keep abreast with the latest developments.

The most ambitious project of communication technology, for which enormous resources have been made available by private enterprise and government agencies, is to make machines accessible to natural languages. Researchers in the fields of Artificial Intelligence, Computer Linguistics, Computer Architecture, and Microelectronics collaborate in order to free those who want to use computers of the need for this purpose to learn complicated programming languages. As soon as it becomes possible for the user to communicate with the machine by means of a variety which approximates his or her own vernacular language, a whole range of other tasks, which ideally the machine should be able to carry out, come within reach. Among them are translating, potent question–answer systems, access to comprehensive data banks, mathematical analyses, and, what is most difficult, problem solving. Rather than consisting in the execution of a given sequence of – maybe extremely numerous – steps in order to arrive at a solution, an operation which computers perform admirably well already, problem solving involves the dividing up of a complex problem into manageable tasks and thus finding a path that leads to a solution. To equip a machine for such a task is a formidable challenge. In order to illustrate the magnitude of the necessary effort, it is useful to refer to an institute which was founded in 1981 by eight Japanese electronics companies with the sole purpose of carrying out the necessary basic research. Some £30 million were spent during the first three years, and the entire budget is estimated as £300 million (Wattenberg 1985).

The above enumeration of innovative language-sensitive products should not lead to the conclusion that language is becoming less important in human communication, that it is being mechanized and even replaced by machine communication. Quite the contrary is the case. To the extent that machines are enabled to perform linguistic functions, language becomes more and more important, because in this way it becomes serviceable in a greater variety of ways. The attempt to use natural language for communicating with machines must not be seen as a corruption and denaturalization of language. The point of this endeavor is to adapt the machine to human requirements, habits, and capabilities, instead of conversely adjusting human behavior to the limitations of the machine and thus becoming enslaved by it. Human language is the most powerful symbolic system known. To the extent that machines are being empowered to perform, or even simulate, functions of natural language, they become more flexible and useful. This is what ultimately justifies the immense investments in this domain.

Private Expenditures for Language – Summary

For a modern economy, that is, a market economy of one kind or another as opposed to a subsistence economy, language is as pivotal as money. Its crucial importance follows from the fact that economic activity consists to a very considerable degree in communication, and that essential parts of economic communication are linguistic in nature.[74] Although there is no economic activity without communication, communication brings on costs, partly on account of the multilingualism of the world. Since the world is polyglot, and since every market is characterized by a specific constellation of languages, there is an ideal communication competence for engaging in economic activities in every situation. The communication competence with which an economic agent is equipped in a given situation can be optimal or sub-optimal. In the latter case, it is necessary for the economic agent to decide whether to tolerate limited efficiency caused by sub-optimal communication competence or to allocate resources for compensating the deficit. How an economic agent decides in such a situation will often depend on the relative costs of the alternatives, where the economic strength of the languages involved can be assumed to play an important role. The acquisition of some languages is more cost-efficient than that of others, depending on the purpose of its employment for company internal communication, the company's communication with its environment, with the market, or as a part of a product. To invest into a language as human capital or as a commodity requires funds, on a smaller or larger scale. Whether or not it makes any economic sense at all to invest into a given language for one purpose or another is the question of costs and benefits, which for private enterprise is even more crucial to consider than for governments.

The Payoff

The above account of language-related expenditures of the public and private sectors is not exhaustive. Hidden language costs among others were disregarded. However, the survey on the preceding pages suffices to demonstrate that language is a cost-factor for both government and private enterprise, deserving more attention than it has often been paid.

Whenever costs are discussed, mention is usually also made of benefits. In the technical terminology of economics it only makes sense to speak of costs when they can be related to expected or actual benefits. For it is important to make a distinction between out-of-pocket expenses and costs. Costs are conceived of as (1) additional outlays which would not have occurred without certain actions, for example, the use or acquisition of a foreign language, the implementation of language laws, the adaptation of language-sensitive products that were developed for one language to another, or the recognition of an additional official language by an international organization; and (2) reduced performance or forgone gains which are caused, for example, by language courses during working hours. Where expenses lead to a direct or long-term improvement of performance, the additional gains thus achieved have to be calculated against the expenses.

It is in this connection that the question of cost efficiency arises, that is, the question of whether the calculable ratio of costs and benefits is such that the latter exceed, or at least equal, the former. In Robillard's words:

> Every time a change is envisioned, the problem is to know whether the situation that will be brought about will really be better in all respects than the present state of affairs, and whether the costs of eventuating the change will not be prohibitive, in other words, whether it is worth the effort.[75]

Efficiency or cost-benefit analyses were first applied to language-related expenditures by Jernudd, Thorburn, and Vaillancourt. Jernudd (1968) examined whether self-study is a more cost-efficient method of foreign language learning than learning by instruction. On the basis of a cost-benefit analysis of real data he arrived at the conclusion that this is the case. Discussing the advantages and drawbacks of using one of the European standard languages as an official language in a Third World country, Thorburn (1971) demonstrated with a hypothetical model how language planning can make use of cost-benefit analyses. And Vaillancourt (1988) has presented a cost-benefit analysis of the Canadian language laws which led him to conclude that the total costs of this policy were high, but that they were relatively low in view of the achieved outcome, that is, the improved competitiveness of the French language and its speakers in Canadian society. Many other authors have also put forth considerations about language problems more or less implicitly based on cost-benefit analyses.[76]

Where cost-benefit analyses can reasonably be applied to language problems is a more difficult question to answer than may seem at a glance. This is so for three main reasons. First, inasmuch as cost-benefit analyses are taken into account for sociopolitical or business decisions, they are typically of a prognostic nature. Thus, while the costs of implementing certain policies can be calculated quite accurately in many cases, as demonstrated by some of the examples discussed above, the calculation of benefits is often characterized by a high degree of uncertainty. Secondly, this uncertainty is further aggravated by the long time frame which has to be reckoned with for political or economic decisions that have a bearing on language. The further a projection reaches out into the future, the greater its imprecision and uncertainty. The general failure of planned languages is clear evidence of the great importance of the time frame of cost-benefit analyses. Proponents of such languages like to invoke efficiency arguments in favor of their promotion and spreading:[77] enormous monies could be saved if the same auxiliary language were used throughout the world, which, moreover, thanks to its regularity and simplicity, is much easier to learn than any natural language. Also its mastery allegedly facilitates the learning of other foreign languages. Thus, Pool (1991) advertises the learning of Esperanto as a way of getting "two languages for the price of one." However, the failure of this line of reasoning to convince the masses, let alone influence their behavior, can be explained on the basis of cost-benefit considerations as well. Here the difference between the interests of individuals and collectivities comes to bear.[78] Half a century ago, Richards pinpointed the insoluble dilemma that stands in the way of the international spreading of planned auxiliary languages. Nothing that the artificial language movement has achieved in the meantime has proved his assessment wrong.

> We may all wish that everyone would learn such a language. But these wishes, however strong they might be, will never be strong enough to make enough people put enough time into learning an artificial language as a speculative investment. If you are going to the trouble of learning a language you need to feel that you will get a return for your toil this very year. (Richards 1943: 11)

Thirdly, the applicability of cost-benefit analysis is not always evident because calculable costs are often related to non-calculable benefits. The following remark by Canada's Commissioner of Official Languages is a case in point:

> It takes money to develop and cultivate linguistic assets . . . Canada's investment in bilingualism has paid important dividends, has helped keep Canada together.[79]

In this connection, "investment" means quantifiable financial outlays, whereas "dividend" is used in a metaphorical sense. Similarly, the 15 million franc (1987) budget of the French Commissariat Général de la Language Française was not made available in the expectation of financial returns of such an amount or more.

Another example is the defense and promotion of multilingualism in the European Community. Economic rationality would seem to dictate the active promotion of a single vehicular language. However, in the minds of many speakers, languages are associated with other than economic values. They believe that, even if this is less efficient than a common lingua franca for all, many languages should be promoted as foreign languages in the EC member states. Thus, Truchot argues:

> The costs of such a programme would be high; they should properly be considered, therefore, not as unproductive expenses, but as an investment. Europe as a whole has at its disposal a linguistic heritage which, if we were to evaluate it, enabled it to expand its influence throughout the world and to forge together the peoples within its boundaries.[80]

Since Truchot refers to financial expenses, "investment" appears to be meant in the literal sense. Yet, it remains unclear what the payoff is expected to be, since the reasons he gives for justifying a financial commitment refer to the past rather than to the future.

Although the material benefits of language policies cannot always be reliably assessed, and although the consequences brought about in the sociopolitical, cultural, or ideological spheres may actually be more important and more highly valued, it is often economic arguments that are resorted to in justifying the financial outlays for such measures. Thus, the head of the department of culture of the foreign ministry in Bonn stated the following motivation for the financial support of exporting the German language abroad: "Those who speak German are more likely to buy German products than those who are ignorant of our language."[81] The conclusion the reader is invited to draw is that it is worthwhile to spend so much money for the promotion of German. There is, however, no rigid cost-benefit analysis underlying this contention.

The lack of foreign language education in American high schools and colleges has often been criticized on economic grounds. "The President's Commission on Foreign Language and International Studies (1979) installed by President Carter came to the conclusion that lack of foreign languages and knowledge of foreign countries and cultures was a serious impediment to American foreign trade. "The tongue-tied American," to quote the title of a book by Senator Paul Simon (Simon 1980), was also blamed for the comparative decline in the quality of US products, because too few Americans are able to take notice of innovative ideas published in a language other than English: Japanese, German, or Korean, for example. In 1982, a bill was put before the American Congress for the improvement of translation and interpretation services, which was argued to be necessary because the availability of language competent personnel is of crucial importance for the national interest in overseas commercial activities (*Channels* 1982).

In this case, as in many others, material interests are invoked in order to defend certain expenditures, yet both sides cannot be related to one another in terms of cost-benefit analysis, because the anticipated socioeconomic repercussions are so diffuse that they are impossible to represent in quantitative terms. Nevertheless, cost-benefit calculations can sometimes be usefully employed.

The point of departure of such an analysis is a situation calling for a decision as to whether or not certain measures shall be implemented or whether alternative measures shall be implemented. The factors to be taken into account in the analysis have to be identified unambiguously. Measures affecting a society's or social group's language use or the communication competence of a company can have multifarious, far-reaching, and very indirect consequences. It is critically important, therefore, to identify the most consequential effects, which for the purpose at hand means those which are quantifiable. Cost-benefit analysis can only be applied if the alternatives for a future course of action are clear, if their respective effects can be predicted within the adopted time frame with a reasonable degree of certainty, and if the anticipated effects are not too diffuse.

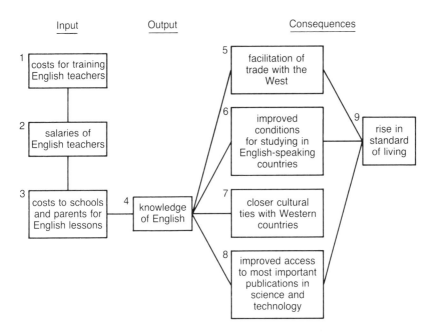

Figure 4.2 Cost-benefit analysis for adoption of English as first foreign language in Poland.

A concrete example may serve to illustrate the difficulties of fulfilling these conditions. As the problem situation to be subjected to cost-benefit analysis let us consider foreign language education in Poland after the end of communist rule and the disintegration of the Warsaw Pact. The alternatives to be considered are the *zero alternative* of leaving school curricula unchanged and the *main alternative* of replacing Russian, as the first foreign language, with English or another Western language. Let us assume, for simplicity's sake, that the zero alternative really does not cause any additional costs. The problem is then to calculate the costs of the main alternative and to relate them to the expected benefits. The various aspects of this problem can be integrated into a graphical model (see figure 4.2). The problem under discussion here is a real problem which Poland had to deal with in 1990.[82] The graph serves to identify in the boxes numbered 1 to 9 the essential components of a solution in accordance with the main alternative. In what follows, these boxes are explained one by one. The costs are divided between the first three boxes, the benefit is given in box number 4, and boxes 5 to 9 contain its anticipated consequences.

1 With regard to the training of English teachers, the existing English teachers must be taken into account. The costs must then be calculated for the number of teachers to be trained in addition to the existing ones. If a target figure is determined, these costs can be estimated with a high degree of accuracy.

2 Similarly, the salaries of the future English teachers can be calculated, although this is a little more difficult, since the projection refers to a more distant future. Assuming that Russian teachers will not be fired, but continue to be paid, this is where the largest costs of the main alternative are incurred. Under this assumption it will be possible to reallocate the monies spent for Russian teachers only very gradually, as retiring Russian teachers are not replaced by new ones.

3 In addition to teachers' salaries, the costs of instruction encompass textbooks and other teaching materials. Yet another factor which could be taken into account is the necessary length of time of instruction. As a Slavonic language, Russian may be easier to learn for native speakers of Polish than English, which implies that more hours need to be spent studying English than Russian for achieving the same proficiency level.

4 The result of the main alternative is a certain level of proficiency in English by a predictable number of high school graduates. This result will have a number of consequences, some of which can be anticipated.

5 For establishing and maintaining international trade contacts, the utility of English is greater than that of Russian not only in Western countries, but also in Eastern Europe. It is, however, difficult to appraise the consequences of the main alternative for expanding trade with the West, because language is not the only or even the most important factor here. Yet, to look at another example, determining the financial benefits of enlarging a highway network or similar public works[83] raises comparable problems, and in such cases it is very common to make use of cost-benefit analysis.

6 A higher level of English language proficiency among high school graduates will clearly ameliorate the possibilities for studying in English-speaking countries. Since this is not only a very diffuse outcome of the main alternative, but also one with a long time

frame, its significance for the national economy is hard to evaluate in quantifiable terms.

7   More intensive cultural relations with Western countries are another expected consequence of the main alternative which, however, cannot be assigned any identifiable function for the national economy.

8   By contrast, easier and more extensive access to English language publications can be expected to have functional effects for the national economy which, however, are once again hard to quantify.

9   The general superordinate motivation for the main alternative is a desire for an improved standard of living. That replacing Russian by English as the first foreign language of school instruction will help to achieve this, is the underlying assumption, whose appropriateness is hard to express in numerical terms; for the time frame of the projection ranges over two decades at least. In retrospect, too, assuming that the standard of living has actually improved, it will be difficult rigorously to assess the contributions of the main alternative to this achievement.

Nevertheless, an analysis of this sort can be useful, not least because it allows for the conditions of the main alternative in terms of its costs to be represented with reasonable certainty. Of course, imponderables cannot be ruled out. To a government burdened with national debts and inadequacies in almost every respect, a project such as the one just discussed may seem desirable, but impractical for lack of funds. Offers by English-speaking countries to train or send English teachers at their own expense can then have a significant influence at the level of decision or implementation. In this way, Poland would be able to acquire the desired product at a discount.

Conceivably, some of the language exporters in addition to Britain and the USA, especially France and Germany, are quite prepared, for their own interests and by their own means, to fill the gap in Poland's foreign language market that opens up as a result of the decreasing demand for Russian. By way of acknowledging historical links with the French language reaching back to the seventeenth century, Poland participates in the Francophonie movement and can presumably expect some support from France. German, on the other hand, is the language of Poland's western neighbor and doubtless increasingly important trading partner. Assuming that French and German compete for second rank in Poland's foreign language market, how can the respective policies be expressed in economic terms?

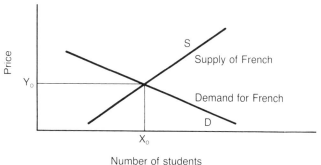

Figure 4.3   Supply and demand of a foreign language.

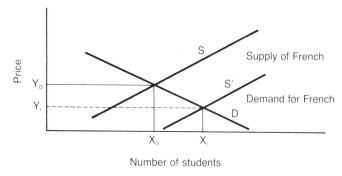

Figure 4.4   Price subsidy for foreign language training.

According to the law of supply and demand, the equilibrium price of a commodity is where supply and demand are balanced. Whenever demand surpasses supply, the price increases until the demand is satisfied, or rather, until further demand is curbed by the increased price. In view of the educational policy and national economic decisions Poland has to confront, a language – i.e., French and German – can be regarded as a commodity, as suggested in chapter 3. The relationship between the price and the number of students studying it as a foreign language can then be depicted in a graph of the standard demand/supply framework (figure 4.3).[84] The demand for French (German) is represented by a falling curve indicating that the number of students increases in correlation with a low price. The supply of French (German) is represented by an ascending curve indicating that supply will grow to the extent that the price increases. The intersection of the supply and demand curves determines the equilibrium price. Financial support by France or Germany enabling Poland to provide more French or German instruction at a lower price, can then be represented by a rightward shift of the supply curve as in figure 4.4. Language export subsidies of this sort serve to prevent a slowdown of increases in demand by rising prices.

That language export promotion measures on the part of France or Germany in accordance with this model could actually have an influence on Poland's educational policy is a realistic possibility, but it would be a mistake to assume a direct relationship between the amount of financial aid and an increase in the number of students studying French or German. For even an artificially low price may be found too high by many individuals or the Polish government, if the *opportunity cost* – that which must be given up to obtain a commodity – is too high. In the case of foreign language acquisition, the opportunity cost can be expressed only partly in money terms and can, therefore, be only partially influenced by means of price subsidies. More specifically, this means that a dumping price for becoming proficient in German or French will not be decisive in motivating potential customers to acquire one or the other, if the alternative of studying English will have to be foregone. The benefits and costs to be calculated against each other are thus the advantage gained by expanding the instruction time of one language and the disadvantage resulting from reducing that of another (or another school subject).

From this follow certain consequences for a cost-benefit analysis of language export promotion. Financial subsidies in accordance with the model depicted in figure 4.4 can have limited effects at best. They would be wasted, to stay with the above example, if applied in order to compete with English in Poland's foreign language market. It would be more promising, probably, to supplement supply-increasing measures such as these with demand-enhancing measures (which would correspond to shifting the demand curve in figure 4.4 to the right). This could be achieved, for instance, by convincing the Polish government of the necessity of letting more pupils study two foreign languages, or by directly appealing to the public with a publicity campaign.

With proper care and certain limitations, cost-benefit analysis can be applied to a wide range of decisions in the area of political and administrative responsibility for language. For example, a journal for executives reports that the Southern California Gas Works were able to save $252,000 per year by using a linguistically more transparent billing form, because, as a result, customer inquiries decreased drastically.[85]

Potential savings were one of the main arguments in favor of the reform of Greek accent writing. Greek pupils were estimated to need 4,500 hours of instruction in order to master the complicated rules of Greek orthography. The introduction of a new writing system called "monotony" writing in 1982 reduced a variety of complicated rules for placing several different accent marks to one simple rule. This measure made possible savings in several domains. Typing time was reduced by up to 35 percent, and printing became less expensive, too. Most importantly, instruction time for mother tongue education could be significantly reduced.[86] Costs of this nature are relatively easy to estimate. Hence, a cost-benefit calculation could be taken into account in the decision process concerning the adoption of monotone writing.

A politically controversial example is a recent proposal by the Dutch minister of education, Mr Ritzen, to introduce English as the language of instruction in Dutch universities.[87] The advantages and drawbacks of this proposal could be examined by means of cost-benefit analysis.

It must be kept in mind, however, that the possibility of applying cost-benefit analysis to language planning and educational policy does not imply that foreign language curricula or language policy measures are always, or even most of the time, determined by cost-benefit analysis. As a matter of fact, language policy is often designed to counter the forces of economic rationality.

The language policy of Kenya, where both English and Kiswahili are recognized as official languages, is a pertinent example. The stated government policy is gradually to reduce the official use of English in order to make Kiswahili the sole official language by the year 2000. This policy runs counter both to the economic development and the economic interests of Kenya, because, as Eastman (1990) has observed, English plays an increasingly important role in Kenya's trade links and business relationships overseas, in Africa, and even in the national context.

The francophone countries of Africa are almost without exception faced with the question of what language(s) to employ in the educational system. Chaudenson (1987: 64) outlines four alternative school types:

1   monolingual French schools without any recognition of African languages;
2   monolingual French schools with regionally adjusted curricula, for instance, by means of contrastive reference to African languages;
3   bilingual schools with balanced instruction in both French and African languages;

4   monolingual African languages schools where French is taught as a subject, but not used as a language of instruction.

On the basis of a cost-benefit evaluation, a school system of type 1 would turn out to be the least expensive, since it can make use of existing teaching materials, tested curricula, and a language which need not prove its suitability for the purposes of academic literacy.

> For the functioning of an educational system, multilingualism is obviously an important cost factor, even if the enormous investments necessary for making languages serviceable are left out of consideration.[88]

In many African countries, school systems of types 1 or 2 are institutionalized because of the economic constraints resulting from the inevitable costs of multilingual school systems rather than political convictions. These options are chosen in plain view of the social costs of a monolingual system, that is, the costs of an elitist system where 25 percent of the national budget is spent for the education of 12 percent of all pupils. Cost-benefit analysis is not designed to reckon with social inequality or deprivation.

To balance economic and social costs or even to give more weight to the latter than to the former is, however, much more difficult for impoverished African states than for advanced industrialized countries. The Netherlands or Canada, for example, can afford to finance language courses for immigrants which puts additional pressure on the national budget, but, in the long run, contributes to social harmony and thus, indirectly, to a growing GNP.[89]

Ireland's language policy, too, is an example of how profitability concerns can be supplemented by sociopolitical considerations. As Commins (1988: 25) has shown, the Gaeltacht, the western region of Ireland where Irish is still natively spoken, exemplifies the dilemma of government control over economic and linguistic development in disadvantaged rural areas. The retreat of Irish began in the eighteenth century, a process which was accelerated during the nineteenth century in the wake of industrialization. Today, only some 2 percent of the Irish population use Irish in everyday life as their first language. This decline is part of the general forces of modernization which are effective especially in structurally underdeveloped regions of Western societies. It has been linked with demographic shifts, that is, urbanization and desertion of the countryside by the young. The Irish Minister for the Gaeltacht explained the connection succinctly as follows:

No jobs, no people; no people, no Gaeltacht; no Gaeltacht, no language. (Commins 1988: 15)

For this reason, it is the ministry of economics which is charged with language policy as part of a regional policy in Ireland. Its declared purpose is to create jobs in marginal areas and thereby preserve the Irish language by way of preserving its original milieu. Thus, this language policy is designed to counter the trends of economic development which are deplored by many. Rather than dealing with language in the abstract, it is concerned with the language of a certain region which is spoken by certain people. In this way, language policy is given an economic rationality which makes it easier to accept and implement than a policy concerned with the preservation of a language of and by itself. However, the economic rationality of regional infrastructure improvements would hardly be enough to make a language maintenance policy acceptable, because the decline of Irish is considered irreversible by most inhabitants of Ireland. They are quite aware of the advantages their native language, Irish English, affords them, making them, as it were, co-proprietors of the economically most potent language on earth, while at the same time allowing them to give expression to their national identity.

However, cost-benefit analysis can be useful not only when an assessment of the economic pros and cons of a language policy blueprint and the decision of whether or not to implement it are at issue, but also for simply analyzing the cost-efficiency of certain measures designed to achieve a recognized goal, for example, supporting a language in retreat (cf. chapter 5). Where resources are limited, cost-benefit analysis can be employed to establish a rank order of priorities and specify the measures which may be taken to attain the stated objectives using a minimum of financial resources (O'Brien 1979: 87).

In addition to cost-benefit analysis, social groups often take other factors into account in connection with decisions concerning language problems. This is particularly likely where the preservation of a language is concerned, no matter whether there is any chance of success, where a language is subject to strong emotional attachment, or closely linked to other social attributes. When considerations of economic utility are unabashedly brought to bear to matters concerning cultural assets, reactions are sometimes vehemently critical. Claude Berri, the French film director, aroused an outcry in the media when he publicly said that there was no longer any future for producing films in French, because the French language was a barrier standing in the way of world-wide distribution.[90]

Other decisions where language is not concerned as the medium of culture are less problematic and, therefore, more susceptible to cost-benefit analysis. For instance, the decision to buy a machine translation system will depend almost exclusively on whether or not the necessary outlays can be expected to yield a return. At the present level of development, this can be determined easily and reliably by cost-benefit analysis. It was more difficult to use cost-benefit analysis for the development of automatic translation systems. As late as 1975, an expert in the field wrote that "there has probably been no other scientific enterprise in which so much money has been spent on so many projects that promised so little" (Kay 1975: 219). Nevertheless, in the expectation of substantial benefits, public and private sponsors were willing to support this research generously. The translation bureau of the Canadian government, for example, from 1973 through 1981, spent some C\$3.5 million to support research and development of automatic translation. In retrospect, these monies were quickly found to be well spent. The investment paid off for the meteorological service Environment Canada alone, which publishes all weather bulletins in English and French.[91] The European Community, in view of the high costs of translating its nine official languages, has also made substantial monies available for developing machine and machine-aided translation programs. First, the EC Commission bought the English–French version of the American SYSTRAN program which, however, proved inadequate for its gigantic translation operations. Then, from 1983 through 1990, it spent some 20.5 million ECU for the multilingual EUROTRA computer translation program. Since the discontinuation of multilingual publication of EC documents is not a politically realistic option, and since the financial and human resources of the translation services are limited, the decision to sponsor this project was well-motivated by cost-benefit analysis, even though the results may not be all satisfactory.[92]

The UN is another international organization which maintains relatively expensive translation services. Under the pressure of the general shortage of funds, there have been repeated demands to rigidly control their cost efficiency. In particular, a program for continuing education designed to reduce the dominance of English and French by making staff members learn at least one additional official language of the UN, was attacked as expensive and inefficient. The general assembly, nevertheless, decided not to abandon this program, because a majority of its members considered the attempt to reduce the linguistic inequality of the organization and to motivate staff members to enrich their language abilities worth the costs. Mahmoud (1987) has interpreted this as the politically motivated refusal to subject the language use and communication competence of the UN to the constraints of cost-efficiency demands.

Costs and Benefits of Language – Summary

The management of language, its cultivation, and its use for purposes of communication, social control, and trade incur costs both to government and private enterprise. Many of these expenses can be related, as costs of measures, to actual or expected gains. This is always the case whenever it is necessary, or possible, to make decisions leading to a change of the existing situation. Although the benefits of language-related measures are more difficult to calculate than the costs, cost-benefit analysis can be usefully employed in connection with the solution of language problems in the public and private sectors. It must not be forgotten, however, that decisions concerning the use, acquisition, or maintenance of a language, though advisable in terms of cost-benefit analysis, may not always be fundable, politically desirable, or acceptable to the public. This is so because, in addition to its economic potential, language is also characterized by political, cultural, and sociopsychological properties which are difficult to evaluate in the same terms. Because of these properties, the consequences of language-related decisions are difficult to predict. Cost-benefit analysis can only reckon with factors which can be operationalized by means of economic value assessments. What it does, therefore, is only to provide an additional piece of information that can be taken into account in decision-making situations concerning language problems; no more, no less. However, as will be demonstrated in the following chapter, in spite of the non-economic values attached to language, what prevails in matters of language is often that which is profitable.

5

Language Careers:
Economic Determinants of Language Evolution

As demonstrated in the preceding chapters, languages are economically valuable, they are traded in a market, they bring on costs, and, through their diversity, exercise an influence on the economic process. But they are also influenced by it. They respond to economic needs. How the career of a language begins and comes to an end; whether it grows to become a multinational concern with subsidiaries and branches in many parts of the world; or whether heading a local general store is the peak of its career; whether and how it is preserved for posterity; all this depends to a significant extent on how it is managed and by whom.

Languages emerge and disappear, their ranges expand and shrink. Often these processes are interrelated. Language contact happens whenever their speakers get into contact with each other. Depending on the nature of that contact, one of the languages involved is superseded, superposed, or supplemented by the other, as the case may be. In short, the relationship between languages can be described as one of competition. Obviously, the universe of languages is not one big competition free for all where every language competes with all others. But shifts of the kind where a language comes into use for certain functions formerly reserved to another can be observed frequently. Since social groups do not increase the number of languages they employ arbitrarily or randomly, the range of usage of a language within a group is typically expanded only at the expense of that of another.

Further, there are at times situations where communities have certain communicative needs, but no language suitable for satisfying them; and others where there is no, or almost no, communicative need for whose fulfillment a certain language is needed. Among the conditions that engender situations of this sort those of the economic environment play a crucial role. They are at the center of the discussion in this chapter. That political and cultural conditions of changing communicative needs and language career chances are mentioned only in passing should, however, not be taken to indicate that they are less important.

Languages are tools, serving certain purposes. If we assume that these purposes can be fulfilled more or less successfully and efficiently, and if we further assume that the users of a tool are inclined to choose one which is suitable to their purposes or to adapt it in such a way as to optimize its suitability for the purpose(es) at hand, then it follows that languages must change whenever the communicative needs change which they are employed to fulfill. This does not mean that languages do not change unless the communicative needs change. Like a knife which, although always employed for the same purpose of cutting, needs to be ground once in a while, there is also wear and tear in language which leads to changes. It is customary, therefore, to distinguish external from internal conditions of linguistic change. Our concern is with the former rather than the latter, that is, with the functions that the speakers of a language must be able to fulfill with it under specific historical conditions. In taking this approach we have made two tacit assumptions, namely (1) that all languages cannot fulfill all functions equally well, and (2) that the communicative needs of any two social groups are not identical. They are not difficult to validate, however, if we think of the concrete functional capacity of a given language at a given time rather than the expressive potential of a language system in the abstract. The many language modernization and reform projects suffice to prove this. There would be no need for them if all languages were equally well equipped for all purposes. That this is not the case is only in keeping with the obvious fact that all languages are different, even unique, for every one is characterized by specific conditions not only in their utilization, but also in their genesis.

Language Birth

Two savages, who had never been taught to speak, but had been bred up remote from the societies of men, would naturally begin to form that language by which they would endeavour to make their mutual wants intelligible to each other, by uttering certain sounds, whenever they meant to denote certain objects. (Smith 1759: 403)

Quoting these lines here is interesting not so much because of their contents as because of their author, Adam Smith, the founder and to many still the unrivalled authority of economics. Like Smith, his most radical and articulate critics, Marx and Engels, took an interest in the origin of language; and like his ideas, theirs point in the direction of a utilitarianistic theory. In a often quoted passage from *Die deutsche Ideologie* they explain:

> Language is as old as consciousness, language *is* a practical, real consciousness which exists both for others and hence also for myself. And language comes into being, like consciousness, only out of the need, the necessity of intercourse with other people.[1]

In the above accounts, "wants" and "need" are to be understood in the economic sense. In order to survive, people must communicate with each other, and that is why the question of the origin of language attracted the interest of Smith as well as of Marx and Engels. What they had to say about this subject was purely theoretical in nature, although Smith developed very specific ideas about the construction of a linguistic system, while Marx and Engels confined themselves to general reflections. However, at the time all theories about the origin of language were speculative, which is what most of them still are.[2] The question how humankind attained speech remains in the dark.[3]

How certain people attained a certain language is not quite as veiled, but here, too, we are faced with grave difficulties. Much can be said, for example, about how the Italians came to speak Italian, but not that they began to speak Italian, say, on September 14, 1321, having used some other language until then. Since languages are passed on from one generation to the next, they change gradually, and only arbitrary decision allows one to draw a sharp line: Here is where Italian begins.

Breaks in Traditions

Only very unusual conditions lead to catastrophic breaks in linguistic traditions that prevent speakers from transmitting their mother tongue to their offspring intact or only slightly modified and, by virtue of "the necessity of intercourse with other people" force them to create a new instrument of communication. This is when pidgin languages are born. Since many of these languages came into existence in the wake of Europe's mercantilist expansion, their origin can be dated rather precisely. Before the first British trading outpost in Guangzhou was established in 1664, there was no Chinese Pidgin English; three or four decades later it was there (Hall 1966: 8). Sranan came into being between 1651 and 1679 in Surinam (Voorhoeve 1983: 42); Hawaiian Creole after 1880 (Bickerton 1981: 1). The origin of none of the great culture languages which are based on an unbroken tradition of several centuries can be pinpointed with similar confidence. That pidgin languages do allow for such precise dating is not because of any of their internal properties, but because of the external, that is, socioeconomic conditions of their genesis; for pidgins are to be understood "as social solutions to the discontinuities in social and linguistic traditions and to the communicative pressure developing in cross-linguistic intercourse" (Mühlhäusler 1986: 94).

It is not without reason that pidgins and creoles are called trade languages, because it was trade that gave rise to their existence. According to Jespersen (1964: 222), the name *pidgin* is derived from the English word *business* distorted in Chinese pronunciation. Thus, Pidgin English is Business English. This etymology which is also given by the Oxford English Dictionary is not uncontested, but two other possible etymologies also link *pidgin* with trade. As reported by Todd (1984: 2), one is the Portuguese word *ocupação* meaning "business, occupation," and the other is Hebrew *pidjom* "barter." The fact that in many parts of the world pidgins function as trade languages suggests that one of these etymologies is correct.[4] This is not absolutely certain, but nevertheless from what was probably its origin at the Chinese coast, *pidgin* has become the general designation of auxiliary trade languages.

Under certain conditions, especially in societies exhibiting great linguistic diversity even on a local level, or in groups who have been deprived of the possibility of using their mother tongue, a pidgin can become "a more valuable instrument than the mother-tongues" (Le Page 1964: 40) of its users. Whenever this is the case, pidgins are put to use for ever more communication functions and gradually penetrate the domestic domain where they acquire the quality of a first language. The next generation of speakers whose only language it may be then expands the pidgin into a full-fledged language. Languages for which this process is evidenced in recent history are called "creoles,"[5] the process itself "creolization." The word *creole* is derived from Spanish *criollo* meaning "domestic, brought up" and originally referred to the white population born and raised in the colonies. Its meaning was extended to include their languages, especially the Caribbean varieties related to French,

Spanish, and Portuguese. Nowadays *creole* is no longer restricted in its meaning to a geographical area or language family, but is generally used as a technical notion in contradistinction to *pidgin*.

Unequal Encounters

Pidgins and creoles are found wherever European merchants established trade links with peoples on other continents: at the West African coast, in coastal regions of India and China, in the Straits of Malakka, in the Pacific, at the northeastern rim of South America and, in great variety, in the Caribbean where Portuguese, Spanish, British, French, and Dutch traders and pirates competed with each other and, from the seventeenth through the nineteenth century, repeatedly used force to seize each other's possessions. Pidginization and creolization have also happened without European participation. Bazar Hindi, a reduced form of Hindi which emerged in the market places of northern India, and Sango, an African creole which is widely used as a vehicular language in the Central African Republic, are often quoted examples. Occasionally trade languages have also emerged in Europe and at its periphery, for instance, Russonorsk, a jargon used by Norwegian and Russian fishermen.[6] Neumann (1966) reports of a Russian–Chinese trade jargon. Sometimes "pidgin" is also used to refer to characteristics of language use which, from an alternative point of view, are described as interference or code switching. For instance, Steinke (1979: 197) explains the influence of Rumanian on the speech behavior of the German-speaking minority in Rumania as follows.

> In the working environment a kind of pidginization sometimes happens, that is, a distinct hybrid language emerges whose technical terms are Rumanian while the sentence frame remains German.

Similarly, the notion of a pidgin has been applied to varieties which have come into existence in the wake of demographic shifts from southern to northern Europe in response to labour market conditions, for example, the German variety spoken by migrant workers.[7] Varieties of this kind as well as other substandard varieties which were brought from the erstwhile colonies to the "mother countries"[8] are now found, increasingly, also in elementary schools of western European countries. However, no matter where they are spoken nowadays,[9] the great majority of the many pidgins and creoles which can be studied today came into existence as a result of the encounter between the Europeans and the peoples of other continents: Pidgin English at the Chinese coast, Krio (English) in West Africa, French Creole in Haiti and on some of the Lesser Antilles, Papiamento (Portuguese/Spanish) in Aruba, Bonaire, and Curaçao, Indo-Portuguese in Sri Lanka, Tok Pisin (English) in Papua New Guinea, Spanish-based contact varieties in the Philippines, Negro Dutch in Virgin Islands (no longer in use), Afrikaans (Dutch) in South Africa, and many others. The fundamental condition of the genesis of these languages is the necessity of adults, who, unlike children, do not have the time to grow into a speech community, to communicate with each other even though they have no common means of exchange at their disposal.

The importance of maritime life has been emphasized by some authors.

> One of the most favourable situations for the formations of such dialects is found aboard merchant vessels which ply the seven seas and ship large numbers of foreign sailors – and indeed the seaman is a figure of the greatest importance in the creation of the more permanent makeshift tongues.[10]

The *Lingua Franca* whose name was transferred to all other vehicular languages was a medieval auxiliary language of Mediterranean traders and the Crusaders. In its time also known as *Sabir*, it is said in addition to its Italian base to have comprised elements of the languages of almost all Mediterranean seafaring peoples: Spanish, Portuguese, French, Turkish, Arabic, and Greek (Whinnom 1977). Hancock suggests that the heterogeneous composition of the crews of British merchant ships and the nautical jargon they used was itself a factor which influenced the formation of English-based pidgins, especially that of western African Krio (Hancock 1976). As a result of the Dutch salt trade with Portugal and because they had manifold, if not always friendly, contacts with the Portuguese both in West Africa and on the other side of the Atlantic in Brazil and in the West Indies, the crews of Dutch merchant ships often used a Portuguese-based pidgin. In this way, Dutch sailors contributed to the spread of Pidgin Portuguese in the Caribbean (Le Page, Tabouret-Keller 1985: 30). And Dillard (1972) argued that Black English derives from the reduced English variety originally used as a trade language at the West African coast, which was then further developed on the transatlantic slave ships, as the Africans they carried had no other shared language.

Pidgins have typically evolved in situations of social pressure and inequality. Lacking as they do the prestige of a literary tradition and socially respected speakers, they are generally despised, a stigma which they usually retain, even if turned into a creole through frequent use. That this reflects their speakers' socioeconomic status and origin rather than systematic properties of the languages is evidenced by the fact that without historical knowledge creoles cannot easily be recognized as such, and that certain other restricted varieties which are used by socially higher ranking speakers are not valued negatively.

Reduction and New Creation

Since they encompass elements of various languages, pidgins and creoles are often simplisticly regarded as mixed languages. If "mixture" is taken to mean only the sum of the composite elements stemming from different sources, this notion cannot do justice to the special nature of these languages. The same can also be said, however, against the alternative view according to which they are merely corrupted varieties of European languages. Father Alonso de Sandoval wrote in 1627 about a creole that is spoken on three islands in the Gulf of Guinea which served as entrepots of the Portuguese slave trade:

> And we call them Creoles or natives of São Tomé. With the communication they have had with such barbarous nations in the time they have been living in São Tomé, they understand nearly all of them by means of a very corrupt and broken Portuguese speech which they call the language of São Tomé.[11]

To Jespersen (1964: 222) Neo-Melanesian, also known as Beach-la-Mar, was

> . . . English, and nothing but English, with very few admixtures, and all of these are such words as had previously been adopted into the English speech of those classes of the population, sailors, etc., with whom the natives came into contact.

Today, more than 90 percent of the vocabulary of Sao Tomese is said to be of Portuguese origin, and English, French, Spanish, and Dutch play a similar role in other pidgins and creoles. This is why these languages are called "Pidgin English," "Pidgin Portuguese," "French," or "Dutch Creole," etc., and from this point of view it is quite plausible to consider them varieties of European languages. Referring to English-based pidgins and creoles, Todd (1984), therefore, speaks of "modern

Englishes." Yet, this approach obscures the innovative nature peculiar to these languages which is emphasized by many creolists. Voorhoeve, for example, writes about Sranan or Surinamese:

> The question of the origin of Surinamese only makes sense because we know with certainty that the forefathers of its present-day speakers spoke a different language: not the same language of an older stage, but an entirely different language.[12]

These seemingly irreconcilable assessments of pidgins and creoles as, on the one hand, substandard varieties of European language, and genuine, self-sufficient languages, on the other, are due to the complexity of the subject matter and to the fact that traditional linguistics, which conceives of languages as tightly integrated systems, lacks the proper means to do justice to it. The methodological axiom of strictly separating systematic and historical descriptions, which implies the fiction of a language system outside time as well as the no less unrealistic assumption of a well-ordered sequence of developmental states of a language, makes it difficult if not impossible to conceptually grasp the dynamics of pidgins and creoles. New Guinean Tok Pisin which emerged around 1880 is at present undergoing creolization (Wurm 1977: 334). Though the mother tongue of some, it is still only a supplementary language for other speakers, used extensively by some and occasionally only by others. Describing it as either the one or the other strips the phenomenon of one of its most interesting aspects: the extreme functional and structural range of variation that distinguishes this language. Put differently, Tok Pisin encompasses synchronic varieties which exhibit characteristics of diachronically successive developmental states of the language. Creolists, therefore, prefer to speak of a continuum of coexisting varieties rather than a sequence of discrete language states.[13] By way of comparison, pidgins and creoles can be located on such a continuum – for example, a full-blown creole such as Sranan as opposed to the unstable jargon known as Gastarbeiterdeutsch – and every one of them can be described in relation to such a continuum.

Synchrony of Different Developmental States

The following stations on a continuum of varieties can be analytically distinguished for the languages that emerged in the said regions following European mercantilist expansion.

1   initial contact between a European and a local language
2   unstable jargon
3   reduced stabilizing pidgin
4   extended stabilized pidgin
5   creole
6   post-creole

These stations are not to be understood as consecutive developmental states, one replacing the other, but rather as co-existing conventions of language use exhibiting a regional and often social distribution. For example, Taylor (1968: 612) writes about the new West Indian languages that "throughout most of their history [they have been] the mother tongue of some, but a second language for other of their speakers." This means that an extended pidgin is not adopted as the family language and hence turned into a creole by all social classes at the same time. Similarly, in the regions where pidgins are spoken, the European languages, which for some speakers function as the super-stratum of jargon formation or an existing pidgin, are at the same time learned and used by the social elite in accordance with the rules of the standard variety. And finally, decreolization, a process which is taking place at this time, for example, in Jamaica where the (English-based) creole is being replaced more and more by English or adjusted to it, can be described as the successive adaptation of the speech of the lower social classes to that of the upper classes.

Thus, starting from a point of origin which can be localized fairly exactly, the multidimensional creole continuum ranges along temporal, geographic, and social scales. In many cases, the time and the place and the social conditions out of which a pidgin emerged are well-known. It is possible, therefore, to give a functional interpretation to the said stations on the continuum which reflect the economic relationships between the speakers involved. This connection is schematically depicted in table 5.1.

The different developmental stages of a pidgin thus reflect the kind and intensity of the economic relationships between European traders, seamen, and plantation workers with the indigenous population. Depending on the nature of these relations, the temporal range of the continuum varies in length. If a pidgin is functionally restricted to cross-linguistic interaction in the domain of trade, it can remain in use as such for several generations of speakers. This seems to have been the case in Cameroon and neighboring regions of the West African coast

Table 5.1   The stations of a creole continuum and the corresponding economic
relationships

European language *local language*	*jargon*	*reduced pidgin*	*expanded pidgin*	*creole*	*post-creole*
primary contact between European traders and indigenous population	sporadic exosocial commercial contacts	extensive exosocial economic contacts	endosocial economic contacts	all socio-economic functions	intensive contacts with society of superstratum language

where an English-based trade language was used as early as the eighteenth
century, which, as the Frenchman Labarthe reported in 1803, was a
great advantage for British traders because they did not need interpreters
(Todd 1974: 68). Nowadays, Cameroon has a bilingual school system
with up to 90 percent of all children being instructed in French and
English, the official languages of the country. Nevertheless, Pidgin
English continues to serve a useful function as lingua franca, especially
across social strata. Chinese Pidgin English, which except for isolated
pockets in Hong Kong seems to be extinct, was similarly used as a non-
native auxiliary idiom throughout the eighteenth century in the vicinity
of the British trading posts and, after 1843, in the so-called contract
ports along the South China coast.

However, socioeconomic necessities can also bring about the creolization of a pidgin within a generation's lifetime. Sranan is an exemplary
case, both as regards the rapidity and the socioeconomic conditions of its
genesis.

An Example: Sranan Tongo

Sranan Tongo, as the language is called by its speakers, came into
existence as a trade language in a twofold sense, as a language of trade
and as the language of those who were themselves turned into a traded
merchandise of the European transatlantic traffic, the African slaves.

European ships visited the coast of Surinam in order to exchange goods with the local Indian population from the early seventeenth century. Through the foundation of sugar plantations around the middle of the century, the European influence in the region changed drastically. Rather than for domestic consumption, the plantations were operated to produce for the world market. The demand for labor was satisfied by importing first English serfs and contract workers and then African slaves of various mother tongues. It was these two groups on the bottom rungs of the social ladder who created the new language. The influence of other speech communities remained almost insignificant by contrast. This is less surprising regarding the small group of Portuguese Jews who in 1665 founded a settlement in Surinam,[14] than regarding the Dutch who seized the colony from the British in 1667 to keep it under their control until independence in 1975. In 1679, the Dutch province Zeeland sold the colony which had been thrown into chaos through the withdrawal of the British, slave rebellions, and attacks by Indians, to the West Indian Company. The Company reached a peace agreement with the Indians in 1686 and from then on ruled the colony. Nevertheless, for reasons to be explained, the Dutch contributed little to the formation of Sranan.

That Sranan is an English-based creole is remarkable, because the influence of English was considerably weakened already in 1667 with the exodus of the English colonists and as of 1680 was virtually nil (Voorhoeve 1983: 39). Barely 30 years of contact on the plantations were enough for a new language to be created, which was not only passed on to newly arriving Africans, but also became the mother tongue of the next generations. It is for two reasons that, although English was natively spoken in Surinam by a small portion of the population for a short period of time only, it could become so crucially important for the development of Sranan. One is that, during the period of British control over the territory, the social group of the planters was linguistically homogeneous, which under Dutch rule was no longer the case. The other has to do with the ratio of white planters and black slaves. According to Voorhoeve's estimate, there were approximately two slaves for every Englishman in 1665. By the turn of the century this ratio had shifted to one of some ten slaves for every European. Moreover, many of the Britons were contract workers who were restricted in their freedom as they were working off a debt or penalty. They were socially closer, therefore, to the black slaves than to the white plantation owners. Hence, during the British time, there was more communication between planters and slaves than after the British had left. At the same time, the need for the slaves to have a common means of communication became more pressing.

Yet, that Sranan, which was hardly stabilized at the beginning of the eighteenth century, was not superseded in the sequel by Dutch or a Dutch-based pidgin, calls for an explanation. One aspect of the answer why this did not happen can be found in Le Page and Tabouret-Keller's (1985) important insight that the stability of pidgins is socially nego-tiated. Where common social aims exist stability of grammar is achieved, whereas lack of social cohesion correlates with instability. Social cohesion among the Sranan-speaking population was unwittingly fostered by the Dutch colonialists who erected social barriers between themselves and the slaves much higher than had separated them from the Britons. Assimilation was, furthermore, inhibited by virtue of the official pre-scription for the Dutch to use Sranan in communicating with slaves, which made it virtually impossible for the latter to learn Dutch. In the nineteenth century elementary education for the slaves was estab-lished on a limited scale, especially for the purposes of proselytism, the language of instruction being Sranan. It was not until 1876 that Dutch was made the only official language of schooling. Today, Dutch is Surinam's national language, but its use accounts for no more than about 50 percent of communication (Campbell 1983: 195). Herein we can detect a distant echo of the communicative conditions in the plantation society of former times. Campbell has portrayed them as follows:

> Prior to 1876, social life in Surinam was structured according to the two-caste system of the plantation model: (a) the upper caste of the Europeans, plantation directors, supervisors, merchants, etc., and (b) the lower caste consisting of Indians and African negroes, the slaves. In this society, Dutch was an exclusive commodity. It was reserved to the upper caste of Europeans only who had to maintain the standards of European culture.[15]

These regulations of the Dutch colonial masters greatly contributed to making Sranan the lingua franca of all of Surinam's population groups, the Africans, the mulattoes, the Indians, the Dutch and Portuguese settlers, and finally, after the abolition of slavery, contract laborers who were brought into the country from other parts of the world with which the Dutch maintained trading relations, especially Asian Indians of various mother tongues, the so-called Hindoestanen, and Chinese from Java. Largely a work of the West Indian Company, Surinam's multilingualism is imported rather than home-grown. In many respects the linguistic conditions of this country are a reflection and a part of its economic conditions. In particular, Sranan, Surinam's most important language, owes its existence to the acute social pressure and communication problems of the slave-driving plantation economy which could be overcome only by means of a contact language.

Linguistic Sedimentation of Economic Inequality

Contact languages always betoken communication impasses or emergencies, and they betoken a relationship of economic inequality between the parties concerned. This is true especially of the pidgins and creoles found in Third World countries today. The socioeconomic conditions pertaining in plantation and trading colonies were a breeding ground of these languages. Sankoff (1979: 24) explains:

> The plantation system is crucial because it was unique in creating a catastrophic break in linguistic tradition that is unparalleled. It is difficult to conceive of another situation where people arrived with such variety of native languages; where they were cut off from their native language groups, where the size of no one language group was sufficient to ensure its survival; where no second language was shared by enough people to serve as a useful vehicle of intercommunication; where the legitimate language was inaccessible to almost everyone.

And Cheng (1982: 127) describes the typical conditions of use of a pidgin language in a trading colony:

> Chinese Pidgin English was mostly a means of communication between foreign masters and Chinese servants, and a medium used in retail shops catering to foreigners.

Plantation and trading colonies were not an environment for contacts between equals. Rather, the Europeans initiated contacts under the premise of actual economic and military superiority and the possession of what they were convinced was a superior culture and religion. Because of this unbalanced relationship between the indigenous peoples and the European intruders, which the latter were never shy to exploit to their own advantage, the bulk of the burden of overcoming the communication impasse fell on the indigenous populations. The fact that European languages furnish the better part of the vocabulary of the newly emerged contact varieties must be understood as the result of the efforts on their part to learn the European languages. Since this had to be accomplished by adults rather than children in the absence of systematic instruction and on the basis of a very limited input for imitation, the acquired words were not used following the grammatical rules of the European languages, or always in their canonical meanings. Because of the peculiar learning situation, the learners could not but rely on the regularities underlying their own languages, which can be recognized as the substratum of later forms of the contact language. The general form of pidgins and creoles borne out of situations of this kind, which exhibits a largely European-origin lexical superstratum and an indigenous grammatical substratum (which is extensively amended and differentiated when creolization takes place) is a reflection of the economically weaker contact partners adapting to whatever extent possible to the economically stronger group.

The predominance of the European languages in furnishing the lexicon of contact languages thus grew out of the need to communicate in a situation of unbridged crosslinguistic contact under conditions of pronounced economic inequity. A structurally similar phenomenon is characteristic of certain language use patterns observed on polyglot market places.[16] Rather than being dominated by the leveling reduction of a single lingua franca for all communication activities, many markets with a linguistically heterogeneous population of merchants and customers display a pattern of language choice which reflects the socioeconomic conditions obtaining in the market. That is, whenever he or she is able to do so, the merchant speaks the customer's language.[17] To be sure, there are also markets in which a lingua franca is used by all participants, especially oligopolistic markets such as the crude oil and grain markets. However, the prototypical market place offers customers the choice between competing merchants which strongly motivates the latter to display an obliging attitude towards the former. One of the most conspicuous ways of doing this is to alert the customers' attention and volunteer information about merchandise, prices, etc. in their language. In this elementary form of marketing an imperfect, broken variety of the customer's language, which is in effect no more than an ephemeral, unstable idiolect, is often used by necessity. Nonetheless, this kind of language choice exhibits a basic relational asymmetry analogous to that of the substratum and superstratum languages sedimented in pidgins and creoles. Hence, the very form of these languages testifies to the specific socioeconomic circumstances of their genesis.

Language Death

Although many pidgins are short-lived and others never cast off the character as makeshift implements, the formation of pidgins and creoles, so characteristic of the age of European expansion, has added to the total number of the world's languages. For these languages do not usually displace others, but emerge in response to new communication needs brought about by sudden economic and demographic shifts. Nowadays the opposite tendency is much more in evidence: the languages of the world are getting fewer. Like pidginization, this is a consequence of asymmetrical contacts of different language groups. At issue are situations where the utility of a language diminishes so that its speakers enlist an additional language for satisfying their communication needs. A foreign medium at first, the additional language gradually penetrates ever more communication domains eventually to replace the original language of the group. That is, as Schiffman (1990) has convincingly argued, language shift takes place domain by domain, rather than speaker by speaker, until no domain at all is left for the abandoned language.

Processes of this kind exhibit a number of systematic characteristics which were first studied extensively in immigrant countries, especially the United States (Haugen 1953, Fishman 1966) and Australia (Clyne 1972). Considering the conspicuity of language as a social feature in these societies and the need to integrate and accommodate ever new waves of immigrants with different mother tongue backgrounds, this is hardly surprising. Yet, language shift is by no means restricted to immigrants or to particular countries but can be observed in many parts of the world.[18]

Language shift is a gradual process which, on one hand, is typical of migrant groups who tend to abandon within a few generations the language they brought with them to their new environment. Since it rarely happens that all speakers of a language emigrate, this usually has no measurable consequences for the language itself. That the Polish immigrants to the Ruhr Territory in western Germany in the early twentieth century had already given up their language after one generation, did not affect the development of Polish. Similarly, that most German-origin Chileans do not speak German any more, does not affect the continuation of German. Even if all expatriate German-speaking minorities[19] were to completely assimilate to their linguistic environments, this would hardly have an influence on the further development of the German language as such. On the other hand, language shift in a speech community that lives in its entirety surrounded by another community speaking a language with greater utility implies that the language will cease to exist. Using a biological metaphor, conditions of this sort have been referred to as "language death."

This metaphor conveys a sense of drama which some authors think befits the phenomenon.[20] But one should not lose sight of the fact that, barring war, genocide, other forms of violence, and natural disaster, language death concerns languages rather than speakers. The metaphor is not without problems therefore. It has been both criticized and expanded. Calvet (1974) speaks of *glottophagie*, language murder, while Denison (1977) considers language suicide a more suitable metaphor than language death, because it is the speakers of a language rather than anyone else who are responsible for its decay. This, in turn, is exactly what some authors deny. The spread of English at the expense of Chamorro in Guam is diagnosed as a case of "linguistic genocide" by Day (1985), because, he explains, the speakers of Chamorro are unaware of the threat that English poses to the survival of their language and that it will eventually cause its demise. A number of studies have discussed the revival of a language for which the by now classical example of Modern Hebrew serves as a general point of reference, although Rabin (1986, 1989) emphasizes that the Hebrew tradition was never completely discontinued and hence proposes "language revitalization" as a more appropriate term. Tabouret-Keller (1981) discusses the "battle for the survival" of the regional languages of France. And Fishman (1985b), deriding the pathetic metaphor, describes the "lively life of a 'dead' language," Yiddish.

Language and Environment

The idea that languages are organisms which implies the metaphor of death is not new.[21] Nowadays it is invoked mainly by those who deplore the decimation of the languages on this planet and, therefore, in the spirit of conservation and environment protection, call for measures suitable to arrest it (Kloss 1969: 287f.). Grounded as it is in linguistic relativism, the wildlife protection analogy claims that with every language not only a unique species of linguistic and cultural evolution is lost, but also a specific way of conceptualizing the world so that with every dying language a singular outlook onto the working of the human mind will be closed for ever.[22] If the survival of the rhinoceros is worth our effort, than surely is that of Irish or Rhaeto-Romance.

Thus where language death is at issue, we are dealing with the relationship of language and environment, with the living environment of a language. This is what Haugen's notion of "language ecology" is about. "Environment" is a many-layered concept. It involves the notion that every species has its environment, its habitat, but also that there is a hierarchy of habitats, an environment of environments. Interpreting the environment concept in terms of the sociology of language, it implies that every language relates to its environment in its peculiar way and is shaped and characterized by the geographic, socioeconomic, and cultural conditions under which its speakers live, as well as by its linguistic environment, the languages with which it is or was in contact. Languages form a part of the life-circumstances of their speakers and, viewed as organisms, they interact within a certain environment with organisms of their own kind.

As ecologists are well aware, an ecology that fails to take into account the economy is doomed to insignificance, and accordingly, transferring the concepts of species and environment to languages only makes sense if the economics of language is also taken into account.[23] The environment is not shaped by economic conditions alone. Economic factors always interact, in different weightings, with geographic, political, socio-psychological and cultural factors in a wider sense. But where the destruction of the environment and the eradication of species living in it are at issue, the economy moves to the center of our attention. For example, the opening up of the Latin American continent for economic development brought with it the eradication of many languages, especially of the Tucano and Jivaro groups together with their speech communities, a process which, owing to the unabated deforestation of the "tristes tropiques" in the Amazon, continues. Very small Indian tribes fall victim to fragmentation, forced assimilation, or physical annihilation. In less dramatic cases, languages of small communities are turned into regressed idioms (Ornstein-Galicia 1989) for lack of need or opportunity to use them for communication.[24] A regressing language exhibits the syndromes of decay prior to its actual extinction, that is, before there is no longer a speech community using it. More than anyone else, Dorian (1981, 1989) has demonstrated that when languages are used less and less, they undergo structural reductions and simplifications in the language system which, to stay with the analogy, can be characterized as symptoms of degeneration. Reductions of this kind have been described as the mirror image of the grammatical expansions typical of creolization (Dressler 1972, Trudgill 1977). In order to explain why and under what conditions the use of a language is cut down, it is, however, necessary to look beyond systematic reductions, since these are the effect, not the cause of the decline.

Loss of Functions and Failure to Adapt

That its use is cut down means that a language is increasingly less employed for certain purposes for which it used to be employed. For example, in the wake of Japan's modernization during the last decades of the nineteenth century, Kanbun, the Japanese variety of the classical Chinese literary language, was gradually driven out of literary and political prose, just as Latin, in the course of the eighteenth century, gradually lost ground in scientific discourse to the European vernaculars. It is important to realize in this connection that usage domains are not eternally fixed. Rather, as a consequence of socioeconomic, technological, and political developments, ever new domains emerge which can become important for the continuation of a language. Today the future of many languages is uncertain not only because their functional range is scaled down, but because they are never used for, and adapted to, newly emerging functions which are from the start associated with another language. Aviation, to mention but one example, has given rise to novel communication needs which almost no language has ever been used to fulfill. More likely than not, the vast majority of all languages existing today will likewise never be used in modern communication domains such as law, administration, science, technology, diplomacy, and higher education. Lack of functional expansion and adaptation is thus a correlate and counterpart of scaled-down use. In conjunction, both contribute to diminishing the serviceability and utility value of many languages.

Which languages are concerned? A drastic reduction of the 5,000 or 6,000 languages that can still be counted on this planet will be inevitable in the global communication community that thanks to intensifying economic interdependencies the world has become. The late Heinz Kloss, one of the keenest observers of language shifts around the globe, surmised that the real question was merely whether in future "we shall, will, and want to deal with hundreds or only dozens of languages"

(Kloss 1969: 294). The majority of the languages whose days are most probably numbered are spoken in the least developed regions of the world by minute speech communities without ever having been written, let alone used for the purposes of modern society. Had not many linguists since the beginning of this century dedicated much of their energy to recording and describing languages in regression, many, especially in the Americas, would have perished unnoticed and without a trace. Chances for the continuation of numerically weak languages of a few thousand or even a few hundred speakers only are clearly extremely slim, once modern civilization has reached the out-of-the-way places where they are spoken. Several well-documented cases such as that of the Ainu language in Japan make their extinction seem inescapable.

The Ainu are a small people living in northern Japan and on the Kuril Islands. Leading a life as hunters and gatherers, they maintained for a long time only loose contacts with the Japanese, since this part of the archipelago was the last to be claimed and colonized by the Japanese. Even though numbering only a few tens of thousands, they formed a homogeneous ethnic group with their own language and culture until the mid-nineteenth century. Then came the forced opening of Japan to the West and the political upheaval known as the Meiji Restoration (1868) whose leaders launched Japan on a course of modernization and industrialization which, among other things, spelled the irreversible eclipse of the Ainu language. By 1937, Murasaki in her description of the language (1976) had to rely on a single informant. When the traditional subsistence economy gave way to other forms of production, social cohesion also crumbled. Wage labor and production for a market necessitated more intensive contacts with the Japanese; intermarriage followed. In 1927, 36 percent of all marriages were mixed, and during the four decades that followed the proportion rose to 88 percent of the Ainu population (Takakura 1960). Since Japanese was economically valuable to the Ainu, whereas the Ainu language was not to the Japanese, language-group exogamy resulted in transitional bilingualism and rapid and complete assimilation of the weaker group. The Ainu language was not passed on to the offspring of mixed marriages, not least because the Ainu were dependent on an exoglossic educational system. Today it is no longer used in everyday communication, being reduced to the status of folkloristic ornament. While this is deplored by some, it was, in retrospect, an unavoidable consequence of the Ainus' integration into the Japanese economy and nation.

Time and Developmental Distance

The decline of Ainu was fast and virtually unimpeded. The Japanese government did nothing to help the Ainu maintain their language, and the speakers themselves parted with it showing little regret or resistance. Excepting some scholars, the idea that the language and culture of a marginal, backward group might be worth preserving was quite alien to both population groups concerned. Nowadays, the application to languages of the call for the protection of threatened species has gained some recognition. In many places the preservation of minor languages has become a matter of public concern. It is highly doubtful, nevertheless, that in the wake of the transition from an agricultural subsistence economy to an industrialized market economy, the underdeveloped regions of India, New Guinea and sub-Saharan Africa will be able to escape language shifts on a massive scale. For the Ainu language industrialization meant that it lost the environment to which it was adapted. The period of time during which the traditional secluded environment was transformed into a modern environment penetrated and dominated by the surrounding society was too short to allow the speakers to adapt their language to the new conditions and thus insure its continuation as a functionally useful means of communication.

In Meiji Japan the clash of traditional society with modernity was particularly vehement, the forced modernization was particularly rapid, uncompromising, and successful. In other parts of the world similar processes have taken place in the past, or are happening at the present time, which are, however, distinguished by different time scales, which means that the length of time available for coping with adjustment problems varies. Europe's modernization took much longer than that of Japan which was underdeveloped by European standards in the nineteenth century. And the developing countries today have even less time for accomplishing this process, if they ever want to reach the developmental level of the industrial world which is already preparing for the post-industrial age. Many of the small speech communities of these countries are likely to be wiped out by the social transformations that rapid development brings about. India alone has more than 1,200 speech communities with fewer than 1,000 members (Srivastava 1984a: 42). Many live in rural areas in circumstances where the introduction of, say, mechanical looms amounts to revolutionizing the conduct of life. The distance to the modern world is too far to be bridged by means of their own languages. Although this does not imply that every single speech community will abandon its language, it is a fact which seriously endangers the continuation of such languages. Modernization means more than the discontinuation of traditional forms of life. In many cases it also means the cessation of an exclusively oral linguistic tradition. Kieffer's description of the mountainous environment of Parāči at the foot of the Hindukush in Afghanistan, and of its economically determined transformation, elucidates the kinds of conditions which are likely to bring about a reduction of linguistic diversity in other parts of the world as well:

> The construction of roads and required military service have recently struck a fatal blow to this refuge area: one entered among the Parāči and left their valleys open from then on. The economic and industrial development did the rest: not only did it create new needs, disturb the traditional net of points of selling and buying, break the equilibrium of the prices of agricultural and industrial products, but it also dismantled once and for all the self-sufficiency and the mountain economy in drawing into the factories and the towns an irreplaceable labor (Kieffer 1977: 97).

That the speakers of Parāči seem to feel little motivation to arrest or try to revert the decline of their language, is explained, soberly but realistically, as follows:

> When one is interested in speaking another language, clearly more profitable economically and intellectually, one is also interested in becoming someone else and in finding more advantageous living space. It is thus vain to defend a language and an ethnic status which would only be old-fashioned folklore (Kieffer 1977: 97).

Industrialization and Language Decay in Europe

Since the number of codified national languages has increased markedly on the European continent from the beginning of the nineteenth century, while only relatively few languages such as Manx of the Celtic family and the Finno-Ugric Livonian and Ingrian have during the same period left the scene of history, the number of European languages that are threatened by assimilation, absorption, or dispersion of their speakers is often underestimated. Yet, in the European context too, the continuance of several languages is in the balance at the present time. Their development is instructive for a general assessment of the prospects of language maintenance in small speech communities, since many of the side-effects of the modernization of Europe will be copied, willy-nilly, in other parts of the world. Moreover, the problem of language decay and disappearance has been investigated more thoroughly in Europe than elsewhere. The phenomenon of regressive use and gradual functional downgrading of minor languages is more conspicuous in Europe than in developing countries. This concerns languages such as Irish, Welsh, Breton, Provençal, Occitan, Rhaeto-Romance, Basque, as well as several minority languages spoken by even smaller groups in almost all European countries. These languages have typically disappeared from public domains and been demoted to home and family languages. Among the ecological changes that have accelerated their retreat, urbanization and industrialization were critical.[25] Over the past two decades or so a considerable body of knowledge about regressing idioms has accumulated, providing a solid starting point for an understanding of the dynamics of these processes. Industrialization poses a threat to minority languages,[26] no matter whether industrial centers are established outside or inside the territory of the language in question; for in either case the erection of industrial production facilities can cause demographic shifts which endanger its continuance. In the former case, industrialization sometimes has the effect that the indigenous language group is turned into a minority in its own territory through in-migration as the new industrial center attracts large numbers of speakers of another language from the outside. And in the latter case, the environment of a language is depopulated through out-migration as its speakers mingle with speakers of other languages in the industrial towns. It also happens that the first process is followed by the second or vice versa. An example may illustrate each of these three scenarios:

1   minorization of the indigenous language group through in-migration caused by industrialization inside its territory;
2   depopulation of a minority language territory caused by industrialization outside it;
3   increasing in-migration and out-migration to/from a minority language territory caused by intensifying economic integration.

Sorbian at the Lausitz   Sorbian (also Wendish) is the last remnant of the Western Slavic languages once present in East-Elbian Germany. Some 50,000 Sorbians live in the marshlands of the Upper and Lower Lausitz near the Polish border. Although the language has a literary tradition reaching back to the sixteenth century, it has been retreating from the

cities, especially Bautzen and Cottbus, ever since the period of pro-
moterism, a process which was accelerated when public use of Sorbian
was made impossible by the Nazis in 1938. The last pre-war census of
1925 lists some 4,000 monolingual speakers, but since the Nazi repression and in spite of the protection the Sorbian minority enjoyed in
the German Democratic Republic, there are only bilingual speakers
now. Miners and farm workers in the countryside continued to use
Sorbian for all purposes of everyday communication until after World
War II. After the foundation of the GDR, a policy of active minority
protection was adopted, including bilingualism in the Sorbian territory
with recognition of Sorbian as the second official language and bilingual
education. Notwithstanding these measures which were desired by only
a part of the Sorbian population, the regression of Sorbian continued,
mainly because of demographic shifts in response to labor market requirements. In order to meet the enormous demand for energy after
World War II, coal production in the mines of the Lausitz area was
drastically increased, leading to the in-migration of many German-
speaking miners. As a consequence, Sorbian was gradually dislodged
from one of the traditional working domains where it used to be the
dominant language. At the same time many young Sorbians gave up
their language, adopting what they perceived as the more prestigeous
and progressive tongue of their wider environment, German. Not only
were they not forced to do so, the lack of language loyalty they exhibited
was in stark conflict with the government policy of bilingualism. In
spite of their stated intentions, the official measures in support of
the maintenance of Sorbian are not suitable to halt its slow but continuing decline. It cannot compete with German, and what is left of
its ethnolinguistic community is being thinned out more and more
by intermarriage.

Basque in Spain   Another example of the threat that industrialization
inside the territory of a minority speech community poses to its continuance is the mountainous region in north-eastern Spain where the
Basques live. The militant ETA movement has incurred them the
reputation of uncompromisingly defending their ethnic identity. But
this should not obscure the fact that ETA is not supported by a majority
of the Basques or that a steadily decreasing number of them consider the
Basque language as an essential part of their identity. Only 25 percent of
all ethnic Basques speak the language, and no more than an estimated
16 percent in the various social domains (Roaetxe 1991).

During the 37 years of the Franco dictatorship, all minority languages spoken in Spain including Basque were brutally repressed, being
prohibited from all public use. The present Spanish government supports the major regional languages – Catalan, Basque, and Galician –
both administratively and financially. But, notwithstanding the official
tolerance democracy brought with it, Basque is becoming a systematically
learned second language for increasingly more Basques. Orwig's (1988:
1) remark that there are "almost 1.5 million Basques who are unable to
speak their native tongue," which is likely to be an understatement,
illuminates what is really at issue. In what sense is a language someone's
"native tongue" who is unable to speak it? The point, then, is the
restoration of a linguistic tradition for its own sake, rather than the
safeguarding of a speech community and its members' right to express
themselves in their own language. One of the problems facing such
revitalization efforts is that the Basques of the older generation who
rightly claim Basque as their native tongue have little or no command of
the written language. In order to cope with this problem, the HABE
institute for the "Alphabetization and re-Basquization of Adults" was
founded in 1983. In collaboration with several other organizations such
as the Basque Language Academy (founded in 1919) and the Secretariat
of Language Policy, it pursues as its main objective the spread of a
normalized standard Basque (Roaetxe 1991). That such a variety is so far
not generally accepted by the entire speech community is because of the
considerable dialect variation among its members.

Another problem is migration. Immigration to the Basque country
during the Franco dictatorship has been described by Roaetxe (1991) as
"one of the measures of de-Basquization." As a result of massive in-
migration there is no monolingual habitat of the Basque language
anymore. More than one million migrants from other parts of Spain have
found work in the shipyards and other factories of the economically
flourishing region. If, as the defenders of Basque advocate, the terri-
toriality principle should determine the status of Basque and the Basque
country should be recognized as the "homeland" of the Basque language,
the migrants, too, should learn Basque, rather than only ethnic Basques
who have limited proficiency in the language. As Spanish is spoken
everywhere in the Basque country, their motivation to do so is, however,
practically nil. Since the end of the dictatorship, Spain's economy has
enjoyed a period of continuous growth of which the Basque country has
had a greater than average share. This has attracted ever more non-
Basque-speaking migrants and continues to do so. It is not without

irony that the democratic state and the expanding economy has created an environment in which the continuance of the Basque language is more at risk than under circumstances of political repression and economic backwardness. However, it is precisely the greater freedom offered by a liberal state that, in spite of a language policy favoring Basque, allows economic developments to take effect more forcefully than under the totalitarian regime where identification with the language was a quasi-natural means of resistance. Basque is not a dead language yet, but, in spite of the purposeful optimism of its defenders, it is moribund, mainly because it cannot withstand the pressure of the unchecked expansion of Spanish inside the Basque homeland.

Breton   Another region at the periphery of the European continent, Basse Bretagne in northwestern France, provides the stage of a well-documented case of language regression. At the beginning of this century, some 90 percent of the ethnic Bretons still spoke Breton, although it was subject to harsh repression by the French government throughout the nineteenth century.[27] With the advent of industrialization in northern France and universal conscription (Weber 1976), French rapidly spread at the expense of Breton. Around the turn of the century, Breton had an estimated 1.3 million primary speakers. By 1952 their numbers had diminished to 700,000, and another 20 years later only 25 percent of the population of Basse Bretagne, most elderly people, used Breton for the purposes of everyday communication. Timm (1980: 30) sketches the fundamentals of the development:

> The last quarter of the nineteenth century brought with it increased industrialization and urbanization, and Breton peasants began abandoning the countryside for the cities, both in and out of Brittany. . . . The great majority of *bretonnants* born after 1900 would learn French before adolescence. Only people living in very remote areas of the peninsula would remain monoglot *bretonnants* throughout adult life. Other Bretons would ultimately supplant their maternal language with French.

Dressler and Wodak-Leodolter (1977: 36) mention a more sophisticated administration and the appearance of the civil service sector as additional factors contributing to the weakening of Breton. This necessitated more exoglossic contacts with French speakers and boosted the economic value of French in Brittany, which made Breton a virtual liability for its speakers. "Getting ahead for Bretons has meant not only

learning French, but getting rid of Breton as a marker of backwardness"
(Kuter 1989: 80f.). Even Bretons of the older generation tend to use
French in these communication domains as well as in situations associated
with progress. Like the Basque language in Spain, Breton is no longer
subject to discrimination by the French state. To some extent it supports
measures designed to reverse, or at least halt, its decline. That they will
be effective is, however, rather doubtful. Industrialization has reached
Brittany itself, attracting foreign labor in significant numbers, especially
from Algeria and Portugal, most of whom have a fair foreign language
command of French but lack any motivation for learning Breton. To the
extent that there will be a continuous presence of Algerian, Portuguese,
and other French-speaking foreign workers in Brittany, this will contribute to a shift in the ratio of Breton speakers and French speakers in
favor of the latter (Timm 1980: 39). An additional, rather peculiar
reason for the limited success of recent language promotion efforts is that
many Bretons seem to have mixed feelings about them, because they
suspect that the French government supports these measures for their
own purposes, namely to impede the spread of English, rather than out
of sympathy for the revivalist cause of the Bretons.

Welsh   Like Breton, Welsh is a Celtic language with a long literary
tradition. Its decline began with Britain's industrial revolution and the
increasing integration of Wales into the British state and economy that
followed it. The government branded Welsh as an impediment to
economic development and a liability for the Welsh population quite
early. In 1846, the government Commission of Enquiry into the State of
Education in Wales stated that

> the Welsh language is a vast drawback to Wales and a manifold barrier to
> the moral progress and commercial prosperity of the people (quoted from
> Wardhaugh 1987: 81).

The Welsh did not really feel a pressing need for moral uplifting,
recognizing the call for progress as an attempt on the part of the British
government to discredit their language as an uncontrollable ideological
force.[28] Yet many of them tacitly agreed with the Commission's assessment of the economic circumstances. For the advance of the capitalist
economic system and industrial production did cause the utility value of
Welsh to erode, while at the same time English became ever more
indispensable.

First, the growing demand for labor in industrialized England drew labor away from Wales to England in great numbers, causing rural depopulation. This was one of the contributing factors of a deep economic depression in Wales during the 1920s, which led to complete economic and infrastructural dependency on England. New traffic links were most indicative of this development, tying as they did various parts of Wales to English towns rather than establishing a more tightly knit network inside Wales. The subsequent industrialization of Wales then induced substantial demographic shifts from England to Wales, accelerating the spread of bilingualism and the ensuing retreat of Welsh. At the beginning of this century, about half of the Welsh population spoke Welsh, a considerable proportion of them being monolingual. But by 1931, the Welsh speakers were only 37 percent of the population, a trend that continued unchecked, reaching 19 percent in 1981. Wardhaugh (1987: 82) now estimates the proportion of monolingual Welsh speakers as a mere 1 percent of the population of Wales. His comments about the reasons for the Anglicization of Wales and the departure of Welsh as a first language turn the above-mentioned analysis of the government Commission on its head. It is not the language, he maintains, that is an impediment of the economy, but "Welsh is disappearing because Wales has been in decline economically" (Wardhaugh 1987: 83). He emphasizes the influence of the economic conditions on the language, while the Commission conversely depicts the language as a factor that influences the economy. However, as the case of Wales very clearly shows, to look at these two points of view as contradictory or alternative explanations cannot do justice to the phenomenon. Language is a factor of the economy which is influenced by it, both in its form and distribution. Moreover, it is not economic slump alone that affects use and dispersion of a language. Economic upswings can also have far-reaching consequences.

Since the 1950s many British companies have come under pressure through intensified competition by European neighbors and newly industrialized countries, forcing many producers of consumer and investment goods to reorganize and relocate their production facilities. Among other things, it became increasingly urgent to reduce labor costs. An effective way of doing this was to move factories from industrial centers to peripheral areas and to hire unskilled, especially female labor. In Wales, too, more industrial plants were established which helped to improve the economic conditions of the region. However, since most of the new plants were subsidiaries of English-owned companies, their establishment was accompanied by an influx of monoglot English-speaking upper and middle level executives responsible for communications with the head offices which are typically located outside Wales. As a result, the social stratification of English and Welsh in Wales has become even more pronounced than it was. In economic contexts English is now the sole language of higher socioeconomic status and of all higher communication functions. "Whether the workers tend to use Welsh or not, the management cling to the use of English" (Lewis 1987: 24). Since social upward mobility has thus become more closely associated with geographic mobility, English could reinforce its status as the language of progress, prosperity, and social advance. The consequences for social life in Wales and the prospects of Welsh are summarized by Williams (1987: 89) as follows.

> The new circulation of capital involved in the restructuring process has been accompanied by a circulation of people. As a consequence, the incidence of language-group exogamy has increased to the point where there are almost as many marriages where only one spouse speaks Welsh as there are those where both speak Welsh. . . . This means that the family is no longer able to reproduce the language.

In keeping with the conciliatory spirit blowing through western Europe as the evening of the twentieth century approaches, various efforts are made in the peripheral regions of the Old World in order to save their traditional tongues from oblivion. Wales is one of them. The most important measures undertaken there are bilingual education, tolerated, if not enthusiastically implemented, by the government (Rawkins 1987), and radio and television broadcasts in Welsh (Lewis 1987). Although they have momentarily given rise to the impression that the revival of Welsh is gaining momentum, it is doubtful whether they will succeed in the long run, because the circumstances described above have aggravated the social gradient between English and Welsh in the economic domain, while at the same time all but eliminating the family as an effective agent of transmitting the language to the next generation.

Syndromes and Prospects of Regressed Languages

Language decay is a widespread phenomenon. The examples discussed above, however few, and although the underlying causes and the manifestations of each of them are peculiar and unique, exhibit a number of common features allowing for some generalizations. The continuance of a language is endangered only in situations of asymmetrical language contact which induces first the elite, then the majority, and finally the totality of the weaker group to become bilingual. Stable intergenerational bilingualism can rarely be maintained. Most of the groups concerned are marginal, both in a geographic and socioeconomic sense. The remoteness of their territories at the peripheries of political, economic, and cultural spheres of influence on islands, in mountainous areas, and in less fertile regions ensured the survival of many minor languages, while the great national languages gained ever wider expanses. Nowadays, their marginal position is an economic disadvantage which lessens the chances for their continued existence. If we look at the global spectrum of languages, irreversible decline is a grave threat to those which (1) retreat from communication functions traditionally fulfilled by them, and/or (2) are not being adapted to newly emerging communication functions.

The first syndrome is in evidence mainly in small languages spoken in isolated areas, or by marginalized groups of the industrialized world. Even a long literary tradition is no effective safeguard against their continuing retreat.[29] Numerical weakness of the speech community, geographic isolation, political marginalization, economic underdevelopment of the language territory, and the resulting stigmatization of the language as old-fashioned rather than merely traditional; the absence of any economic incentive to learn the language combined with the economic necessity for its speakers to learn the dominant language; all of these factors must compromise language maintenance measures and impair the chances of many minor languages to hold their own, even within the private domain of the family, in competing with the big national languages which are favored by government, economy, and society.

The prospects of the many unwritten languages of developing countries of which the second syndrome mentioned above is typical are hardly brighter. Their chances of ever being expanded to become modern standard languages are extremely slim. They are spoken by small marginal speech communities in the most impoverished regions of the Third World. In most cases, their speakers have a vital economic interest in acquiring a second language with a wider range, which, although it will not necessarily supplant the native language of the group in all communication domains, will effectively block any further development of it.

It must be noted for both kinds of cases that not all of the communities concerned have an active interest in a language policy designed to strengthen their language, reverse its attrition and, maybe, better its chances for survival. Such measures are not always desired, but sometimes perceived with skepticism or outright hostility by the groups in question as restricting their access to economic progress and social participation. Language preservation and revival movements, therefore, often lack the support of major parts of the speech community.

On the other hand, the economic causes and correlates of language regression and disappearance are comparable to those of dialect leveling, which have been observed in Europe for a long time. In this connection Hartig (1990: 129) speaks of "the typical reduction phase characterized by high language loyalty coupled with only limited active language competence."[30] However, the disappearance of a dialect is generally not felt to be as dramatic an event as that of a language (Hoenigswald 1989: 348), not least because many dialect speakers gradually replace their basic dialect with a dialectally colored variety of the standard language, and thus hardly notice the change. Language decay also does not happen overnight but as a gradual process restrained and mediated by mechanisms of adjustment to the dominant language. Yet, to the outside observer at least, because of its finality, it appears to be a more serious incident. A tradition comes to an end, and that which is really unique about it cannot be preserved to live on in the garment of another.

Interaction of Linguistic and Extra-Linguistic Factors

Four levels can be distinguished in which the decline of a language manifests itself: (1) the speech community, (2) communication domains, (3) the speaker, and (4) the language system. The numerical dwindling of the speech community is clearly an important factor, but it must not be considered in isolation. It typically interacts with the retreat of the language from communication domains and the regression of the corresponding registers. For unwritten languages, retreat from the domain of primary socialization usually means the end of the tradition, whereas languages with meaningful literary traditions can lose this domain and continue to function in others, for example, cult. On the individual level, the retreat of a language from communication domains prompts increased codeswitching from the regressed to the dominant language, especially in instances where topics associated with the dominant language are discussed in a domain in which the regressed language is commonly used. On the level of the language system this translates into an increase of transfer and interference. Welsh, for example, has adopted phonetic properties of English, just as Breton has been influenced by French, and both languages exhibit a progressive tendency for lexical borrowing from the dominant language. During its terminal phase, a regressing language loses many of the features which distinguished it when it was used in all, or nearly all, communication domains, serving its speakers as their chief means of communication. Viewed from a systematic point of view, language decay is thus a self-reinforcing process.

So far as the above observations go, languages do not only disappear because they are spoken by ever fewer speakers; but the fact that they are used in fulfilling an ever narrower range of communicative functions brings with it systematic decay of grammar and lexicon. There is hence a subtle interaction between the socioeconomic potential, the communicative serviceability, and the systematic differentiation and flexibility of a language. That the regressed language and its speakers become increasingly more dependant on the dominant language echoes and reinforces the weaker group's growing economic dependency on the stronger group. This perspective on language decay is not intended to establish a monocausal explanation, nor does it imply that a community's consciousness about, and attitude towards, its language is determined by economic conditions alone. Ideological motives, especially those related to religion, ethnic identity, and nationalism, often provide the foundations of language loyalty strong enough to resist the forces of economic development. But wherever languages retreat or disappear, economic development is an important, often decisive factor. It usually acts as the trigger of language regression which takes place in speech communities that were able to protect their language from the coming onslaught of modern civilization by erecting an ideological fence around it.

Language Spread

That two languages are in competition with each other does not always entail the submission of one to the other by way of being supplanted (language shift) or absorbed (de-creolization) by it. However, shifts in the allotment of functional roles of languages in competition can be observed almost everywhere. Since speech communities rarely exist in complete isolation, but tend to have various sorts of contacts with each other, and since many societies make systematic use of several languages, the languages also interact. As Kloss (1969: 556) once put it, languages "cannot leave each other alone; one always tries to drive out the other, geographically or in a functional sense." In the present context, such a formulation which makes languages appear like agents with the capacity to act offers itself, because changes in the allotment of communication domains to languages are caused only partly by conscious intervention on the part of their speakers. Language spread is a partially unguided process which happens just as much as it is intentionally brought about. Where language spread is not based on a deliberate policy with corpus planning and status planning, it makes just as much sense to say that a language acquires additional speakers as that speakers acquire an additional language.

Social Factors of Language Spread

The most important social factors contributing to the spreading of a language are conquest, mass migration, colonization, proselytism, official language planning, as well as traffic and trade. These factors rarely become effective independently. More often they interact or appear one after the other. For example, Lingala, a Bantu language spoken on both sides of the Zaire river, in its pidginized variety known as Bangala fulfilled the functions of a vehicular language for trade across linguistic and ethic boundaries even in pre-colonial times. Missionaries then contributed decisively to the standardization of the language by reducing it to writing. The Belgian colonial government further promoted Lingala, which now had a written variety, by using it in elementary school and for the military. Largely on account of increasing trade, the post-colonial era witnessed further spread of this language, especially in larger towns in Zaire and the Congo (Calvet 1987: 107f.). Thus, trade and traffic, mission, and colonial government all had a part in the spreading of Lingala.

Real success in language expansion hinges on its being used and promoted in all of the said domains, government, law, economy, military, religion, education. But usually the factors behind the spreading of a language differ in weight and impact. Hindi (including Urdu and the medieval literary languages Brajbhasa, Avadhi, and Dekani) owes its spread across the northern part of the Indian subcontinent largely to the political power of the Great Moguls who in the sixteenth century used it to administer their vast and linguistically heterogenous empire. The dispersion of Arabic from the Arabian penninsula to the Atlantic coast and Spain, to Asia Minor, Central and Southeast Asia is a direct concomitant of the triumph of Islam and, like Christian Latin and Buddhist Pali, typifies religiously driven language spread. Low German in northern Europe, Malay in Southeast Asia, Swahili in East Africa, and Hausa in West Africa may be cited as examples of language spread by trade and commercial traffic. Before taking a closer look at the expansion of both the territorial range and the functional potential of these languages and discussing how exactly the geographic and demographic evolution of speech communities is linked to economic development, let us first consider some general aspects of the relationship between economy and language spread.

Demographic and Functional Language Spread

A distinction must be made, first of all, between language expansion caused by the demographic growth of its speech community, on one hand, and language shift, that is, the gaining of additional speakers from other speech communities, on the other. For both cases there are economic correlates which are often referred to more or less implicitly in historical-reconstructive arguments. For illustration consider the attempt to draw conclusions from the present geolinguistic situation in Africa about the spread of Bantu languages in former times. The generally accepted view is that the Niger-Congo languages of West Africa expanded to the east and southeast at the expense of the Nilo-Saharan languages. This is taken to indicate that

> the black peoples living in the western half of the Sudanic belt were more successful in the transition to food production in moist woodland conditions than those living in the eastern half, and so were able to press with expanding numbers into a wide zone to the south of the second group. (Oliver and Fage 1978: 18)

In this argumentation economic causes are assumed to underlie the eastward expansion of the Bantu languages. Since the events under consideration here took place a long time before historical tradition on the black continent began, language distribution patterns provide the only available evidence. Investigations of the relationships between the various Bantu languages by means of philological and glottochronological techniques[31] lend support to the hypothesis that these languages developed out of a common proto-language spreading from west to east during a dispersal period of some 2,000 years. That this period also saw language shifts to the benefit of the Niger-Congo languages cannot be ruled out, but need not be assumed to explain their spread.

Recently, a change in economic conditions has also been cited as triggering the initial spread of the Indo-European languages. Diverging from longstanding views according to which this process is to be explained by mass migration movements and conquest, Renfrew (1989) presents an elaborate theory arguing that the Indo-European proto-language hails from Anatolia from where it spread, peacefully, in the sixth millennium to Greece and the European continent. This was possible and bound to happen, Renfrew claims, as a result of sedentary agriculture which made possible demographic growth on a larger scale than an existence based on hunting and gathering. According to this theory, then, the elaboration of farming led to the dispersion not only of a new form of economic life, but also of people and the language they spoke. This happened not through dramatic mass migration, but gradually with small, local movements of small groups advancing slowly to create more arable land that could support their growing numbers.

The other type of language spread is exemplified by numerous cases of utilitarianistic language shift whereby a language gains additional speakers quite independently of any demographic growth of its speech community. Just as a language's utility is the prime reason for learning it as a foreign language (Weinreich 1966: 77), the direction of language shifts in language contact situations is determined by the utility and prestige gradient characterizing the relationship of the two languages in question. Especially in the case of young languages there is hardly any interference by cultural factors. Mühlhäusler's (1986: 58f.) description of the situation in colonial Samoa under German administration highlights the crucial point:

> Samoan Plantation Pidgin English was the first language of many children on the German plantations of Samoa, but proved of little use to their later life . . . Consequently these creole speakers adopted the more useful Samoan language as their exclusive means of communication.

Samoan, it is argued here, acquired additional speakers because it was more useful than another language which coexisted in a contact situation with it.

Although they often interact, demographic growth and language shift are independent factors of language spread if looked at from a systematic point of view. Population growth does not necessarily contribute to strengthening a national economy, and in some overpopulated countries such as Bangladesh even becomes a liability and, indeed, the most pressing economic problem. In the same vein, language spread based solely in demographic growth cannot be equated with an increase of the language's economic strength. China's population increase of 1.2 percent annually[32] means that Chinese acquires some 12 million new speakers every year, but this does not affect its geographic and functional distribution. As compared to its colossal demographic gains, those motivated by language shift are negligible. China's 55 officially recognized ethnic minorities are demographically unimportant, and no cases are known outside China where Chinese absorbs functions of other languages.

The reverse is true of English. At 0.1 percent in Great Britain and 1.0 percent in the US, the demographic growth rate of the native speech community is very modest. Moreover, in both cases growth is due largely to immigration. Nevertheless, English penetrates functional domains of other languages in many parts of the world. As Perren and Holloway (1965: 32) observed, the expansion of world trade during the nineteenth and early twentieth century was instrumental in making English a world language. In the meantime, it has become by far the most important language of international trade. In many countries where it used to play a rather marginal role it has also made important advances in the work domain. In Singapore, for instance, "the most important language in work situations is without doubt English" (Kwan-Terry 1991: 70). In Fiji, English is said to be "the language for any white-collar employment" (Siegel 1989: 57). And in Samoa, Samoan is the language of local governance and social interaction, but "the worlds of commerce and trade dictate the use of English" (Huebner 1989: 61).

After English, the next contenders to economic status are French, German, and Japanese, because of the substantial trade volume of the most important countries of these languages; but they lag far behind English, to some extent because, in conducting their trade, these countries, too, rely partly on English. Accordingly, Truchot (1990: 90) calls English their "language of export." In contradistinction to German and Japanese, but like English, French is to some extent used as a lingua franca of trade. The Franc Zone which is composed of thirteen countries once controlled by French or Belgian colonial administrations, is dominated by French, the official language of these countries, although it is not spoken by the majority of the population in any of them. The function of mediating between speakers of third languages, which also constitutes the strength of English, still secures French an important position as an international language. However, a comparison of the trade volume of the anglophone and the francophone countries of the world reveals a major reason why French stagnates, whereas the spread of English continues. The former account for as much as one third of the world trade in goods and services, but the latter only for one fifteenth. This imbalance finds expression in the international language competition, among other things, in that the 96 members of the General Agreement on Tariffs and Trade (GATT) handle their business in English alone.

Observations of this kind underscore the importance of distinguishing demographic from functional language spread, since they illustrate that the size of a speech community can vary without having any effect on the functional spread of a language. Yet it is worthwhile to reflect on the consequences of demographic language spread. From the viewpoint of the ecology of language, the North–South problem implies that a few languages of the have-nots of the southern hemisphere are rapidly becoming the most populous languages of the world. Natural population increase in the Arabic world is 3 percent, making Arabic the language of wider communication with the greatest growth rate. Assuming that the population increase of the speech community of Hindi/Urdu is not lower than the average of India's (2.2%) and Pakistan's (3%) demographic increase, this language grows almost as rapidly. By way of contrast, the growth rates of the industrial countries is below one percent throughout and in some cases even negative (Japan 0.7%, France 0.5%, Italy 0.3%, Germany –0.1%). The only European languages which exhibit significant growth rates are those which also became languages of the Third World, Spanish (2.1%) and Portuguese (2.2%). Since the beginning of this century, the number of Spanish speakers has undergone a fivefold increase – corresponding to a growth factor of 5.7 – while that of English speakers only doubled, although English has gained most in terms of functional domains.[33] During the same period of time, the French and German speech communities increased by only about 20 percent. From a global perspective this means that, measured in terms of primary speakers, the internationally most important European languages are losing ground, while the weight of some Third World languages increases steadily. Arabic, Hindi, Bengali, Spanish, and Chinese are the languages of major demographic expansion. If the size of a speech community plays any role at all in determining the significance of a language (cf. chapter 3, pp. 58ff. above), the significance of these languages will continue to grow relative to others.

Mackey (1976: 203f.) advanced the idea that the international rank of a language should be computed by multiplying its demographic strength with the average per capita income of its speakers. Applying such a calculation, for example, to German and Chinese, results in a ratio of G 138 : C 29.[34] Intuitively this might indicate the global significance of the two languages quite well, but the same calculation yields an index of 189 points for Japanese, which would thus appear to outrank German and even more decisively French with an index of only 70. Clearly this kind of reckoning does not reflect the present conditions of the distribution and significance of these languages, although it may be of some prognostic value with respect to the weak position of French in the global language competition. It must be noted in this connection that the strength of French is based partly on the fact that it has traditionally been the most important foreign language of English-speaking countries, and it is here that it can be expected to erode, as other languages such as Japanese gain more recognition.

Ranking languages according to an index calculated on the basis of number of primary speakers and per capita income provides only limited evidence, because in the first place functional language spread is not a matter concerning primary speakers. Rather, processes of this sort typically take place in situations of complex multilingualism where individuals are in a position to choose between several languages. This leads us to the second distinction that has to be taken into account in discussing language spread, that between increases in the number of primary speakers and secondary speakers. Among the secondary speakers, again, those initiating a language shift should be distinguished from those adopting an additional language, integrating it into a configuration of social multilingualism. The latter is typical for the functional and geographic spread of the range of a vehicular language, for the importance of which the number of secondary speakers is more consequential than that of primary speakers. As a result of their wide distribution among secondary speakers, such languages often prompt language shift which then leads to an increase of primary speakers as well. Once again economic factors act as major motives here.

The Spreading of Vehicular Languages

The term "vehicular language" is used in different ways. In a wider sense it is synonymous with "lingua franca," while designating a particular type of lingua franca in its narrower sense. Samarin (1968: 661) lists four alternative and partly overlapping notions which are referred to under the cover term "lingua franca." (1) A *contact language* is one which is not used habitually in daily life. (2) An *international language* is a lingua franca whose use is virtually international. (3) An *auxiliary language* is an artificial language which offers a means of simple communication between speakers of mutually unintelligible mother tongues. And (4) a *vehicular (or trade) language* is a lingua franca not included among the few world languages which is used regionally as a second language across linguistic boundaries in commercial situations. Samarin (1968: 661) points out that all trade languages are lingua francas, and although not all lingua francas are used in trade, many of them emerged in this domain. Another feature of vehicular languages which has often been remarked is their low prestige. Spengler's critical appraisal of some trade languages known from history is representative:

> In the upper classes of cosmopolitan populations emerges an intelligent and practical koine averse to dialects and poetry, such as belongs to the symbolism of every civilization; something wholly mechanical, precise, cold, and with a gesture reduced to a minimum. These final languages without home or roots can be learned by any merchant and coolie, Hellenic in Carthage and at the Oxus, Chinese in Java, English in Shanghai; and "speaking" is irrelevant for understanding them. Looking for their actual creator, one finds that it is not the spirit of a race or religion, but merely that of economics.[35]

What is surprising in this account is that it identifies the upper classes as the originators of these "koines," while at the same time crediting the motivation underlying their genesis, namely the practical concerns of economic operations, with the fact that they can be learned by the uneducated and hence uncultured lower classes, the merchants and coolies. That economic necessity can influence language development and even bring languages into existence is recognized, but disapproved of, since languages are conceived of essentially as the product of the spiritual strength of a people or religion. Hence, it is *"merely* the spirit of economics'* which, from a neo-Romantic point of view, is pitted against that of aesthetics and poetry. Yet, Spengler realized an important point, that koines result from the convergence of different varieties and are thus nobody's mother tongue. That they originate in commercial interaction is a feature they share with pidgin languages.[36]

As discussed in the first section of this chapter, trade is an activity which in certain conditions leads to the emergence of new languages. That it is also an important force behind the spread of languages and their penetration into functional domains other than commerce itself shall be illustrated in the following by means of the rise of three vehicular languages on three continents, Low German in the ports of the North and Baltic Seas, Swahili in East Africa, and Malay in Southeast Asia.

Low German as the Tongue of the Hanseatic League   From the twelfth to the sixteenth century, the North Sea and the Baltic Sea were the realm of the operations of the Hanseatic League. A union of tradesmen first and then of cities, the League was a loose organization devoted exclusively to the expansion and protection of trade links. The important role it played in spreading Low German throughout the region is documented in Ureland (1987). Its rise to become the "koine of commerce in late medieval northern Europe" (Friedland 1987: 15) is closely linked with the formation of the Hanseatic League.

Already with the eastward advance of Germanic peoples across the Elbe beginning in the twelfth century (*Ostkolonisation*), Low German was carried to the east, especially by trading families hailing from Lübeck who played an active role in founding new cities in Slavic-speaking areas at the southern coast of the Baltic Sea – Rostock, Stralsund, Danzig (Gdansk) – and further to the northeast where they came into contact with Finnougric and North Germanic languages, Finnish, Estonian, Lithuanian, Old Prussian, and Swedish in Riga and Reval, to mention but the most important ones. In many of the new settlements various patterns of multilingualism emerged, depending on the composition of the population, but Low German invariably came to occupy the topmost position in the social pecking order of languages. During the twelfth and thirteenth centuries Riga was largely dominated by it, whereas Reval became a multilingual city where it co-existed with Swedish and Estonian.

At that time, the written language of the League was still Latin, but as a spoken language Low German became ever more important. A relatively uniform variety of the language spread across a wide area and could eventually claim currency from the trading offices in Bruges and Cologne in the west to those in Königsberg and Reval in the east. This was partly a consequence of the fact that "the merchants engaged in long-distance trade formed a homogeneous elite related to each other by kinship" (Peters 1987: 69). Again, decisive impulses emanated from

Lübeck where, thanks to the mixed composition of the city's population, linguistic convergence and accommodation had already given rise to a compromise variety of the language. From the second half of the fourteenth century, the League's offices increasingly employed this variety of Low German for written communication, too.

> On account of its importance for the correspondence of the Hanseatic League, the written language of the leading Hanseatic city rose to interregional preeminence. The Lübeck variety of Low German became the international means of communication in the northern part of Central Europe, the Baltic countries, Scandinavia, and in the trading offices. (Peters 1987: 74)

Only in Nowgorod (St Petershof), the eastern outpost where the League kept offices for the trade with Russia, Low German was not widely spoken. Russian was used instead. The League tried to monopolize access to Russian language skills, making sure that other traders, especially from southern Germany and the Netherlands, had to depend on their good offices. The language was so critically important that "a monopoly of interpreter training was virtually tantamount to a monopoly of trade" (Ureland 1987: xxiii).[37]

Low German kept its predominant status as a means of international communication in northern Europe for about 200 years from the fourteenth through the sixteenth century, when High German spread to Low German regions and gradually became the dominant written language. Much like its rise, the decline of Low German was brought about largely by economic factors. In the fifteenth century the Hanseatic League had passed the peak of its power, as the focus of commercial activities in Europe shifted from the League-controlled east–west trade to north–south traffic. The transition from Low German to High German as the dominant written language followed with some delay after the decline of the Hanseatic economic system during the decades around 1500 (Peters 1987: 85). In the wide areas which the Hanseatic League had helped to develop, Low German continued to be spoken for centuries, but the diminution of the League's economic clout gradually stripped it of the foundations of its prestige and of the impetus to continue to spread.[38]

Swahili in East Africa   The more than 50 million inhabitants of the three countries summarily referred to as East Africa, Kenya, Tanzania, and Uganda, speak some 170 different languages none of which counts more than five million native speakers (Merritt and Abdulaziz 1988: 51). Swahili is one of them. It is the mother tongue of only a small part of the population along the coast from southern Tanzania to southern Somalia and on Sansibar and other offshore islands.[39] However, the spreading of Swahili has been progressive for a long time, and at present it is one of the most vigorously expanding languages in the world, both demographically and functionally. It is spoken habitually in everyday life by some 30 million people (Jungraithmayr and Möhlig 1983: 234) and is used occasionally for certain purposes by an even larger number. This makes it easily the leading language of the region with English as its only significant competitor. Swahili owes its dissemination in the first place to the intense multilingualism of the region, secondly to the fact that like it the great majority of the region's languages belong to the Bantu family, and finally to its being employed in commercial traffic and in the market place.

Though Swahili arrived at the coast from interior Africa more than 1,000 years ago, it first spread along the coast through maritime trade where alongside Arabic it gradually became the second important trade language. For a long time there was intensive language contact between the two, and it is assumed that some form of Swahili–Arabic bilingualism existed. Swahili was first written with Arabic letters and has incorporated a great deal of Arabic vocabulary, especially in the field of religion. To the extent that trade expanded from the coast to the interior, Swahili gained ground both vis-à-vis Arabic and regional languages. The fact that Arab merchants also used Swahili contributed to its spread, but in some places also to its being stigmatized as the language of the slave traders. The increasing trade throughout the region was largely controlled by Arabs who formed caravans for carrying ivory, animal skins, and slaves from the interior to the coast. Slave trading outposts established during the eighteenth and nineteenth centuries in the interior as far away as present-day Zaire grew into small towns in which Swahili became the major language of communication (Massamba 1989: 60). It was used by the Arab traders from the coast and their middlemen in the interior, by liberated slaves, and the Islamized offspring of various ethnic groups. Thanks to its currency in the emerging towns it also gained importance for the trade between town and countryside as well as for inter-tribal communication. When the European colonialists arrived, Swahili was already the most important trade language in the region.

The German colonial government realized the importance of Swahili,[40] and although it was only short-lived, it was instrumental in further spreading the language by using it for establishing an administrative infrastructure. Tanzania, the former German East Africa, is still the country where the spread of the language is most advanced. After World War I, the German colonial masters were succeeded by the British. In keeping with their policy of divide and rule, they promoted local vernaculars and English, instead of Swahili. Today, the consequences of this policy are more clearly visible in Kenya and Uganda than in Tanzania. Although in post-colonial times Swahili was proclaimed Kenya's national language as well, it could not displace English there in the domains of government and education as successfully as in Tanzania, but it plays an important role in the economy. In Uganda, Swahili has very little prestige, because it was for a long time associated with slave trade. English and some of the more important local languages (Luganda, Soga, among others) were therefore promoted at the expense of Swahili, which for some time was even excluded from school curricula. That Swahili is more widely spoken in Tanzania than in Kenya and Uganda is also due to the differing linguistic situations of the three countries. In British Tanganyika it faced little competition from other large vernaculars and thus was accepted in addition to, rather than instead of, the many smaller Bantu languages. In Kenya and Uganda, by contrast, Kikuyu, Luganda, Luo, among others have relatively numerous speech communities with which Swahili had to compete.

However, despite the limited official support Swahili received by the British, it continued to spread under their rule because of its importance for trade in Tanganyika and throughout the region. In certain professions it became the preferred language everywhere in East Africa. With the extension of the railway network track layers carried it to the interior, and as the language of the miners it once again advanced as far as Zaire, since Belgian mine owners recruited labor in eastern territories and, in addition to French, used Swahili themselves in public life, business, and in the market place. Especially in the industrial province Katanga it is nowadays an important vehicular language, albeit in a variety distinctly different from Kiswahili, literally "the language of the coast," as it is known by its speakers. Since independence Swahili has, therefore, been one of the four national languages recognized in addition to French. (The others are Tshiluba, Kikongo, and Lingala.)

Swahili has not gained prominence as the language of a demographically important group of native speakers, or because of its valuable literary tradition. Its early association with Islam did not do much to promote its spreading and in some parts became a drag which had to be cast off. And for political purposes it was employed only when its usefulness in East Africa could no longer be overlooked. The major moving power behind its expansion was the economy, trade in particular, for which it came to serve as the principal language of wider communication across linguistic and ethnic boundaries. At the same time, the expansion of economic structures across larger areas and migration in response to labor market demands played an important role as well. Excepting the domain of university education, Swahili is nowadays unchallenged in Tanzania. It is the titular national language of Kenya where, notwithstanding the strong position of English, it is also the most widely used language of cross-linguistic communication. It fulfills important functions in the southeast of Zaire and, therefore, enjoys official status in this country, too. This is now also true of Uganda where it is used extensively in regional and domestic trade across linguistic boundaries, although English is still the dominant language of government and education and Swahili is hence not associated with education and higher socioeconomic status there, as it is in Tanzania. It also serves as a trade language in parts of Rwanda and Burundi.

In spite of its relatively small number of mother-tongue speakers, Swahili has thus become the most important language of East Africa. The increasing urbanization of the region can only reinforce this development, as ever more speakers of differing mother-tongues interact in the urban centers. This tendency which is observed throughout Africa strengthens the indigenous vehicular languages more than the former colonial languages.[41] For, although the latter are commonly associated with the prestige of learning, modern life, and higher social status, social advancement through education is an avenue which is expensive and open to only a select few. A more promising and for many the only practicable approach leads into the world of business and markets, that is, the spheres dominated by the regional vehicular languages. Moreover, for speakers of different but more or less closely related languages, the regional vehicular languages are easier to learn than the European languages. It is for this reason that languages which are insignificant on a global scale can successfully compete regionally with the world languages English and French, and in some cases even drive them back. In Uganda, Kenya, and Tanzania, Swahili competes with English and in Zaire with French. Especially in Tanzania it has taken on functions which during the second phase of the colonial period used to be fulfilled by English. The price to be paid for this is a decline in the level of

English language proficiency, the reward, a higher level of national integration. Similarly, in West Africa, Wolof, being the language of business, spreads more rapidly than the more prestigious French in the urban regions of Senegal and the Gambia. And for the same reason, despite the colonial heritage, Hausa could spread beyond its mother-tongue speaker base in northern Nigeria to wide stretches of West and Central Africa, above all, in the cities from Brazzaville in the south to Tripoli in the north, to become a vehicular language as important as Swahili is in the eastern part of the continent.

Malay in the East Indies   The dynamics of the spread of Malay on the Malayan peninsula and the Indonesian archipelago exhibits certain similarities to the spread of Swahili. In the service of trade in an extremely multilingual environment[42] it was able to rise to become the principal regional language for wider communication which absorbed some of the functions of a national language. Alisjahbana (1976: 32) describes the functional demands to which Malay has adapted over the centuries:

> Because the extensive area of Indonesia and Malaysia is fragmented into hundreds of geographical, cultural, and most important, linguistic units, there has been from time immemorial a need for a single common language which could be understood not only by the natives of the archipelago but also by the constant waves of foreigners attracted by celebrated riches.

This role devolved upon Malay, since Malays dwelled on both sides of the Strait of Malacca as well as in Sarawak. For many centuries the Strait of Malacca was the principal thoroughfare of commercial traffic in Southeast Asia, which was largely dominated by the inhabitants of the Malayan peninsula and Sumatra. Malayan merchants and seafarers carried the language to all ports of call where it was picked up by other tradesmen, sailors, and pirates operating in the region, at least to the extent that was necessary for their business. Moreover, long-distance trade from Arabia, India, and later Europe in the west to China in the east also led through the Strait of Malacca. The seasonal changes of the monsoon made it impossible to complete the journey to China without seeking shelter in the Malayan ports, sometimes for several months. These conditions made Malay the quasi-natural trade language of the region. The history of its diffusion is not well documented, but it is known to have fulfilled this function as early as the sixteenth century when the first Europeans reached East India (Teeuw 1959).

Alisjahbana (1976: 33) reports that, in the seventeenth century, Malay enjoyed a reputation comparable to that of French in Europe. This can hardly have been true of the reduced and bastardized varieties known as Bazaar Malay which served the various population groups of the region as a link language. Bazaar Malay and the cultivated written variety of the language co-existed in a diglossia setting, and it was principally the low variety which spread in the wake of trade. Therefore, the other great regional languages, especially Javanese as the medium of an old and sophisticated culture, but also Sundanese, Achinese, Madurese, and Balinese, all of them with several million speakers, were considered more prestigious not only by their own speakers but by others as well. Their currency, however, is limited to the regions occupied by their native speakers, whereas Malayan varieties could spread along the coast relatively independently of local cultures. Not being the language of a demographically significant group or an exclusive ethnic or cultural tradition predestined it to become a means of cross-linguistic communication and allowed it to prevail over culturally and demographically more powerful competitors, with most of which it is genetically related. For example, Javanese with a speech community of 70 million (1988) distinguishes itself by a complex honorific system which, because of its sociocultural loading, makes it hard for outsiders to learn and unsuitable for inter-ethnic and cross-linguistic communication. By contrast, Malay offers itself for these purposes, since its development was shaped less by the court culture of the Islamic sultanates on the Malayan peninsula than by the outward oriented seafarers and traders. Anderson underscores the "democratic" qualities of Malay which it owes to the fact that "as an 'inter-ethnic' language . . . it had *ipso facto* an almost statusless character . . . and was tied to no particular regional social structure."[43]

In the colonial period, the region where Malay is spoken natively and as a vehicular language came under Dutch and British control. As Lowenberg (1988) has pointed out, the differing language policies of the colonial administrations have left traces in the language. The Dutch found Malay extremely useful and in 1865 adopted it as the second official language of the East Indies. Pursuing a largely segregationist policy, they used Malay as the language of instruction for the vast majority of the population, reserving Dutch-medium schools for themselves and a tiny coopted indigenous elite. In Malaya and Singapore, the British took a different approach, promoting, as they did, English on a large scale. As a consequence, the standardization of Malay advanced more vigorously under Dutch than under British rule.

Table 5.2   Mother-tongue speakers of Malay in four countries

	Population (m)	Malay mother-tongue (%)
Brunei	0.25	60
Malaysia	17.50	45
Singapore	2.60	15
Indonesia	171.40	7

(After Prentice (1990: 187); demographic data from *Fischer Weltalmanach (1990)*)

It is because of this discrepancy and because of its diffusion through trade over a vast and disparate area that Malay still exhibits a wide spectrum of varieties today. National varieties, on one hand, and social varieties, on the other, are clearly distinct. In the four countries where it enjoys the status of national or official language, it is known by three different names: Bahasa Indonesia ("Indonesian language"), Bahasa Malaysia ("Malaysian language"), and Bahasa Malayu ("Malayan language"). Owing to their respective contact histories with Javanese and Dutch in Indonesia and Arabic and English in Malaysia, these varieties differ mostly in the lexicon and are mutually intelligible (Prentice 1990). In the social ranking order, Bazaar Malay ranges at the bottom, and the standard language which is oriented to the literary variety now called "classical," at the top. Standardization is not yet complete, since the technical vocabulary in particular is still to be augmented and harmonized. However, its cultivation as the national language of the four countries mentioned above as well as its systematic instruction in all schools helps to further promote the spread of Malay. Through this process, Bazaar Malay, which was so critically important for its diffusion initially, is gradually superseded by the standard variety.

Now as before, the secondary speakers of Malay outnumber its mother-tongue speakers by a large margin, and this is unlikely to change significantly in the near future. Only in tiny Brunei is it spoken natively by a majority of the population. In the other three countries the proportion of mother-tongue speakers is much smaller, as shown in table 5.2. In spite of these low figures, especially in Indonesia, the most populous country of the region, increasing economic and political integration of the four countries has made it the most important means of communication for the almost 190 million inhabitants of this multilingual region not only in the spheres of economy and government, but also in education and the mass media. For wider communication throughout the region it is more important than any other language, but on the national level it is indispensable as well. In Malaysia, this is evident because of the demographically and politically dominant position of its mother-tongue speakers, but also because it is the language of greatest serviceability.[44] In Singapore, where English is the chief means of inter-ethnic communication and the major language of work and business, it is less important as a link language. But since its native speakers were resident in Singapore long before the economically dominant Chinese and the other population groups and are, moreover, disinclined to exogamy, the language also has an undisputed position in the modern city state, which is even enhanced to some extent by language shift on the part of inhabitants of South Asian extraction. In the long run, language shift also works in favor of Bahasa Indonesia. For the reasons discussed in the next section of this chapter, many of the minute speech communities of Indonesia will abandon their languages and, after a period of transitional bilingualism, eventually adopt the national language as their principal or only means of communication. Indonesia's larger speech communities will not give up their traditional languages for the benefit of Malay. Rather, these languages will co-exist with it in situations of function-specific bilingualism, though urbanization and the greater geographic and social flexibility of Bahasa Indonesia can be expected to further strengthen its position.

Conclusions

A number of conclusions can be drawn from the above observations. Those pivotal to the problems of language spread discussed in this section can be summarized in five points.

1   Language spread is often an indication of economic conditions and in some cases the result of economic developments. For changing conditions of the economy force societies to readjust their speech repertoires and patterns of communication. This is evidenced most clearly by vehicular languages whose range expands, initially at least, primarily through commercial traffic, while the political power of their speakers, their aesthetic-cultural esteem, and their symbolic value as a catalyst of individual, social, or national identity formation are of little consequence. The principal determinant of the progressive spreading of vehicular languages is the economy.

2   That the utility of a language does not depend on the demographic strength of its mother-tongue community is also most forcefully demonstrated by vehicular languages. This is true both of relatively small languages in terms of number of mothertongue speakers such as Swahili, as well as for big ones such as English. For a proper understanding of the dynamic spread of a language, the demographic strength of its primary speech community is less important than its geographic and socioeconomic distribution. Low German which in the initial phase of its spread was almost entirely restricted to commercial circles is a case in point. In situations of unstable multilingualism, the number of mother-tongue speakers of a language may vary more strongly than can be explained by natural demographic changes alone; for an expanding language acquires additional speakers through language shift.

3   Even more significant than the growth of the mother-tongue community of a language is its increasing use as a second language. In multilingual settings so complex as those that emerged in recent decades in the newly urbanized regions of Africa and Southeast Asia, the acquisition of a vehicular language is for many a matter of economic survival. Depending on the mother-tongue, and the kind of language contact thus established, the acquisition of such a language is the first step towards language shift or, alternatively, the emergence of a stable function-specific pattern of bi- or multilingualism. Both will strengthen the position of the vehicular language. In multilingual environments the communication needs in commerce and business as well as in the expanding labor markets are particularly pressing. Languages by means of which these needs can be fulfilled acquire additional secondary and primary speakers who, in turn, enhance their utility value.

4   The scenes where language spread happens are manifold. Only very few languages take part in language competition on a global scale, maybe the six official languages of the United Nations. However, the international weight of these languages does not imply their superiority on a regional level. Regional languages can prosper alongside them, and under certain conditions even spread more vigorously, since they are more suitable for the communication demands at hand. Once again, intra-regional, as opposed to world trade and the increasing need of mobility in the labor market, are critical factors here.

5   Language spread must, therefore, be measured not only demographically and geographically, but also in terms of the functions a language fulfills. Thus an expansion pattern for every language results, indicating by how many primary and secondary speakers it is spoken, in

which communication domains, for what purposes, at what level of proficiency, and where it is expanding.

Language Perpetuation

Functions of Writing

The technological innovation which makes it possible to perpetuate the ephemeral word, writing, must be counted among the most dramatic stations of language history. Breasted (1926: 53f.) emphasized its far-reaching importance for civilization in general in his often quoted statement that "the invention of writing has had a greater influence in uplifting the human race than any other intellectual achievement in the career of man." Since this influence has a correlate in the history of language, the distinction between invention and evolution is an important one for us to make: language evolved, writing was invented. No other single achievement has had greater consequences for language. Writing has influenced people's relationship to language as deeply as it has influenced individual language careers. While the expression of ideas by means of the spoken word is bound to the here and now and its passing-on depends on an unbroken tradition, "the preservation of the spirit in writing directly ties times and distances to each other." Since Wilhelm von Humboldt (1963 [1822]) wrote this, generations of linguists, historians, cultural anthropologists, and sociologists have tried to understand the role writing played in the development of language awareness, norm formation and standardization, the development of novel linguistic functions, the modes of existence of languages, and the differences its use makes vis-à-vis languages transmitted only orally.[45]

Jespersen (1933: 670) called written language "an unnatural substitute of the spoken word." Although there are good reasons to consider written language as an extension rather than a substitute of speech, Jespersen's characterization of written language as unnatural is quite apt. He picked up the threads of a long tradition. Dante had already contrasted what he called *lingua naturalis* with *lingua artificialis*.[46] Through writing, the natural faculty of language which finds expression in every language is supplemented by an artificial element. As collective products, languages are rendered artefacts by being given a written form. Through the availability of a codifiable and potentially objective standard their development can be controlled in a manner quite different from unwritten languages. In contradistinction to speech which is part of the basic human equipment, writing is an artificial tool whose habitual use leaves traces in the medium to which it gives form. Accordingly, Paul (1909: 414) called written language straightforwardly "an artificial language." For, as one contemporary author puts it, "the distinctive traits of standard languages reflect a cultural intervention against the normal development of language (Joseph 1987: 19)."[47]

Kloss (1978) has demonstrated that reducing a language to writing is essentially an instrument of language constitution which both manifests and confirms the claim for a variety to be recognized in its own right and without which it cannot be elaborated into a common language in the sense discussed in chapter 2. Writing also secures the survival of languages; not only in the sense that Sumerian exists today, while countless other languages vanished without leaving a trace, but also as a means of upholding a tradition. What would Latin be today without its rich literature? How could Hebrew have endured its long journey through the millennia to eventually be re-employed orally without the prop of writing?

Writing is a communication technique which opens up an entire spectrum of novel communication functions. A speech community's adoption of this technique alters its communicative habits and potential as drastically as it affects the environment of the languages concerned, the one that is elevated to written status as well as those with which it is in contact. To this day, only a small fraction of all languages have ever been used in writing, and it is sensible for us to suspect that the great majority of the world's languages never will be. The question of why this is so cannot be answered unless we investigate the purposes served by writing and written language. In this pursuit we quickly and inevitably run into economic constraints, no matter whether we inspect the earliest documents of literate culture or direct our attention to the conditions of successful literacy campaigns and the introduction of hitherto oral societies to the art of writing in our times. What is it that writing does which cannot be done in oral societies? And under what conditions is it necessary to do what can be done by means of writing only? In our discussion of this question we shall not take issue with the many hypotheses concerning the enigmatic origin of writing; for our purposes, what gave rise to the invention of writing is less important than how, and in response to what kinds of needs, the achievement, once accomplished, was put to use.

Beginnings of Writing

The three major early literate cultures exhibit a number of commonalities. They emerged in fertile river basins – at the Euphrates, the Nile, and the Yellow River – in densely populated areas whose inhabitants produced more than was necessary for their own reproduction. Property came into existence, as well as the desire to mark it as such. Moreover, the increasing complexity of socioeconomic structures which came along with surplus production, called for an objective medium of recording, which detached information from the individuals possessing it and made it possible for a message to be preserved and transmitted independently of them. The division of labor and the emerging forms of social life which came in the wake of increasing population density and the formation of cities in the earliest high cultures of Sumer, Egypt, and China, are inconceivable without writing.[48] Forms of trade transcending immediate exchange of goods in barter, collectively organized irrigation and the production for stockpiling that it made possible, inventory control, a developed taxation system, regular evidence of ownership and transfer of property, a more than rudimentary system of credit and loan, as well as the bureaucratization of government either presuppose writing or are raised to a qualitatively new level of sophistication by it. Although the beginnings of writing in Egypt and China, to the extent that they are known, suggest a relation to cult, its significance for creating an organized economy and erecting a bureaucratic state is beyond question.[49] The nexus of literary culture and economy is in evidence even more strikingly where a full writing system was developed first, in Mesopotamia. In the temple economy of the cities in ancient Babylonia we find the earliest instance of the Weberian paradox that the economic rationality of administering worldly goods issues from the seat of the administration of irrational transwordly goods.

The Letters of Economy and the Economy of Letters

The Sumerian writing system dates from the late fourth millennium, hailing from a city, perhaps Uruk, as is generally assumed and which has recently been argued convincingly once again by Powell (1981). At the center of Uruk and later cities of the region was the temple which accumulated considerable riches through taxation, donations, and labor carried out for its benefit. Administering these riches must have played a decisive role in the development and diffusion of writing. As early as

1936, when Falkenstein published a report on the most archaic Uruk tablets, he emphasized the importance of book-keeping for the development of writing,[50] and subsequently Gelb (1963: 62) pronounced without reservation that "Sumerian writing owes its origin to the needs arising from public economy and administration." Green (1981: 347) specified the tasks for whose execution writing was needed in ancient Babylon:

> The cuneiform writing system functioned as a device to record transactions of the Sumerian administrative bureaucracy. It enabled that bureaucracy to expand vastly its basic resources and production processes – the control and distribution of information, labor, goods, and services.

The force of these arguments was recently corroborated in a number of important studies Nissen (1985)[51] conducted on the basis of much more comprehensive data than were available to Falkenstein. 85 percent of the more than 4,000 clay tablets from the Uruk period (3300–3100 B.C.) were found to be economic records. The sheer number and the contents of the texts lead Nissen to link the development of sedentary life in Babylonia during that period, increasing population density, and the emergence of defined standards as controlling devices of a growing economy, to the advent of Babylonian writing. The new communication technique, Nissen (1985: 352) argues, was appreciated from the outset "as the ultimate answer to the problems of controlling economic life."

That writing was controlled by the temple thus does not imply that its uses were primarily religious, since the economy, too, was controlled by the temple, and for administering it writing was much more important than for cult. The many documents which have come down to us, thanks to the virtually indestructible medium of clay, leave no room for doubt. Upwards of three fourths of the 150,000 or so tablets excavated in Mesopotamia pertain to economic and administrative matters. The importance of an objective system of keeping records, which made the many members of the administrative bureaucracy both accountable and replaceable as individuals, cannot be estimated too highly.[52] Through the recording of business transactions, tax payments, debts, dealings in futures, among others, the economy of letters gradually penetrated social life, even in the private domain, or more appropriately, perhaps, it thus created a private domain. In addition to inventories, contracts of purchase and lease, lists of goods received or to be delivered, rations for slaves, marriages and adoptions were confirmed in writing, and wills were drawn up disposing of one's possessions. Later documents from the period of the Akkadian King Saragon (2334–2279 B.C.) indicate that the centralized temple economy took on ever more secular and private traits. Near the end of the third millennium, writing had become such a matter of course in everyday life that it was possible to stipulate by law that every business transaction be recorded in writing. Obviously, not everybody could write. Though literacy was taught in schools[53] and had been diffused beyond the bureaucratic apparatus (Chiera 1938: 67), it remained the privilege of an elite. A new profession, therefore, came into existence, the scribe, who took care of the correspondence and book-keeping of businessmen amongst each other and with the temple.[54]

This was all the more important since the cities of the ancient Orient knew no market places (Oppenheim 1964: 129). In view of the size and typically prominent position of such places of exchange where they do exist, the fact that archaeologists have not found any speaks against the assumption that they were there at all. The documents contain no references to market places either which would suggest that lack of archaeological evidence is coincidental. The explanation that historians feel compelled to accept point in a different direction: "Babylonian trade and business activities were not originally market activities" (Polanyi 1957: 25). The extensive trade in which the cities had to engage for the procurement of both building materials and luxury items because their local environment, though fertile, was poor in raw materials such as stone, metal, and timber, was contract trade rather than market trade. As opposed to the exchange of goods in the market place which brings together the parties of the transaction, this form of trade is necessarily verbal, involving promises and communication over a distance. The deal is not completed at the time the agreement is reached. Durable records of the transaction were, therefore, necessary. The mediation office was a public agency – the temple, the palace, or the city – where all obligations against third parties had to be registered. The contracts that were closed for this purpose were described by Polanyi as follows:

> The documents themselves were set out with a brevity and precision which enabled the public trustee – the *tankarum* – to take action at all times if enjoined by an interested party in legitimate possession of a copy of the relevant document. (1957: 24)

Prices too, if this notion is applicable in the absence of a universal means of exchange,[55] as well as measures and interest rates were controlled publicly. From the rich stock of different adjectives relating to equivalencies in the Sumerian formulary, Polanyi (1957: 20) concludes "that the handling of 'equivalencies' must have been subject to administrative rules of an intricate kind."

Through risk-free trade controlled and backed up by public agencies which at the same time functioned as trustees, the cities of Babylon were in contact not only with Susa, the center of nearby Elam to the north of the Persian Gulf, but also with more distant parts of the world such as Ebla in northern Syria and Egypt. These contacts, attested already in the third millennium, may have been instrumental, as some historians believe, in spreading writing throughout the Fertile Crescent even prior to the formation of the mature Babylonian–Assyrian cuneiform system. Because of the conspicuously different graphical appearance of the Egyptian hieroglyphs, no immediate influence on the development of writing in Egypt can be ascertained, but many researchers nevertheless hypothesize that the idea of writing was brought to Egypt through the trade links with Mesopotamia.[56] The diffusion of cuneiform writing from Sumer to Elam and Ebla is established beyond doubt. In Elam it appears as early as the middle of the third millennium (Powell 1981: 434), and soon thereafter in Ebla. In northern Syria, Italian archaeologists have excavated a comprehensive archive of some 15,000 tablets with cuneiform inscriptions containing contracts, ledgers of tax dues and receipts, as well as trade agreements dating from between 2400 and 2250 B.C. (Biggs 1980).

The advance of literacy in the ancient Babylonian cities was driven by the economy – book-keeping, taxation, organized production – and pushed up to higher levels by it, especially through trade which also carried writing from Mesopotamia to other lands. For a long time, the economy was not only the chief domain of Sumerian writing, but its exclusive field of use. It was only later, after the Akkadians had penetrated the region and gained political influence, that it began to be employed in other domains as well. Under the Akkadians, the Sumerian city states were expanded to cover wider areas making written communication increasingly indispensable in government. As a consequence, the status of medium of diplomacy and international treaties accrued to the Akkadian written language (Hawkes and Wooley 1963: 504). Around the middle of the second millennium it was used for correspondence with Mesopotamia even by Egyptian chanceries. In the cultural sphere, writing began to draw initial lines of differentiation. Medical texts and botanical lists were compiled as well as cook books (Bottéro 1987);

hymns, rites and astrological omens were recorded for posterity; and recent research has discovered "apocalyptic" or "prophetic" texts "with decidedly political overtones" (Sack 1981: 410). And eventually, what could not have been *avant la lettre* appeared, literature, the Gilgamesh epos of the third dynasty of Ur (around 2000 B.C.) being the most magnificent example. Civic life became subject to lawful regimentation where the need to control economic relations continued to be of paramount importance as the moving force for the development of a literate culture. The Assyrian law collection of the eighteenth century, the famous Codex Hammurapi, which was compiled when Babylon's grandeur was at its peak, incorporates the first codified commercial law.

The Most Precious Language of the World

We are now in a position to identify two accomplishments of writing which are at the center of its economic significance. (1) Writing enables the scribe to take stock of the world. (2) Writing creates pre*scriptions*. This does not mean that before the introduction of writing human society was without knowledge of the world or without order; but only written recording makes it possible to accumulate knowledge and to perpetuate standards detached from, and independent of, its individual adherents. The continuity of the conduct of life thus gained and the conservatism of writing are documented by the fixed formulae professional scribes used in redacting commercial and diplomatic contracts, some of which were handed down in their verbatim form from one generation to the next for several centuries.[57] These two accomplishments of writing which can be equated with its encyclopedic and normative functions, particularly important in the present context, also apply to that which writing represents, language. On clay tablets the ephemeral word is captured, reified for the first time, and, as a tangible object, ready to become the subject of contemplation and investment.

If writing did not create meta-linguistic discourse, it surely raised it to higher levels of insight and systematicity. The scribes were quick to produce the auxiliary means they needed for their work and for training, reference works such as lists of signs along with their pronunciation, synonym lists, as well as bilingual Sumerian–Akkadian word lists (Sack 1981: 410). One of the longest known cuneiform documents is such a dictionary.[58] As pointed out repeatedly by Goody (e.g., 1977: 74ff., 1986: 54ff.), lists are the model case of decontextualized and asyntactic language. Their occurrence among the earliest Sumerian documents is so very important, because they bring language itself to the focus of attention, providing as they do the means both to inventory and to standardize it. On tablets used for training, which are also attested as early as the third millennium, we find the first evidence of language cultivation in the repeated copies by the apprentice of what the teacher had pre-scribed. Their language, Sumerian, thus became the most valuable language of the world. The first language of the ancient Near East to be reduced to writing became the model of written language as such, which was to give it an enormous competitive edge over other languages. Its career exemplifies the triumph of artificial selection as no other language ever since, excepting, maybe, Chinese with its written tradition of three millennia. Though Sumerian ceased to be passed on as a mother-tongue by 1800 BC at the latest, the Sumerians having assimilated to the Akkadian usurpers, it continued to be used as a written language for another one and a half millennia down to the Seleucid period.

When the Akkadians began to dominate economy and government, they first used, by necessity, only Sumerian for correspondence, yet, once they had learned to write their own language by means of the Sumerian writing system, they still continued to use the Sumerian culture language. This language contact gave rise to a situation of bilingualism with diglossia, Sumerian functioning as the prestige language. The Mesopotamian scribes were bilingual,[59] establishing a pattern of language use which was to be followed almost invariably wherever writing was introduced into an oral environment, and which we still recognize today in many societies where the written language differs from the vernacular not only superficially in style but genetically, as is the case in many Third World countries.

The fact that Sumerian was the first language of the ancient Orient to be given a written form had another important consequence for its continuation. Since the adoption of the cuneiform writing system first for Akkadian and later for other languages, too, was effected by way of learning the Sumerian written language, Sumerian became a resource for the development of many other languages, or, to put it differently, cuneiform became the transmission belt for the incorporation of Sumerian words into these languages. Even texts in the languages whose reduction to writing led to the most extensive modifications and simplifications of the cuneiform system,[60] contain Sumerograms, Sumerian loanwords, that is, which in the recipient language are written in the same way as in Sumerian. This practice too set an often-repeated precedent: the terminological resources of a cultivated written language are tapped by others. This process is embodied in Sanskritized varieties of Hindi and other Indian languages, as it is in the Chinese stratum in the lexicon of East Asian languages such as Vietnamese, Korean, and Japanese, and in the Greco-Latin stratum of Germanic languages. In this way, languages typically remain indebted to the ones through which they came by writing.

From the point of view of the language it represents, writing thus proves to be a double guarantor of its perpetuation, or at least, as an artificially created adaptive advantage. It enables a language to be maintained and cultivated after its natural tradition, unguided by instruction, has come to an end, and it makes sure that a language lives on in others, since it permits language contact in the absence of mother-tongue speakers, making that language accessible to others as a resource for enrichment.

By reifying it, giving it a lasting, unalterable form of existence, by making it visible and tangible, writing renders language a valuable good on a qualitatively new level. In Mesopotamia, its individual and social possession was for the first time in history an expression and a constituent factor of affluence. Ever since the age of literacy was irreversibly ushered in there for all of humanity, it became ever more a precondition thereof.

Written Language and Poverty

The above statement concerning the nexus of written language and affluence calls for further specification. Individual and social acquisition of literacy surely is no sufficient condition for affluence. And, considering the many contemporary business people and politicians whose command of computer literacy would seem to be just as low as that of ancient merchants and medieval princes of the writing technologies of their times, one could be led to conclude that literacy is not a necessary condition for wealth and power either. However, this is only to show that it is possible to have the technology at one's disposal without mastering it oneself. The scribes who had mastered the technical skills stood at the top of the social hierarchy in antiquity no more than secretaries do today, but they never stood at the bottom either. Especially where there is little social affluence, participation in a written language guarantees higher social status, for under such circumstances literacy is usually restricted to a small segment of the society. From the

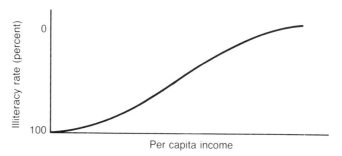

Figure 5.1   Unrealistic correlation of illiteracy and social affluence.

point of view of those who have no written language at their disposal,
directly or indirectly, the correlation is more conspicuous; as individuals
and social groups they are economically impotent and immobile.

Written Languages   If participation in a written language means the
expansion of one's communication range, access to objectified knowledge, and increasing social integration and differentiation, not all languages which have been reduced to writing can count as written languages.
Languages recently reduced to writing in the course of this century by
missionaries or linguists, mainly for their own purposes, without being
used in writing to any significant extent, or exhibiting a body of
literature worth mentioning, are not considered written languages in the
present context. Rather, the notion of written language is taken to cover
only languages which acquired a written form in conjunction with the
differentiation of economic, sociopolitical, and cultural structures, or
which, in spite of their recency, are widely used having assumed important functions of written communication within their speech community.
Thus, languages used only as a "bridge"[61] for literacy education to
facilitate mastery of a more widely used written language, or fulfilling
mainly decorative functions, are excluded.

Both on the individual and social level, possession of a written
language must be conceptualized as a graded notion. At one end stand
illiterates, at the other literati, and in between the two there is a wide
spectrum of varying literary skills. Likewise, there are societies such as,
for example, Finland, where virtually everyone partakes in the written
language, and there are those where, as, for example, in Afghanistan,
literacy is reserved to a tiny elite; and again there is a graded continuum
of literacy levels in between. Both individual and social possession of a

written language correlates positively with material welfare. UNESCO pointed out long ago that the world map of illiteracy is largely congruent with the world map of poverty.[62] Global correlations of illiteracy and gross national product are indicative at a level of 0.8 or more. However, such general correlations hide as much as they reveal (Foster 1972: 593), for increasing literacy rates and increasing social affluence do not correlate exponentially. It would be misleading, therefore, to represent this relation graphically as an S-shaped curve as in figure 5.1, which would indicate that illiteracy in a society decreases to the extent that wealth, in terms of, say, per capita income, increases and vice versa.

The most literate man is the wealthiest man no more than the country with the lowest illiteracy rate has the highest per capita income. Those who can barely write their name do not have significantly better economic chances than those unable to write at all. On the social level, affluence does not imply general literacy; witness the United States where mass functional illiteracy is, maybe, indicative of the unequal distribution of wealth, but not of social wealth as such. On the other hand, the reduction of illiteracy from 50 percent to 40 percent which was accomplished in Nicaragua by a literacy campaign during the 1980s will likely have no immediate or medium-term consequences for the development of social wealth in that country. Thus the socioeconomic value of literacy cannot be measured on a scale with linear progression. The correlation is really only evident at the extremities: in the 25 poorest countries of the world with an annual per capita income of $500 or less, illiteracy rates are above 60 percent of the population 15 years of age and older, whereas the 20 richest countries with a per capita income in excess of $10,000 have illiteracy rates below 10 percent.[63] If these quantities are to be related to each other in a graph in such a way that the axis of X measures per capita income and the axis of Y literacy rate, and the coordinate plane is divided into quadrants, then there will be concentrations of coordinate points in the lower left and the upper right quadrants as in figure 5.2. The concentration in the upper right quadrant represents the industrial countries and that in the lower left one the poorest countries of the Third World. By and large, these concentrations coincide with the extremities of the S-shaped curve in fig. 5.1, but such a curve only results when the widely scattered coordinate points in between are abstracted. There are coordinate points both in the upper left and the lower right quadrants, which indicates that the correlation is much weaker in the center of the coordinate plane where middle-income countries with moderate illiteracy rates are located. In the lower right

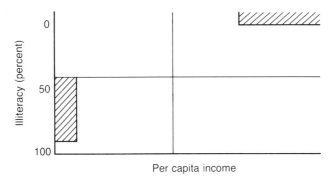

Figure 5.2   Participation in a written language and social affluence.

quadrant, for instance, countries such as Saudi Arabia would be located whose per capita income comes close to that of the industrial countries, but which has a much lower literacy rate. In the upper left quadrant countries with low per capita income but relatively high literacy such as Sri Lanka would be located.

Explanations for these "deviations" are not far to seek. The prosperity of the countries in the lower right quadrant, rather than being a result of domestic socioeconomic development, was brought about suddenly in the course of this century by developments in which they played no active part, the paradigm case being oil-rich states of the Arabian peninsula. Looking at the countries in the upper left quadrant, another relationship becomes apparent which is of interest to our present considerations. Cuba, Laos, Sri Lanka, and Vietnam are some of the countries in question. What they share in common is that they have low per capita incomes in spite of relatively high literacy rates. Another conspicuous feature of these countries is their linguistic homogeneity and the fact that the dominant written language is the mother-tongue of the majority of the population or closely related to it.

Endoglossic and Exoglossic Written Languages   These observations suggest a conceptual differentiation which enables us to determine more accurately the economic preconditions and consequences of the social possession of a written language: where the dominant written language is the language of the majority of the population or closely related to it, this language shall be called "endoglossic written language" (example: Swahili in Tanzania). Conversely, an "exoglossic written language" shall be one which is not the language of the majority of the population or related to it (example: Portuguese in Mozambique). It now turns out that the 20 richest countries of the world, without exception, possess endoglossic written languages, while in 20 of the 25 poorest countries exoglossic written languages are the major means of written communication. In 70 percent of these countries, illiteracy ranges between 40 percent and 90 percent of the population 15 years or older. This does not imply that an exoglossic written language is the sole cause of these countries' high illiteracy rates; but these figures do suggest that the acquisition of universal literacy by a society, which allows the advantages of this communication technique to be fully exploited, is made more difficult by an exoglossic written language.

Economic Development Precedes Literacy The unequal distribution of wealth between the countries of the world is reflected, among other things, by the distribution of endoglossic written languages which, in turn, relates to literacy levels. Illiteracy has been aptly called "the tip of the iceberg of underdevelopment" (Slaughter 1985: 134).[64] Although in the beginning the formation of written languages was an effect of economic developments as much as it helped to stimulate them, the universal spread of literacy across all social strata is a modern, very recent phenomenon founded on socioeconomic realities some of which took many generations to accomplish. It is a mistake, therefore, to assume that development in western industrialized countries was possible thanks to high literacy rates. Yet many developing countries conduct literacy campaigns in the expectation to thereby improve their economic performance. Literacy campaigns are viewed as investments, the anticipated return being a better standard of living. Underlying this perspective is a causal interpretation of the coincidence of social affluence and general access to a written language which is so conspicuous in the advanced countries. Yet it is by no means clear, as some believe, that there is a threshold literacy level above which economic development takes off.[65] With a few exceptions such as Sweden, it is true of the advanced countries that economic development led to widespread literacy, not vice versa. Daswani (1991) has, therefore, rightly called into doubt the implicit assumption that literacy campaigns in Third World countries will help to generate input conditions for economic development after the western model. It is not high literacy that boosts development, but rather economic demand for literates that promotes literacy.

However, the causality in this direction is limited, too. What, maybe, the American example illustrates more clearly than any other is that a high level of economic and technological development is not incompatible with relatively high rates of illiteracy. As a matter of fact, in virtually all advanced countries that have taken the trouble to investigate the matter, it was found in recent years that functional illiteracy is much more pervasive a problem than had previously been thought. A recent Canadian study by the federal government agency Statistics Canada found that as many as 38 percent of Canadians had reading limitations that could affect their work opportunities. It would be unreasonable to think that Canadians are less literate than people in other advanced countries, but reliable surveys are hardly available (Hirsch 1991). On the economic level, OECD has in 1991 for the first time carried out a major study on the effects of adult illiteracy on economic performance, presenting evidence that functional illiteracy incurs losses to businesses in the order of magnitude of billions of dollars annually (Benton and Noyelle 1991). On the social level, much attests to the validity of Hammink's (1987) analysis of functional illiteracy as rooted in social inequality, which would predict that illiteracy would be highest where social inequality is most pronounced – witness the United States – and lowest where social inequality is most limited – witness, for example, Sweden and Japan. Thus, if the economy is the engine that initiates the drive for literacy, it does not by itself bring about a fully literate society. Universal literacy can only be achieved if the political will is there, and if there are the financial resources necessary for establishing a system of universal education that does not allow for anyone to fall through the net to become functionally illiterate as an adult. In this pursuit, an endoglossic written language is an asset, facilitating as it does the definition and implementation of standards.

For a variety of reasons concerning the exchange of goods, people, and information, the spread of endoglossic written languages coincided historically with economic advance. That many developing countries will be able to replicate, or even significantly stimulate, such an advance by importing an exoglossic written language seems doubtful. An exoglossic written language does not serve well the purpose of literacy campaigns, and, because of its typical social restrictedness to a small portion of the society, its potential for production, commerce, administration, and social integration cannot be fully exploited. Such a language helps to erect rather than bridge social barriers. The dilemma, however, is that in many countries no promising alternative is in sight. Languages newly reduced to writing, although, maybe, facilitating the acquisition of literacy by their speakers, are not heavy-duty languages, since they lack the functional range of languages with a literary tradition, especially the European written languages. They offer little in terms of access to the various channels of information and objectified knowledge, or for the vertical integration of society. It is mainly for this reason that, rather than elevating vehicular languages such as Bambara, Ewe, Hausa, Kinyarwanda, Kirundi, Yoruba, and West African Pidgin English to the dominant medium of literacy instruction and written communication, the great majority of the multilingual countries of Africa have adhered to the exoglossic written languages they inherited from colonial times, while at the same time promoting literacy in newly written languages. This policy seriously compromises the integrating effect of written language as such and the unfolding of its socioeconomic potential.

The Competitive Edge of Written Language – Summary

As a means of perpetuating language, writing incorporates the first communication revolution in human history. Since the Sumerian pioneers, humankind has never dispensed with this valuable instrument. The early phase of literate society is still instructive for a proper understanding of the economic aspects of linguistic communication. From the outset, the nexus of economy and written language has been one of mutual influences.

On the social level, written language was created and spread in response to communication demands rooted in economic necessities. By virtue of its indifference to spacial and temporal distance it enables the individual and the social group to expand the range of communication beyond the shared environment of co-present interactants. To create such an expanded communication range in the absence of economic conditions requiring it does not necessarily cause writing to be adopted widely as a technique and means of communication, as attested by the many literacy campaigns that came to nothing. The social acquisition of a written language is part and parcel of its economic, social, and political development, and to the extent that advances are made in these areas it becomes an ever more important and valuable component of the socioeconomic infrastructure. Therefore, the prospects for the spread of exoglossic written languages are not good, because they do not emerge in conjunction with the communicative demands and the underlying economic necessities, but have to bring them about or expedite their development.

For a language it is a competitive advantage to be used in writing in response to existing demands and thus to be gradually rendered a written language. By being given a written form, a language gains a dimension which makes it objectively more useful than unwritten languages. The letter helps to accumulate the value of a written language. The first written language acquired by a social group is hence hard to replace, since an established written language is of and by itself valuable. The longevity of the first great literary language, Sumerian, is already evidence of this. The deepening of literate culture in the course of the centuries and the increasing dependency on writing as a means of controlling economy and society has made the advantage of the language which a community first used for written communication even more commanding. For today the function of written language to provide access to information is much more important than the ability to express one's own thoughts in writing, and this function is best fulfilled by established written languages, the European common languages in particular. Chances that, as the next millennium draws near, new written languages will come into existence that are equally useful must, therefore, be judged as exceedingly slim.

These two aspects of the conservatism of written language interact. The long-term dilemma for the communication economy of many Third World countries is that the chances for spreading exoglossic written languages and the chances for the coming into existence of efficient new endoglossic written languages are equally poor. The European written common languages have been adapted in the course of industrialization and modernization to the demands of contemporary communication requirements. They are thereby secured a lead in advance over most other languages which will be almost impossible to make up for.

The Role of the Writing System

One more aspect of written language and its consequences for language careers needs to be discussed here, the writing system. Ever since Diringer (1948) christened the alphabet a "democratic script" as opposed to the "theocratic scripts" of the ancient Near East, it has often been claimed that the alphabet was a breakthrough in the development of literary culture with revolutionary consequences both for language careers and the impact of literacy on economic and social life.[66] The argument underlying this view assumes a causal link between the structural make-up of writing systems and literacy levels achieved in the societies using them, taking the size of the inventory of basic signs as the critical variable. The alphabet's alleged simplicity is taken to be its major virtue, since it makes it easy to learn.

On the face of it, this would appear to be not only plausible but almost self-evident. Assuming that a given writing system A of complexity level X takes three years of systematic schooling to master, while another, B, of complexity level Y takes four years, it is to be expected that, everything else being equal, we will find a higher number of people who fail to master the task in the B-group than in the A-group. Hence we would have a direct correlation between the relative complexity of a writing system and the literacy rate of its users. How convincing is this assumption? In order to answer this question, it is necessary to scrutinize the argument more carefully and to consider the evidence. The basic claims on which the argument hinges are three. (1) It is assumed that the quality of writing systems is determined by structural properties, the basic unit of representation and the size of the inventory of basic signs that follows from it being considered crucial. (2) The fact that the alphabet prevailed over other writing systems is attributed to its quality in this regard, much as marketing experts will explain why a personal computer that is cheaper and weighs less will drive out a competing model which is heavier and more expensive. (3) Structural properties of the alphabet are credited with the exploitation of the socioeconomic and cultural potential of written language, because it is the alphabet alone that allows for the universal spread of literacy. Alphabetic literacy is, therefore, regarded as qualitatively different from literacy under the conditions of other writing systems.

Clearly, every one of these three points calls for criticism. The internal economy of the inventory of basic signs, to which we will have occasion to return for more detailed discussion in chapter 6, is a problematic yardstick for assessing the quality of writing systems. For one thing, it fails to specify for whom a writing system is good or better than another. A small set of signs is an advantage for learning a system, not necessarily for using it; the writer benefits much more from it than the reader. Moreover, the same number of letters can be used to form systems differing greatly in their respective complexity.

Even if we accept without further qualification that the alphabet is simpler than several other writing systems, this does not imply that the alphabet prevailed *because* of its simplicity and therefore marked a turning point in the history of humankind. Other factors are more important for the spread of writing systems, above all the principal functions written language serves to fulfill, those of trade, religion, and empire:

the maritime trade of the Phoenicians in the case of spreading their alphabet throughout the Mediterranean world; the Islamization of northern Africa and many parts of Asia in the case of the Arabic alphabet; and the consolidation of the empire of the Han in the case of the Chinese script, to mention but three prominent examples. This brings us to the most problematic part of the said argument, the alleged causal relationship between the internal economy of writing systems and the social diffusion of literacy and its impact on economic development.

That ancient Greece owed economic prosperity and cultural progress to the alphabet is doubtful. For, in spite of the often repeated claim that around Plato's time writing was diffused through the population,[67] we do not really know how widely literacy was spread or whether the level of reading and writing skills was higher than in Babylon with its cuneiform script, which in the sense under discussion was doubtless more difficult and less economic than the Greek alphabet. The laws of King Hammurapi were chiseled in stone for public display proclaiming:

> The man who has been wronged, who has a grievance, let him come before my statue, "King of Justice," and read forth my inscribed stele and hear my precious words, and let my stele show him the grievance. (quoted from Powell 1981: 436)

From this it cannot of course be concluded that everyone in Babylon could read and write, as we already noted above; but the literacy level must have been high enough for everyone to have access to the written language, at least indirectly, and thus make it possible and meaningful to commit the entire population to the letter of the law which could be inspected and appealed to without guidance or consent of the authority. In this sense Oppenheim (1957: 28) can call Babylon "a literate civilization." There is no evidence to suggest that the civilization of classical Greece was on a higher level in this regard. Hence, we have to put aside as mere speculation this variety of the claim that writing systems are more or less successful, according to their relative complexity, in producing mass literacy and thereby promoting socioeconomic development.

More or less the same argument has also been advanced from the opposite direction, that is, while the alphabet is credited with speeding up development if not causing it, other writing systems are blamed for blocking it. The Chinese script in particular has often been made responsible for China's restricted literacy (e.g. DeFrancis 1950: 93;

Goody and Watt 1968). Thus, one of the foremost students of Chinese declares: "If [the Chinese] maintain the quintessentially Chinese system of characters as the exclusive means of writing, it seems certain that many if not most of the people will be doomed to perpetual illiteracy and that China's modernization will be seriously impeded" (DeFrancis 1984: 287). Again a causal relationship is construed between the complexity of a writing system and socioeconomic development, but the condemnation of the Chinese script in this version of the argument is hardly more credible than the praise heaped upon the alphabet in the other. The validity of DeFrancis' claim is most obviously called into question in Taiwan and Japan.[68] While the Japanese writing system is different in important respects from the Chinese, it is certainly not easier or more economic, and there can be no doubt that mastering written Japanese is a more formidable task than becoming literate in virtually any alphabetically written language. Yet, Japan had achieved a literacy level comparable to that of western European countries already by the mid-nineteenth century. Moreover, its complex writing system has evidently not hampered her advance to the very forefront of development. As for Taiwan, functional illiteracy is a marginal problem there today, whereas it still is a characteristic feature of China's rural population and is by no means eradicated in the cities. In this regard China differs little from India where much easier writing systems have been in use for many centuries. The complicated Chinese and Japanese writing system which make written language more difficult to process, have no more stood in the way of economic and technological progress in Taiwan or Japan than the simple Indic systems have helped to push it ahead.

Considering the evidence, the argument that links structural features of writing systems with socioeconomic developments does not hold water, whichever way we turn it. What is crucial for effecting economic and social changes is the written language, not the writing system. Whether or not the potential of written language can be fully exploited depends on a variety of factors of which the writing system does not seem to be one, not an important one anyway.

For this reason it must also be denied that structural features of writing systems have a crucial influence on the carrying-on of a literary tradition and hence the perpetuation of a language. Powell (1981: 43f.) has rightly criticized the prevailing view that cuneiform as a system of writing declined and was eventually abolished because it was less practical and less easily learned than the alphabet. In his view, the role the alphabet played in the history of literacy has been hitherto as much overrated as that of cuneiform has been underrated. Mass literacy is a function of economic development, not vice versa.

The idea that structural features of the various writing systems have a bearing on the diffusion of a literary tradition and, through it, the chances for the continuation of a language has a parallel with respect to the linguistic system; that is, the notion that structural features of languages have a bearing on their competitiveness and hence on their careers. This raises the question of whether there is a relationship between the external and internal economy of language, that is, between the functions, the fulfilling of which makes a language useful, and the systematic properties allowing it to fulfill them. When our century was still young, the great linguist Otto Jespersen thought he knew the answer. About the emerging world language he remarked: "It would be unreasonable to suppose, as is sometimes done, that the cause of the enormous propagation of the English language is to be sought in its intrinsic merits" (Jespersen 1926: 228). Whether in this intricate question his lucid words can stand without qualification is the subject of the next chapter.

6

Economy in Language:
Economic Aspects of the Language System

That language is said to have its own economy and that linguistic means are employed more or less economically, has been understood occasionally as merely a coincidental equivocation of the term "economy." This chapter is an attempt to demonstrate that this is a misconception. It is argued that there is more than a coincidental interrelationship between linguistic economy and the economics of language.

Language as such is a prerequisite of social life and every language is the product of social life. Economics is the quest for parameters of optimizing the efficiency of means—ends relations in performing tasks. Since all languages are used purposefully as means towards certain ends, every language can be assessed with regard to its virtues for achieving these ends and thus be subjected to an economic analysis of the kind that, as one economist has called it, belongs to the normative branch of communication economics, that is, the "search for communication systems best suited to a given scale of values" (Marschak 1965: 136). This branch of communication economics and, by implication, the economics of language, is normative inasmuch as it deals with ideal rather than real systems. Investigations are concerned with features a language should have in order to meet certain requirements as defined, for example, by a stated language policy.

The economics of language also deals with actual systems. Its central concern here is with the question why individual languages are as they are, that is, why certain features have prevailed, while others have not. Although this approach evaluates real rather than projected systems, it is concerned with basically the same kind of parameters, namely those which determine the viability of a system. Viability conditions are hence not different in kind from efficiency conditions. In this sense, the question of the viability of a language can be understood as an economic question.

External and Internal Economy of Language

As should have become evident in the previous chapter, individual language careers interact in manifold ways with economic processes. On several occasions we came across interconnections between (extra-linguistic) factors of the economics of language and (linguistic) factors of the economy of language, without, however, discussing these connections at length. To recapitulate only the most conspicuous examples, the emergence and regression of languages mark extreme points not only in their external sociocommunicative development, but also in their internal structural development. Where contact between speakers of different languages is restricted as, for example, in sporadic trade across linguistic boundaries, the fact that little is communicated has a correlate in the restricted expressive power of the code that is being used, which is, perhaps, a language in the making. Conversely, the regression of a language which is being stripped of its economic foundations of use, finds expression not only in the fact that its speech community dwindles, but also in the expressive impoverishment of the code, which is, perhaps, a language on the way out.

Proceeding from these extremes, it would seem reasonable to look for other connections between the socioeconomic conditions of the use of languages and their internal structural properties. Some of the questions that suggest themselves in this regard are as follows:

Is there any correlation between the size of a speech community and the size of the lexicon of its language,[1] and if so, what is the nature of the correlation?

Do structural features of languages have any bearing on their competitiveness in the world market of languages?

Or conversely, do the economic necessities which demarcate the fundamentals of human existence determine the structure of possible languages, defining ideal types which are approximated by real languages?

Do writing systems or orthographies affect the survival chances of languages?

Is there any connection in language contact situations between the relationship of donor and recipient languages, on the one hand, and the economic relationship between their respective speakers, on the other?

Do changing communication and documentation practices conditioned by economic developments engender new functional requirements to which languages must adapt, thus influencing their development?

From these and similar considerations one general question can be extracted: Does not the fact that languages are a factor of the economy imply an economic rationale underlying their internal logic of operation, and hence an interrelation between the external and internal economy of language? In what follows arguments are presented for answering this question in the affirmative.

Economic Notions in Linguistics

Linguistics is literally unthinkable without economic concepts. This has been argued emphatically by Bourdieu (1977, 1982) among others, and already at the beginning of our considerations concerning the exchange of material and intellectual goods in chapter 1, it became apparent that at many points the analysis of linguistic communication draws on that of economic interaction. Referring once again to these metaphorical points of contact we will now inspect the most important economic notions that the science of language has requisitioned for its own purposes and examine their contents and the reasons for their employment.

Value

Two linguistic notions of value can be distinguished, both of which are metaphorically derived from the original economic notion, though they differ in content. A first differentiation to be made is that between a descriptive and a normative notion. The former refers to language as a symbolic system, the latter to language as a social institution. Accordingly, the descriptive notion of value can be assigned to linguistics proper, while its normative counterpart belongs to the conceptual equipment of various disciplines dealing with the use of language by society. We will here single out only two of them, language criticism and the investigation of language attitudes. In both cases the concern is with the evaluation of language, the object being linguistic products in

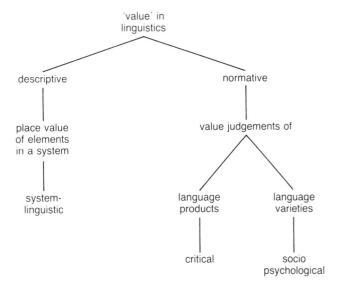

Figure 6.1   The notion of value in linguistics.

the former and linguistic features as indices of social identity in the latter. These various applications of the notion of value in linguistics are summarized in figure 6.1 and further explained in the sequel.

Place Value in the Linguistic System   The descriptive notion of value as defined by Saussure is a cornerstone of structuralist linguistics. To him "language is only a system of pure values" (Saussure 1974: 111), a structure characterized by the relationships between its components, each of which is defined negatively by being that which all the others are not. Every element enters into relationships with others in systematic ways determining how it can be connected with or replaced by them. These relations are characteristic of all levels of the linguistic system. Saussure, whose ideas we already had occasion to discuss in chapter 1 (see p. 9f. above), explains his notion of value by considering the question of what a word is.

> A word can be exchanged for something dissimilar, an idea; besides, it can be compared with something of the same nature, another word. Its value is therefore not fixed so long as one simply states that it can be "exchanged" for a given concept, i.e. that it has this or that signification: one must also compare it with similar values, with other words that stand

in opposition to it. Its content is really fixed only by the concurrence of everything that exists outside it. Being part of a system, it is endowed not only with a signification but also and especially with a value, and this is something quite different. (1974: 115)[2]

Saussure's notion of value is value-neutral, not in the sense that it refers to a value scale rather than to one of its extreme points, but in the sense that it is not related to a value scale at all. A more appropriate term for the notion of value in the Saussurean sense is "place value" which, instead of referring to the evaluation of linguistic elements against a given standard, captures the systematic nature of language, namely the fact that every linguistic element obtains its functions only from the relationships into which it enters.

In this sense of systematic place value, Saussure's notion has been applied in various branches of linguistics. Trubetzkoy defined phonology as a theory of "abstractive values." "Above all these values are relationships, oppositions, etc., non-material objects, that is, which cannot be perceived or investigated by means of the sense of hearing or touch" (Trubetzkoy 1958: 16). The whole point of his phonology is to determine the phonematic values of linguistic sounds in individual languages which are to be described phonetically by means of universal features.[3] Trubetzkoy refers to mother-tongue interference in foreign language learning in order to explain the difference between language-specific values and universal features. This phenomenon illustrates that the correct articulatory realization of a foreign speech sound does not by itself guarantee its proper use, unless its place value in the foreign sound system is recognized and applied whenever the sound in question is to be contrasted or identified with others, rather than using it in accordance with the place value it has in the native sound system.

It is not enough to adjust the speech organs to a new articulation, one has to also adjust one's phonological consciousness to correctly assign to this new articulation its monophonematic or polyphonematic value (Trubetzkoy, 1958: 59).

Other disciplines of the humanities, cultural anthropology and sociology in particular,[4] have borrowed the structuralist abstractive notion of value from Trubetzkoy's phonology. What, if anything, is there that it shares with the economic notion of value?

To Saussure, who must get a hearing here once again, "value" was far from being merely a label borrowed from the terminology of economics and provided with a contents all of its own. On the contrary, we must assume that he basically saw only one concept which, he explained, had a role to play both in political economics and linguistics.

> Both sciences are concerned with a *system for equating things of different orders* – labor and wages in one and a signified and signifier in the other. (Saussure 1974: 79)[5]

Further, Saussure recognized in the difference between political economics and economic history an exact parallel of the distinction between diachronic and synchronic linguistics which he considered so important.

> For a science concerned with value the distinction is a practical necessity and sometimes an absolute one. In these fields scholars cannot organize their research rigorously without considering both coordinates and making a distinction between the system of values per se and the same values as they relate to time. (1974: 80)[6]

Saussure's strict divorce of system and change in language belongs to those aspects of his teaching which have been criticized most severely. That historical linguistics ought to be a discipline in its own right is less controversial in this regard than that an abstract system of language as such, without any temporal coordinates, should be considered the proper subject matter of synchronic linguistics. The crucial question is whether a model that does justice to its object, language, can be construed at all where the dimension of time is left out of consideration, that is, whether it is possible under these conditions to correlate historical and systematic descriptions of language. With his notion of "diachrony within synchrony" Coseriu (1974) has convincingly argued against the assumption that the systematic place value of a linguistic sign can be determined on a purely synchronic basis, or rather, a-chronically. For this approach repeats a mistake for which the proponents of a synchronic structuralist linguistics criticized historical comparative linguistics, namely the mistake of abstracting from essentials, though in this case the essential in question is not the systematic but the historical context of the linguistic sign. Similarly, variation linguistics of the Labovian kind insists on incorporating into the systematic analysis of linguistic signs the dimension of value changes, thus recognizing their historical depth, without, however, denying that the objective of historical linguistics is not the same as that of systematic linguistics.

In the economic sciences similar conditions obtain. To be sure, economic history is concerned with questions quite different from those pursued in economics. However, the latter, while focussing on the systematic interrelations between resources, production, prices, the distribution of wealth and income, and other factors shaping economic events, cannot disregard completely the historical framework within which these factors interact, precisely because it deals with values, and with variations in values, at that. How economic value systems – say, the currency and stock markets – work is impossible to explain without referring to value fluctuations, gains and losses, and to this end, time has to be taken into account. This is what might be called the diachrony within the synchrony of economics. As W. Kula has written, "the notion that economic history is a science of the past and economics a science of the present just won't bear scrutiny."[7] All value systems are mental entities and hence bound to time, as are those who create or adhere to them. Even non-historical analyses of value systems, therefore, cannot disregard time.

Value Judgments of Linguistic Expressions   A normative notion of value comes to bear in linguistics when language is analyzed as a social institution. The fundamental fact to which sociolinguistics owes its existence is that the heterogeneous realizations of linguistic expression are indicative of social differentiation, mapping social hierarchies and thus functioning, in Halliday's (1978) terms, as a system of "social semiotic." Since the use of different speech forms or varieties defines social groups, these varieties are associated with social values determining status, stigma, and standard.

Social structures are basically hierarchical in nature, which implies that their reflection in language can be related to value scales. As the investigation of language attitudes has demonstrated in many studies, value judgments of speech varieties in accordance with socionormative (right – wrong), aesthetic (pleasing to the ear – ugly), or pragmatic (plain – incomprehensible) value scales, typically cover social prejudices, on one hand, and speaker status, on the other.[8] However, and this is what makes language attitude research difficult and interesting, evaluations of speech varieties are not fixed in time or across groups of speakers. A case in point is the Saxon dialect which, within a few generations, underwent a dramatic deterioration of its social value from the most prestigious to the most despised and ridiculed German dialect. And at a given point in time, what for one social group is a prestige form to be aimed at, for another group may be a socially unacceptable variety to be avoided (Halliday 1978: 156). Finally, in-group and out-group evaluations of speech varieties also vary.

The phenomenon of social evaluation of speech forms is of considerable importance for all linguists working with empirical data, because the assumed or actual prestige value of a given variety can influence the authenticity of speech samples. In this connection, Löffler (1985: 46) has pointed out that too little attention has been paid to the problem of how evaluations of speech varieties on the part of their speakers can be measured, a problem which "so far, has been wrongly relegated to the corners of sociopsychological and commercial-demoscopic research."

In the field of linguistic criticism, twentieth-century linguists have adopted a very restrained posture. While in earlier times language cultivation was one of the main concerns of those dealing scientifically with language, especially in the context of the formation of the European common languages, it is, for reasons not to be discussed at this point, no longer considered proper for linguists to engage in such a pursuit. The generally accepted and undoubtedly reasonable principle that discovering the norms underlying language must have priority over stipulating the norms guiding its use, as well as the well-founded criticism of allegedly objective (but too often ideologically motivated) standards of goodness such as purity, elegance, and perfection, have led most linguists to turn away from applying the means of their own discipline to the search for criteria that will enable a critical evaluation of language. Yet, without a foundation of linguistic criticism in linguistics, language planning is doomed to remain a more or less arbitrary endeavor. It is of practical importance, therefore, to confront the question of what linguistics has to contribute to a rational foundation of value judgments about language.

Actually, language evaluation is a very common activity, practiced as a matter of daily routine not only by teachers, but also by compilers of dictionaries, newspaper editors, and other "censors" of printed products. By refusing to take part in the difficult search for standards of evaluating language, linguists adopt too simple a position. They should instead accept the responsibility that follows upon their expertise, since they have a better understanding of why languages change and how they adapt to changing requirements. As will become more evident below, an analysis of the various levels of the language system in terms of linguistic economy can reveal which of its systematic properties lend themselves to optimizing the efficiency of a language as a system of communication and should hence be evaluated positively in language criticism. The point here is not to champion efficiency at the expense of other (for example, aesthetic) value scales. It is rather to make sure that in normative decisions, which are informed by a whole cluster of different values, functionally valuable properties are recognized so that they can be taken into account for what they are.

Function (Work)

Functionalism is one of the important schools of thought in linguistics, and although *function* is too general a term to bear any specifically economic connotations, one of the principal works of functionalism started out from an economic concept. This is Karl Bühler's book *Sprachtheorie* (1934) which, though less well-known and translated into English only in 1990, is no less profound than Saussure's *Cours*. Bühler's concern was with incorporating the theory of language into a psychological theory. His lead question was what the linguistic sign does, how it works, rather than what it is. At the center of his theory of language is what is known as the "organon model" of the linguistic sign which is analyzed as a tool with three basic functions, expression, appeal, and representation (Bühler 1934: 28). These functions belong to situated speech rather than the linguistic system in the abstract.

Bühler's notion of functions of the linguistic sign is inconspicuous to the English reader, although the term *function* captures very well what Bühler had in mind, except that it does not carry the economic connotations of the German word *Leistung* of which it is the translation. *Leistung* is a household word in German with a wide range of meanings including "achievement," "performance," "output," "work," "power," and "efficiency." *Leistung* has decidedly economic overtones, indeed, the underlying concept is first and foremost an economic concept.

Bühler's axiomatic theory was not the first attempt or the last to establish a theory of language with the notion of *Leistung* as its foundation. Humboldt's interpretation of language as *energeia* (Greek "activity, power") is a close cognate which was further elaborated by Leo Weisgerber (1962) who however, unlike Bühler, focussed on the language system rather than the speech act. Directly related to Bühler's theory is Roman Jakobson's model of language functions. Although it is more differentiated than the organon model, posing six instead of

Bühler's three functions, it pursues the same approach of capturing the essence of language by analyzing how it works and what it achieves.

Production

The actual realization of speech is also often analyzed in terms of instrumental functions. The linguistic sign process is seen as requiring mental and physical work: planning the contents and structure of the utterance and modulating the voice to form speech sounds. Taken together, these activities enable the production of linguistic signs, a process which is executed in real time and thus subject to the constraints of natural laws. What, in Bühler's sense, language does, it can do only inasmuch as linguistic signs are materialized, that is, given a material form as tokens of the types they embody. The necessary phases of speech production are characterized by the principle of maximizing efficiency. On the level of brain work which does not lend itself easily to experimental investigation,[9] the necessary effort is assumed to be expended in accordance with a "minimax principle" which is explained as follows.

> The speaker attempts to minimize the surface structural complexity of the utterance while maximizing the information communicated to the listener. It is obviously in the speaker's interest to communicate effectively while not unnecessarily burdening himself in the process. (Bever, Carroll, and Hurtig 1977: 168)

What these authors consider obvious is the equilibration of the two basic needs the linguistic sign process must fulfill in communication, those of the speaker and those of the hearer. Simplifications, abbreviations, reductions and losses of inflexions, and similar processes which facilitate speech but, at the same time, potentially interfere with comprehensibility,[10] demonstrate that these needs of coding and decoding do not coincide.

Optimizing production also means minimizing effort; for from a physiological point of view the production of speech sounds is work that consumes energy. Certain aspects of the functioning of the speech apparatus suggest that the principle of least effort, to which we shall return in a different context below (pp. 235f.), played a significant role in its evolution. Like all mechanisms, the speech apparatus needs a supply of energy to be activated. The source of energy of the speech apparatus is an organ which, by maintaining the oxygen exchange in the blood, primarily fulfills an essential function in keeping the body alive; only secondarily do the lungs function for activating the speech apparatus.[11] Although it is physically possible to talk as breath is being taken in, this is not what typically happens. Rather, the body first secures the supply of oxygen and only uses the act of disposing of the waste products for operating the speech mechanism.

The power for speech thus comes from exhalation, a process which is coordinated minutely with the mental side of speech production (Fry 1977: 23f.). The average rate of quiet breathing is about 15 breaths per minute with inhalation and exhalation taking roughly the same amount of time. In speech the rhythm of breathing changes, because otherwise continuous speech would be impossible. In order to prevent interruption of the stream of speech, the rhythm of breathing is altered in such a way that the moments at which breath is taken in are made to coincide with syntactic junctions of the utterance, that is, they are synchronized with the structure of the utterance. This means that the control of respiration is guided by the mental planning of the utterance structure, both in terms of the energy supply of the speech apparatus and in terms of the time spent for producing utterances; a very economic procedure indeed.

Economy

On the level of the language system too, economy has often been topicalized, or rather, emphasized as a formative principle, an economy of the formal means used for representing a given meaning. Paul dedicated one of the best chapters of his major work to it, entitled Sparsamkeit im Ausdruck ("economy of expression"). He reflects:

> Whether linguistic means are employed economically or more copiously depends on the needs. It cannot be denied that these means are often used extravagantly. However, by and large, our speech bears the features of a certain thriftiness.[12]

So far, his considerations refer to speech, the contextual and situational needs at hand to which the utterance must be adjusted. Yet, Paul never loses sight of the interconnection of speech and the language system, and the formation of the latter by the former. Hence he continues:

> Everywhere forms of expressions must evolve containing no more than is required by their comprehensibility to the hearer.[13]

In his discussion of economy of expression, Paul treats a number of phenomena which are hard unequivocally to assign to the level of the language system or to language use and, therefore, expose the problematic nature of their analytic distinction. Central to his thoughts about mechanisms located somewhere between grammar, stylistics, and the analysis of situated speech are ellipsis (Greek *elleipsis*, "lack") and completion which demonstrate that grammaticalized elliptic constructions are a sediment of the completion of the sense of utterances by their contextual environment and their embedding in a speech situation.

Much like Paul, Jespersen assigns economy of expression a central role in his thinking about the nature of language. In his opinion, language change is essentially a manifestation of the universal tendency towards economy of effort.[14] In contradistinction to Paul, however, Jespersen (1924: 263f.) was concerned mostly with the language system. Interlinguistic comparison reveals that grammatical means such as tense and case are made use of more or less economically. Case marking in German, for instance, which applies to noun, article, and attribute, is in this sense uneconomical.

Theories of linguistic economy such as those by Paul and Jespersen have been criticized occasionally. Moser (1971), for example, charged that they rested on a conception of humanity where *homo ludens* and *homo cogitans* have to play second fiddle to a domineering *homo faber*. Linguistic evolution, he maintained, is not driven exclusively by improving the utility of the tool language. At the same time, Moser (1971: 91) remarked that: "the phenomenon of linguistic economy has been paid relatively little attention," a shortcoming he sought to correct by proposing a typology of kinds of linguistic economy. Surprisingly, Moser never mentions the most important work in this field of inquiry, George Kingsley Zipf's book of 1949. Yet he is indebted to it indirectly through Martinet whose work he does acknowledge. Moser distinguishes three kinds of linguistic economy. They are

1   the tendency to use linguistic means sparingly and thus reduce the physical and mental effort necessary for producing speech, as well as for elaborating and adjusting linguistic means;
2   the striving for improving the efficiency of linguistic means;
3   the trend towards levelling regional and social norm differences in order better to meet communication demands (Moser 1971: 92).

In the above (1) refers to the economy of the language system, (2) to the economy of information transfer, and (3) to an economical expansion of the range of a standard language. Moser fails to explain why he sees the requirements of *homo ludens* and *homo cogitans* with regard to language at variance with those of *homo faber*, that is, why linguistic economy should not also be conducive to thinking and aesthetics. He suggests that the striving for economy in language will never attain its goal, because natural language is "a collective product" (*Kollektivgebilde*) constructed by many who, sometimes, work in opposite directions' (Moser 1971: 116). From this it does not, however, necessarily follow that the speech of some members of the community will undermine or counteract the tendency toward greater linguistic economy. For, as Moser (1971: 113) points out himself, the economy of the linguistic system has a counterpart in the economy of learning which is of utmost importance in handing down a language from one generation to the next.

Evaluation and the Lex Parsimoniae

Every language allows for a variety of analytic descriptions. No one has taken the selection of the correct one more seriously than Chomsky who made this the critical issue of linguistic methodology. For him this decision has to be made on rational grounds, for which Chomsky has proposed formalized evaluation procedures using simplicity and elegance of description as his main criteria.

The simplicity criterion is a new variation on an old theme, the *lex parsimoniae* proposed by the Schoolmen which demands economy in theory formation.[15] Its significance for Chomsky's theory of language lies in his conception of the relationship between meta-theory and language description. Different answers are conceivable to the meta-theoretical question of what a grammar should describe. Chomsky's unusual and original answer is that in order to fulfill the requirement of explanatory adequacy, a grammar must map the functioning of the language acquisition device.

> The problem of internal justification – of explanatory adequacy – is essentially the problem of constructing a theory of language acquisition, an account of the specific innate abilities that make this achievement possible. (Chomsky 1965: 27)

Chomsky thus defines the grammarian's task as that of reconstructing what children accomplish when acquiring their first language, that is, forming hypotheses about the grammar of the language on the basis of the linguistic data to which they are exposed, in order to discover the underlying system. Whether there really is a specific language acquisition device as opposed to the more general cognitive architecture, including the capacity to learn, with which human beings are naturally equipped, is none of our concern here, but the assumption of such a device by Chomsky reveals the great importance attributed in his theory to the law of parsimony. It is one thing to prefer one theory to another because of its simplicity, as has been common practice since Scholasticism. There can be various reasons for doing so concerning, for example, aesthetics or the comprehensibility of the theory. But it is something quite different to link the simplicity postulate with the claim that the relatively greater simplicity of the theory has a correlate in reality and is hence demanded by reality. This is exactly what Chomsky does by postulating that a grammar should represent the rules that are operative in the language acquisition device. To him this an empirical question:

> A proposed simplicity measure . . . constitutes a hypothesis concerning the nature of such a device. Choice of a simplicity measure is therefore an empirical matter with empirical consequences. (1965: 38).

This evidently implies the assumption that the language acquisition device will in any event follow the simplest, most economical path, to reconstruct which is the grammarian's business. Thus the reason why the simplest grammatical description is theoretically preferable is that it represents reality more faithfully, the reality that human beings have a tendency to look for the simplest solution to the tasks with which they are confronted and thereby to maximize the efficiency of their effort.

The discussion of economic concepts in linguistics could easily be continued. Notions such as "productivity," "borrowing," "language needs," "language processing," "the treasury of words," among others, originate from the terminology of economics just like "value" (*valeur*), "function" (*Leistung*), "production," "economy," and "evaluation," the ones here discussed. They are manifest proof of the fact that economic notions have an important role to play on every relevant level of linguistic theory, reducing, as they do, the question of why this is so, to a rhetorical question. The answer is evident: because the subject matter requires it. Rationalists and empiricists, ideationalists and materialists, hard-core grammarians and variationists, in short, linguists of all theoretical affiliations use economic notions because they cannot dispense with them. Language system and language use, language change and language acquisition expose the characteristics of a tool which to acquire and use human beings as a species must economize their effort in the interest of survival. How this fundamental condition is reflected in systematic properties of language is the subject of the following pages.

Economy in Language

The Principle of Least Effort

The most comprehensive attempt to date to explain the economy intrinsic to language and to relate it to a general ecological theory of human behavior is Zipf's book *Human Behavior and the Principle of Least Effort* (1949). Though famous, it has not been taken seriously enough in the linguistic sciences. Zipf's ambitious goal was to present convincing evidence for his conviction that "every individual's entire behavior is governed by the Principle of Least Effort" (Zipf 1949: 6). This venture cannot be appreciated properly if it is put aside without thorough inspection as a utilitarianistic reduction of the human nature to laziness and apathy or, perhaps somewhat less disparagingly, to optimizing chances of survival. Rather, it must be recalled that in Zipf's theory, minimizing effort does not mean the tendency to expend as little work as possible at any moment, but that a *"person's average rate of work-expenditure over time"* (1949: 6) is minimized. Zipf thus reckons with foresight and the ability to expend work in order to save work at a later time. He also acknowledges the possibility of miscalculation, that is, an expenditure of energy which is not balanced by an anticipated energy saving. In the long run, however, he sees the Principle of Least Effort being effective in a process of adaptive evolution.

An essential aspect of this adaptation consists in developing suitable instruments for the objectives at hand as well as employing existing instruments for pursuing the objectives for which they are suitable. Instruments must be matched to objectives and vice versa. Adaptation then also means to improve the functionality of instruments and to facilitate access to them in such a way that the necessary effort of handling them is minimized.

To illustrate this abstract principle, Zipf refers to the concrete example of the tools on a carpenter's work-bench. Working with tools involves not only operating them but also the work that is necessary for their procurement, maintenance, and modification. For every individual carpenter and for carpentry as a craft the Principle of Least Effort will have the result that the most frequently used tool will be subject to most modifications, making it the tool that is smallest, lightest, and easiest to handle. There is thus an economy of increasing the frequency of use of the easiest tool, which will be that which has been most often redesigned. Another consequence will be that all tools will be arranged on the work bench in such a way that distance from the carpenter's hand is inversely related to frequency of use: the least frequently used tool will have its place at the greatest distance from the working hand. A certain feedback effect comes to bear here, inasmuch as the carpenter will tend to use most that tool which is nearest, since reaching for the tool is an energy-consuming part of the total work-usage.

Use of a number of different tools in accordance with the Principle of Least Effort can be illustrated if it is assumed, for simplicity's sake, that the work of using a tool consists of the work of moving it once from its place on the work-bench to the carpenter's lap and back to its place on the bench. Work, w, is then equal to the product of the mass of the tool, m, multiplied by the distance between the tool's place on the bench and the carpenter's lap, d. If f is the frequency of use of a tool r during a fixed time period of measurement, then the total work-usage of this tool for that time period, w_r, is equivalent to the product of its f, m, and d. This is what Zipf (1949: 59) calls the "minimum equation of arrangement:"

$$w_r = f \times m \times d$$

In order to organize work in the carpenter's shop following the Principle of Least Effort, the sum of the products $f \times m \times d$ for each of the n tools must be minimized. An additional factor to be taken into account is the size of the tools, s, for the smaller the tools, the more closely they can be arranged on the bench, which translates into a reduced distance from the carpenter's lap and hence a reduced total work expenditure. There is hence an economy in a small size.

As for the economy of f, the Principle of Least Effort demands an increase in the frequency of use of that tool whose product of m and d is smallest, which in turn implies that this tool should be modified in such a way that it can absorb jobs of other tools, thereby increasing its own frequency of use still more. This relationship which Zipf has called the Law of Abbreviation says that m, d, and s are correlated positively with each other and negatively with f, that is, in the arrangement of the tools on the work-bench, the tools' mass, size, and distance from the working hand increase, while their frequency of use decreases.

Further, another consequence of applying the Principle of Least Effort to working with tools is the Law of Diminishing Returns of Tools (1949: 66). It concerns the total number n of tools on the carpenter's bench. Since n is related to d – every additional tool pushes the farthest tool further down the bench – there is an economy in keeping n small, if not reducing its size. Though a new tool can be useful for certain jobs, the addition of every new tool also has a negative effect on the work economy of the shop which must be averted or redressed; for the greater the size of n, the smaller the advantage of an additional tool.[16] It is possible to reduce n by increasing the functionality of individual tools and by combining several tools to do the job of a very specialized tool in accordance to what Zipf called the Principle of the Economical Permutation of Tools. In this context "permutation" means combining a tool with another in a non-arbitrary way. Permutation correlates with distance which is to say that the tools closest to the carpenter's hand will enter into permutations most frequently thereby absorbing functions of more distant tools and making some of them superfluous. An immediate consequence of this for the durability of a tool is that the carpenter is less likely to part with a tool that is used and permutated frequently than with others less frequently used. This implies as a general tendency that frequent usage correlates with age, for the value of keeping any given tool is directly related to its relative frequency of usage. Any given tool is used frequently either because the job it does occurs frequently or because its versatility allows it to do a great variety of jobs. In any event, frequency of usage correlates with utility.

Of course, the number and variety of jobs to which a tool can be adapted and which can be performed by permutating existing tools are not unlimited. In spite of the Law of Diminishing Returns, it would be counter-intuitive for n to approximate 1 which would mean that only a single polyfunctional tool will be left; and conversely, it is unlikely that, in order to keep n small, the number and complexity of the permutations of a given tool can be increased indefinitely. Both of these aspects, that is, the number of jobs for which a given tool can be used and the permutations into which it enters with others in order to perform additional jobs, may be summarized under the notion of the *functional load of a tool*. The Principle of Least Effort dictates for every tool that its functional load will be increased only to the extent that the total work to be done in the shop will thereby be reduced. If a permutation is so complex that its execution consumes more energy than is necessary for producing a new tool, and if it is easier to produce and use a new tool for a given job than to redesign an existing one, the new tool will prevail in the workshop. The Principle of Least Effort demands that a balance be struck between the tendency to reduce the number of tools and the necessity of keeping the functional load of every tool manageable. Put differently, for every n there will be an ideal constellation of tools with higher and lower functional loads, where the former are at the same time the smallest, lightest, most frequently used, and oldest tools.

Zipf's theory, which he needed a lengthy monograph to unfold, cannot be explained here in due detail. This brief recapitulation must suffice as an introduction to his approach, and its significance to language will become apparent in the following sections. After discussing some of the phenomena which most clearly testify to how language is affected by the Principle of Least Effort, we shall return once again to the issue of whether and how external and internal economy of language are interrelated.

Abundance and Thrift in the Lexicon

Let us begin with a simple question: Why is it that the lexicons of all languages are not equal in size? Even if the assumption implicit in this question is granted, its impact will be softened immediately upon recalling the notorious difficulties encountered in the seemingly simple business of counting words. A conceivable answer to our question would then be that differences in the size of the lexicons of different languages are due to the vagueness of the notion of what a word is, on one hand, and to differing criteria for identifying words, on the other. It is also well known that the division of labor between grammar and lexicon is subject to ample variation across individual languages and language families. That one language possesses more words than another, therefore, does not mean very much, because both can yet be equally efficient and on a par as regards expressive power, if "expressive power" is defined as verbalizing a given content at a given expenditure of energy. However, is it really possible then to do away with our initial question by withdrawing to such a relativistic position?

Leibniz acknowledged the importance of lexical differentiation.

> Richness is what is of principal importance in language, and it consists
> in an abundance rather than a scarcity of adequate and forceful words

suitable for all occasions, in order that everything can be represented vigorously and properly and depicted in living colors, as it were.[17]

Leibniz was fully aware of the problems of counting words and thus assessing the relative wealth of the lexicon of a language, but he also pointed out a way of dealing with it, namely language comparison by means of translation:

> The true touchstone of a language's abundance or scarcity is found in translating good books from other languages into it. . . . Meantime, the richest and most adequate language is that which lends itself most easily to verbatim translation and is able to follow the original step by step.[18]

This method uncovers asymmetric relationships between any two languages where it is easier to translate from one into the other than in the opposite direction. For example, as Leibniz had noted, German suffered from a deficit in comparison with other European languages, which is why he made a plea for the deliberate enrichment of the German lexicon. Similarly, we can nowadays observe that many languages spoken in the pre-industrial world show a considerable lexical deficit in comparison with those European common languages which were serviceable in mastering the lexical needs generated by industrialization.

Hence, there are differences between the lexicons of different languages which are quite independent of the problem of segmentation. By using the orthographic word as the basic unit of comparison, we admittedly disregard a number of problems having to do with different writing systems,[19] writing conventions,[20] and lexicographical traditions.[21] Still Leibniz's method makes possible a comparison of the relative richness of the lexicons of different languages. The emerging differences can be accounted for and even predicted on the basis of the functional demands that different languages have to meet. If an attempt has never been made to discuss problems of semiconductor technology in a language, it can be expected that it will lack the suitable vocabulary. There can be no doubt not only that different languages are confronted with different functional demands, but also that the ranges of functional demands vary across languages.

This is of some importance with respect to the validity of the Law of Diminishing Returns referred to above in the realm of language. It predicts scarcity rather than abundance in the repertoire of lexical tools, because the extra benefit of every additional item decreases steadily. The

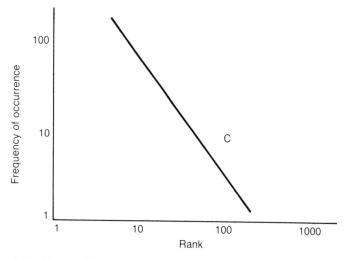

Figure 6.2   The Zipf function of rank-frequency distribution. (Adapted from
Zipf 1949: 85.)

validity of this law, however, is not absolute but relative to the jobs at
hand. The fact that the lexicons of individual languages differ in size
thus does not mean that the economic aspect of the tool analogy does
not apply to the lexicon, but rather that the total amount of work that
speakers must be able to accomplish with linguistic means is not the
same for all languages. This is most clearly evidenced by the enormous
lexical growth in recent decades characteristic of all modern common
languages. The relevant question, therefore, is not that of how many
tools are needed in order to be able to verbally communicate, but the
more specific question of how many tools are needed in order to be able
to accomplish a given total of communicative work efficiently by means
of language. Assuming that the Law of Diminishing Returns is valid
and hence equally effective in all languages, it can then be expected that
lexicons of different languages (at any given point in time) differ in size.
Nevertheless, lexicons are structured following an internal economy of
which the Law of Diminishing Returns is a part. This is revealed by
certain statistical properties of lexicons and the usage of their elements.

  One relationship which is of particular importance is what has come
to be known as Zipf's Law. Based upon observations by Estoup (1916),
Zipf was able to demonstrate that the relationship between a word's
frequency of occurrence, *f*, and its rank on a frequency scale for a given

corpus, r, is always approximately the same for all texts and for all languages. The function $f \times r$ is in other words a constant which can be represented graphically as a declining curve as in figure 6.2. What it says is that there are a small number of high-frequency words and a large number of words with a low frequency of occurrence.

Zipf has tested this function across a wide variety of culturally distant and genetically unrelated languages including Gothic, Nootka, Plains Cree, Chinese, Old English, and German. Other scholars followed in his footsteps checking the validity of his law against yet other languages,[22] and proposed certain refinements and modifications.[23] But on the whole, testing results have been so remarkably uniform that it is justified to regard the function as a law.

The constant distribution of rank on a frequency scale and the frequency of occurrence of lexical items across languages can be interpreted as testifying to the force of the Principle of Least Effort. It reflects the economically ideal relationship between the total number of words in a text corpus – i.e., the word tokens expended for a given total of communicative work – and the frequencies of occurrence of all words types in the corpus – i.e., the number of times each tool is used.

The tool analogy is further supported by a correlation that holds between polysemy and frequency of occurrence of lexical items. In the analogy, orthographic words correspond to tools and their meanings to the jobs for which the tools are suitable. Now it hardly comes as a surprise that words with more than one meaning should occur more frequently than those with a single meaning only, or conversely, that it is the more frequent words which are associated with several meanings. But it is an interesting aspect of the internal economy of language, which is far from being self-evident and could not have been uncovered by structural analysis alone, that the statistical correlation between the number of different meanings of a word and its relative frequency of occurrence is a constant function with the number of different meanings of a word being equal to the square root of its frequency (Zipf 1949: 76).

Furthermore, Guiraud (1959) discovered a correlation between word length (measured in terms of number of letters or phonemes), l, and frequency, which also fits into the analogy. The shortest words are the most frequent ones: $l \times f = C$. Once again, the function is a constant, which implies that the most frequently occurring meanings are expressed by means of the shortest word forms.

The number of morpho-syntactic permutations into which a word form can enter also correlates positively with its frequency of occurrence. This correlation corresponds to the Principle of Economical Permutation of tools. It entails that a word form which can enter into a great number of formal permutations will also have a rich semantic potential.

In continuation of Zipf's work, Mandelbrot (1954) elaborated the theory and more explicitly exposed the significance of the above inter-relationships for communication economics. Using an operationalized concept of information, he introduced the notion of "minimizing the costs of communication" (*minimisation du coût*), taking into account the costs of both encoding and decoding. Starting out from the assumption that the "cost" of a word, with an information content which is held constant, increases with each additional letter or phoneme, Mandelbrot arrived at the conclusion that the rank-frequency distribution of words revealed in studies of the kind referred to above is ideal in an economic sense, that is, it is as it would be if a language were constructed from scratch according to the demands of communication economics. With Mandelbrot's improvements certain deviations from Zipf's rank-frequency function can be explained and subsumed under the Principle of Least Effort. He proposed that pragmatic conditions of communi-cation should be taken into account which may outweigh the dis-advantages of delay and increased effort brought about by using a long word more frequently than would be predicted by the constant, by offering additional advantages, for example, increased precision.[24] At the same time, this introduces an imponderable factor into the model which can explain cross-linguistic variations in the rank-frequency relation without calling the general validity of the underlying principle into doubt.

The said correlations of frequency, rank, length, number of mean-ings, and formal permutations of a word have an important dynamic aspect which has a bearing on the development of the lexicon. Whenever a new word enters the lexicon, its frequency of occurrence changes and it also changes its form, semantic potential, and permutability. There is a tendency toward abbreviation: *telephone* > *phone*, *omnibus* > *bus*, *refrigerator* > *fridge*, *high fidelity* > *hi-fi*, not the other way around. Another feature of structural economy on the lexical level is the ten-dency toward the unalterable word form. It enhances the permutability of words, as can be seen in English where it is further advanced than in other European languages. This tendency finds expression both in the fact that words can easily change their grammatical roles or parts of speech, e.g., *the baby*, *to baby*, and enter into a great variety of com-

binations, e.g., *baby-sit*, *babyish*, *babyhood*, *baby beef*, *baby grand*, etc.
The same tendency is at work in other languages too, for instance,
in Dutch and German, where Dutch with its reduced system of morphological case and gender occupies a position midway between English
and German which maintains the richest inflectional morphology. But
even in German certain developments such as the disappearing *-s* of the
partitive genitive – *eine Tasse Tee*, "a cup of tea", instead of *Tees* – as well
as that of the possessive genitive – *der Kurs des Dollar*, "the dollar rate" –
can be attributed to this tendency.

Changing a word's part of speech has an influence on its frequency of
occurrence and its permutability, for example, when an intransitive verb
is assigned an additional role as a transitive verb, as happened with
English *to walk* – *walk someone to the station*. Such an extension of its
functional potential makes a word more versatile.

Generally speaking, exploiting the possibilities for functional
extension, simplification, abbreviation, and systematization wherever
they arise is part of the continuous adaptation of the lexicon to its users'
communicative needs. Considered in isolation, the truncation of *omnibus*
to *bus* and the valency expansion of *to walk* are rather trivial phenomena,
to be sure; but as an expression of a general tendency governing the
evolution of the lexicon, they exemplify an essential principle which
cannot be ignored in trying to explain why a given lexicon is structured
as it is. Saying *bus* instead of *omnibus* saves energy which is thus set free
for doing other jobs. The composition of the vocabulary of a language as
well as that of a given text corpus is such that the communicative needs
at hand can be met at a minimum expenditure of energy. Optimizing
this property is in the best interest of securing the continuation of a
linguistic tradition and the society of its speakers.

Economy of Speech Sounds

One remarkable property of the sound systems of human languages is
that their constitutive elements have differing frequencies of occurrence.
This raises the question why this is so, that is, why the phonemes of a
language are not all used with approximately the same frequency. For an
answer we once again have to turn to the Principle of Least Effort.

From the point of view of articulatory phonetics, phonemes are
conventionally represented as clusters of distinctive articulatory features.
Articulation is a sequence of muscle movements activating the various
speech organs. Intuitively the different nature of the muscle movements

involved in producing different phonemes leads us to suspect that the energy expenditure for the corresponding speech sounds varies: realizing one phoneme takes less energy than another. The problem is to turn this intuitive idea into an empirically testable hypothesis, in other words, to define criteria for measuring energy expenditure in articulation. If two phonemes differ only in that one has an extra articulatory feature which the other has not, it is also intuitively clear that the one with the extra feature is more costly to produce. Of course, whether this plausibility is corroborated depends in some measure on how the features in question are defined; but where a feature is involved that describes a muscle contraction rather than its omission, its realization can safely be said to account for an extra energy expenditure. One such feature is aspiration. In Chinese, where aspiration is phonemic, the non-aspirated stops /p/, /t/, /k/, among others, were found to occur two to three times as frequently than their aspirated counterparts /pʰ/, /tʰ/, /kʰ/, etc., while conversely no aspirated sound occurs more frequently than its non-aspirated phonemic counterpart (Zipf 1949: 101). Further, the bilabial nasal /m/ is easier to articulate than both dental and alveolar /n/, since the latter require an additional movement of the tongue. In this connection Zipf (1949: 104) found /m/ to be much more frequent than /n/ in 22 languages of different language families.

Observations of this sort suggest that there is a general correlation between ease of articulation and frequency of phonemes which can be attributed to the effectiveness of the Principle of Least Effort on the phonological level. There are other indications pointing in the same direction, for instance, the well-known yet surprising fact that phoneme systems consist of a small inventory of between 20 and 70 rather than hundreds or thousands of elements. Obviously, this order of magnitude is adapted to the human organism, allowing it to reduce the work of articulation as much as possible without hampering the work of decoding which consists largely in discriminating sounds and therefore favors a relatively large set of distinct elements. Thus the size of existing phoneme systems strikes a balance between the conflicting requirements of ease of production and ease of decoding.[25]

Martinet made the cornerstone of his phonological theory the insight that on the level of speech sounds a principle of economy is at work. He first formulated his approach following Zipf, in an article about language change in 1955. Above all, his theory is concerned with phonological evolution, the main force behind which, as he sees it, is the perennial conflict between the language users' communicative needs and their inclination to minimize physical and mental effort.[26] Language appears as a self-regulated system which is subject to two opposing forces, the first being the speakers' tendency to maximize the efficiency of the system, that is, to realize communication at a minimal energy expenditure, and the second is the wish to be understood. The first tendency aims at reducing redundancy, the second at increasing it. Assuming that both forces are always at work, it follows that the redundancy of linguistic systems is approximately constant. Although we lack theoretically well-founded and methodologically reliable means to measure the redundancy of linguistic messages, this is surely a plausible assumption.

The idea that language change is always a reflection of the antinomy of inertia and communicativeness is not the only point at which the Principle of Least Effort comes to bear on the phonological level. In addition, what, according to Martinet, is the most important structural property of human language is also motivated by the forces of linguistic economy. This is the principle of duality of patterning, also known as "double articulation," which allows for linguistic units to be segmented into meaningful units on one level, *monemes* in Martinet's terminology, and meaning-differentiating units, that is, phonemes, on another. He explains:

> The evident advantage of the second articulation is economy. The first articulation is economical in the sense that it is possible by means of a few thousand not very specific monemes to realize an infinity of different messages. In the same manner, the second articulation is economical inasmuch as a judicious combination of some dozens of phonemes permits man to keep all of the monemes apart that he needs. In view of the variety and the richness of human communication, double articulation is a necessary trait of human languages.[27]

The structural property of double articulation, Martinet (1969: 36) argues, is of such fundamental importance that the evolution of humanity is inconceivable without the economy achieved by segmenting monemes into phonemes.

The segmentation of linguistic units into smaller elements continues on the level of phonemes which, consisting as they do of specific combinations of articulatory features, also exhibit internal structure. Theoretically a phoneme system is conceivable whose every element differs from all others with respect to all articulatory features. Speakers would then have to distinguish with their articulatory organs as many articulations as their language has phonemes. However, this would be tantamount to a highly redundant differentiation of the phonemes of the system and hence be very uneconomical. In reality no such phoneme systems exist. Rather, from 80 percent to 100 percent of the phonemes of a system are realized by combining articulatory features occurring in more than one of them. Martinet (1975: 168) calls this multiple use of distinctive features "feature economy." The relationship between phonemes and distinctive features varies across languages: the greater the number of phonemes that can be distinguished by means of a given set of features, the greater the feature economy of the system. From the fact that languages differ in terms of feature economy, it must not be concluded that the principles according to which features are combined to form phonemes have nothing to do with the economy of the language system, but rather "that the economy of phonological systems is an extremely complex matter involving a wide range of factors" (Martinet 1975: 173).

Assuming that a system consisting of a larger number of phonemes is more difficult to handle than one with a smaller number and that, furthermore, a larger number of distinctive features composing a phoneme renders it more difficult to differentiate than a smaller number, it follows that it is economical to minimize both phonemes and features. Although, as noted above, there is a wide range of variation, the small number of both in all languages testifies to the fact that the Principle of Least Effort, which governs the speakers' communicative work expenditure, is reflected through the perpetual process of language change in the linguistic system. The observable range of variation on the levels of phonemes – roughly from 20 to 70 phonemes per language – and distinctive features – about 10 to 30 features per phoneme system – indicates that there is an upper limit of articulatory differentiation in terms of the system's economy, while the lower limit is indicative of the hearers" minimal requirements of the articulatory differentiation of utterances for securing uptake.

At the lexical level, one could interpret over-differentiation, the presence of synonyms and words that are similar in meaning, as an exceeding of the upper limit of the lexicon as it would be defined following the criteria of communication economics. Such an excess can be motivated by extra-economic, for instance, aesthetic criteria and be the result of deliberate language planning designed to expand the vocabulary and provide the flexibility and abundance Leibniz envisioned.

At the phonological level this is not possible because articulation is largely removed from conscious control and phonemes cannot easily be added, erased, or modified by intentional intervention into a phonological system. In spite of the range of variation in the phonological structure of languages, economical principles of the kind described above can, therefore, take effect on the phonological level even more directly than in the lexicon. It is for this reason that languages are much more similar in their phonological than in their lexical equipment.

Economy of Writing

Like speech, writing involves work, maybe even more obviously so. The Principle of Least Effort can therefore be expected to also affect the production of visible language. Indeed, economy of effort is in evidence both on the level of producing visible signs and on the level of writing systems. Let us first consider the production of written signs which is similar in some respects to the production of speech sounds.

We do not know how phoneme systems evolved, but since writing is so much younger than speech and since, unlike speech, it leaves behind traces of its own genesis, we have a fairly good understanding of the evolution of writing systems. The best documented case is that of Mesopotamian cuneiform. A largely commercial and administrative script (cf. pp. 203–7 above), it evolved from pictographic origins into a highly standardized medium of written communication. In the above account of the economy of speech sounds we argued that phonological systems have an inherent tendency toward simplification and increasing ease of production. The same can be said with some modifications about writing systems, although the medium spells out certain physical conditions which are characteristically different for speech and writing. Speech uses air, writing a solid surface; speech is realized by the larynx, the tongue, the lips, and the other parts of the articulatory tract, writing by the hand which is guided by the eye. There is hence a parallelism between oral and dexterous articulation movements, as there is between hearing and vision, phonetics and graphetics.

The early Sumerian glyphs were pictorial representations of concrete objects. They were incised on clay tablets with the tip of a stylus. The characteristic wedge-shaped impressions from which cuneiform gets its name only appeared at a later stage, around 2500 B.C., when the scribes began to use the angular end of the stylus pressing it into the clay, instead of tracing its pointed tip over the surface. This made for neater and more regular signs which initiated a process of standardization and simplification. The drawn line was broken up into segments, each consisting of a wedge-shaped impression. The various wedge positions which resulted from the irregular (semi-)pictorial signs of the earlier period were the distinctive features of cuneiform glyphs. The next step brought a reduction of wedge positions. In a meticulous study of the impact the mechanics and control of the hand had on the development of writing, van Sommers (1989) has shown this reduction to be a result of formal articulatory constraints and principles of economy. As he explains, the scribes first used a great variety of stylus angles to produce wedge positions extending around 270 degrees. The writer's hand in manipulating the stylus "had to move quite radically to achieve the full 270 degree range of orientations. It is hardly surprising therefore that this range quickly contracted" (1989: 7). What remained were four wedge positions arranged within a quarter-circle of 90 degrees only with the perpendicular and horizontal orientations being dominant in use.

Van Sommers (1989: 7) goes on to point out that "further contraction was probably halted as a concession to readers, that is for reasons of legibility." Again we can recognize an exact parallel to the production of speech sounds here. As we saw in the previous section, what makes economic sense for speakers does not necessarily meet the demands of hearers. The relationship of writers and readers to their medium of communication displays the same need for striking a balance between ideal conditions of coding and decoding. This also has a bearing on the evolution of structural features of writing systems to which we turn next.

Conceivably a graphic code could be developed which equals natural languages in expressive power without being derived from any of them. However, the history of writing only shows faint traces of such a development. The case can be made, credibly and with good arguments, that writing evolved above all for the preservation and communication of information rather than for the representation of the sounds or other units of a language, hence that it was initially quite independent of language[28] and could have been developed into a visual means of communication in its own right not based on the structural properties of another system of communication. Yet the history of writing took a different course. The graphic codes that were created or adopted soon took their pattern from the languages of those using them. The failure, in creating a new system of communication, to relate to the most powerful one available, would have been a much greater waste of intellectual energy than the proverbial re-inventing of the wheel. Consequently what we find is that all writing systems irrespective of the specific circumstances of their creation have become instruments for recording linguistically coded information. This is a first hint that economic principles were at work in the genesis and development of writing systems. The level of communication power once achieved by the human species (language) was capitalized on in creating a new code, rather than trying to replicate that level by starting from scratch in a different medium.

In this sense, writing systems are subsidiary. Scholars who emphasize the derived nature of writing and attribute little importance to the new possibilities and constraints that come with the new medium of communication for its systematic development, have interpreted the history of writing as a teleological development driven by the dictate of economizing effort which brings about a reduction of the inventory of elementary signs. According to this view, the alphabet is the ultimate long-term goal of the development of writing toward which it was headed from the outset. The principal argument advanced in support of this view is that the alphabet's inventory of basic signs is smaller than that of other writing systems. Gelb, the most prominent advocate of this position, has postulated a "principle of economy" which aims "at the effective expression of the language by means of the smallest possible number of signs" (Gelb 1963: 72).

This principle is invoked for explaining a variety of phenomena, for example that in Hittite hieroglyphic no distinction is made between voiced, voiceless, and aspirated consonants (Gelb 1963: 83), and that the number of homophone signs in Old Babylonian cuneiform was reduced (Gelb 1963: 109). Plausible though it seems, Gelb's hypothesis about the principle of economy underlying the history of writing is problematic because his notion of economy of writing is too narrowly restricted to the economy of the inventory of basic signs. The size of this inventory thus becomes virtually the only criterion for assessing the quality of writing systems.[29]

Evidence suggests that the inventory of basic signs is only one of the factors determining the quality of a writing system. It interacts in complex ways with others, especially simplicity, unequivocalness, and faithfulness. These parameters must be determined in relation to the level on which the writing system operates. Thus, a syllabic system, Japanese Kana, for example, can be more or less economical, simple, unequivocal, and faithful, just as much as a morpheme-based system such as the Chinese, or an alphabetic system such as that of English. Simplicity and unequivocalness have to do with the relationship between signs and their referents (morphemes, syllables, phonemes). A biunique relationship between a letter and a phoneme or a Kana and a syllable is simple. By contrast, if a letter denotes several phonemes or a phoneme is represented by several letters, the relation is complex. Faithfulness has to do with how precisely and completely a writing system allows linguistic units to be represented.

The alphabet is commonly said to be superior to other writing systems because it is economical, simple, faithful, and efficient, thus maximizing all of the said properties.[30] This appraisal, however, is based on the problematic assumptions that, one, a good writing system is an isomorphic representation of the language for which it is used, and two, reducing the number of basic signs is an unqualified advantage. Both are only partly correct, for optimizing one of the said parameters often goes at the expense of another. For example, improving the faithfulness of a system may imply an increase of the number of basic signs or increased complexity in their relationships with their referents.

Furthermore, the decisive steps in the development of writing were accomplished not so much by economizing existing systems as by adapting them to other languages. By applying Sumerian cuneiform to Akkadian, the system was transformed from a logographic into a syllabic script with logographic residues. Similarly, the Japanese syllabic Kana systems resulted from representing Japanese words with Chinese characters. In both cases the inventory of basic signs was drastically reduced. Yet it cannot be overlooked that the increased economy of the systems thus achieved was not fully exploited and, in some measure, even counteracted by antithetical tendencies. The complexity of the mapping relations between signs and linguistic units is greater in Akkadian than in Sumerian. And the equally simple and faithful Kana system could not replace Chinese characters in Japan whose literati continued to use them, and in a way that makes for much more complex mapping relationships than in Chinese.

As for the alphabet, its evolution also testifies to the interaction of the said factors. Its transfer from Phoenician to Greek resulted in a slight increase of the sign inventory (from 22 Phoenician to 26 Greek letters) which at the same time made a more faithful mapping of the language possible. With this the development had by no means come to an end. Rather, the alleged simplicity and economy of the alphabet did not interfere with the coming into existence of writing systems exhibiting radically different levels of complexity. The English spelling system, for instance, is often said to operate on a "deep" level of morpho-phonological representation. From the point of view of the graphic unit of the alphabet, the letter which supposedly represents a phoneme, this implies a very uneconomical mapping relationship. By counting the phonemes that each letter represents and the letters used to represent each phoneme, Nyikos (1988) demonstrated that in relatively frequent English dictionary words the 40 phonemes of English correlate with as many as 1,120 graphemes (letters or combinations of letters). The duality of patterning, thanks to which the English sound system gets by with just 40 units, thus has a spectacularly bad counterpart on the level of its written representation.

This example clearly illustrates that the economy of a writing system's inventory is only one of a number of interacting factors which determine the quality of a writing system and the economy of written communication. If the size of the inventory were to be the only yardstick for evaluating writing systems, the English alphabetic system would be judged more economical than, say, Japanese Kana. But if simplicity, unequivocalness, and ease of learning are also taken into account, Kana are clearly superior as regards minimizing the effort necessary for achieving individual and social literacy.

The merits of inventory economy have also been misjudged in connection with the Chinese writing system. For instance, Goody and Watt's (1968: 36) contention that it takes some 20 years to master the Chinese script with its immense inventory of more than 50,000 characters is doubly misleading. For one thing, at no time have more than 5,000 to 8,000 characters been in use. Nowadays, a much smaller set of perhaps 2,000 characters is sufficient for reading 90 percent of all contemporary texts. For another, to contrast 26 alphabetic letters with 50,000 characters is not a meaningful comparison because Chinese characters are internally structured, consisting of a fixed set of building blocks sometimes called "radicals." This set comprises only 214 elements, a number which is evidently of an altogether different order of magnitude than the 50,000 or so characters that ever existed. To have 50,000 different *elementary* signs would be very uneconomical indeed, but this is not how the Chinese writing system works. Instead, all characters consist of a combination of some of the 214 radicals, some of only one. What this means is that a principle is at work in the Chinese writing system which, as we have seen above, is part of the foundation of the economy of language, namely duality of patterning. Notice, however, that the duality of patterning of Chinese characters bears no relation to the duality of patterning of the Chinese language. It is purely a duality of graphic articulation.

Another aspect of the internal economy of the Chinese script finds expression in a correlation between frequency of use of characters and number of constituent strokes, that is, graphic complexity: the characters consisting of the smallest number of strokes are used most frequently. Further, Zipf's observations of what he calls "the versatility of words" (1949: 75) also apply to Chinese characters. There is a correlation between the frequencies of occurrence of characters in running text and the number of different meanings that can be represented by them.

This teaches us that as they evolve, writing systems follow their own inherent laws which have to do with their structural make-up. The allegedly natural tendency of aiming at the smallest possible number of signs was certainly not the only or decisive force underlying the development, as Gelb contends. Evolutionary jumps, leading to the emergence of new types of systems, happened whenever other factors came into play, especially the transfer to other languages. This is also evidenced by the Egyptian hieroglyphic system which in spite of its high complexity never changed its type during the 3,000 years it was used; although it was at the threshold of phonemic representation already in its earliest form.

Granted that something like the principle of economy assumed by Gelb was one of the forces that shaped the history of writing, it must yet be appreciated that other factors interfere with this tendency more than in other linguistic subsystems. The principal reason for this is that, as the literally most visible part of a language, the writing system lends itself most easily to linguistic conservatism. Once established, writing systems are extremely stable and resistent to change.

The Chinese and other users of the Chinese writing system have known the alphabet for many centuries. Moreover, an alphabetic orthography for Chinese, *hanyu pinyin*, has not only been available for decades, but actively promoted by the Chinese government.[31] Yet, except for demonstration purposes, it remains virtually unused. That the Chinese instead cling to their traditional script requires explanation, especially if it is assumed that there is a single history of writing which is governed by the all-important principle of economy. As I have argued elsewhere (Coulmas 1991b), there are two possible answers. One is that the grindstones of the Principle of Least Effort turn slowly but unfailingly, that not enough time has passed for hanyu pinyin to compete successfully with Chinese characters, but that eventually the principle will prevail, and the latter will be abolished in favor of the former. The other is that other factors interfere with the Principle of Least Effort, not temporarily but as rival precepts of the human condition.

Every writing system has its own history which is intimately linked with the language for which it was developed. In contradistinction to the development of other subsystems of language, this history is partly subject to conscious formation. Economy is then often sacrificed to other merits. That is, conscious traditions interfere with the pursuit of increasing system economy. It is for this reason that the history of writing is not the history of the universal diffusion of whatever system happens to be the simplest and most economical. The principles of communication economics are therefore more important within the context of the history of every individual script than they are for explaining the assumed but highly problematic teleological development of writing from word over syllable to phoneme representation. Every writing system has its own inherent economy, no matter on what level it operates.

The fact that writing systems and orthographies are open to deliberate formation implies, on one hand, that economic principles can be consciously brought to bear in writing reforms and, on the other, that quasi-natural economic developments, as observed in other subsystems of language, can be constrained. That this actually happens is vividly illustrated by the heated debates which usually accompany even moderate spelling reform proposals, witness recent recommendations for both French and German which came to nothing. As soon as economy of effort is brought into the discussion, it is also called into doubt as an unconditional criterion. That certain changes would render an orthography more regular and unequivocal and hence simpler is for many not a sufficient reason to accept such changes. So far we have no more than an embryonic understanding of what the ideal writing system, that optimizes the demands of both the writers and the readers of a given language, would look like. There is good reason therefore for skepticism that conscious control of the development will yield optimal results. The history of writing knows of many cases where systems became more complex and cumbersome rather than simpler, as the

Principle of Least Effort would predict. The Egyptian, the Chinese, and the English writing systems are three examples, yet different types of systems.

Nevertheless, there are some universal features of the economy of writing. All writing systems are underdetermined. Which is to say that they do not represent all of the distinctions of the linguistic level on which they operate. Consonant alphabets leave out vowel phonemes; languages written with full alphabets usually have more phonemes than letters; likewise, in syllabic systems, the syllables of the language typically outnumber the syllable signs; and morpheme-oriented systems are far from representing all morphemes of the language for which they are used each with a different sign. Faithfulness is generally subordinate to economy. This makes pragmatic sense because the typical user of a script knows the language it is used to write and can hence easily compensate for reduced redundancy caused by incomplete representation.

The fact that writing systems leave many distinctions of speech unrepresented also implies that they develop a system-inherent economy of their own, which must not be regarded as deficient relative to other structural levels of language. Most existing writing systems could be more efficient and economical than they are, had they been constructed following the dictate of maximizing efficiency. That they are not ideal from an economic point of view is counter to expectation, because writing systems can be intentionally shaped more easily than other linguistic subsystems. Writing is also much more a product of culture than, say, phonology and syntax. Rather than being the result of conscious planning, the economy that distinguishes the other subsystems reflects developmental tendencies that are hidden from conscious observation. In terms of communication economics writing systems are sub-optimal. This can be understood as an expression of the fact that it is the essence of culture to partly resist the subordination of social behavior to the Principle of Least Effort.

Useful Talk: The Rationality of Discourse

The Principle of Least Effort can affect the language system only as the result of collective, cooperative language use, although the subsystems of language can be investigated without paying much attention to this fact. Phonological systems can be conceived of, in the absence of speakers using them, and the same can be said of lexicon, syntax, and writing system. There is no compelling need for an analysis of these systems to be guided by the insight that they are collective products. This is different with discourse, the fabric of speech that is woven jointly by two or more speakers working together.

Traditionally, discourse, the basic site of language use, has therefore been conceptually opposed to language as depending on it and making use of it. Statements about economy or excess in discourse were understood as referring to *parole* rather than *langue*, for instance as stylistic descriptions or rhetorical directives. The view that discourse is no more than the realization of the structural principles of the subsystems of language has been challenged recently. As a result of the increased attention pragmatics has received during the past two and a half decades or so, the conceptual relationship between language and speech, *langue* and *parole*, has been transformed and become more intricate. The existence of formal constraints and regulations beyond the sentence frame is now generally acknowledged, as is the legitimacy and necessity of general principles and specific rules of discourse organization being taken into account in a comprehensive description of the language system. The question of how discourse works is recognized as a part of the question: "What does it mean to know a language?" in contradistinction to the social rules governing language use.

Philosophers of language and linguists have spent much energy exploring the underlying regularities of discourse organization. A proper point of departure for the discussion are the maxims which, according to Grice (1975), normal speakers, under normal circumstances, adhere to in conducting a conversation. The essential part of "normal circumstances" is that the participants are, and mutually expect each other to be, cooperative. On the assumption that this "Cooperative Principle" holds, Grice proposed four categories of discourse organization under which fall a number of more specific maxims. The categories are called Quantity, Quality, Relation, and Manner. The following two maxims fall under the category of Quantity:

1 Make your contribution as informative as required (for the current purpose of the exchange).
2 Do not make your contribution more informative than is required. (Grice 1975: 45)

Evidently, these two maxims are in accord with the Principle of Least Effort. The measure of what is "required" in (1) is the energy expenditure that can reasonably be expected of the hearer for decoding the utterance, while (2) relates to the speaker's energy expenditure for formulating the message. Since (1) and (2) oppose each other, an equilibrium must be found. As Leech (1983: 67) put it:

> In practice, a balance has to be struck between saving time and effort, and maintaining intelligibility.

In discourse organization, the tendency toward reduction of expression is always in conflict with the need for perspicuity (a maxim which falls under Grice's category of Manner). Reducing one's contribution by means of pronominalization, ellipsis, and other shortcuts is in concordance with the rationality of discourse only inasmuch as it does not compromise the purpose of the utterance, especially by rendering it ambiguous or incomprehensible.

What Grice strives to explain is that normal speech is highly implicit and indirect. In actual conversational settings, utterances typically mean more than is entailed by the meaning of the sentences and the logical relations between them. It is neither the lexical meaning of the words nor a logical conclusion in the strict sense that allows us to interpret an utterance such as *The garbage can is full* as a request to empty it. Yet this intention is easily understood, indeed, making it explicit would often be perceived as marked if not deviant. The question then is, "deviant relative to what," which is to be answered with Grice as follows. Overexplicitness violates the logic of conversation which is not the logic of calculable implication but the logic of implicature, that which is recognizably intended. The axiom of this logic is that people behave rationally. As listeners, participants assume that utterances are made with a purpose in mind, and as speakers they will not take the trouble of saying anything which is understood without being put into words. In this sense, speakers expect each other to voice useful words only. Hence, the logic of conversation is ultimately utilitaristic and based on a principle of economy.

Grice presents his insights in the form of theoretical maxims which are not prescriptive norms for speakers to consciously adhere to, but principles he recognizes as generally valid guidelines underlying the organization of discourse. These maxims seem to take the Principle of Least Effort for granted. There is, however, also some rather specific empirical evidence testifying to the fact that it is also at work on the level of discourse organization.

Olson (1970) and Krauss and Glucksberg (1977) found that in

verbally referring to objects which are known by various names, speakers tend to prefer the shortest possible nominal label which enables the listener to identify the intended object in the given context.

From a study of declarative sentences such as *I must request you to sit down immediately*, which are called "hedged performatives" because they are used for enacting orders, warnings, requests, etc., Fraser (1975: 195) derives a Principle of Efficiency which says:

> Given nothing to suggest the contrary, whenever a further utterance would be redundant one can infer that the speaker need not make the utterance but that he will operate as if he had made it and will expect the hearer to operate similarly.

Further, in an empirical study of business negotiations, Stalpers (1992) demonstrates that redundancy reduction in discourse is negatively affected by external factors such as use of a foreign language. Where the language used is a foreign language for one of the speakers, discourse sequences in which one speaker completes another's utterance require an additional step, the acknowledgment of acceptance of the completion. As Stalpers found out by interviewing participants of business negotiations, it was because of differences such as these, between conversations involving mother-tongue speakers only, on one hand, and those involving foreign language speakers also, on the other, that the latter were experienced as tiresome and uneconomical. Such observations indicate that speakers are sensitive to relatively minor deviations from the efficiency requirements which govern normal cooperative discourse behavior caused by special conditions, such as use of a foreign language.

Further, the results of an experimental study by Clark and Wilkes-Gibbs (1986) indicate that discourse work is performed under the restrictions of economy constraints. They describe the making of a definite reference in discourse as a collaborative process where each participant behaves in such a way as to minimize the necessary joint effort. Clark and Wilkes-Gibbs emphasize that the Principle of Least *Joint* Effort is not the same as the Principle of Least Effort governing the individual's behavior in Zipf's sense, and that their principle must be assumed in order to explain certain features of referring, or rather establishing reference, to objects in a manner mutually accepted by all. They thus accentuate the cooperative nature of discourse. It would be misguided, however, to interpret the Principle of Least Effort too locally with respect to the discourse behavior of individual speakers as implying that each contribution must be as economical as possible at every given point in a conversation. Since every participant incorporates the discourse roles of speaker and hearer, the measure for what is necessary to say is always the other's potential for uptake and comprehension. Every conversation is cooperative work and perceived as such by its participants. In the organization of discourse it is important for the participants to minimize the effort necessary for getting this work done. It is immaterial whether the inclination to do so, which is a key prerequisite of rational discourse behavior, is attributed to the Principle of Least Effort or its more specific derivative, the Principle of Least Common Effort. What both theoretical analyses and empirical studies confirm, is that speakers mutually expect their contributions to be rationally calculable, that is, ultimately accessible to cost-benefit analysis. This is the foundation of mutual understanding. With this in mind, Kasher (1985: 247) proposed to replace Grice's cooperative principle by a more general principle governing conversational conduct. In a nutshell it encapsulates the economy of discourse:

> Given a desired end – a minimal purpose – make that linguistic action which most effectively and at least cost attains that purpose.[32]

Economy of the Linguistic System – Summary and Conclusions

Economy principles permeate the linguistic system on every level: the structural foundation of the duality of patterning and the ratio of distinctive features and phonemes; the correlations of word length, frequency of occurrence, polysemy, and the numerical ratio of frequent and rare words that characterize the lexicon; relative simplicity and parsimony as the criterion of determining the validity of rival syntactic structures; the dependency of writing on levels of linguistic structure and the underdeterminacy of individual writing systems relative to the level on which they operate; and finally, the striking of a balance between costs and effects as the basic rationality of discourse. All of these phenomena attest the pervasive influence on language of the Principle of Least Effort. In the final analysis, this principle is grounded in the limits of human life which makes time a scarce resource. Hence it flows from one of the basic conditions of human existence. The economy of language is a consequence of the necessity to economize speech; for the manner in which every individual, by necessity, handles speech, namely economically, translates into systematic properties of language, namely its internal economy. Much like a speaker who makes no greater effort than is necessary to attain a given communicative purpose, a language at every point in time affords only the expressive power which is necessary to fulfill the communicative needs of its speech community.

This forces us to embrace an evolutionist view of language which assumes that speech communities adapt their languages to the communicative needs at hand, which in effect means that the external economics of languages eventually, if, perhaps, very indirectly, makes itself felt in their internal economies. A more far-reaching conclusion is that, as a reflection of specific historical and socioeconomic conditions, there are always some languages which are better adapted and more powerful than others. Statements such as this are often not well received and invite the reproach of Social Darwinism, more specifically the reproach that the essence of language is thus reduced to an instrument in the social struggle, rather than a means of giving form and expression to the human mind. These are, however, hardly incompatible qualities. Language is certainly both, and saying that some languages are, at a certain point in time, more powerful than others is no more than pointing out the obvious, although linguists have demonstrated a marked lack of interest in the fact that languages are unequal in the expressive possibilities they afford their speakers. What do the actually existing differences in the serviceability of individual languages imply for their development? This question is discussed in the final chapter.

7

Language Adaptation:
Differentiation and Integration

Normally, language adaptation[1] happens continuously as a process which secures the efficiency of a language in a changing world with changing communication needs. It is not usually noted by the speakers of the language in question. A language can be said to be well-adapted if, with respect to the communication needs of its speakers, it is

1 *referentially adequate*, that is, it can without difficulties denote all objects which need to be verbally distinguished;
2 *sufficiently standardized*, that is, a common form of the language is universally accepted by its speech community; and
3 *sufficiently differentiated*, that is, it affords access to functionally specific particularistic speech forms.

That these conditions are satisfied is the ideal normal case. Since socio-economic and linguistic developments do not always coincide, the actual circumstances of a language may only more or less approximate this ideal or, indeed, be far removed from it. Speech communities are then faced with a language crisis brought about typically by external disruptions of their sociolinguistic ecologies such as, for example, war, conquest, colonization, or enslavement. As a result, the need for language adaptation becomes a matter of conscious concern. For instance, near the end of the seventeenth century, Leibniz diagnosed serious shortcomings of the German language which paled in comparison with French with respect to the lexicon, which suffered from deficiencies in abstract terminology,[2] as well as grammar, which lacked differentiation and standardization.[3] Some 250 years later, Gandhi passed a similar judgment on the big literary languages of India, especially deploring their impoverishment in terminology.[4] In such situations a language's maladaptedness becomes generally noticeable, and the task at hand is not so much to maintain its serviceability as to (re-)build it. Borrowing the sociological concepts of integration and differentiation discussed in chapter 2 (pp. 36f.), maladaptedness can be described as lack of differentiation – the functional range of a language is too narrow – or as lack of integration – the available registers for the various communicative functions are too disparate. Whenever language adaptation succeeds and a higher level of differentiation and integration is accomplished, as was the case, for instance, for German during the eighteenth century, the difference between the state of the language before and after the process is very conspicuous. For, "if we concede (as we must) that languages adapt to needs, it follows, on any reasonable evolutionary view, that before the adaptation the language is not as well adapted as after it."[5]

Language adaptation is generally accepted as a meaningful concept in one area of language evolution which is often, I think erroneously, considered as a special case: the expansion phase of a pidgin language. That pidgin languages are functionally restricted is evident, since both their grammar and lexicon are comparatively inflexible and poor. Yet, this is unproblematic because, by definition, these languages are not mother-tongues and hence not their speakers' only languages. Their limitations imply nothing, therefore, about their speakers' communicative capacity. However, a pidgin which by changing circumstances is pressed into heavier duties than that of satisfying the restricted communication needs of sporadic cross-linguistic contacts in trade is a different matter. When pidgins become the sole or principal means of communication of a new generation of speakers, they must be adapted. The most widely accepted view is that by being turned into creoles they overcome the limitations characteristic of pidgins. Additional grammatical distinctions are introduced into the system; the lexicon is expanded to achieve referential adequacy; tendencies of leveling and standardization make themselves felt. The conditions of interaction and communicative exchange between the speakers, that is, eventually the external economics of the language, are thus reflected, indirectly, perhaps, but recognizably, in their internal economy, their lexical and grammatical structures. At the opposite end of the linguistic life cycle, the impact of socioeconomic factors on the use and transmission of languages are similarly evident, as was demonstrated in chapter 5 (pp. 167–74). When the economic foundations of using a language are removed, it not only loses speakers, but also grammatical and lexical differentiations.

Both expanding pidgins and regressive or terminal languages can thus be described as maladapted in the sense that they cannot fully satisfy their speakers' communicative needs. The question that now arises is how language adaptation should be understood in theoretical terms. Should we look for adaptation level thresholds such that qualitative differences between adapted and maladapted languages can be identified which are similar in nature to the qualitative differences motivating the distinction between pidgins and creoles? Or should adaptedness be conceived of as a scalar property such that all languages can be characterized as more or less well-adapted, both with respect to the communicative needs of their speech communities and with respect to the maximal communication needs given at a certain time? From this follows another question, namely that of whether languages differ in their ability to adapt. There can be no doubt that the difficulties of maladapted languages to adapt vary. But whether this is because some languages are less well-adapted than others or because some adapt more easily than others, we do not know. At the present state of knowledge, we are not in a position to decide whether languages differ in their adaptability by virtue of their structural make-up.

Assuming a threshold implies that there is a difference in kind between language adaptation and regular language change and that languages are usually well-adapted. A scalar notion of adaptedness, by contrast, means that it is always possible for a language to further approximate the ideal level of adaptedness and that languages can hence differ in terms of relative adaptedness. In languages that exhibit a high level of adaptedness, the internal economy of the language system does not interfere with the functional requirements imposed on it by its external economics. A language that meets these conditions is efficient.

Among linguists who subscribe to cultural relativism of one variety or another, there is a general reluctance to part with the view that languages are usually well-adapted. This assumption relieves them of the need to seriously examine the implications of the possibility that some languages are better adapted than others and hence more useful to their speakers than are others to theirs.[6] The existing lack of theoretical means for comparing individual languages in terms of their relative efficiency is partly due to the reluctance to deal with such considerations which run counter to the egalitarian ethos prevailing in linguistic research. But it must also be attributed to the great complexity of language, thanks to which comparable functions can be carried out in different languages by quite different means, as well as to the difficulties of defining a metric concept of efficiency which is applicable to linguistic work.[7]

To say that language A is more efficient relative to certain purposes than another B, in other words, that it is better adapted to the requirements of a certain communication domain, say, fishery, causes no difficulties as long as it can be argued that this difference reflects a difference in the importance of the communication domain in question to the two speech communities. For example, if the speech community of A lives at the coast and that of B up-country, such a difference is no more than would be expected. However, it would be much more difficult to explain that A is more efficient in a given communication domain than B, if this domain is of equal importance to the speech communities of A and B. For this would entail, or at least make it highly probable, that A possesses certain inherent features making it more adaptable than B. This would be a manifest advantage with respect to language expansion as well as a good reason to suspect that language spread is caused not by language-external factors alone.

Considerations of this sort are at odds with the current paradigm of linguistic thought which asserts the fundamental equality of all languages and stresses the insignificance of interlinguistic differences as opposed to the importance of the commonality of the human brain endowed with the generic faculty of language.[8] The resulting interest in universal features of language is as reasonable as it is meaningful, but it should not provide a pretext for branding as illegitimate the question of whether the evolution of human language has resulted not only in varying degrees of adaptedness in individual languages, but also in differences in their adaptability.

There are good reasons to assume that the Principle of Least Effort is effective in language adaptation, too. That language change always happens as a tug-of-war, as it were, between the two factors identified by Martinet, economy of effort and communicativeness,[9] follows from the fact that they govern speech behavior, for it is only through speech that languages can be changed and adapted. Notwithstanding this universal principle underlying all specific adaptation mechanisms, it is possible to distinguish degrees of well-adaptedness of different languages: they differ with respect to the level of differentiation and/or integration. The question then is whether these differences are occasioned exclusively by external socioeconomic and cultural factors of language use, or whether language-internal conditions also have a part to play. In the final analysis, what we need are criteria for assessing the internal economy of languages. By way of complementing the observations reported in the previous chapter, the following sections discuss two major mechanisms of language adaptation which highlight the importance of incremental differentiation and integration, large-scale borrowing and the formation of languages for special purposes.

Borrowing

Natural languages have a continuous need for lexical innovation caused, on one hand, by the wear and tear of words, which has been called "the depreciation of once valid vocabulary" (Seibicke 1959: 71), and by changing communication needs resulting from the discovery, invention, and adoption of new things and ideas which must be labeled, on the other. The main strategies of meeting the lexical demand thus incurred are derivation, composition, and borrowing.[10] For our purposes, borrowing is of special interest because its investigation highlights a point where the interconnection of the external and internal economy of language becomes apparent.

Loanwords are subject to many prejudices and misconceptions. One of the most common has grown out of the ideology of purism, the linguistic counterpart of racialism. It is the idea that loanwords contaminate the assumed purity of the recipient language, not only violating its dignity, but also compromising its serviceability. In 1557, Sir John Cheke, a classicist, wrote about English:

> Our tung shold be written cleane and pure, vnmixt and vnmangeled with borrowing from other tunges, wherein if we take not heed bi tijm, euer borowing and neuer payeng, she shall be fain to keep her house as bankrupt. (Quoted from Moore 1910: 5)

Borrowing without paying back means to run into debts which is not only morally objectionable, but also gets oneself into trouble. The non-scholarly discussion of linguistic borrowing has often been informed by a rather too literal interpretation of the metaphor underlying the expression *loanword* which has, therefore, been criticized as misleading. Haugen (1950: 211) called it absurd, "since the borrowing takes place without the lender's consent or even awareness, and the borrower is under no obligation to repay the loan." This can hardly be denied. Furthermore, the creditors suffer no loss even if they are not repaid. Nonetheless, the metaphor is more germane than may appear at a glance.

Borrowing refers to the lexicon of a speech community rather than to the language use of an individual speaker, though individual usage is always the beginning. Thus there is no liable borrower, because he or she who first uses a given lexical item within the context of another language has no means of controlling what the speech community will do with it. Individual control over lexical items would be incompatible with the social nature of language. Partly similar conditions obtain with respect to collective borrowers such as countries or their governments. There is no individual liability and, as is well-known, many large-scale loans are never repaid. In recent years, enormous debts were remitted and converted into development aid.[11] This is exactly what loanwords are: development aid for languages which are to a greater or lesser degree referentially inadequate.

On the other hand, it is not always true that loanwords are not returned. For example, Modern Greek borrowed *cybernetics* from English, but the English word originated from the Ancient Greek word *kubernetes* ("helmsman") which through Latin mediation also gave rise to various other words such as *government*, *governor*, etc. This case is not exceptional or especially complex. Rather, borrowing is frequently a multi-level process of recycling where the languages involved change places repeatedly, functioning alternately as donor and recipient. In order to better understand the role of borrowing in the interaction of the external and internal economy of language, it must suffice in the present context to establish its main determinants. To this end, the following compact question may serve as a useful guideline: Who borrows what, why, how, from whom, and under what circumstances?

Who? Borrowing is a universal phenomenon, which is already a general answer to the first element of our question. Every language comprises loanwords, every speech community borrows lexical items from others. Further qualifications of this general statement become possible in connection with other components of the question.

What? The general answer to the question of contents is that speech communities borrow labels for objects, in the widest sense, for which their own language has no name or appropriate designation. However, a number of additional factors interfere with this seemingly straightforward rationale. These have to do primarily with the prestige gradient characterizing the relationship between donor and recipient language, as well as formal constraints of the recipient language on the introduction of elements from other languages. As a general tendency, nouns are borrowed most frequently. Analyses of loan vocabularies across languages reveal that nouns account for a higher percentage of loans than all other form classes combined. While verbs and adjectives are often derived from loan nouns, words of these form classes are rarely borrowed themselves.[12] Of course, this also reflects the fact that nouns usually constitute the largest part of the lexicon.

Why? The various reasons for borrowing lexical items from other languages can be assigned to two categories, sociopsychological and socioeconomic reasons. The former have to do with prestige and fashion, which in many cases motivate speakers to intersperse their speech with foreign words in the absence of any real lexical deficit. The crucial socioeconomic motivation for borrowing, on the other hand, is the need to secure the language's utility, that is, more specifically, its referential adequacy. Referential adequacy can also be achieved without borrowing by relying on the lexical and morphological means of the language itself. This points to the *how* of the borrowing process.

How? There are various patterns of the mechanics of linguistic borrowing. The most important ones are the following: (1) adopting the donor language word with appropriate modifications in accordance with the phonological, orthographic, and morphological regularities of the recipient language, for example, *leitmotif* from German *Leitmotiv* or *moxa* from Japanese *moe kusa* ("burning herbs"); (2) loan translation or calque such as German *Wolkenkratzer*, French *gratte-ciel*, Spanish *rascacielos*, and Japanese *matenrô*, modeled on *skyscraper*, or German *Ente* modeled on French *canard* ("false story"), which English adopted as such; (3) hybridization where the recipient language reproduces a lexicalized concept of the donor language by combining native and foreign elements, for example, English *mis-fortune* (English + Latin), *sketch-book* (Italian + English), or Japanese *genshi-enerugii* ("atomic energy": Sino-Japanese + English).

Languages differ in their preferences for any of these patterns. In Chinese, for instance, calquing (2) is by far the most common strategy of lexical innovation under foreign influence, while English shows a marked preference for adoption (1). Such preferences are a result of both sociocultural and structural features of the recipient speech communities and languages, respectively. Explanations for the Chinese preference for (2) must be sought, on one hand, in the traditional self-centeredness of Chinese culture and, on the other, in the Chinese writing system which does not lend itself easily to integrating words written in other scripts or to representing foreign words phonetically. That English, by contrast, is very open to accommodating borrowed forms in accordance with (1) reflects both its historical development since the Norman conquest, especially its prolonged intensive contact with French, and its simple morphology thanks to which foreign forms can be integrated effortlessly into the grammatical system.

It can be argued that the preferred strategy for lexical enrichenment by tapping foreign resources is determined in each language by an interaction of external and internal factors. Once again, a principle of economy makes itself felt here. To mention but one specific example, De Vries (1988: 125f.) has demonstrated how complex Indonesian calques of Western notions were replaced by Dutch loanwords such as *politik* (Du. *politiek*), *demokrasi* (Du. *democratie*), among others, because "the principle of economy prefers the use of one word instead of a phrase."

Which strategy prevails is thus eventually a question of the costs that it involves. Depending on the state of the existing infrastructure, either importation or local reproduction of a foreign product or word is simpler and more cost efficient. English is an import language, Chinese a reproduction language. Although such preferences can be very pronounced at any given time, they are not unalterable.

From whom? Usually borrowing happens inadvertently.[13] Hence, what determines the choice of a donor language are not consciously weighed efficiency criteria. Yet, generally speaking, the most likely donor language is that which furnishes the closest and most profitable source. Truly global communication networks are a very recent phenomenon still limited to certain areas such as science, finance, and maybe fashion and tourism. Here it has become possible for the English language to be tapped more or less simultaneously by a variety of recipient languages. But apart from these areas, borrowing is a local process. While it would be foolish to deny that a language sometimes borrows from several other languages at the same time, its main source will be that language which is most easily accessible to the speech community and offers most.

Under what circumstances? The fundamental condition for borrowing to take place is that there is contact between donor and recipient language. As Weinreich emphasized again and again,[14] this presupposes bilingual individuals, where "bilingual" is understood in a wide sense of varying degrees of proficiency in the languages involved. Typically, but not exclusively, borrowing happens between neighboring speech communities. In this connection it must not be forgotten that neighborhood relations are often brought about by migration or colonization which in turn engender bilingual mediators between the population groups thus brought into contact. There would be no French loan words in Vietnamese if it was not for the presence of French colonial officers and merchants in Vietnam and mother-tongue speakers of Vietnamese who had learned French in their dealings with them. The role of bilingual individuals for lexical expansion cannot be estimated too highly. Even a small number of individuals can exercise considerable influence on the development of a language, a point which will be illustrated below by the Dutch–Japanese language contact which was limited to a single trading post in western Japan. This is even more apparent in cases where language contact is restricted to the written medium alone without any physical contact between the speech communities involved.

We can now draw some conclusions which will be illustrated in the following with a concrete example. Like pidginization, borrowing results from the interaction of speakers of different mother-tongues and is thus an expression of language contact. Language contact involves at least two parties linked together in what is typically an asymmetrical relationship. Borrowing, or rather its result, the languages' stock of loanwords, is indicative of the nature of the relationship between the speech communities involved. Although, in language contact situations, both languages are potentially donor and recipient languages simultaneously, the give and take of loanwords is not usually balanced. Rather, the exchange is such that one language is predominantly giving and the other predominantly receiving. In the following language pairs, for example, the first members have adopted incomparably more loans from the second than vice versa: Rhaeto-Romance < German, Welsh < English, Breton < French, Sardinian < Italian, Basque < Spanish. Every language contact situation thus has a dominant donor language and a dominant recipient language, reflecting the socioeconomic and cultural power relation between their speech communities.[15] Sharpening the answer to the first part of our question, it can be said that it is those speech communities that borrow which stand in need of doing so. Although there is no evidence to suggest that large-scale borrowing is an indication or part of incipient language decline, it is frequently perceived as such. In France, the condemnation of loanwords as a threat to the integrity and welfare of the national language is at present a regular part of public discourse.[16]

A synchronic review of the loan-vocabularies of two languages in contact can make it seem that there is an equilibrium between them, that is, that the total stock of loanwords they took from each other is about equal in size. Still, their mutual influence at any given point in time is lopsided; for the roles of donor and recipient language can be reversed. French was for centuries the main donor language for English without adopting many English words. Now the two languages have changed places and the opposite is true. The relationship between Chinese and Japanese is of a similar nature. Since the end of the nineteenth century, Chinese increasingly borrowed words from Japanese, while the latter at the same time turned away from Chinese as its main source of lexical enrichment. The reasons for this are not far to seek. The lexicon of a language always reflects the level of socioeconomic and cultural development. A suitable donor language can therefore only be one which is spoken by a speech community that is, in this sense, superior, a language, namely, that comprises the linguistic conceptualization of the higher level of development at the time. Wherever a difference in the level of development exists, the major flow of loan words will be in the direction of the language of the less developed group. Loans will invariably occur under such circumstances even if this flow has to be channelled through a passageway as narrow as the eye of a needle. For borrowing is not so much the linguistic analogue of the international division of labor as it is part of it. Every country produces those commodities for whose production it has the greatest comparative advantage. Words are the products of a speech community. Just as the objects they denote, their appreciation finds expression in the demand for them under the existing trade conditions.

Deshima

The Japanese vocabulary includes many words of Dutch origin. Vos (1963) provides a list of more than 400 items consisting mostly of Dutch words in the strict sense, as well as words of other languages such as Portuguese which came into Japanese through Dutch, plus a few hybrids. Place names such as *doitsu* < *duits{land}* (Germany) and *toruko* < *turkije* (Turkey) which were also borrowed from Dutch in considerable numbers are not included. How did Dutch become such an important donor language for Japanese?

Owing to its insular position east of the Asian continent, Japan's contact with other countries was limited for many centuries to China and Korea or to their mediation. The first Europeans to reach Japanese shores in 1543 were Portuguese missionaries, followed a few decades later by their Spanish competitors. The first Dutchmen arrived in 1600 on board the *Liefde*, a commercial vessel of a Rotterdam trading company. Unlike the Catholic Portuguese and Spaniards, the Protestant

Dutchmen were less concerned with the spiritual salvation of the Japanese than with trade, for which the latter, too, had more understanding. The Portuguese and the Spaniards were, therefore, expelled from the country, and they and other Westerners were barred from entering Japanese ports. The Dutch alone were permitted to retain their trading concession. As a consequence, they enjoyed a trade monopoly with Japan for a period in excess of 200 years, from 1640 to 1854. During that time, the Dutch were the sole conduit for commercial and cultural contacts between Japan and the West. These contacts, however, were held under strict control. In order to keep a lid on the influence that could emanate from the Dutch trading post, the factory was placed on an 130 acre artificial island in the harbor of Nagasaki, liked with the city only by a guarded bridge. This island was called Deshima.

Because of this very special situation and the great distance between Japan and the Netherlands, Deshima provides laboratory conditions as it were for the study of linguistic borrowing. We know the motivation, the physical circumstances, the length of time, and the intensity of the Dutch–Japanese language contact and are hence in a position to determine how reliably it is attested by the loanwords which resulted from it.

The Dutch Factory of the East India Company (VOC) which was staffed by a director and a few employees never numbering more than 20 was the only site of the language contact. Communication between the foreigners and the native population was subject to strict supervision. The Japanese government issued regulations forbidding any Dutch to leave the island without permission. Accordingly, contacts between the Dutch and the Japanese were very limited, too limited to give rise to a Dutch–Japanese trading pidgin. Instead, eager to control as much of the necessary communication as possible and to use it to their own advantage, the Japanese had a number of officials trained in Dutch who came to be known as *oranda tsûji*, the Dutch-language interpreters. Their task was to serve as go-betweens and eventually as customs officials and superintendents of the trade with the Dutch. In the course of time, the *oranda tsûji* gained considerable power and influence. In keeping with the social practice of the feudal system, the post of chief interpreter became hereditary in designated families. By the middle of the nineteenth century when Japan's policy of seclusion came to an end, he headed an office with a staff of some 140 assistants. It was these interpreters who did the actual borrowing by translating freight inventories and trading contracts, as well as Dutch books on ship-building, weaponry, medicine, and other fields where Europe was ahead of Japan, and by compiling dictionaries.[17] The crucial role Dutch played in the technology transfer from Europe to Japan is well illustrated by the hybrid form *rangaku* (*ran* < *Holland* + *gaku* "study") which meant "Western studies." During the eighteenth and first half of the nineteenth century, *rangaku* was Japan's only source of information about the outside world.

At the same time the trade with Japan was highly profitable for the Dutch, indeed it was the main pillar of the dealings of the VOC. Their trading posts in Southeast Asia enabled them to import lucrative merchandise into Japan, especially raw silk, textiles, sugar, medical drugs, sappanwood (of a tree from Southeast Asia used for its red dye), pepper, glass, and books. Export of silver, copper, camphor, porcelain, and lacquerware was even more gainful. For present standards, the volume of traded goods was small. Rarely did more than ten Dutch ships per year enter the habor. Yet, the trade was so profitable that it provided the Dutch with the motivation to put up with the monotonous and restrained life in the factory and the obligation to report to the government in Edo (present-day Tokyo). Deshima thus existed for two centuries by virtue of the mutual agreement and interest of the Dutch and the Japanese.

The traces Deshima left behind in the Japanese language testify to the specific needs of the Japanese during that time. Larger groups of loanwords include terms for technical implements and tools, chemical substances, diseases and medical instruments, weights and measures, weapons, textiles, and foodstuffs.

Technical implements: *buriki* < *blik* "tin(-plate)", *konpasu* < *kompas* "compass", *okutanto* < *octant* "octant", *ponpu* < *pomp* "pump", *môru* < *moer* "nut (of a bolt)", *renzu* < *lens* "optical glass".

Chemical substances: *arukari* < *alkali* "alkali", *arukôru* < *alcohol* "alcohol", *gasu* < *gas* "gas", *kobaruto* < *kobalt* "cobalt", *richûmu* < *lithium* "lithium", *sojûmu* < *sodium* "sodium".

Medicine: *chibusu* < *typhus* "typhoid", *hipokonderî* < *hypochondrie* "hypochondria", *infuruenza* < *influenza* "influenza", *katêteru* < *katheter* "catheter", *kirisuteru* < *klisteer* "enema", *marariya* < *malaria* "malaria", *moruhine* < *morphine* "morphine", *pesuto* < *pest* "pestilence", *supoito* < *spuit* "syringe".

Weights and measures: *garamu* < *gram* "gramme", *onsu* < *ons* "ounce", *pondo* < *pond* "pound", *ton* < *ton* "tonne, tonnage".

Weapons: *kanon-hô* < *kanon* "cannon" + Sino-Jap. *hô* "barrel", *pistoru* <

pistool "pistol", *ransetto* < *lancet* "lance", *sâberu* < *sabel* "saber". Textiles: *furanneru* < *flanel* "flannel", *rinneru* < *linnen* "linen", *seirasu* < *zelas* "Ceylon silk", *zukku* < *doek* "cloth". Food stuff: *bîru* < *bier* "beer", *bisuketto* < *bischuit* "rusk", *bôteru* < *boter* "butter", *kôhî* < *koffie* "coffee", *sarada* < *salaad* "salad", *shiroppu* < *siroop* "syrup", *wâfuru* < *wafel* "wafer".

Together with the objects, the Japanese adopted their Dutch names. By so doing, they acquired knowledge and skills and added a new pattern of borrowing to their language. For since the adoption of the Chinese script in the fifth century, Chinese had been virtually the exclusive source of loans. Enough Chinese words had been integrated into Japanese to form a Sino-Japanese stratum which became productive in the language. Today it accounts for about 40 percent of the entire lexicon. This stratum of Sino-Japanese morphemes provided the infrastructure for language adaptation. Chinese was the quarry for the building material of lexical innovation. The two centuries during which Japan's contacts with the outside world were mediated by the VOC and filtered through the Dutch language ushered in a change of orientation. The Dutch loanwords which infiltrated Japanese at the hands of the *oranda tsûji* were the harbingers of a veritable flood of words of other European languages which were adopted to satisfy the increasing lexical demand, once Japan was forced to end its isolationist policy in the middle of the nineteenth century. As a consequence of the initiation of trade relations with the United States and European powers, the Dutch lost their monopoly position. Their trade with Japan diminished, and English displaced Dutch as the chief Western donor language for Japanese. Although Dutch continued to be used until 1870 as the language the Japanese employed for diplomatic negotiations, it rapidly lost its exclusive value after Japan's opening to the West. The stream of Dutch loanwords dried up. Many of them were indeed replaced by new loans from English or German, or were reinterpreted as English or German loans.

Together with the trade, the language contact was reduced to insignificance. How strongly the latter was dependent on the former is also evidenced by the traces left behind by the Dutch–Japanese relationship at the other end. There are hardly any loanwords of Japanese origin in Dutch. This can be read as reflecting the fact that the VOC transacted by far the largest part of the trade with Japan within Asia rather than within the Netherlands. Moreover, it testifies to the technological and

socioeconomic disparity between the modern European trading nation
and the introvert East Asian feudal empire. Except for profits, Japan had
little to offer to the Dutch. In this regard the Dutch–Japanese language
contact is not exceptional. Only a few words were borrowed into Dutch
from other languages spoken on the Indian subcontinent and in Southeast Asia where the Dutch had major trading posts. In view of the
commercial nature of the relationships the Dutch maintained in this part
of the world, it is not surprising that these are primarily appellations of
objects that they first imported to Europe.[18]

Lexical loans from other languages are adopted whenever there is
a need. This need can be of various kinds, being grounded in an
economic, cultural, or political-military imbalance between the speech
communities of donor and recipient languages. Trade is not the sole
transmission belt of lexical import, but it does play a decisive role for
setting off developmental differences in many areas such as production
and technology. Where there is trade, there is language contact. Large-
scale borrowing of lexical items for the purposes of language adaptation
is one of its consequences. The example of Deshima teaches that minimal conditions as regards the number of bilingual individuals and the
opportunities for contact suffice for borrowing to take place to the extent
that there is a need for it. The mutual enrichment of the languages
involved is hence no more balanced in quantity and quality than the
commercial exchange between two trading partners. Rather, borrowing
fulfills the purpose of balancing a lexical deficit and thus adapting a
language to a higher level of differentiation in areas relevant to overall
socioeconomic development.

Languages for Special Purposes

Special activities require special forms of expression. This has long been
recognized. Leibniz himself realized the relevance of technical terms for
language adaptation and therefore recommended

> an inspection and investigation of all German words which, in order to be
> complete, must concern itself not only with those used by everyone, but
> also with those peculiar to certain arts and walks of life.[19]

He also realized that to this end the lexicographer must lean on the
expertise of specialists

versed in the nature of things, especially herbs and animals, fusing and chemistry, arithmetic and mathematics, as well as architecture and other arts that depend on it, weaving and so-called manufactures, commerce, navigation, salt and other mining, and the like.[20]

Leibniz was concerned with technical terms of the German language which, as was pointed out earlier, he thought in need of enrichment and improvement. In keeping with this approach, we will here consider as languages for special purposes, varieties which, while transcending the speech of everyday communication, at the same time, like it, belong to a modern common language. The relation of belonging is to be defined in greater detail below. Suffice it to say for present purposes that, as opposed to the learned languages of pre-modern times under conditions of function-specific bilingualism, languages for special purposes in this sense are accessible from a modern common language. The formation of technical jargons and languages for special purposes in their relationship to the common language is a continuous process of differentiation and integration. Conrad described technical language as "an instrument wrought into perfection by ages of experience, a flawless thing for its purpose" (quoted from Coleman 1985: 118). In his history of the German language, A. Bach observes that trades and professions, social ranks and groups have provided the general public with new words (Möhn 1981: 189). Thus, while a higher level of division of labor and specialization brings with it the formation of specialized registers, these registers also interact with the general language, enriching it whenever specialized knowledge is diffused and acquires the status of common knowledge (Hüllen 1981). Integrating the respective terms into the common language is then again followed by continuing specialization of the communication needs of individual disciplines and thus also leads to increasing differentiation. This is the mutually reinforcing process of repetitive cycles of differentiation and integration on the level of language.

Social and linguistic integration and differentiation are here clearly intertwined; the multitude, nature, and stage of development of the specialized registers belonging to a language are a reflection of the level of division of labor of its society. In the course of industrialization, first the formation and then the scientific investigation, coordination, and planning of languages for special purposes became a matter of economic necessity; just as the problem of systematically forming and labeling new concepts became a crucial concern of technology and science. Special forms of expressions used by guilds and other groups defined by their position in the process of social reproduction are an old phenomenon.[21] Yet, the increasing differentiation of languages for special purposes is a process of "intellectual rationalization" (Möhn 1977: 71) characteristic of modern times. It was boosted immensely by industrialization to become both a forerunner and manifestation of the post-industrial information society.

The enormous development of science and technology and the deluge of industrially produced goods prompted an unprecedented need for new terms. At the same time, access to the conceptualization of the world that had already been accomplished became an increasingly important factor of social well-being and economic progress. It was felt by many that the communication needs and hence, indirectly, the material needs of modern society could no longer be satisfied without consciously planning and guiding language innovation and adaptation. In the 1930s, this impression gave rise to a new branch of applied linguistics which came to be known as *Wirtschaftslinguistik* ("economic linguistics").[22] While relatively short-lived and not attracting much attention, it was a sign of impending problems. Linguistics was slow to accept any responsibility in dealing with them. It was in industry that the first attempts were made at standardizing concepts and terms in order to overcome the inaccessibility of technical terminologies of different fields and to facilitate the dissemination of information. This is understandable, since the communicative aspects of the various phases of the economic process from planning and production to distribution and customer service clearly bring to light the importance of suitable terms for concepts and products. Industry needs languages for special purposes as tools of information management. It, therefore, has a vital interest in carefully observing and, sometimes, actively influencing the development of specialized terminologies.

> Here the technical term serves to designate the various relationships of products to the production sphere and in the market. Thus it has to answer the needs not only of science and technology, but also of the language of work, the language of business, and the language of the consumer, where each of these have different demands on precision, unequivocalness, uniqueness, memorizability, publicity value, etc. (Drozd 1981: 132).

In addition to the practical problems of communication within and across scientific disciplines and industries, theoretical questions relating to the formation of languages for special purposes have attracted a great deal of attention of late. The main issues are epistemological problems such as the dependency of knowledge on the systematic conceptualization of a given field of inquiry, the intercommunicability of the findings of different scientific disciplines tackling the same phenomenon from different directions, as well as specific concerns of lexicology, ontology, and semiotics. This gave rise to the new field of terminology and terminography which works at the interface of linguistics, logic, and information theory. By investigating existing terminologies, it uncovers the principles that can be applied in forming new ones.

This is not the place to provide even a cursory account of the manifold tasks of terminology formation and knowledge engineering. However, that this is a real concern, may be illustrated by a few figures. In 1982, the Tokyo publishing house *Shuppan Nyūsusha* brought out a list of dictionaries and references works of various sizes. Almost all of its 6,092 entries are monolingual or multilingual dictionaries pertaining to special fields. This number increases steadily with a total annual output of some 200 specialized dictionaries. The Japanese Ministry of Education regularly publishes lists of Japanese scientific terms as well as guidelines for the formation of terms.[23] This one example which has many counterparts in other languages is clear evidence of the fact that languages for special purposes are of major importance for the internal economy of every language used in science, technology, and other fields requiring special modes of expression. Two aspects of languages for special purposes and the terminologies that form their backbone are especially relevant here. These are the questions (1) how languages for special purposes and general language are interrelated and (2) how the systematic efficiency of technical terminologies can be optimized.

Languages for Special Purposes and General Language

By "general language" we shall here mean language for general purposes, that is, as it were, the core of a common language which is shared by most members of the speech community. To begin with, the relationship of general language and language for special purposes is to be assessed in quantitative terms. Language for special purposes is like a microscope. Its function is to look at a small fragment of reality closely. In areas where technical registers develop, likewise only small fragments of reality are made the subject of discussion, and from a very peculiar viewpoint at that. Yet, the vocabulary that is necessary for taking part in such a discussion is far greater than the lexicon of general language. It is quite insufficient, therefore, to describe languages for special purposes, as is sometimes done, as special forms of a (common) language, for this suggests a smaller segment of something larger. Rather, languages for special purposes are extensions of general language, much like a microscope is an extension of the naked eye. They are precision instruments allowing their users to penetrate a given subject matter more thoroughly and to open up entirely new fields of inquiry. The natural sciences and technical disciplines alone make use of millions of concepts. This is many times the size of both individual speaker vocabularies and the collective lexicon of any language for general purposes. Languages for special purposes are hence to be conceived of as varieties encompassing general language whose grammar and lexicon they use selectively, rather than each forming a segment of general language. Conversely, the general language can be said to open into more specific registers, though no sharp line can be drawn between it and these varieties. General language is thus where languages for special purposes overlap, and in some cases their intersections go beyond it.

In order to satisfy the requirements of linguistically representing conceptual differentiation and innovation, new terms are coined continuously. The masses of concepts and terms of the various disciplines have become impossible to handle without systematic management in clearly defined nomenclatures. In some fields the immense demand for new designations necessary for labeling, representing, and ordering new objects (in the epistemological sense) goes beyond the capacity of language. Nonlinguistic symbols are therefore increasingly made use of in the respective languages for special purposes.

The enormous size of specific terminologies and the continuous need for new designations also carry certain qualitative implications. How are terminologies structured, and how should they be? How exactly do they relate to the lexicon of the general language? Some characteristic features of technical terms which have often been noticed are the following: they are (ideally) unequivocal, referentially precise, free of emotive connotations, and, in many cases, their meaning is fixed by explicit definition and/or integration into a concept system. How this is done is subject to the peculiar conditions of individual languages, such as patterns of word formation and the accessibility of a classical language.

The lexicons of some languages incorporate a stratum of lexemes and morphemes which are removed from everyday speech and therefore suitable for the formation of technical designations free of undesired connotations. This lexical stratum is supplied by a classical language such as Latin, Sanskrit, Chinese, Aramaic, etc., a language, that is, which once served as the vehicle of education and culture. Such a classical stratum may have come into existence as the result of prolonged language contact, as is the case with the Greco-Latin stratum in the Germanic languages, or because a modern language is, in one sense or another, the offspring or continuation of a classical language, as is the case with Modern Hebrew. In any event, a classical stratum is an advantage for terminology formation. The manner in which this stratum is integrated into, or linked with, the general lexicon has a bearing on the relationship between languages for special purposes and the general language, and on the relative transparency of the technical vocabulary.

The technical vocabulary is not homogeneous in itself. It consists of lexical items understandable to experts and scholars only and others which are generally understandable. On one hand, the understandability of terms depends on the degree of specialization – e.g., *potato chips* vs *blue chips* – and on the other, on the lexical stratum to which it belongs – e.g., *word* vs *lexeme*. The organization of lexical strata within the general and specialized lexicon varies across languages. For example, *tonsillitis* is a technical term both in English and in German, but it is a generally understandable term only in English. In German, another word, *Mandelentzündung*, is used outside the medical professions. The same is true of many other medical terms in German. Thus, the relationship between the generally understandable and the not generally understandable parts of the specialized vocabulary is not the same for all languages. In terms of the model here proposed, the fact that the specialized vocabulary of a language consists, to a relatively large extent, of generally understandable terms can be interpreted as a high level of integration. The obvious advantage of such a situation is that it facilitates access to languages for special purposes from the basis of the general language. The disadvantage is the danger of technical terms being semantically contaminated by the non-technical concepts which they designate in general language use.

So far, there has been precious little research on how, or even whether, the relationship between the generally understandable and not generally understandable parts of technical vocabularies can be optimized. With respect to the augmentation and innovation of the specific vocabulary this problem would seem to be tantamount to the question of which lexical stratum should be the preferred resource to this end. One argument favoring the exploitation of the classical stratum, especially the stock of Greco-Latin morphemes of the European languages, is their internationality. This helps to reduce communication barriers in scientific and technical discourse. It must not be overlooked, however, that using the same morphological material in different languages is no more a guarantee for sameness of meaning in specialized vocabularies than it is in the general lexicon. False friends are frequently encountered. Their dissimilarities often go unnoticed. Wüster[24] (1959: 550), one of the pioneer advocates of terminology standardization, mentions the word *deformation* for illustration. As an internationalism it exists in many European languages, but it does not always mean the same thing. For example, in German it means the plastic distortion of an object's natural shape, while in French its meaning also includes disfigurement by cutting. In technical use, it is precisely such relatively fine differences in meaning which are critical. For technical terms of different languages, identity of internal form, that is, conceptual content, is more important than identity of external form. For this reason, in determining the criteria of terminology formation for a language, its relationship to other languages should not be of great weight. The Greco-Latin lexical stratum is firmly integrated into the European culture languages. If we look at the details, however, we find that it is assigned a somewhat different role in each. International standardization and unification of technical terms and the optimization of the relationship between the generally understandable and the not generally understandable parts of the specialized vocabulary of a given language must hence be treated as separate problems.

The situation is different in non-European languages such as Indonesian and Chinese which suffer from a backlog demand of terminology, since in these languages all of the Greco-Latin based terms, borrowed into them from modern European languages, belong to the not generally understandable part of the specialized lexicon. Thus, here the alternative "international or native" more or less coincides with the divide between that which is generally understandable and that which is not. Whether international or native forms should be preferred then depends on how highly internationality of technical terms is valued and on how difficult it is to integrate the Greco-Latin forms into the lexicon.

Indonesian language planners, for example, adopted a strategy of large-scale import of international terms, from Dutch at first and then from English.[25] In Chinese, by contrast, and in keeping with its characterization in the previous section as "a reproduction language," the other strategy is predominantly applied, that is, utilization of autochthonous material.[26] In other languages both strategies are pursued in various combinations. However, no matter how terminology formation is realized and to which lexical stratum technical terms belong, and no matter how the lexical strata of a language relate to the generally understandable and not generally understandable parts of its specialized vocabulary, technical terminologies have to meet certain essential requirements. To them we turn next.

Systematic Efficiency of Languages for Special Purposes

Every language has but a few thousand morphemes. With these, millions of concepts have to be designated (Wüster 1959: 550). This general fact implies, first, that the individual disciplines are forced for their terminologies to draw on the material of the general language which is then integrated into the technical language by explicit standardization (Möhn 1977: 69). Secondly, it follows that no simplex terms are available for the great majority of all concepts that need to be designated, which, thirdly, entails the imperative of using the available linguistic forms (including those not yet coined) economically. In research on terminology and language for special purposes, this imperative is generally recognized.[27] A good language for special purposes is one that is economical. This general requirement can be subdivided into four more specific criteria. The issue here is not, however, whether or not, but to what extent these criteria are met, for they also hold for the general language. Languages for special purposes thus differ from general language in degree rather than kind. The four criteria are:

1 avoidance of synonyms;
2 avoidance of homonyms;
3 an economic ratio of technical terms with their constituents;
4 limitation of the length of technical terms.

Examinations of individual languages for special purposes have repeatedly shown that (1) and (2) are often violated. Möhn (1977: 71) cites a report by the Federation of German Industries (VDI) where it is pointed out that as many as six different designations are commonly used for the clearly defined concept of a "reduction valve." These are *Überdruckventil* "high-pressure (relief) valve," *Druckbegrenzungsventil* "pressure restriction valve," *Sicherheitsventil* "safety valve," *Überströmventil* "overflow valve," *Vorspannventil* "relay valve," and *Druckregelventil* "pressure regulation valve". Such a state of affairs interferes with attempts at establishing a terminological system. Moreover, in stock-keeping, recording and handling orders, and other activities concerning the management of industrial products which increasingly rely on electronic data processing, such a multiplicity of synonyms is an avoidable obstacle. The general requirement thus is: a single designation for every concept.

Homonymity, that is, multiple concepts designated by the same form, also causes problems. A common type of homonymity is using a generic term for several specific concepts, for instance, *nozzle* for *high-speed nozzle*, *injection nozzle*, and *discharging pipe*. In disjunctive fields homonyms do not hamper communication. If used within one field or in two overlapping fields, however, such ambiguity of technical terms compromises the quality of product descriptions, instruction manuals, information material for customer service, as well as the translatability of such texts. Hence, the next requirement is: a single concept for every designation.

Criteria (3) and (4) have to do with the construction of technical terms by means of compounds and syntactic groups, as well as with the morpheme material for these operations. As noted above, most technical terms are compounds or syntactic groups such as, for instance, *speed regulator* or *integrated field regulator*, respectively, rather than simplex terms, such as *regulator*. This raises the question of how many morphemes a given terminology should do with, that is, how productive the constituent morphemes should be, individually and in combination.

Feng (1988) has examined the Chinese terminology of data processing. Chinese is a language well suitable for statistical investigation of this kind, since as an isolating language it does not pose the hairy problem of different word forms. Feng proposes an economical efficiency index for terminological systems along the following lines. Let T be the total set of the terms of a terminological system and M the set of the constituent morphemes, then the economical efficiency index E can be represented as the quotient value of T and M:

$$E = T/M$$

For most terminologies (as for the general lexicon), it holds that $E > 1$. Were it the case that $E \leq 1$, the average frequency of occurrence of all morphemes would be smaller than the average number of morphemes of which technical terms consist. Hence, every morpheme has a formation frequency F, which is indicative of its capacity to produce terms. If the value of F is high, the respective morpheme occurs in many different terms. As has been established by Zipf (1949), the morphemes with high formation frequency values account for only a small part of all morphemes of a given system. The formation of new terms causes changes in both F and E. If new terms are created without introducing additional morphemes into the system, E will grow and the average length of terms L, measured as number of morphemes per term, will increase. This tendency raises the efficiency of the system; yet, reinforcing it unconditionally is not desirable, because if a term is too long it is not practical to use and to remember.

Thus, there are three factors which play a role in the systematic organization of terminologies: the economical efficiency index E, the formation frequency of morphemes F, and the average length of technical terms L. The total number of terms constituting the system is an additional variable. Where it is very small, in a system, say, that encompasses only a few dozen terms, E cannot have a high value. Generally speaking, the economical efficiency index of terminology systems increases together with the total number of terms. How F and L are affected thereby is a matter of decision, at least where we are dealing with planned terminologies, as opposed to terminologies which have grown out of a general lexicon more or less spontaneously. Feng (1988: 179) has proposed that, for the purposes of terminology planning, E should be considered as a function of F and L. In the form of "the economic law of term formation" he formulated:[28]

> In a terminological system, the product of the economic index E of the system and the average length L of terms is exactly equal to the formation frequency F of morphemes composing these terms.

$$F = E \times L$$

This function implies two possibilities of improving the efficiency index of a terminological system: (1) reducing the average length of terms and (2) raising the formation frequency of morphemes with the average length of terms held constant. In actual terminology work both possibilities are exploited. It is eventually a psychological question whether preference should be given to one of them. This question involves an additional factor which Feng has not taken into account, that is, the differentiation of terms from each other. Minimal differentiation in this regard means that every term of a terminological system differs from any other term of that system only in a single constituent. Evidently, this is a system with minimal redundancy. There are two ways of increasing the differentiation of terms without increasing the total number of morphemes of the system. One is to extend the average length of terms, and the other is to change the rank order of the frequency of occurrence of the morphemes in such a way that low-frequency morphemes are used more often. Whether the first or the second strategy should be pursued then depends on what is easiest for human beings to handle. More specifically, this is the question of how average length of terms, their differentiation, and the size of the total set of morphemes should be related in order to be ideal for human perception, memory storage, and cognition.

Conclusions

Linguistic borrowing is a necessity and so is the formation of languages for special purposes. The reasons for this lie in the functional requirements put on every language as a means of social exchange under the specific conditions of socioeconomic, political, and cultural development in which it exists. Both borrowing and the formation of specialized registers, particularly the establishment of standardized terminologies, are instrumental in maintaining or enhancing the utility of languages.

For economic exchange between groups to take place, there must be differences in overall or sector-specific development. Such differences always exist, and therefore, unless artificially restrained, economic goods are always exchanged, which provides the opportunity for language contact and hence borrowing. In addition to the exchange of goods (which in many cases embody knowledge), there is transfer of knowledge, which nowadays more than ever is represented linguistically. Likewise, the acquisition, processing, and transmission of specialized knowledge has become highly dependent on mastering languages for special purposes. It is for this reason that the formation of languages for special purposes and borrowing often go together. For technical registers have become the principal channels for absorbing foreign lexemes. Borrowing reflects developmental gaps and the contacts suitable for closing them.

Incorporating loanwords and expanding technical registers are major ways of enriching languages. Both effect more differentiation, making communication in the domains in question more efficient. At the same time, they bear the risk of erecting new barriers for interdisciplinary communication and the popularization of specific knowledge. These barriers must be reduced by integrating the foreign word, thus stripping it of its alienness, and by making technical discourse permeable to the general language.[29] This is accomplished by the constant influx of technical terms from professional registers into the general language. In this way, borrowing and the formation of languages for special purposes are essential mechanisms of language adaptation, which takes place, to once again pick up the Parsonian terms, as a perpetual interplay of differentiation and integration.

Language Adaptation and Language Spread

Let us now return to the question of what follows from the differing efficiency of different languages. From the point of view of individual languages, language adaptation is a process of differentiation and integration suitable to improve the languages' utility. As pointed out in the previous section, in many cases another language which is more highly developed and better adapted serves as a point of reference in this process. Language adaptation as an orientation toward another language in this sense is a micro-sociolinguistic process. It has a macro-sociolinguistic counterpart on the level of the speech community, namely the acquisition of other languages by its members, for purposes of communication with other speech communities or with each other. What kind of relationship is there between these two processes?

That they should be unrelated seems implausible. An obvious fact which contradicts such an assumption is that borrowing and language spread exhibit a certain parallelism. More specifically, there is a tendency for languages which are expanding on the micro-level, that is, languages functioning as donor languages for others, to also be expanding on the macro-level by way of functionally supplementing other languages in certain communication domains or superseding them altogether.

Just as every language can be described as a donor or recipient language with respect to other languages with which it is in contact, for every historical moment, speech communities can also be characterized as donors or recipients. They give off elements of their communication repertoire to others and take in such elements from others. Speech communities differ, however, on a wide scale with respect to what they give off and take in. This scale ranges from isolated loan items over large-scale borrowing of technical terminologies and domain-specific registers to the extreme case of adopting an entire language. In order to adapt its communication repertoire to its communication needs, one speech community borrows a few words from another language; another adopts a foreign language for specific functions – for example, in the nineteenth century, the Japanese speech community used Dutch for purposes of international communication; and yet another speech community replaces its language by another in all communication domains – for example, the Manchus, whose Ch'ing dynasty ruled over China from 1644 until 1911, allowed their language to retrogress to the status of a foreign language for themselves. Though Manchurian was the officially recognized language of power, they adopted Chinese instead. The language that prevails on the macro-level as on the micro-level is that which is more advanced and better adapted to the relevant domains and functions of communication. That a language is expanding, that it is used increasingly, in whole or in part, outside its primary speech community, finds expression in a number of phenomena testifying to its superiority relative to others in terms of development and adaptedness. It is the more highly developed and adapted languages which

1   are studied as foreign languages;
2   represent the superstratum where pidginization takes place;
3   serve as donor languages in linguistic borrowing;
4   cover the domains of public, formal, and technical communication in codeswitching routines;
5   furnish the goal of language shift.

These are dominant tendencies rather than exceptionless patterns. No more is (1) meant to suggest that a speech community never learns a foreign language which is less adapted than its own than (3) should be taken to mean that a donor language (i.e., one that predominantly functions as such) includes no loans from less developed languages. The above five phenomena can be investigated separately. However, as indicators of a gradient in the overall functional potential of different languages they are also related to each other. The relationship that holds between them can be represented as a probabilistic implication in the opposite direction of their enumeration above. Thus, while habitual codeswitching in a speech community cannot be taken as a certain sign of incipient language shift, a process of completed language shift justifies the assumption that it was preceded by widespread codeswitching. This in turn makes it likely that the abandoned language was a recipient language relative to the adopted language. Further, a give-and-take relationship between languages implies that, where pidginization occurs, the donor language will supply the superstratum. And finally, (1) is presupposed by (2), (3), (4), and (5), where the results of learning a language vary broadly, ranging from the adoption of isolated words to that of the whole language with all the trimmings.

Whichever steps are taken, they all serve the adaptation of the speech community's communication repertoire. Where a language is too difficult to adapt to novel communication requirements because of extensive functional deficiencies, or where the costs of language adaptation seems too high, the speech community will adapt its communication repertoire by adopting another language, in addition to its own or in its place.

The Adaptedness of the World Language

To illustrate this general abstract connection, we shall now consider the above five points with regard to English, the most vigorously expanding language of our age. (1) English is by far the most widely studied foreign language and the most sought-after vehicle of international communication the world over (McCallen 1989: 12–20). Since the locus of language contact is the language-using individual, this warrants the assumption that English is in contact with more languages than any other language. (2) Contact with English has yielded more pidgins than have resulted from language contact with any other modern language. It has, moreover, invariably furnished the superstratum of the newly emerged languages.[30] (3) In the course of the last 50 years, English has become the most prolific donor language of the world. In a comprehensive study of "the English elements in European languages," Filipović (1982) has demonstrated that English words can be found in every continental European language from Iceland to Albania. No similarly detailed studies are available for other continents. But the existing contacts with numerous languages in Africa and Asia leave no room for doubt that on these continents, too, English is at present the most important donor language. (4) In many Third World countries English serves as the dominant vehicle in higher communication domains such as science, government, and law, which has given rise to habitual patterns of codeswitching. And in industrialized countries, too, certain domains have developed quasi-institutionalized as well as spontaneous codeswitching patterns where English is increasingly used, especially in science, technology, finance, but also tourism. English has become a fixed part of the communication repertoire of Swedish companies, in the lecture halls of Dutch universities, at the stock exchange in Zurich, and even in French research laboratories. (5) Finally, English is the goal of language shifts in regressive speech communities on all continents.[31]

Clearly, the spread of English to which these five phenomena bear testimony, cannot be explained by a single cause. Rather, it must be attributed to a concert of socioeconomic, political, and cultural factors, as were discussed in chapter 5. The question is whether the language itself has a part to play in this concert, that is, whether it can be argued, reasonably, that, contrary to Jespersen's above-quoted assessment (see p. 220), certain structural features of English concerning its adaptedness and adaptability are also conducive to its spread.

"English is already the best language that man has yet evolved" (Paget 1930: 80f.). On first impulse, we are tempted, to be sure, to ban such global judgments from scholarly discourse and file them away as evidence of prejudice and imperialistic arrogance. Yet, even if the quoted statement belongs to this category, there could be some truth in it. Whether or not this is so can only be determined on the basis of examining specific properties of the language that make it comparable to others. Paget identified two such properties that make English stand out in comparison to French and German, word order and lexicon.

> In English the [word] order is more natural and logical than in either French or German, German being the greater offender owing to its old habit of putting the verb at the end of the sentence.

> English, owing to its mixed parentage, is exceptionally rich in words, the Latin parentage giving us a large vocabulary of abstract terms to add to our Saxon heritage of words of concrete meaning. (Paget 1930: 69)

Both of these properties have been emphasized repeatedly in the meantime outside ideologically tinted contexts. Although research in this area is still in its infancy, many linguists now recognize as legitimate and important the quest for uncovering criteria of the naturalness of linguistic structures.[32] The vastness of the English lexicon is undisputed, and that it feeds on two main sources is generally seen as one of the factors accounting for it. With respect to linguistic hybridization, Décsy (1973:

184f.) distinguishes "hybrid," "neutral," and "introvert" languages. In hybrid languages such as, for instance, English, French, Rumanian, and Japanese, the foreign element is extensive, occupying a prominent position. By contrast, its representation in introvert languages such as German, Finnish, Icelandic, and Chinese is below average. Hybrid languages are more accommodating, taking in foreign lexical items more easily than introvert languages. The percentage of direct borrowings from Latin in English is estimated as ranging between 22 and 28 percent (Braun 1989: 163). Moreover, the English language, or rather Anglophone lexicographers, continue to adopt and integrate words from many different languages without provoking a discussion about the pros and cons of admitting them.[33] This means that English is able to serve as the resourceful donor language it is thanks to its speech community's readiness to assimilate on a large scale loanwords from other languages. Owing to this enormous lexical turnover, English has become the medium of innovating the world vocabulary.

Another strength of English which has often been noted, for instance in Viereck (1988: 141) and Braun (1989: 163), is its simple and flexible morphology. On one hand, this makes for ease of learning and thus expansion on the macro-level. On the other hand, it equips English with a virtually unlimited potential for functional shift, word-formation by means of derivation, affixation, and compounding, as well as semantic expansion and specialization of words. As Viereck (1988) has remarked, finding substitutes in other languages for the results of this productivity is often difficult, if not impossible. This explains, partly at least, why so many English neologisms are quickly borrowed or calqued into other European culture languages, thereby again reinforcing the influence of English on the micro-level. Its uncomplicated morphology must also contribute to its prominent position in advertizing and naming new merchandise produced in non-English-speaking countries. The Japanese *walkman* which lost no time making its way around the world is but one example.[34]

Other authors cite further structural features of the English language as boosting its world-wide advance.

> English is relatively easy to pronounce, having, for example, few of the tongue knotting consonant clusters of a language such as Russian, or the subtle tone shifting requirements of Chinese. The basic syntax is fairly straightforward, as is the fact that English has dispensed with the informal vocation and gender systems that most other languages such as

French and German possess and that many students find confusing. The Roman alphabet upon which English is based is also considered to be more efficient and economical than the Arabic equivalent; and English is easier to learn than the ideography of Chinese. (McCallen 1989: 23f.)

Each of these arguments can be contested, for reasons some of which have been addressed in preceding chapters of this book. No one familiar with grammar research during the past 20 years or so will accept McCallen's remark about English syntax, not least because grammarians find it difficult to mark off what is basic in the syntactic system. Likewise, considerable problems are involved in determining whether a language as a whole is easy or difficult to pronounce. And as regards writing, McCallen ignores the fact that the English orthography is extremely complex and more difficult to learn than other Latin orthographies. However, it is questionable whether this kind of criticism of detail, warranted though it is, really gets to the bottom of the issue. For individual speakers are not concerned with the overall complexity of the language which linguists must keep in mind in order to escape simplification and unfounded generalization. Rather, they are concerned with those aspects and fragments which offer access to the domains most relevant to them and which enable them to cope with the communicative tasks which they would normally encounter. The higher the level of a language's differentiation, the more varied its specific possibilities in this regard; and the tighter its integration, the easier it is for its speakers to expand their communication proficiency into other domains. Steiner (1975: 468) offers the following considerations about the spread of English:

> There is ample evidence that English is regarded by native speakers of other languages whether in Asia, Africa, or Latin America, as easier to acquire than any other second language. It is widely felt that some degree of competence can be achieved through mastery of fewer and simpler phonetic, lexical, and grammatical units than would be the case in North Chinese, Russian Spanish, German, or French (the natural rivals to world status).

Steiner's argumentation is more cautious than McCallen's, since what McCallen presents as established facts, he qualifies as opinions and attitudes on the part of the many students of English throughout the world. But the message is essentially the same: "A large part of the impulse behind the spread of English across the globe is obviously political and economic. . . . But the causes of universality are also linguistic" (1975: 468). They have to do, above all, with the fact that English is relatively easy to learn. Linguists shy away from judgments of this sort. Like the question of the value of a language discussed in chapter 3, they have by and large ignored that of an effective standard for measuring the difficulty of a language, or expelled it from their sphere of expertise, partly, no doubt, because they are more clearly aware than others of the enormous complexity of any linguistic system. Researchers of neighboring disciplines have fewer reservations to recognize properties such as the simplicity and expressive richness of a language as contributing to its spread, maybe because they are less concerned with structural analyses, focussing instead on aspects of language use, and because they are satisfied with inductive evidence of which attitudes and judgments of language learners are a part. For instance, from a sociopsychological point of view Tabouret-Keller (1991a) argues that the strength of English is the result of a variety of language-external causes, but that "the simplicity of its morphology and syntax" should also be taken into account.

Appraisals of this sort are yet too vague and fuzzy to allow for objective verification. But this can be no reason for not taking them seriously. Developing more rigorous and testable criteria for assessing expressive richness, grammatical simplicity, and efficiency of languages is a challenge for linguistics proper, as is the development of a conceptual framework for the kinds of adaptive changes that are possible.

Adaptation makes languages better; better, in any event, relative to certain purposes. As regards the multiple purposes and needs of communication of modern society, English nowadays presents itself as the language which, thanks to its rich lexicon, its uninhibited openness to borrowing, its simple phonology, morphology, and syntax, and its extensive repertoire of technical registers, is most advanced in the perpetual process of differentiation and integration. Language adaptation takes place wherever there is a need and opportunity for it. A language's adaptedness is a function of the communicative tasks for which it is enlisted and the number of individuals using it in carrying them out. Hence, the large size of a speech community is an adaptive advantage of its language not only for demographic and socioeconomic reasons, but also because it accelerates its adaptation to changing needs. For if we assume (as we must) that language adaptation is effected by repeated use, that is, eventually, through every speech act, then the number of speakers translates into the total length of time a language is put to use. Viewed from this angle, the adaptedness of English is no more than should be expected.

That, at a given point in time, a language has risen to become the most advanced and adapted language in the world does not mean that it will occupy this position forever. Many factors not directly related to language can lead to the decline of its speech community or major parts of it, making it less attractive to learn as a second and foreign language. The pressure put on it to adapt may lessen as a result. But once a language has been put, in the course of events, in the top position, a reduction of its significance and its impact on other languages will follow such a decline only with great delay, because on account of the structural properties it has acquired by being adapted to so many purposes, such a language is extraordinarily valuable of and in itself. In this regard languages behave like other social achievements which have grown out of the cycles of differentiation and integration. To this day, the Lombard Street at the heart of London's financial district and the Lombard Bridge in Hamburg speak of the financial activities of northern Italian merchants in the fourteenth and fifteenth centuries. And similarly, internationally important currencies continue to function as valuable means of exchange long after the economic power of their principal holders has dissipated – the pound sterling after World War I – or started to show serious weaknesses – the US dollar today. No great risk is involved, therefore, in predicting that for the next generations English will continue to be the best adapted and most widespread language of the world. The principal reasons for this are that its high level of differentiation allows it to promote a more integrated world economy, which for the first time ever is deserving of this name, while at the same time becoming ever more differentiated as a result of its enormous diffusion across the globe.

The Bottom Line

Language adaptation concerns every speech act as well as the language system as a whole. It thus combines in it the individual and the collective of language. The basic function of language is to mediate between the one and the other, for the sake of which it must be adapted continuously. This makes it the subject matter of scientific inquiry in which many different disciplines take an interest, testifying to its great importance for human existence. An exclusive claim to knowledge about language is even less tenable than about other phenomena peculiar to humanity. For *homo loquens* appears in a different light as a species, a social animal, or an individual, depending on the point of view of different scientific disciplines. They all contribute to a comprehensive understanding of his tool, human speech.

In the foregoing chapters, we have discussed language from an economic viewpoint, and economic aspects of language. This is not an attempt to explain everything on the basis of a single principle. No economic reductionism is intended. Rather, the purpose is to familiarize ourselves with yet another perspective which allows us to perceive interconnections between language as a highly abstract structure and the concrete conditions of its possessors' existence. As languages are put to use as tools by their communities, both are being interconnected. The main thesis advanced in this book is that there really is a non-trivial connection between the two sides, that is, that the formation and development of languages are affected by the way human societies interact with their physical, socioeconomic, and linguistic-cultural environments, and that, conversely, certain formal features of individual languages have an influence, however subtle, on how their users relate to these environments. In order to substantiate this argument, both analogies between linguistic and economic systems were investigated and points of contact where language becomes immediately relevant to economics, and vice versa.

We looked at the dynamics of expanding markets and language spheres, arguing that the rise of the European standard common language and the standardization of currencies were necessary concomitants of the emergence of national markets. In more than a metaphorical sense, discourse and trade were the media of intellectual and material enrichment, respectively. When they were extended across national and linguistic boundaries, dramatic changes were effected in the communication habits of those concerned: in order to cope with new communication needs, new means of communicative exchange were brought into existence by hybridization; many old ones were wiped out or abandoned. Long-distance trade made language itself a commodity. A market of languages came into being which nowadays exhibits both regional and global dimensions. There is competition between languages not only in the largely institutionalized foreign language market, but also inasmuch as languages, as they are handed down from one generation to the next, gain or lose speakers. This macro-level is where an economic evaluation of languages is feasible. Their spread is indicative of their utility, their economic success, which is dependent upon the socioeconomic conditions of their respective speech communities. However, as tools for acquiring knowledge and exchanging information, languages are an integral part of these conditions. Their competitiveness also depends on their goodness, on how well-adapted they are to the communication requirements of their speakers. Just as economic agents adjust their communication competence to their communication needs, societies proceed with their communication repertoires, their languages. They bear the necessary costs, make investments for the maintenance, cultivation, and *Ausbau* of individual languages and their entire repertoires, perhaps discarding unprofitable languages in the process. In this way, there is an interaction between the levels of differentiation and integration in society and language.

The world of today is characterized by what some fear is a widening gap between developing and advanced countries in socioeconomic and scientific-technological development. At the same time, the growth and geographic expansion of multinational enterprises, in conjunction with modern means of transport and communication, have resulted in more tightly integrated global economic relationships. Even small ethnic groups living in remote areas are increasingly drawn into the economic process and, by necessity, establish communication links with the outside world. It is from this interaction with more advanced societies that the pressure to adapt is born. Since many small languages suffer from severe deficits with respect to the functional requirements of modern communication and, therefore, are of limited value for those wishing to take part in modern life, not a few of them will in future be used less and less by their speakers or altogether disappear from their communication repertoires. What, in the present age, causes changes on the world map of languages more than anything else is their economic utility. I have tried in this book to present evidence for the claim that one constituent of the economic utility of languages is their internal economy which, in the final analysis, grows out of the necessity for human beings to apply the means for achieving communication economically. As yet, it is not very clear how exactly this necessity affects the structural possibilities of linguistic systems, and likewise knowledge about languages as a factor of the economic process is embryonic. Thus, no final balance is presented here, but a temporary account waiting for critical auditing.

Meanwhile learning progresses, slowly, and once we know more about how language and economy interact, we will be able better to economize on words.

Notes

Chapter 1 At Face Value

1   Proverbs 10: 20. Historians might question the legitimacy of interpreting the silver in Solomon's dictum as money, since the earliest archeological finds of coined money in ancient Lydia date from 625 B. C., considerably later than Solomon. However, unstamped money was common much earlier, and precious metal is known to have played a significant role as such (cf. Smith 1904: chapter 4; Keynes 1932: 181f.). The only precondition for fulfilling this function was a system of weights and measures, which had been developed in Mesopotamia as early as the third millennium B. C., cf. Seelow (1990).

2   "Und wie aus einem Beutel mancherlei Art von Münzen herauskommt, entweder güldene oder silberne oder kupferne, so auch kommen aus einem Munde Aussprüche und andere Worte von größerem oder geringerem Wert" (Stefano Guazzo, *De civili conversatione, Das ist: Von dem Bürgerlichen Wandel und zielichen Sitten.* In die Hochdeutsche Sprache gebracht von Nicolaus Rücker 1626. Quoted from Schmölders (1979: 132)). All translations of quotations are by myself, unless indicated otherwise.

3   Quoted from Burchfield (1985: 20).

4   "Daher braucht man oft die Worte als Ziffern oder als Rechenpfennige anstatt der Bildnisse und Sachen, bis man stufenweise zum Fazit schreitet und beim Vernunftschluß zur Sache selbst gelangt. Hieraus erscheint, ein wie Großes daran gelegen ist, daß die Worte als Vorbilder und gleichsam als Wechselzettel des Verstandes wohl gefaßt, wohl unterschieden, zugänglich, häufig, leichtfließend und angenehm sind" (Leibniz 1983: 7).

5   The reason for Leibniz's concern was the fact that German enjoyed only little prestige among the intellectual elite of his time and was, therefore, for higher communicative functions often replaced by the more highly respected French language. For a detailed account of Leibniz's efforts cf. Coulmas (1989c).

6   Similarly, Hegel argues that "money is not one particular type of wealth amongst others, but the universal form of all types so far as they are expressed in an external embodiment and so can be taken as 'things'" (Hegel 1854; trans. Knox 1953: 194f.).

7   "Das Geld und die Sprache sind zween Gegenstände, deren Untersuchung
     so tiefsinning und abstrakt ist, als ihr Gebrauch allgemein ist. Beide
     stehen in einer näheren Verwandschaft, als man muthmaßen sollte. Die
     Theorie des einen erklärt die Theorie des anderen; sie scheinen daher aus
     gemeinschaftlichen Gründen zu fließen. Der Reichtum aller menschlichen
     Erkenntnis beruhet auf dem Wortwechsel. . . . Alle Güter hingegen des
     bürgerlichen oder gesellschaftlichen Lebens beziehen sich auf das Geld als
     ihren allgemeinen Maasstab" (Hamann 1761/1967: 97).

8   Herder, who was strongly influenced by Hamann, also adopted this meta-
     phor. In his *Fragmenten* of 1767 he refers to the empty phrases of social
     intercourse as "the most frequent small coins of the oral and literary
     commerce" of his contemporaries, thus criticizing the artificial ways of
     speaking of modern times. In contrast, the genuine usage of the ancient
     Hebrews and Arabs was as if "gold coins were exchanged" (Herder [1767]/
     1985: 195). What he had in mind, it seems, was the analytic and concrete
     vocabulary of the oriental languages which stand out for the many mono-
     sememic terms for all natural objects, whereas European languages tend to
     use more general terms which are modified for the particular case at hand.

9   Onomatopoeia, or sound imagery, was already known to ancient Greek
     grammarians and has since deeply influenced reflections about the origin of
     language. Giving expression to a typically romantic sentiment, Herder
     theorized in his famous treatise on the origin of language: "These sighs,
     these tones are language. There is hence a language of feelings which is
     genuine law of nature" (Herder [1771]: 138). Much later, but in not too
     different a manner, the early ethnologists of the "century of imperialism"
     were fascinated by the formative power of sound symbolism which they
     thought they could detect in "primitive languages." Lévy-Bruhl (1918),
     for instance, interpreted the sound imagery of some African languages as
     vocal gestures which, he maintained, could lead to an understanding of the
     magic use of these languages. The most thorough criticism against this
     view of language formation is provided in Bühler (1934: chapter 13) where
     he explains why the question of whether the world can be depicted by
     means of sound images has to be answered in the negative.

10   Recall the beginning of Genesis. Cassirer (1925) reports on surprising
     parallels between this story of the creation of the world which accords the
     word such a prominent role and less highly developed religions and
     mythical systems where the word is revered in a similar way as the power
     which imposed order on the original chaos.

11   "Les mots sont comme les monnaies: ils ont une valeur propre avant
     d'exprimer tous les genres de valeur" (de Rivarol 1906: 125).

12   "Changer le sens des mots d'une langue faite, c'est altérer la valeur des
     monnaies dans un empire" (de Rivarol 1906: 122).

13   "Die Ideen werden nicht in der Sprache verwandelt, so daß ihre Eigentüm-
     lichkeit aufgelöst und ihr gesellschaftlicher Charakter neben ihnen in der

Sprache existierte, wie die Preise neben den Waren. Die Ideen existieren nicht getrennt von der Sprache. Ideen, die aus ihrer Muttersprache erst in eine fremde Sprache übersetzt werden müssen, um zu kursieren, um austauschbar zu werden, bieten schon mehr Analogie; die Analogie liegt dann aber nicht in der Sprache, sondern in ihrer Fremdheit" (Marx 1953: 80).

14 Still the most ingenious discussion of the implications of dialectical materialism for the philosophy of language is in Voloshinov (1973) where he expounds, among other things, how the linguistic sign is to be understood in terms of the theory of base and superstructure.

15 Above all and most convincingly Quine (1960) has argued that linguistic communication consists, first and foremost, in ascertaining that one's interlocutor refers to the objects of the physical world in a way compatible with one's own. Even establishing stable reference for one's own purposes is a process which he calls "radical translation." Cf. also Steiner (1975).

16 "Wie meine Gedanken die Form der allgemein verstandenen Sprache anneh man müssen, um auf diesem Umweg meine praktischen Zwecke zu fördern, so muß mein Tun oder Haben in die Form des Geldwertes eingehen, um meinem weitergehenden Wollen zu dienen" (Simmel 1977: 205; trans. 1978: 210).

17 ". . . ein ausschließlich soziologisches, in Beschränkung auf ein Individuum ganz sinnloses Gebilde, [das] irgend eine Veränderung gegen einen gegebenen Status nur als Veränderung der Verhältnisse der Individuen untereinander bewirken [kann]" (1977: 143).

18 ". . . pourquoi le fait social peut seule créer un système linguistique. La collectivité est necessaire pour établir des valeurs dont l'unique raison d'être est dans l'usage et le consentement général; l'individu à lui seul est incapable d'en fixer aucune" (Saussure 1972: 157; trans. 1974: 113).

19 The function of the concept of value for the theoretical development of linguistics is further discussed in chapter 6, pp. 223–9.

20 "Pour déterminer ce que vaut une pièce de cinq francs, il faut savoir: 1° qu'on peut l'échanger contre une quantité déterminée d'une chose differentente, par example du pain; 2° qu'on peut la comparer avec une valeur similaire de même système, par example une pièce d'un franc, ou avec une monnaie d'un autre système (un dollar, etc.). De même un mot peut être échangé contre quelque chose de dissemblable: une idée; en outre, il peut être comparé avec quelque chose de méme nature: un autre mot. Sa valeur n'est donc pas fixée tant qu'on se borne à constater qu'il peut être 'echangé' contre tel ou tel concept, c'est-à-dire qu'il a telle ou telle signification; il faut encore le comparer avec les valeurs similaires, avec les autres mots qui lui sont opposables. Son contenu n'est vraiment déterminé que par le concours de ce qui existe en dehors de lui" (Saussure 1972: 160; trans. 1959: 115).

21 "Daß das Geld Tausche vermittelt und Werte mißt, ist gleichsam die

Form, in der es für uns existiert; . . . Gewiß muß auch dieser Wert des
Geldes einen Träger haben; aber das Entscheidende ist, daß er nicht mehr
aus seinem Träger quillt, sondern umgekehrt der Träger das ganz Sekun-
däre ist, auf dessen an sich seiende Beschaffenheit es nur noch aus tech-
nischen, jenseits des Wertempfindens liegenden Gründen ankommt"
(1977: 196; trans. 1978: 203).

22   Early forms of moneymediated trade were rooted in the instantiation of
money as a tangible object. The use of precious metals for this purpose was
already an advanced stage. For a long time commodities such as salt, bales
of cloth, hides, or cattle (cf. Latin *pecunia* < *pecus* "cattle") were used as the
means of exchange, obscuring through their utility value the essential
difference between commodities and money. To advance from the notion
of money as a special commodity to that of money as a pure measure of
values was a great achievement of abstract thinking.

23   "Das Pendant zum Zeichenverkehr ist der *Güteraustausch*. Machen wir uns
an einem schematischen Vergleich deutlich, wie es bestellt ist mit der
Formalisierung der drei Verkehrsdinge: *Markenware, Münzen, Wörter*" (Bühler
1934: 60).

24   "Die Münze hat ein Gepräge, das ihr vom Münzstock verliehen ist; beim
unbesorgten Kaufakt prüft man nicht lange, sondern verläßt sich auf das
Erkennen des ersten Blickes. Aber wenn Echtheitszweifel aufsteigen, ist es
doch geratener, das Stück zu prüfen oder abzulehnen. Im unbesorgten
Sprechverkehr riskiert man im allgemeinen keinen späteren Verlust und
wenn ich nur genügend sicher weiß, was eine phonematisch schlecht geprägte
Münze sein *soll* nach der Intention des Sprechers, darf ich sie hinnehmen;
wenn nötig präge ich sie meinerseits richtig, sei es zur Sicherung gegen
Mißverständnisse oder zur Belehrung des Sprechers" (Bühler 1934: 60f.).

25   Book money is, of course, not a recent invention, but it is only of late that
some banks have ceased to deal in cash altogether.

26   In this case it is not really an abstract model, but the one concrete copy
which has been recorded together with certain parameters of variation
which define the extent of the admissible deviation.

27   Barkan (1980: 141), for instance, explains: "Language itself correlates with
a socially shared world . . . so as to achieve identification of what is the
same across varying experiential contexts." Unfortunately, she fails to
disclose the particulars of how this is accomplished.

28   Of late, Searle (1984: 26f.) has adopted this position. Summarizing his
ideas on the mind–body problem, he states:

> On my view, the mind and the body interact, but they are not two
> different things, since mental phenomena just are features of the
> brain. . . . Suppose we define "naive physicalism" to be the view that
> all that exists in the world are physical particles. . . . And let us

define "naive mentalism" to be the view that mental phenomena really exist. . . . . Naive mentalism and naive physicalism are not only consistent with each other, they are both true.

29   The consequences of this important fact are discussed in chapter 6.

30   "La langue est à chaque moment l'affaire de tout le monde; répardue dans une masse et maniée par elle, elle est une chose dont tous les individus se servent toute la journée. Sur ce point, on ne peut établir aucune comparaison entre elle et les autres institutions" (Saussure 1972: 107; trans. 1974: 73).

31   "Man könnte das Geld höchstens nach mancher Richtung hin der Sprache vergleichen, die sich ebenfalls den divergentesten Richtungen des Denkens und Fühlens unterstützend, verdeutlichend, herausarbeitend leiht. Es gehört zu jenen Gewalten, deren Eigenart gerade in dem Mangel an Eigenart besteht" (Simmel 1977: 533; trans. 1978: 470).

32   Galbraith (1976: chapter 6) presents these experiments in a more favorable light, crediting paper money as an important instrument of social change without which the French or the American Revolutions could not have been accomplished.

33   In German *Geld* "money", rather than *Gold*.

34   Und meinen Leuten gilt's für gutes Gold?
Dem Heer, dem Hofe gnügt's zu vollem Sold?
So sehr mich's wundert, muß ich's gelten lassen.
        (*Faust* II, 6083−5; trans. Philip Wayne)

35   Unmöglich wär's, die Flücht'gen einzufassen;
Mit Blitzeswink zerstreute sich's im Lauf.
Die Wechslerbänke stehen sperrig auf;
Man honoriert daselbst ein jedes Blatt
Durch Gold und Silber, freilich mit Rabatt.
        (*Faust* II, 6086−90; trans. Philip Wayne)

36   Hörisch (1990) provides numerous examples of the diabolic character attributed to money in European literature from antiquity to modern times. His focus of attention is on the symbolic affinity of greed and lust. As evidence of the ignominy of money he quotes a number of verses from another scene of *Faust* which, however, because of their obscenity, were never published.

37   "Nach Golde drängt, am Golde hängt doch alles! Ach, wir Armen!" *Faust* 2802−4; trans. Philip Wayne.

38   Schüler: Doch ein Begriff muß bei dem Worte sein.
Mephisto: Schon gut! Nur muß man sich nicht allzu ängstlich quälen;
        Denn eben wo Begriffe fehlen,
        Da stellt ein Wort zur rechten Zeit sich ein.
        Mit Worten läßt sich trefflich streiten

Mit Worten ein System bereiten,
An Worte läßt sich trefflich glauben,
Von einem Wort läßt sich kein Jota rauben.
                    (*Faust* I, 1993–2000; trans. Philip Wayne)

39   One need not believe, as Lakoff and Johnson (1980) have tried to convince their readers, that we "live by metaphors," in order to appreciate their cognitive significance. Ignoring as they did more than two thousand years of research, Lakoff and Johnson have reinvented the wheel of metaphoricity by pointing out that "most concepts are partially understood in terms of other concepts" (p. 56). Since my interest is not in the theory of metaphor, but in the pertinence of one particular metaphor, there is no pressing need here to discuss the shortcomings of their approach. Rather, the reader might benefit from referring to Weinrich (1958) who explored the analogy of language and money from the point of view of a theory of metaphor, treating the image of the word-coin as the central element of what he called "an image field." His concern is less with the factual significance of the homology of language and money than with the conceptual conditions of metaphor formation. His main point is that, much like semantically related words, metaphors are not isolated, but, in conjunction with others, constitute an image field. In his discussion of the metaphors which belong to the metaphorical system of the word-coin he provides a great number of examples, especially from belles-lettres.

Chapter 2   "*Language is an Asset*"

1   Sources for number of languages: Grimes (1988); for population and per capita income statistics: World Bank and *The World Almanac and Book of Facts 1991*.

2   Per capita income is normally defined as the total income of the residents of an economy divided by the total population. An important defect of per capita income as a measure of economic development is that only marketed products are taken into account. Especially with respect to developing countries where a relatively large portion of the economy operates at the level of subsistence production, this results in a somewhat distorted picture.

3   In the absence of detailed studies, it is often difficult to know how closely languages are related to each other, especially in the case of unwritten languages. Whether two varieties should be considered independent languages or dialects of one language is a question that may not be answered uniformly by their speakers, linguists, or politicians. Cf. Haugen (1966), Coulmas (1985: chapter 1).

4   Cf. Linguistic Minorities Project (1985: 50).

5   At a time when the last European multilingual empire, the Hapsburg monarchy, crumbled, Max Weber (1978: 395) commented on the relationship between nation, state, and language as follows: "Indeed, 'nation state' has become conceptually identical with 'state' based on common language."

6   According to Décsy (1973: 176f.) the mother tongue of 88 percent of the population of European states is identical with the official language of their country.

7   I have on various occasions argued against the neglect of writing in linguistics. In Coulmas (1989a) I have tried to demonstrate that writing does not only exercise an influence on linguistic analysis, but on language itself. The rather extensive recent literature is reviewed there in some detail.

8   Writing was recognized as the crucial difference already by Spengler. He called it "the great symbol of the distant, thus the will for eternity" and "one of the first indications of historical aptitude" (1922: 180). In his cyclical philosophy of history, historical consciousness is viewed as the watershed between primitive life which is grounded in the present, and a civilization designed for continuation: "The word belongs to man; writing belongs to civilized man alone" (1922: 180).

9   "Die Frage nach den Triebkräften der Expansion des modernen Kapitalismus ist nicht in erster Linie eine Frage nach der Herkunft der kapitalistisch verwertbaren Geldvorräte, sondern vor allem nach der Entwicklung des kapitalistischen Geistes" (Weber 1920: 53; trans. 1930: 68).

10   ". . . die Ersetzung einer höchst bequemen, praktisch damals wenig fühlbaren, vielfach fast nur noch formalen Herrschaft durch eine im denkbar weitgehendsten Maße in alle Sphären des häuslichen und öffentlichen Lebens eindringende, unendlich lästige und ernstgemeinte Reglementierung der ganzen Lebensführung" (Weber 1920: 20; trans. 1930: 36).

11   Eggers (1969: 145) cites the number of 1,120 print shops in 260 European towns for 1500.

12   According to Pörksen (1989: 130) the number of German prints surpassed that of Latin ones only during the last two decades of the seventeenth century.

13   For instance, Ickelsamer's *Teutsch Grammatica* of 1527 which, for promotion purposes, was provided with the promisory subtitle *Die rechte weis aufs kürzist lesen zu lernen* "the proper way of learning to read quickliest." Cf. Giesecke (1979).

14   Paul (1909: 420) pointed out that "if the advantages of printing were to take effect, a single print must suffice for the entire language area, which implies that the language put down in print is understood everywhere." Similarly, von Polenz (1978: 86) emphasized the importance of the press for the emergence of the German common language.

15 Merchants, too, were actively involved in this process. As Cipolla notes, merchants' manuals providing detailed information about countries and measures, merchandise, trade practices, monetary exchange, etc. were among the first printed materials which were put on sale with great success. 'Between 1589 and 1640, John Browne's *The Merchant Avizo* went through six editions, and J. De Savary's *Le Parfait Negociant*, published at the end of the seventeenth century, was also frequently reprinted" (Cipolla 1991: 157).

16 To be sure, the contributions of individuals must not be overrated. One person cannot create a common language valid for a whole nation. Nevertheless, Luther played an outstanding role, because he was both influential in the religious–political domain and highly creative in his linguistic usage. His writings provided the process of linguistic compromise (*Ausgleich*) with a direction. In 1822 Jacob Grimm, therefore, remarked in the preface to his grammar of the German language "that one may, indeed, call new high German the protestant dialect" (Grimm 1822: xi).

17 "Gemeinsamkeit der Sprache, geschaffen durch gleichartige Tradition von seiten der Familie und Nachbarumwelt, erleichtert das gegenseitige Verstehen, also die Stiftung aller sozialen Beziehungen, im höchsten Grade" (Weber 1956: 22; trans. 1978: 42).

18 "Die Orientierung an den Regeln der gemeinsamen Sprache ist primär also nur Mittel der Verständigung, nicht Sinngehalt von sozialen Beziehungen" (Weber 1956: 23; trans. 1978: 43). In view of the ideological instrumentalization of languages for nationalistic purposes, Weber's assessment clearly provokes far-reaching criticism. Since this problem has only indirect bearing on the economic aspects of language development, it shall not be addressed here. Cf. Fishman (1972), Weinstein (1983), Coulmas (1985: chapter 2) for further discussion.

19 In the Austro-Hungarian Dual Monarchy, for instance, Latin was still the official language at the time of the Congress of Vienna (1814–15).

20 Abbé Grégoire in his report of June 6, 1794 informed the National Convention that

> one can assure without exaggeration that at least six million Frenchmen, especially in the provinces, are ignorant of the national language; that an equal number is incapable of holding a sustained conversation; that in the last analysis, the number of those who speak it fluently does not exceed three million, and probably the number of those who write it correctly is still smaller.
> (Quoted after Jacob 1990: 50)

21 That dialects are best preserved in isolated rural areas is the obvious correlate of the link between industrialization and language standardiz-

ation. It is well known that dialect leveling is largely motivated by economic forces. As Leopold (1959: 140) remarks, social and economic reasons often require complete conformity in language.

22 Cf. Jakobson (1945).

23 Cf. Burchfield (1985: 20ff.).

24 Commins (1988) explores the socioeconomic background of the failure of Ireland's language policy in maintaining, or reviving, Irish.

25 Cf. Van de Craen and Willemyns (1988).

26 In passing it is of some interest to note that the variety of Buddhism most characteristic of Japan, Zen, has cultivated a working ethos of self-supply and knows no mendicant friars.

27 Cf. Coulmas (1988).

28 Cf. DeFrancis (1984).

29 "In Quebec . . . the entire educational system was designed for a population made up exclusively of English Protestants and French Catholics" (Mackey 1984: 160). Cf. also Esman (1985) and chapter 4, p. 92ff. below.

30 The implications of the formation of languages for specific purposes for the language system are discussed in chapter 7.

31 Cultural anthropologists usually take a close relationship of commodity exchange and communication for granted, so much so that the two sometimes seem hard to distinguish. For example, according to Lévi-Strauss (1969), beneath the contingent organization of social life, there is "exchange, always exchange." Systems of marriage, transfer of property, and linguistic communication are all analyzable in terms of generalized exchange. I do not wish to pursue this avenue of approach, because the point at issue here is that communication, with language as its most important means, is part of the economy and that, on the other hand, economic principles are found to be at work in language (see chapter 6 below), but that both are, nonetheless, distinct.

32 "Le troc . . . est une forme d'''échange qui ne necessite aucune pratique linguistique et s'accomode fort bien du commerce à la muette" (Calvet 1984: 56). Mühlhäusler (1986: 51–3) discusses the question to what extent gesture can accomplish communication across linguistic boundaries. He conjectures that, in the absence of a common linguistic means of exchange, communication was impaired by frequent misunderstandings, which is why communicative pressure quickly leads to the development of a jargon. Cf. also chapter 5 below.

33 In their investigation of language use on multilingual markets in Ethiopia, Cooper and Carpenter (1969) found that merchants tend, to the best of their abilities, to adjust to the mother tongue of their respective customers.

34 "Je mehr Menschen miteinander in Beziehung treten, desto abstrakter und allgemeingültiger muß ihr Tauschmittel sein; und umgekehrt, ist erst einmal ein solches geschaffen, so gestattet es eine Verständigung auf sonst

unzugängliche Entfernung hin, eine Einbeziehung der allermannigfaltigsten Persönlichkeiten in die gleiche Aktion, eine Wechselwirkung und damit Vereinheitlichung von Menschen, die wegen ihres räumlichen, sozialen, personalen und sonstigen Interessenabstandes in gar keine andere Gruppierung zu bringen wären" (Simmel 1977: 377; trans. 1978: 347).

35   In 1793 Père Grégoire in his report to the National Convention on "The need and the means to eradicate the patois and to universalize the use of the French language" suggested that all citizens should be able to communicate with each other. As one of the reasons for this suggestion he explicitly states that "for the territory of the whole nation *every language is paramount to a trade barrier*" (emphasis added, cf. de Certeau et al. 1975: 300ff.)

36   Quoted in Galbraith (1987: 39).

37   *Disme* is derived from French *dixième* "tenth" and became *dime. Dollar* is derived from German *Taler*. Cf. Mencken (1945: 116).

38   Quoted in Mencken (1945: 10).

39   The French-franc zone cannot obscure this fact. Formed in 1948, it comprises 13 francophone African countries whose currencies are tied to the French franc by a fixed exchange rate. Although this linkage was intended as a means of disciplining the monetary policies of these countries, devaluation and inflation could not be averted. Cf. The *Economist* July 21, 1990: 82.

40   Quoted in Panikkar (1969: 246).

41   Cf. p. 25, and, more recently, Pool (1990: 250f.).

42   Hoogvelt (1978: chapter 3) provides a useful overview of current theories of development.

43   Lévi-Strauss' *Tristes tropiques* (1955) may be quoted in this connection. Although development was hardly an issue when he wrote it, the underlying idea of this book is the destruction of traditional structures by the unchecked advance of civilization. For an account within the framework of the sociology of development cf. Mair (1963).

44   These problems are dealt with in *Capital*, vol. 3. Another important article is "The Government of India" which Marx wrote in 1853 for the New York Daily Tribune. For a critical account of recent dependency theories concerning structural imperialism and "the development of underdevelopment" cf. Wesseling (1988: 264ff.).

45   In 1937, Gandhi wrote: "I insist so much on language because it is a powerful means of achieving national unity" (Gandhi 1965: 45). Weinstein (1983: 138) explains the importance of a common language for nation building as follows: "Efforts to save and use each and every language for all the same political and economic functions disrupt efforts to build and maintain national solidarity. A multiplicity of official tongues makes communication over a large area impossible; it encourages fissiparous

forces, wastes resources, and ultimately vitiates integrating efforts." Cf. also Fishman et al. (1968).

46 "Nous nous exprimons en français, parce qu le français est une langue à vocation universelle, que notre message s'adresse *aussi* aux Français de France et aux autres hommes. . . . Chez nous, les mots sont naturellement nimbés d'un halo de sève et de sang; les mots du français rayonnent de mille feux, comme des diamants." Quoted in Ngūgī (1986: 19).

47 See also Pattanayak (1981) and Khubchandani (1983) for critical discussions of the equation of modernization with the elimination of multilingualism.

Chapter 3   The Value of a Language

1 "Daß Nationen von glücklicheren Gaben und unter günstigeren Umständen vorzüglichere Sprachen, als andere, besitzen, liegt in der Natur der Sache selbst" (Humboldt 1963a: 20).

2 Early European students of non-European languages were often deeply impressed by the systematicity of their make-up. Du Ponceau, for example, made the following remak about one of the Delaware languages:

> Who can say what Homer would have produced if he had had for his instrument the language of the Lenni Lenape? . . . He would have been able to say more in fewer words, than even in his own admirable Greek. (Zeisberger 1830: 95f.)

3 Linguistic aspects of qualitative language valuation are treated in more detail in chapter 7.

4 The metaphorical extension of the economic concept of value was initiated during the 1890s by the philosophers Alexius Meinong and Franz Brentano and further elaborated into a general theory of values in the works of Max Scheler (1921) and Nicolai Hartmann (1926). Moritz Schlick (1934) then developed a meta-normative theory of values concentrating on the epistemological status of value predicates and sentences. This approach is influential in the philosophical discussion of values (e.g. Apel 1976).

5 Conceivably, this emphasis on verbal skills is a characteristic of our loquacious times. In premodern cultures it is not at all common that everybody has to say something on every possible occasion. This has been stressed time and again by Lévi-Strauss, who nevertheless views language as the ultimate paradigm of structuring reality (Lévi-Strauss 1958).

6 Even for the Roman people Rhaeto-Romance is only "the language of the heart," while German is that of "one's daily bread," as Solèr (1986: 289) pointedly put it. He also points out that in the nineteenth century

RhaetoRomance was recognized as an obstacle to economic development.

7 Gorter (1987) gives 400,000 as the number of speakers of Western Frisian in the Netherlands and 10,000 for the Northern Frisian dialects in Germany.

8 The importance of mobility for modern economic life can hardly be over-emphasized. With respect to development Moore (1961: 71) bluntly stated that "if one were to attempt a one-word summary of the institutional requirement of economic development that word would be 'mobility'."

9 As a result of the globalization of television, Icelandic is coming under increasing pressure from English. Until recently, English language broadcasting was strictly limited in Iceland, but the Gulf War of 1991 opened the door to virtually unlimited consumption of American and British TV products.

10 Analyzing the difficulties immigrants are confronted with in Western Europe, Castles and Kosach (1973: 181) point out that language is their first and most urgent problem upon arrival and that many immigrants never completely master their linguistic difficulties. In Japan, too, immigrants have to be content with jobs for which many of them are highly over-qualified because of insufficient language skills (Kimura 1987).

11 The EC Commission repeatedly deplored inadequate foreign language skills as a major obstacle on the way to realizing the legal possibilities of free movement of persons and ideas throughout the Community (e.g. Documents COM (88) 841: 1989). The Community's initiatives concerning the improvement of foreign language education are discussed in more detail in chapter 4 below.

12 Robert L. Cooper (personal communication); these statistics are for the Jewish year beginning in September or October.

13 By contrast, the diffusion of Arabic as a second language in Israel has been described as "a non-profit investment," because its linguistic capital value in Israeli society is low, if not negative (Ben-Rafael and Brosh 1991).

14 The fact that China had monolingual dictionaries much earlier than that cannot be explained away by pointing out that, owing to the nature of the Chinese writing system, the earliest Chinese dictionaries were character dictionaries. Professor Wu Tie-ping of Beijing Normal University has kindly called my attention to the earliest known character dictionary, the *Er ya* of 206 B.C., which contained 3,600 entries. The 10,000 entries of the famous etymological dictionary *Shuo wen jiezi* of 120 A.D. is already organized in accordance with the main principles of all subsequent Chinese lexicography.

15 Like science in general (cf. Solla Price 1963), lexicography is strongly centered in the present. It must not be overlooked, however, that the first step of lexicographically recording a language is always the most difficult and most important one. Dictionary work is more cumulative in nature than other scientific work, even though careful selection and prudent limitations are crucial for the production of good dictionaries.

16 Languages that use different writing systems, say English and Chinese, illustrate the fundamental difference between dictionaries of the two kinds. In a Chinese–English dictionary for Chinese users the entries are given in Chinese characters, but in a dictionary of the same language pair for primary speakers of English they will be alphabetically transliterated.

17 Zgusta (1971) is a useful overview of the problems and methods of lexicography providing many detailed references.

18 Japanese publishers benefit from this situation, since, by default, many English-speaking learners buy dictionaries made for Japanese users which are still better than none. With less distant language pairs, the functional difference of bilingual dictionaries for primary speakers of the one or the other are not so conspicuous. As Hausmann (1985: 378) points out, bilingual dictionaries of the great European standard languages are, therefore, usually marketed in both countries.

19 Occasionally bilingual dictionaries are compiled with a normative purpose in mind. This may be the case where a language without a well-defined standard is related by means of a dictionary to a highly standardized language which, as it were, then functions as a scaffold. For example, E. Annamalai, the director of the Central Institute of Indian Languages, explains the purpose of a modern Tamil–English dictionary as "aiming at defining and legitimising modern Tamil" (Annamalai, personal communication August 18, 1989).

20 It must be recognized, of course, that the compilers of dictionaries do not necessarily regard their work as an investment. Especially in the case of first dictionaries for languages not hitherto recorded, the primary motivation is not usually the expectation of financial returns, but scientific or missionary zeal.

21 Included among the monolingual dictionaries are the character dictionaries peculiar to Japanese in which the Japanese and the Sinojapanese strata of the vocabulary are related to each other (*Jiten jiten sôgô mokuroku* 1989).

22 It has been demonstrated in some detail, for instance in Saitô (1977) and Yanabu (1977), that the Japanese translation zeal ever since the Meiji period has left distinct traces on the Japanese language.

23 This trend is particularly conspicuous in the natural sciences where German scientists publish more original research results in English than in German (Skudlik 1990). The changing status of German as a language of scientific communication has attracted some attention lately. Cf., for instance, Klaverkämper and Weinrich (1986), Ammon (1990), Coulmas (1990).

24 By presenting these two graphs together, I do not want to suggest that the tendencies they display are causally related. It is hardly farfetched, however, to assume that their synchronous appearance is not coincidental. Rather, the underlying reasons for the increasing appreciation of the yen and the Japanese language are the same: during the decade in question Japan has become an economic superpower. As one relevant indication it is

useful to note that Japan has emerged as the biggest aidgiver in the world. By 1986 it had become the chief benefactor of 25 countries throughout the world (McCord 1991: 157). The growing demand for Japanese as a foreign language, therefore, does not come as a surprise. Cf. Coulmas (1989b) for more details on the surge of Japanese.

25 In 1988, 151 countries were members of the International Monetary Fund.

26 It is not possible accurately to determine the total of international foreign exchange reserves, because central banks do not usually reveal their holdings and to estimate those of private banks is even more difficult. The above statistics are therefore given in percent rather than in absolute numbers.

27 In a report on foreign language needs, Oud de Glas (1983) lists more than 100 titles on this topic.

28 In the 1960s educational policies in the Netherlands were adjusted to market developments. Choice of the first foreign language was decontrolled which led to English becoming by far the most popular first choice and French being displaced to the third rank behind German. In 1975 an analysis of language needs in the Netherlands was carried out by the Institute of Applied Sociology of the University of Nijmegen. It was found that the greatest demand was for English, German, and French, in this order. For example, all students of the economic disciplines read educational materials in English, 75 percent in German, and 35 percent in French. There was some variation in the respective figures for other disciplines, but the rank order was the same throughout. This is a strong indication that foreign language choice is determined rather directly by the perceived utility of the languages in question (Oud de Glas 1979).

29 This question has been asked explicitly by Strevens (1982) and by Haberland (1990). The latter was not aware, it seems, of Strevens's concern with the problem to which he, too, directs his attention, that of who should have the prerogative of determining the standard of the modern world language. Interesting as it is, this discussion amounts to little more than hair splitting if it fails to take into account the economic dimension of this question.

30 The market for EFL textbooks and other educational materials made in Britain is estimated at 1 billion. Further, more than 20,000 Britons are employed in EFL teaching and other language jobs overseas. English as a commodity now also has its own fair, the English Language Fair, first held at the Institute of Education, University of London (*The Linguist* 28/4 (1989) p. 111).

31 Popular and, maybe, also plausible as this assumption is, there is no empirical evidence to support it. The question whether one language is easier to learn as a first language than another is as simple to ask as it is difficult empirically to investigate. That there is virtually no research

about this is due to the fact that it is extraordinarily difficult, if not impossible, to control all of the relevant variables which bear on language acquisition as part of a culturally specific socialization in order to thus make the first acquisition of two languages truly comparable.

Universalists who, like Chomsky, emphasize that language acquisition is a natural process virtually unaffected by sociocultural variables therefore find it easy to claim, or implicitly assume, that all languages are equally easy or difficult to acquire as first languages. However, as long as there is no empirical evidence supporting this assumption, we should not preclude from our reasoning about how languages are similar and different from each other the possibility that some are easier to acquire than others.

Chapter 4   The Costliness of the Polyglot World

1   Although Breton (1978) does not mention Max Weber, his account of nationalism and language policies in Canada calls to mind a comparison between the Protestant Anglo-Canadians and the Franco-Canadians who decidedly opposed the "Protestant ethic". Cf. p. 26ff. above. It is interesting to note in this connection that Ó Riagáin (1991: 257) makes a similar point about the Catholic church in Ireland where, in the eighteenth century, language shift to English was slowed down, as "Catholics, and therefore Irish-speakers, [were prevented] from participating in economic and political life."

2   For a detailed albeit somewhat dated analysis of the economic conditions of Franco- and Anglo-Canadians see Raynauld and Marion (1972).

3   Quoted from Daoust (1990: 108). Vaillancourt (1978) analyzed the social implications of the Charter immediately after it was passed into law, and Daoust (1990) presents a critical assessment of its effects after a decade.

4   Article 46 of the Charter is very explicit in this regard as it prescribes French for all written communication between employers and their personnel, and forbids employers to require of job applicants knowledge of a language "other than the official one," unless they can prove that knowledge of such a language is essential for the job in question (cf. Daoust 1990: 111).

5   Those responsible for these policies have never hesitated to admit this. A former Quebec Minister of Culture for instance declared "Nous savons de quel prix il faut parfois payer – voire douloureusement – le maintien d'une langue et d'une culture nationale" [We are well aware of the price that, hard as it may be, it is occasionally necessary to pay in order to maintain a national language and culture] (Richard 1984: 32).

6   All three agencies were created through the 1977 Charter: a, the task of

l'Office de la langue française is to make sure that French becomes the language of communications, of work, commerce, and business in the public sector and private enterprise, which includes the formation of appropriate terminologies by the Banque de terminologie du Québec; b, the Commission de protection de la language française concerns itself with violations of the language laws and their corrections or penalties; finally, c, the Conseil de la langue française was established to advise the government on questions of language policy. For further details see Daoust (1990: 113f.).

7   Four of Belgium's seven government crises since 1979 were provoked by the perennial language strife.

8   In 1988, about 11 percent of the American population, that is, some 27.6 million people, spoke languages other than English as their first language (*Britannica World Data Book* 1988).

9   Baetens Beardsmore and Kohls (1988: 67) have rightly pointed out that the primary concern of school systems which have been evolved for coping with several languages within a given country is typically that of fostering national cohesion. By contrast, the system of European Schools established in 1953 does not serve the integration of marginal groups, but rather pursues the ambitious aim to eliminate ethnolinguistic prejudice and make sure that all students become proficient in more than two languages. There are European Schools in five countries with a total population of 12,000 students. These schools are publicly funded and, not surprisingly, because of their multilingual operation, are particularly expensive.

10   Some readers may be surprised to learn that English is not the official national language of the United States. The political controversy about US English and other groups committed to the idea that the United States needs an official language is well documented in Marshall's (1986) thorough article and in Adams and Brink (1990).

11   For further allegations that Spanish-speaking immigrants to the United States create "barriers to assimilation" cf. also Bikales and Imhoff (1985: 8–10).

12   In their campaigns at national and state levels, US English habitually appeals to social greed by calling attention to the tax monies which, as they see it, are wasted for bilingual education (see, for instance, Diamond 1990).

13   Cf. Jernudd and Jo (1985) for a similar argument.

14   Cf. Lee McKay and Wong (1988) for the US, Brook (1980) for Britain, Extra and Vallen (1988) for the Netherlands, Kerr (1984) for Sweden, Nelde et al. (1981) for Germany, Bentahila (1983) and Fitouri (1983) for Morocco and Tunisia, Gonzales (1978) for several South Asian countries, and Lewis (1977) for some cross-national comparisons.

15   Notice that in another dominantly English-speaking country where multiculturalism has become more widely accepted as a social ideology

of late, the government takes a very different stance toward foreign language education. The government of Australia recently established the well-funded Languages Institute of Australia designed to improve the quality of language education in Australia, "in keeping with the goals and principles of the National Policy on Languages and Australia's social, economic and cultural needs" (*New Language Planning Newsletter* 4, 2: 3–5).

16 *Ministerie van Welvaart, Volksgezondheid en Cultuur* Fact Sheet-1-E-1986.

17 This figure is an estimate by Friedrichsverlag, the largest German publishing house for pedagogical journals. Since elementary school teachers teach all subjects, it is difficult to make a more specific statement.

18 This figure was provided by the Secretary of the Permanent Conference of Ministers of Culture in Bonn; personal communication March 19, 1990.

19 Cf. Weinrich (1985), especially his comments on "linguistic culture in the school," pp. 27–32.

20 Harald Koch (personal communication), a lawyer who specializes in legal problems of language use, has pointed out to me that even legal documents such as contracts or bills often contain meaningless terms such as "a country's mother tongue" giving rise to difficult forensic problems. Cf. also Le Page and Tabouret-Keller (1985: 188ff.) and Skutnabb-Kangas and Phillipson (1989).

21 The Swiss census, for example, does not allow for multiple answers to the mother tongue question, forcing Rhaeto-Romance speakers most of whom also speak German to make a choice, which does not reflect the reality of their bilingualism from birth.

22 Article 2 stipulates that these children shall be given compensatory teaching in the host country's language, and Article 3 provides that they shall receive formal schooling in their (parents') mother tongue.

23 There is a growing need for funding German language training for migrants with a claim on German nationality. The latest available figure of public funds allocated by the German government is for the first half of fiscal 1984: DM 95.6 million (Deutscher Bundestag 1986: 334).

24 For a discussion of the most commonly cited definitions of language planning cf. Cooper (1989: 29–45).

25 Rubin (1979) lists 152 organizations in 75 countries. In the meantime new organizations have come into existence, for example, the Bureau for Lesser Used Languages sponsored by the EC, which on the basis of a 1981 resolution passed by the European Parliament was established in Dublin; or the Comité International pour la Sauvegarde de la Language Bretonne in Brussels. The rising tide of nationalism in eastern Europe and in the republics of the former USSR has also brought with it renewed institutional care for various languages.

26 The tasks of the *Bord na Gaeilge* is described in some detail by Tovey (1988).

27   This unofficial and unpublished estimate for the years 1983–5 suggests that expenditure on the Irish language is running at less than 0.1 percent of total government expenditure. This does not, however, include incalculable hidden costs. (P. Ó Riagáin, personal communication, March 13, 1990.)

28   According to a calculation by Robert Cooper, personal communication.

29   I have not been able to determine the annual budget of the Académie française, although I have been assisted in my quest by some French colleagues.

30   According to Article 6 of its statute, the task of the Commissariat général is "to support and coordinate activities of the administration and other public and private organs which are designed to spread and defend the French language" ("d'animer et de coordonner l'action des administrations et des organismes publics et privés qui concourent à la diffusion et à la défense de la langue française").

31   For more details on script and spelling reform projects cf. Coulmas (1989a: chapter 13); for German cf. Kommission für Rechtschreibfragen (1988); and for Dutch de Rooij and Verhoeven (1988).

32   The problems of adapting Arabic to the communicative needs of modern society are discussed in Ibrahim (1989). Seckinger (1988) provides an in-depth account of the specific problems of Morocco's Arabization policy.

33   Altoma (1974) discusses a problem of the Arabic script which is often mentioned in this connection. The different shapes of Arabic letters in initial, medial, and final position are uneconomical, hard to handle by machines, and difficult to learn.

34   For details cf. Misra (1982) and, more generally on the problems of modernizing India's great regional languages, Daswani (1989).

35   Cf. Instituto della Enciclopedia Italiana (1986).

36   Cf. Tovey (1988) for details on the Irish campaign, Anderson (1987) on the Indonesian language month, and Cooper (1986) for a general assessment of the significance of public relations work for language planning. The Euskara Congress is documented in *II. Euskal-Bilzarra*, three luxurious volumes published by the Servicio Central de Publicaciones del Gobierno Vasco 1988.

37   In fiscal 1989; cf. Witte (1989) and Ammon (1989) for a survey of the Federal Republic of Germany's language export policy up to 1985; for documentation of the opinions of law makers and experts invited to report their view on this matter to a parliamentary committee, cf. Deutscher Bundestag (1986).

38   Cf. Ridler and Pons-Ridler (1986: 50) for this estimate and further details.

39   "'Accepter le monopole linguistique de l'anglo-américain constitue un appauverissement culturel sans précédent.'. . . M. Chevènement voudrait impulser une politique diversifiée des langues vivantes, composante essentielle de notre force de frappe économique'" (*Le Monde* 1985: 31).

40   *Français du Monde* (1982: 13).

41   "Le lien entre la language et le commerce ne peut être durablement établi que dans la mesure où un certain nombre de préjugés seront progressivement abandonnés: préjugé matérialiste vulgaire quant à l'activité économique, conception passéiste de la culture, séparation radicale de l'échange culturel et de l'échange commercial. C'est dire qu'un immense travail de démonstration est à faire quant à l'utilité économique et commerciale de la langue française" (Renouvin 1989: 75).

42   Cf. Lewis (1972).

43   NRC-Handelsblad May 25, 1990.

44   Gage (1986: 374) compares the major languages of the world from the point of view of their productive power. According to his criteria, German and Japanese are "languages of high-tech industry." It is in keeping with this assessment that for both languages specific educational materials have been developed recently. The Goethe-Institut now offers a diploma for business German for which it developed a curriculum in collaboration with the German Chamber of Commerce.

45   "Die Bundesregierung wird Deutsch nicht nur fördern, wo Nachfrage nach Deutschunterricht besteht. Sie wird versuchen, in den wichtigen Partnerländern aktiv Interesse zu wecken" (Deutscher Bundestag 1986: 265).

46   "Werbung für die deutsche Sprache als Marketing, etwa sogar durch eine Werbeagentur, ist abzulehnen. Die besten Werbeagenturen für die deutsche Sprache sind die deutsche Literatur und die in den deutschsprachigen Ländern betriebene Wissenschaft. (Deutscher Bundestag 1986: 196)

47   "Das ist ökonomisch und hat mit auswärtiger Kulturpolitik überhaupt nichts zu tun" (Freimut Duve in Deutscher Bundestag 1986: 17).

48   Cf. Boeglin (1987), Bowen (1987).

49   The Committee on Youth, Culture, Education, Information and Sport gives the following percentages for the language costs of the various EC institutions' administrative budgets: Parliament 60%, Council 60%, Court of Justice 50%, Commission 33% (EC Document 1–306/82, p. 31). A more recent estimate puts the proportion of language costs of the operational expenditures of these institutions at between 35% and 65% (Vollmer 1989: 85). Cf. also Kusterer (1980) who refers to "the astronomical costs" generated by the EC's official multilingualism. The *Economist* (July 18, 1987) also comments on the language costs of the EC.

50   Barrera i Vidal (1991) describes the post-Franco situation of Catalan and summarizes the arguments for its recognition on the EC level.

51   For a discussion of the ideological background and the economic consequences of the EC's language policy problems cf. Coulmas (1991a).

52   For example, bomb attacks on British broadcasting installations or the painting over of signposts in Wales; cf. Baker (1985).

53   dpa February 1990; under the heading "Deutsch please", the daily *Die Welt*, September 6, 1989 made a similar plea, praising the then-minister

of economics, Haussmann, for demanding "more weight for German in the EC," a request which was repeated once again in the *Frankfurter Allgemeine Zeitung* of July 8, 1991, p. 10.

54 "Une économie 'ideal' supposerait une langue unique à travers le monde" – thus Chaudenson (1987: 55) in a research paper about language, education, and development in Africa, in which he also refers to *babélisme* as a problem.

55 A report of the British Government Committee for Education for Sales-manship commented that "in almost all markets it is a damaging and often fatal handicap if representatives cannot converse freely with the customer in his own language, as well as read his newspapers and trade journals" (quoted from Lowe 1982: 23). Cf. also Håkausson (1982).

56 Bowen (1980).

57 Stalpers (1992) is a discourse-analytic study of language barriers in negotia-tions of Dutch and French businessmen.

58 In 1988, British exports had a total volume of $145,151 billion with a population of 56.9 million, as compared to a population of 14.7 million Dutch whose exports totalled $103,561 billion.

59 Truchot (1990: 94) reports on a study of General Motors France in Strasbourg which reveals a similar attitude: "Il ne viendrait jamais à l'idée d'un Américain d'apprendre le français pour communiquer avec des mem-bres du personnel de General Motors France." [The idea to learn French in order to communicate with the company personnel of General Motors France never occurred to any of the Americans].

60 Cf., e.g., Erlinghagen (1975), Hayashi (1988), Neustupný (1989). Tsuda (1984) is an ethnographic study of characteristic differences in the style of Japanese and American sales talk.

61 This figure is based on the 1991 price of ¥4,000 for a small group lesson at the Berlitz School in Tokyo. Three hours per day, five days a week adds up to ¥2,880,000 or 11,000 at current exchange rates. A price of ¥6,000 to ¥7,500 is charged for private lessons.

62 However, in certain industries such as the securities business which is involved in daily transactions across national borders and time zones, it is above all proficiency in English which is indispensable. The *Economist* (July 21, 1990, p. 18) pointed out that "the use of English as the market's *lingua franca* . . . has disadvantaged smaller Japanese brokerages."

63 Cavanagh (1988), Coulmas (1989b).

64 Quoted from Matthews and Nakamura (1989: 17f.). These and many other comments as well as my own observations make Holden's (1987: 129) claim seem quite dubious. Largely inspired by Miller's (1982) often tendentious account of Japan's linguistic culture, he maintains that a fluent command of Japanese can be "totally counterproductive" for business.

65 Marketing Semiotics is being conceived by some as a subdiscipline in the

making, where semioticians and marketing specialists develop new inter-disciplinary theoretical and methodological approaches for a formal investi-gation of the sign processes in the market (Umiker-Sebeok 1987). Cf. also Vestergaard and Schröder (1985).

66   Hagen (1988) provides an account of the foreign language needs of com-merce and industry in Britain.

67   According to the theory of human capital, every individual is endowed with native and acquired faculties which taken together constitute the human capital. Human capital thus combines physical constitution, strength, and intelligence with knowledge obtained through experience and learning, as, for example, that of foreign languages. Cf. Becker (1975).

68   The translation system Metal is sold with a price tag of DM80,000.

69   As yet machine translation programs are to be considered as an auxiliary device rather than a substitute for human translators. It is beyond doubt, however, that their productivity is greatly enhanced by the various pro-grams that are available today. Hutchins (1986) and Large (1983: 88–116) are instructive accounts of the research history of automatic translation.

70   "Gute Qualität zu niedrigen Preisen, mit anderen Worten: Rationalisier-ung der Arbeitsabläufe – das ist das Ziel, dem sich alles unterordnen muß, was im Betrieb geschieht. Auch die Sprache hat überall, wo sie im Betrieb gebraucht wird, diesem Ziel zu dienen" (Häfele 1977: 86).

71   L'Association générale des usagers de la language française. For additional examples of France's language inquisition see L'Express (1984).

72   For a discussion of the allocation of language risks in cross-border sales transactions and further references cf. Koch (1991).

73   Commission des Communautés européennes, SG (85) 8781, December 8, 1985.

74   More detailed studies of economic aspects of language problems are pro-vided in the documentation of an international conference on language and information in economy and society which was held in 1985 in Hamburg (Bungarten 1988); cf. also ENCRAGES (1986).

75   "A chaque fois qu'on envisage un changement, le problème est de savoir si la situation d'arrivée sera vraiment meilleure à tous régards que le présent état des choses, et si le coût à encourir pour effectuer ce changement n'est pas prohibitif: en d'autres mots, si le jeu en vaut la chandelle" (Robillard 1987: 31).

76   For example, Ben-Rafael and Brosch (1991) describe the diffusion of Arabic as a second language in Israel as "a nonprofit investment," because the linguistic capital value of Arabic in Israeli society is low, if not negative.

77   Cf., for example, Sakaguchi (1989) with many references; also Large (1985). In this connection it is of some interest that one of the creators of a

planned language was treasurer in the French ministry of finance, Joachim Faiguet de Villeneuve, who presented his design for the *Langue nouvelle* in volume IX of the *Encyclopédie*.

78 This means that the so-called "marginal-cost conditions" of supply and demand and the retail price of a commodity do not hold here, not in any event in the same way as they hold for material commodities; for the individual's marginal value and opportunity costs do not coincide with the marginal value and opportunity costs of the collectivity.

79 Quoted in Pons-Ridler and Ridler (1987: 101).

80 "Le coût d'un tel programme serait élevé; il convient donc de le considérer non comme une dépense improductive, mais comme un investissement. L'Europe dans son ensemble dispose d'un patrimoine linguistique qui, s'il était valorisé, lui permettrait à la fois d'accroître son rayonnement dans le monde et de souder les peuples à l'intérieur de ses limites" (Truchot 1990: 366).

81 "Wer Deutsch spricht und versteht, der kauft auch eher deutsch als der unserer Sprache Unkundige" (Witte 1987).

82 Other Eastern European countries where Russian used to be the first foreign language since communist regimes were installed there had similar problems. In 1989, Hungary decided to retrain 1,000 Russian teachers as German teachers (*Süddeutsche Zeitung*, October 17, 1989).

83 In his account of the unfolding world economy, Stadermann (1988: 5) observes with respect to ships and caravans that "the existing institutions and means of transportation have at all times determined to what extent economies could be organized in a transregional way." From this perspective, languages, too, are to be conceived of as means of transportation, a view which, to the extent that geographical distance is less and less important, becomes increasingly pertinent in modern times.

84 Following the standard graphs used in economics for representing supply and demand; cf., e.g., Woll (1981) and Ridler and Pons-Ridler (1986) who have developed an economically informed approach for a solution of Canada's language policy problems; also Vaillancourt (1991: 35).

85 *Personal Report for the Executive* (1986).

86 Cf. *Language Planning Newsletter* (1983).

87 *De Volkskrant* (1989).

88 "Le plurilinguisme est évidemment un facteur important d'accroissement du coût de fonctionnement d'un système éducatif même lorsque ne sont pas à réaliser d'énormes investissements dans l'instrumentalisation des langues" (Chaudenson 1987: 66).

89 In keeping with this kind of reasoning, Frideres (1988: 96) even made the suggestion that immigrants in Ottawa should not only receive English instruction free of charge, but also be compensated by the government, partly at least, for foregone gains during the time of ESL training.

90   The *Japan Times* (1988).

91   The system "accomplishes with a limited staff of seven a task that under optimum conditions would require at least twenty persons" (Landry 1987: 50).

92   For details cf. Vollmer (1989), who points out that the expected benefit of EUROTRA is not only a long-term reduction in the expenses of the translation services of the EC. "EUROTRA will be a means of overcoming communication and trade barriers in a multilingual community, and will, moreover, enhance expertise in computational linguistics and language processing throughout the Community" (1989: 94).

Chapter 5   Language Careers

1   "Die Sprache ist so alt wie das Bewußtsein – die Sprache *ist* das praktische, auch für andere Menschen existierende, also auch für mich selbst existierende wirkliche Bewußtsein, und die Sprache entsteht, wie das Bewußtsein, erst aus dem Bedürfnis, der Notdurft des Verkehrs mit anderen Menschen." (Marx and Engels 1969: 30)

2   In 1866 the Linguistic Society of Paris decided to disallow all talks about the origin of language, because they saw no way of testing any of the hypotheses that had been put forth. Cf. Hockett (1960).

3   This holds true, I believe, although we know much more today, for instance, about the phylogenetic evolution of the speech apparatus than was known at the time of Adam Smith. Cf. Landsberg (1988).

4   In their thorough and well-documented account of the sociolinguistic development of Chinese Pidgin English, pointedly entitled "From Business to Pidgin," Baker and Mühlhäusler (1990) also arrive at this conclusion.

5   Creoles which came into being in the more distant past are not usually designated as such. French, for instance, is not called a Latin creole, because more than a thousand years have passed since French emerged as a language in its own right, separate from Latin.

6   Cf. Neumann (1965). The term "jargon" is used by creolists to refer to unstable hybrids preceding or introducing pidginization. Cf., e.g., Mühlhäusler (1986: 5).

7   Cf. Clyne (1968); Heidelberger Forschungsprojekt "Pidgin Deutsch" (1975).

8   Cf., e. g., Le Page (1981).

9   Some pidgins are known to have been displaced together with their speakers, for example, Jamaica Pidgin to England, Black English to the Bahamas, and Gastarbeiterdeutsch to Australia (Clyne 1975).

10   Reinecke (1937: 434).

11   *Lungwa san tome* in Sao Tomese; quoted from Le Page and Tabouret-Keller
     (1985: 28).

12   "De vraag naar de oorsprong van het Surinaams is alleen zinvol, omdat wij
     met zekerheid weten dat de voorouders van de huidige sprekers een andere
     taal spraken: niet een ouder stadium van de huidige taal, maar een geheel
     andere taal" (Voorhoeve 1983: 38). Cf. also Bickerton (1981), Hill (1979).

13   Mühlhäusler (1986: 55f.) suggests relating the dimensions of stabilization
     (temporal) and remoteness from an assumed center of the spread of Tok
     Pisin (geographic) with each other. On the basis of his model conclusions
     can be drawn from geographically remote varieties on earlier forms of the
     pidgin in more central locations.

14   According to Voorhoeve (1983: 44) between 4.5 and 5 percent of Sranan's
     basic vocabulary is of Portuguese origin.

15   "De Surinaamse samenleving van vóór 1876 was gestructureerd volgens
     het plantage model. De plantage samenleving was een twee kastensysteem:
     a de hogere kaste (Europeanen: plantage directeuren, administrateurs,
     kooplieden, enz.) en *b* de lagere kaste (Indianen en Negers uit Afrika: de
     slaven). In deze samenleving was het Nederlands exclusieve koopwaar. Het
     was uitsluitend bestemd voor de hogere kaste van Europeanen, die de
     Europese cultuur in stand moest houden" (Campbell 1983: 191).

16   Cf., e.g., Cooper and Carpenter (1969); Calvet (1984); also chapter 2,
     pp. 38–42 above.

17   This principle also determines language choices where the spheres of
     production and distribution are linguistically distinct. For example, Floc'h
     (1981) describes the language behavior of Breton fishermen who speak
     Breton aboard ship, whereas they negotiate the sale of their catch in
     French.

18   Cf., e.g., Ureland (1978), Haarmann (1980), Williamson and van Eerde
     (1980), Nelde (1980), Kloss (1984).

19   The most up-to-date report of the size and assimilation tendencies of
     German-speaking minorities in 27 countries is provided in Born and
     Dickgießer (n. d.). They reckon with between 2.7 and 3 million German
     speakers for these countries.

20   Kloss (1969: 293) invokes the notion of "mass-extinction of languages;"
     with her work Dorian (1973, 1977, 1981) has contributed more than
     anyone else to establish "language death" as a generally recognized topic in
     discussions about language maintenance and shift. Cf. also Dressler and
     Wodak-Leodolter (1977).

21   During the nineteenth century, in particular, when linguists began to ally
     their discipline with the natural sciences, languages were conceived of as
     natural species. For example, Schleicher (1873: 6) explicitly links linguis-
     tics to Darwin's theory of evolution: "Languages are natural organisms
     which, having evolved in the absence of human control, have grown and

developed following certain laws, and which will age and die away."

22   This view has been eloquently expressed by Steiner (1975: 470): "[The destruction of natural linguistic diversity] is, perhaps, the least reparable of the ecological ravages which distinguish our age."

23   Denison (1982: 9f.) has emphasized this point with regard to multilingualism in Europe, arguing "that a linguistic ecology without a linguistic economy is not possible. Linguistic diversity involves costs, both of a material and of a social kind, of which would-be linguistic ecologists must be aware."

24   Ornstein-Galicia (1989) discusses mainly languages and varieties of language islands which have come into existence through migration, for example, Portuguese in Goa, the southwestern variety of US Spanish, and French in Missouri. However, his notion of "regressive idiom" can be applied to other languages, too, although the final consequence of regression, the exitus, would appear to be more dramatic where languages are concerned as opposed to the levelling of dialects.

25   Cf. Fasold (1984: 217), Verdoodt (1980), Price (1979).

26   Much has been written about the problematic notion of minority language, cf., e.g., Coulmas (1985: 100ff.). This is not the place to continue the discussion. Suffice it to say that, in the present context, we focus our attention on minority groups whose first language is none of the European national languages. Our concern is thus not with language islands – e.g. German speakers in Rumania – or extensions of major language groups beyond national boundaries – e.g. Turkish speakers in Greece.

27   The universalistic drive of the French Revolution meant hardship for the not so universal minority *patois* which were perceived as barriers to French national unification. In 1794, speaking before the Convention, Barrère characterized Breton as the language of federalism and superstition. He demanded that it should be smashed together with the other harmful instruments of counterrevolution. Until very recently, French governments have not departed much from this line of thinking.

28   The political and ideological aspects of the disparagement and repression of Welsh on the part of the British government are documented in Khlief (1980); cf. also Grillo (1989: 55–60).

29   All of the European languages discussed are marked by an old literary heritage: that of Welsh goes back as far as to the sixth century; Sorbian was first written in the fifteenth century; and the earliest written documents in Basque and Breton date from the sixteenth century.

30   It has long been recognized that dialect leveling has important economic causes. For example, discussing the decline of German dialects, Leopold (1959: 140) pointed out that it is economic and social reasons which demand uniformity.

31   Glottochronology or lexico-statistics is a controversial method for recon-

structing linguistic genealogies. It proceeds from the assumption that changes in the basic vocabulary through time are roughly the same for all languages occurring at a rate of 14 percent per thousand years. The number of shared items in the basic vocabulary of any two languages then justifies statements about their relatedness and the point in time when they started to drift apart. We are not concerned here with the reliability of this method, which has been questioned for good reasons (cf. Haarmann 1990), but with the kind of argumentation for which it is employed.

32   Average growth rate 1980–1986; all demographic data after *Fischer Weltalmanach* 1990.

33   Cf. Jespersen (1926: 229), Gage (1986: 379).

34   The number of speakers of German is taken to be 100 million and the 1987 average per capita income of FRG and GDR $13,800; the demographic strength of Chinese is assumed to be one billion and the average per capita income of its speakers $290, also for 1987.

35   "Es entsteht in der Oberschicht weltstädtischer Bevölkerungen eine gleichförmige, intelligente, praktische, den Dialekten und der Poesie abgeneigte Koiné, wie sie zur Symbolik jeder Zivilisation gehört, etwas ganz Mechanisches, präzis, kalt und mit einer auf ein Minimum beschränkten Geste. Diese letzten, heimat und wurzellosen Sprachen können von jedem Händler und Lastträger gelernt werden, das Hellenische in Karthago und am Oxus, das Chinesische auf Java, das Englische in Schanghai, und das 'Sprechen' ist für ihr Verständnis bedeutungslos. Fragt man nach ihrem eigentlichen Schöpfer, so ist es nicht der Geist einer Rasse oder einer Religion, sondern lediglich der Geist der Wirtschaft" (Spengler 1922: 188).

36   The functional similarity of koines and pidgins is mentioned by Samarin (1968: 662) who also points out that the Greek koine was spoken by both tradesmen and scholars from 300 B.C. to 500 A.D. in "the civilized part of the Mediterranean world," and not only by Greeks, but also by Egyptians, Persians, and Arabs.

37   "The refusal to provide foreign language training, the safeguarding of their Russian language monopoly, served the members of the Hanseatic League as a means of obstructing competitors and maintaining their trade monopoly in Russia" (Peters 1987: 83).

38   Bluntly, but much to the point, Ureland (1987: ix) insists: "Without trade there is little communication, and without communication there is no real understanding."

39   Estimates of the number of native speakers of Swahili vary greatly: Grimes (1988) cites 1,300,000, Gage (1986) 4 million, and Jungraithmayr and Möhlig (1983) refrain from giving any figure.

40   The University of Berlin established a chair for Swahili as early as 1887.

41   Cf. Scotton (1982) for other examples illustrating the function of vehicular languages for economic integration. Calvet (1987: 107–20) demonstrates

that African vehicular languages take precedence over French in the market place in some francophone countries. Cf. also Djité (1992) who, accordingly, presents an argument for the adoption of these languages instead of European languages for the purposes of economic and national integration.

42   Grimes (1988) lists more than 600 languages for Indonesia and 140 for Malaysia. In addition there are Brunei with 17 and Singapore with 24 languages. That some of the languages have very small speech communities, and that others are spoken in more than one country, so that these figures cannot simply be summed up, does not change the fact that this is one of the linguistically most diverse regions of the world.

43   Quoted from Lowenberg (1988: 152).

44   This was demonstrated by Kuo (1979) in a study measuring the communicativity of six languages in Singapore and Malaysia. These were English, Malay, Chinese (Mandarin), Cantonese, Hokkien, and Tamil. For Kuo communicativity is a metric notion, namely the probability of being able to communicate by means of these languages with a random population.

45   Historians, anthropologists, and sociologists were always aware of the fundamental significance of writing. An avalanche of linguistic publications during the past two decades underscores what 19th-century linguists took for granted, but has been called into doubt in 20th-century mainstream linguistics, namely that writing and written language are legitimate objects of linguistic study. Baum (1987) provides a highly informative discussion of written language. Glück (1987) is a presentation of the problems in the field of writing still waiting for a solution. Coulmas (1989a) and DeFrancis (1989) are up-to-date accounts of research on writing systems. And Goody (1986) recapitulates recent and more dated studies on the social implications of writing.

46   Dante (1890), cf. also Baum's (1987) discussion of Dante's *De vulgari eloquentia*.

47   Joseph (1987: 19) accuses grammarians who ignore the special character of standard languages of producing analyses which are "as misleading as a geologist's attempt to deal with Mount Rushmore, Stonehenge, or St. Paul's Cathedral as if they were natural rock formations."

48   Childe (1982: 31) called writing "a necessary by-product of this urban revolution which ushers in *civilization* and initiates the historical record."

49   For Egypt cf. Schenkel (1983: 52): "The use of writing for the marking of 'economic' goods is as old as its application to the fixation of historical data . . . The uses of writing for the purposes of 'economy' are of an administrative-legal nature" Cf. also Oppenheim (1964: 230f.). Evidence for China is more problematic, since the majority of the earliest inscriptions were divinations; but some documents, also dating from the Shang period (1200–1045 B.C.), register the receipt of valuable items (DeFrancis 1989: 92).

50   In this connection it is of little importance whether the origins of cunei-

form writing can be traced to an accounting system of geometric clay tokens, as claimed by Schmandt-Besserat (1978, 1979). Lieberman (1980) has called this theory into doubt.

51   Cf. especially Nissen, Damerow, and Englund (1990).

52   Kramer (1963: 230) asserts that record keeping was an important part of every Mesopotamian city state.

53   Many of the clay tablets contain lists of cuneiform signs which were copied by the pupils over and over for practice. Cf. Vanstiphout (1979: 125f.) and Falkenstein's (1953) still authoritative account of the Babylonian school.

54   The Sumerian *edubba* ("tablet house") or archive was first established "for the purpose of training the scribes necessary to satisfy the economic and administrative needs of the land" (Kramer 1963: 230).

55   Silver was used as a standard means of exchange throughout the known history of Mesopotamia, although gold was also recognized for a short time in the Middle Babylonian period (Oppenheim 1964: 86).

56   Gelb (1963) who subscribes to a theory of monogenesis of writing, which according to him originated in Sumer and only there, is not the only one to make this assumption. Scharff (1942), Ward (1964), and Hodge (1975), among others, also reckon with a Sumerian influence on the development of writing in Egypt.

57   "The regulations that governed Sumerian trade were adopted by independent kingdoms; actually we find in treaties of the second millennium BC expressions taken *verbatim* from those in a treaty of Naram-Sin of Akkad in the twenty-fourth century BC" (Hawkes and Wooley 1963: 507).

58   The Sumerian–Akkadian dictionary known under the title á = A = nâqu [a (Sumerian pronunciation) = (the cuneiform sign) A = (Akkadian) "to cry"].

59   "The traditional bilinguality of the Mesopotamian scribe was maintained by the training in which a great deal of Sumerian material was used" (Oppenheim 1964: 249).

60   Especially Elamitic; cf. Jensen (1969: 98), Lieberman (1977).

61   In keeping with the axiom, long championed by UNESCO, but really lacking both good reasons and sufficient evidence, that mother-tongue literacy is easiest to learn and, therefore, best, literacy campaigns in minority language groups are often initiated in their own languages, though the ultimate goal is to facilitate access to a more widely used written language. In India, in particular, mother-tongue literacy has often been promoted as a "bridge" in this sense. Cf. Jalaluddin (1983), Srivastava (1984a).

62   UNESCO (1964); cf. also Oxenham (1980: 2ff.) for a discussion of some exemplary cases.

63 Statistical data on illiteracy are notoriously unreliable, mainly for two reasons. One is that there is no generally accepted definition of functional literacy, and the other is that, in most societies, illiteracy is strongly stigmatized and therefore hidden. Enormous discrepancies are very common. To illustrate, Freyenhagen (1981) cites "almost one million" citizens of the Federal Republic of Germany who are unable to read and write", while Grundmann (1985) speaks of three million German illiterates. Cf. Giese and Gläss (1989) for data on other western European countries and many references.

64 The available statistics, although often no more than "guesstimates," convey an idea of the extent of the problem. For 1990, proclaimed "International Literacy Year" by the United Nations, UNESCO reckons with some 900 million adult illiterates, 300 million more than 30 years ago. This in spite of gigantic efforts to ameliorate the situation, which, for example, have improved initial school enrolment in developing countries from 50 to 95 percent. More than half of the pupils, however, drop out or leave school functionally illiterate.

65 A literacy level of 40 percent of the adult population has been considered the threshold by economists above which a positive impact on the economy can begin to be effective. Cf., e.g., Anderson (1966).

66 Among those who have grossly overestimated the superiority of the alphabet in comparison with other writing systems are McLuhan (1962) and Goody in his earlier works, for instance Goody and Watt (1963), where the authors speak of "alphabetic" rather than "literate" society. The overrating of the alphabet takes on well-nigh comic proportions when Illich and Sanders (1988: 9), echoing McLuhan's earlier pronouncements, declare that "alphabetic writing can be spoken of as bringing the human race into existence."

67 For example, Havelock (1963), Ong (1982), Illich and Sanders (1988).

68 Singapore and Hong Kong could also be mentioned in this connection, but because of their colonial history, the multilingualism it produced, and their urban character they constitute very special linguistic and economic environments which are hard to compare with other countries.

Chapter 6   Economy in Language

1 To Wilhelm von Humboldt the existence of such a correlation was self-evident: "Die Mannigfaltigkeit der Welt und die Tiefe der menschlichen Brust sind die beiden Punkte, aus welchen die Sprache schöpft. An je mehr und verschiedeneren Menschennaturen sich daher die Gegenstände spiegeln, desto reicher ist der Stoff, desto größer die Kraft der Sprache bei

übrigens gleichen Umständen." [The multiformity of the world and the depth of the human soul are the two sources from which language draws. The greater the number and variety of the people reflecting the objects, the richer the substance and the greater the power of the language, everything else being equal] (Humboldt 1963c: 252).

2 "Un mot peut être échangé contre quelque chose de dissemblable: une idée; en outre, il peut être comparé avec quelque chose de même nature: un autre mot. Sa valeur n'est donc pas fixée tant qu'on se borne à constater qu'il peut être 'échangé' contre tel ou tel concept, c'est-à-dire qu'il a telle ou telle signification; il faut encore le comparer avec les valeurs similaires, avec les autres mots qui lui sont opposable. Son contenu n'est vraiment déterminé que par le concours de ce qui existe en dehors de lui. Faisant partie d'une système, il est revêtu, non seulement d'une signification, mais aussi et surtout d'une valeur, et c'est tout autre chose" (Saussure 1972: 160).

3 With respect to suprasegmental phenomena, Martinet (1975: 160) stated analogously that the linguistic value of accent, like that of phonemes, lies in its presence or absence.

4 Influenced by Trubetzkoy's phonology, Lévi-Strauss, in an article about structural analysis in linguistics and anthropology, wrote: "Comme les phonème, les termes de paranté sont des éléments de signification; commes eux, ils n'acquièrent cette signification qu'à la condition de s'intégrer en systèmes." [Like phonemes, kinship terms are elements of meaning, and like the former the latter acquire that meaning only by virtue of being integrated into a system] (Lévi-Strauss 1958: 40f.).

5 "Dans les deux sciences, il s'agit d'un *système d'équivalence entre des choses d'ordres différents*: dans l'une un travail et un salaire, dans l'autre un signifié et un signifiant" (Saussure 1972: 115).

6 "Pour les sciences travaillant sur de valeurs, cette distinction devient une nécessité pratique, et dans certains cas une nécessité absolue. Dans ce domaine on peut mettre les servants au défi d'organiser leurs recherches d'une façon rigoureuse sans tenir compte des deux axes, sans distinguer le système des valeurs considérées en soi, de ces mêmes valeurs considérées en fonction du temps" (Saussure 1972: 116).

7 Quoted from Cipolla (1991: 6).

8 Notice that some speech therapists make a living by helping speakers to get rid of their low-prestige varieties. Cf. Conniff (1988) for an example.

9 The most important empirical data on which speech production models have been based are speech errors. It is assumed that different types of speech errors can shed light on the organization of speech production on the mental level. Berg (1988) presents a new spreading activation model that views speech production as a parallel rather than serial operation.

10 To cite just one specific example, Mühlhäusler reports that in Tok Pisin

the adjective ending *pela* can be shortened to *pla*, and the preposition *bilong* is also realized as *bolong*, *blong*, *blo*, or even *bl*. He comments: "Although such changes promote optimalization of production, especially in allegro speech, there is a considerable price to pay, namely that of decodability" (Mühlhäusler 1986: 70).

11 In Fry's (1977: 22) lucid words: "We could live without talking but we certainly cannot talk without living."

12 "Die sparsamere oder reichlichere Verwendung sprachlicher Mittel für den Ausdruck eines Gedankens hängt vom Bedürfnis ab. Es kann zwar nicht geleugnet werden, dass mit diesen Mitteln auch vielfältig Luxus getrieben wird. Aber im Grossen und Ganzen geht doch ein gewisser haushälterischer Zug durch die Sprechtätigkeit" (Paul 1909: 313).

13 "Es müssen sich überall Ausdrucksweisen herausbilden, die nur gerade so viel enthalten, als die Verständlichkeit für den Hörer erfordert" (Paul 1909: 313).

14 Jespersen formulated his ideas most clearly in what he called the "Ease Theory." He wrote: "I am not afraid of hearing the objection that I ascribe too great power to human laziness, indolence, inertia, shirking, easy-goingness, sloth, sluggishness, lack of energy, or whatever other beautiful synonyms have been invented for 'economy of effort' or 'following the line of least resistance.' The fact remains that there *is* such a tendency in all human beings, and by taking it into account in explaining changes of sound we are doing nothing else than applying here the same principle that attributes many simplifications of form to 'analogy'" (Jespersen 1964: 263).

15 *Entia non sunt multiplicanda praeter necessitatem* [i.e., no entities should be assumed to exist unnecessarily]. This is the most concise formulation of the principle also known as "Ockham's razor," although William of Ockham does not seem to have used these words himself.

16 The law of diminishing returns makes itself felt wherever work is done with limited resources in a limited field. It states that as extra units of one means of production are employed, with all others held constant, the output produced by each extra unit will eventually fall. Zipf's application of this law to the use of tools in a shop follows standard economic explanations.

17 "Reichtum ist das erste und nötigste bei einer Sprache und besteht darin, daß kein Mangel, sondern vielmehr ein Überfluß erscheine an bequemen und nachdrücklichen Worten, so zu allen Vorfälligkeiten dienlich, damit man alles kräftig und eigentlich vorstellen und gleichsam mit lebenden Farben abmalen könne" (Leibniz 1983: 27).

18 "Der rechte Probierstein des Überflusses oder Mangels einer Sprache findet sich beim Übersetzen guter Bücher aus anderen Sprachen. . . . Inzwischen ist gleichwohl diejenige Sprache die reichste und bequemste, welche

am besten mit wörtlicher Übersetzung zurechtkommen kann und dem Original Fuß vor Fuß zu folgen vermag" (Leibniz 1983: 28f.).

19 Chinese lexicographers, for instance, traditionally count *Hanzi*, that is, Chinese characters which usually denote a morpheme rather than a word.

20 Compounds are always written as one word in German, but not usually in English.

21 The Academy Dictionary of the Russian Language (Moscow 1950–65) contains some 120,000 entries, whereas the Van Dale (Utrecht, Antwerp 1984) has 230,000 entries for Dutch. It would surely be a mistake to conclude on the basis of these figures alone that the lexicon of Dutch is almost twice the size of that of Russian.

22 E.g., Guiraud (1959) for French, Kabashima (1979) for Japanese, and Billmeier (1969) once again for German.

23 Mandelbrot (1954: 20) pointed out that the Zipf function had a tendency to become rather diffuse in the range of the least frequent words, and Frumkina (1970) was able to show that it was valid without condition for the interval of $50 \leqslant r \leqslant 1{,}500$ only.

24 Mandelbrot (1954: 10f.) emphasized that Zipf's Law must not be interpreted as saying that the occurrence of a given word in a certain context is a function of its rank on the frequency scale. For ". . . il est clairement absurde de supposer que les fréquences des idées suivent une loi quelconque" [it is obviously absurd to assume that the frequency of ideas depends on such a law]. A theory designed to explain the statistical distribution of words should therefore apply to empty word forms. In Shannon and Weaver's mathematical theory of communication he found an approach that satisfied this requirement.

25 In Bolinger's (1980: 61) graphic words: "You want to speak with least effort, so you speak sloppily; I want to hear with least effort, so I listen with half an ear."

26 "Afin de comprendre comment et pourquoi une langue change, le linguiste ne doit jamais perdre de vue deux facteurs antinomiques toujours présents: tout d'abord les nécessités de la communication, le besoin, pour le locuteur, de communiquer son message, ensuite le principe du moindre effort, qui lui fait réduire sa production d'énergie, à la fois mentale et physique, au minimum compatible avec la réalisation de ses desseins" [In order to understand how and why a language changes, the linguist must never lose sight of two conflicting factors which are always present: first, the necessities of communication, that is, the speaker's need to get his message across, and then the principle of least effort which makes him reduce his mental and physical energy expenditure to the minimum compatible with the realization of his purposes] (Martinet 1969: 166f.).

27 "L'avantage évident de la deuxième articulation est l'économie. La première articulation était économique en ce sens qu'avec quelques milliers

de monèmes peu spécifiques il était possible de réaliser une infinité de communications différentes. De la même manière, la deuxième articulation est économique puisque la combinaison judicieuse de quelques dizaines de phonèmes permet à l'homme de maintenir distincts tous les monèmes dont il a besoin. Etant donné la variété et la richesse de la communication humaine, la double articulation ne pouvait d'être un trait des langues humaines" (Martinet 1969: 35).

28 This is argued by Harris (1986) and Feldbusch (1985), among others.

29 Cf. Coulmas (1989a, chapter 3) for a more detailed discussion of Gelb's theory.

30 Cf., e.g., Diringer (1948), Gelb (1963), McLuhan (1962).

31 All writing reform schemes for Chinese are motivated by economic considerations. For detailed discussion cf. DeFrancis (1984), Coulmas (1989a, chapter 13).

32 In a different context, Kasher has described what he considers the main problem of rational discourse behavior in similar terms. The crucial question, he maintains, is this: "What determines, in our rational use of language, the equilibrium points of effectiveness and cost?" (Kasher 1986: 110f.).

Chapter 7   *Language Adaptation*

1 The notion of language adaptation is discussed from various angles in the contributing chapters to Coulmas (1989c). In the following I draw on this discussion, while shifting the focus to the problem of the economic serviceability of languages.

2 "Es ereignet sich aber einiger Abgang bei unserer Sprache in den Dingen, so man weder sehen noch fühlen, sondern allein durch Betrachtung erreichen kann." [There is, however, a deficit in our language in those things that you cannot see or feel, but attain by contemplation only] (Leibniz 1983: 8).

3 "Ob nun schon wir Deutschen uns also desto weniger zu verwundern oder auch zu schämen haben, das unsere Grammatik noch nicht in willkommenem Stande, so dünkt mich doch gleichwohl, sie sei noch allzuviel davon entfernt und habe daher eine grose Verbesserung nötig." [While we Germans thus need not be surprised or ashamed that our grammar is not yet in a welcome state, methinks it is still too far off the mark and, therefore, greatly in need of improvement] (Leibniz 1983: 42).

4 "The languages of India have suffered impoverishment. . . . There are no equivalents for scientific terms. The result has been disastrous. The masses remain cut off from the modern mind" (Gandhi 1965: 5).

5   Whinnom (1971: 110). This paper, which describes pidginization and creolization by analogy to the biological theory of evolution as adaptation processes, came to my attention only recently, after I had independently developed a similar concept of language adaptation which, however, does not refer to pidgins and creoles in particular (cf. Coulmas 1989c).

6   Whinnom's (1971: 110) considerations about creoles are exceptional. He suggests that "modern linguists may have been dangerously sentimental about creole languages, which, with only a few notable exceptions, constitute in most communities a distinct handicap to the social mobility of the individual, and *may* also constitute a handicap to the creole-speaker's personal intellectual development." This is not the place to assess whether or not this is actually true, but Whinnom is certainly right in demanding that these questions be investigated.

7   In spite of the many projects designed to adapt languages on every continent to modern communication requirements, the extensive language planning literature does not offer any such notion either. Occasionally the notion of efficiency is employed in connection with language planning, for instance in Desheriev (1973), but it is never clearly defined, let alone operationalized as a metric concept. Conversely, linguists have failed to provide language planners with the devices they need, a fact which is acknowledged and deplored only rarely. "The refusal to comment on qualitative matters has made linguistics a less useful source of information to those who need it most, the language planners' (Mühlhäusler 1982: 105). However, Mühlhäusler (1982: 106) also cites one of the reasons why it is so difficult to make any statements that imply value judgments: "To claim that either Tok Pisin or one of its varieties is good or bad because of its referential potential ignores the fact that the potential of all varieties is continuously changing."

8   Expanding and contracting languages are clearly the most disturbing phenomena for the equality claim. "What extreme cases like this [language death] show is that we need to rethink our claim about linguistic equality" (Hudson 1990: 833). Self-evident as this would seem, Hudson's is decidedly a minority position.

9   Martinet (1969: 166f.); see above chapter 6, note 11.

10 The literature on borrowing is boundless. Deroy (1980) lists more than 1,500 titles. There has been extensive research in this field ever since from lexicographic, sociolinguistic, and historical linguistic points of view.

11 In 1987, Canada canceled all debts of African countries, and two years later President Mitterand announced that France would write off the debts of Africa's 35 poorest countries worth 16 billion francs. Recent debt deals of Western countries and Japan with Mexico (1990) and other Latin American countries first and then Eastern Europe and the remains of the Soviet Union for debt and debt service reduction, rescheduling, and debt-equity swaps are other examples.

12 The extent to which words of different form classes are borrowed is a reflection of their integration in the structural organization of the language. Form classes can thus be ordered for each language along a "scale of adoptability" (Haugen 1950: 224). Generally speaking, content words are borrowed more freely than function words, and among the former, nouns are more numerous than verbs, which in turn outnumber adjectives.

13 This is true in spite of the fact that achieving referential adequacy is among the most consciously pursued goals of language planning. Cf., e.g., Marina (1987).

14 According to the definition Weinreich (1966: 1) provided at the outset of his seminal study, languages are in contact "if they are used alternately by the same persons. The language-using individuals are thus the locus of the contact."

15 Bloomfield (1933: 458) described loanwords as traces of cultural diffusion which "show us what one nation has taught another." Similarly, Jespersen (1964: 209) opined that "loan-words always show a superiority of the nation from whose language they are borrowed, though this superiority may be of many different kinds."

16 Deniau (1983: 118), for instance, warns: "We cannot maintain our francophone identity by tolerating Franglais or defective speech" [Ce n'est pas en tolérant le franglais, ou une language défecteuse, que nous pourrons conserver l'identité francophone]. For a detailed discussion of linguistic purism and a number of specific cases cf. Jernudd and Shapiro (1989); Kirkness (1975) for German.

17 The first Dutch–Japanese dictionary, the *Haruma wage*, was at the same time the first comprehensive dictionary relating Japanese to a European language. It was complied on the basis of François Halma's [< *haruma*] *Woordenboek der Nederduitsche en Fransche Taalen* (Dutch–French dictionary) by Inamura Sampaku, one of the most talented *oranda tsûji*, and first appeared in 30 copies in 1796.

18 Polomé has investigated the contact of Dutch with Indian languages. Summarizing his observations, he remarks: "The contacts of the Dutch with the Indian subcontinent have left some traces in their language. They may not be many, but they are instructive, and they often illustrate the important role of intermediate agents that the Dutch have played in bringing new products and their names to western Europe" (Polomé 1986: 147).

19 "Musterung und Untersuchung aller deutschen Worte, welche, dafern sie vollkommmen, nicht nur auf diejenigen gehen soll, die jedermann braucht, sondern auch auf die, so gewissen Lebensarten und Künsten eigen" (Leibniz 1983: 17).

20 "so in der Natur der Dinge, sonderlich der Kräuter und Tiere, Feuerkunst und Chemie, Wißkunst und Mathematik und daran hängenden Baukünsten und anderen Kunstwerken, Weberei und sogenannten Manufakturen,

Handel, Schiffahrt, Berg- und Salzwerksachen und was dergleichen mehr, erfahren" (Leibniz 1983: 25).

21 For example, according to Schirmer's commercial dictionary *Wörterbuch der deutschen Kaufmannssprache*, the beginning of a German terminology for trade dates back to the early second millennium, "when trading in kind was being superseded by money economy and trade and business concentrated in the flourishing cities" (Schirmer 1911: xvi).

22 Cf. Drozd and Seibicke (1973: 68ff.).

23 Gakujutsu shingikai gakujutsu yôgo bunkakai (1983).

24 An engineer himself, Eugen Wüster began in the 1930s to lay the groundwork for a general theory of terminology whose principles he developed in numerous publications. His two volume book of 1979 offers the most comprehensive approach. Felber's *Terminology Manual* (1984) is an important continuation of Wüster's work. Felber was director of Info-term (International Centre for Terminology), which in 1988 helped to establish TermNet, an international terminology network. TermNet offers practical services for the recording of terminological data, the establishment of terminological data banks, and for translation-oriented terminology work (cf. Galinski and Nedobity 1989).

25 "The majority of the words belonging to this group [i.e., scientific and technical terms] are international words of Greco-Latin origin and have been coined by language engineers" (De Vries 1988: 132).

26 This has been demonstrated in some detail for the Chinese terminology of economics by Louven (1983). In a more dated study Gao and Liu (1958) investigated the source languages of technical terms of various fields which have entered the Chinese language as loan translations.

27 "A language for special purposes is supposed to accurately designate and differentiate working processes and results, though at the lowest possible cost" (Ploß quoted in Möhn 1981: 176). Similarly, Wyler (1987: 79) states: "LSP is a type of language based on the two requirements 'precision' and 'economy' or, more clearly, 'precision' and 'economy of expression'."

28 Notice that Feng (1988) has formulated his economic law of term formation taking words as minimal units. For Chinese this is less problematic than for languages with many bound morphemes.

29 "No discipline can afford to work in complete isolation. This is where the obligation to provide, and the demand to receive information meet, which implies a most important linguistic task for modern publications: They have to popularize, in the best sense of the word, the progress of the sciences" (Möhn 1981: 205).

30 English-based creoles are the mother tongues for the majority of the population of as many as nine countries. These are the Bahamas, Barbados, Belize, Guyana, Jamaica, Papua New Guinea, St Lucia, St Vincent, Trinidad and Tobago.

31 In Europe, this holds particularly for the Celtic languages of the British isles. In North America, many Amerindian languages have yielded to the pressure of English and most of the remaining ones continue to decline. The Franco-Canadian speech community is also on the defensive. In the Caribbean and on the South American mainland, various English-based creoles increasingly adapt to English. In South Africa, English is on the advance vis-à-vis Afrikaans, and in Namibia where it recently acquired the status of official language, it is also expanding. In Asia, English is expanding in various situations despite small numbers of primary speakers, as in Singapore and the Philippines, to mention but two examples.

32 The notion of iconicity plays an important role in this discussion. It applies to the mapping relation between linguistic structures and structures of the phenomena in the world around us. Cf., e.g., Van Langendonck (1988) and other research findings about iconicity in language presented at the International Congress of Anthropological and Ethnological Sciences 1988 in Zagreb, the proceedings of which are under preparation for publication in a volume edited by Marge E. Landsberg entitled *Syntactic Iconicity and Freezes*.

33 In this connection, Viereck (1988: 150) criticizes "the hunt for the foreign vocabulary" in recent English dictionaries which often fail to indicate "what is more or less permanent and what only ephemeral usage in English."

34 Whereas its French claque *baladeur* will doubtless be confined to the Gallic province of an imaginary *pureté de la langue*.

Bibliography

Adams, K. L. and Brink, D. T. (eds). 1990. *Perspectives on Official English: The Campaign for English as the Official Language of the USA*. Berlin, New York: Mouton de Gruyter.

Alisjahbana, S. Takdir (ed.). 1967. *The Modernization of Languages in Asia*. Kuala Lumpur: The Malaysian Society of Asian Studies.

Alisjahbana, S. Takdir. 1976. *Language Planning and Modernization: The Case of Indonesian and Malaysian*. The Hague: Mouton.

Alisjahbana, S. Takdir. 1984. The Concept of Language Standardization and its Application to the Indonesian Language. In Coulmas, F. (ed.) *Linguistic Minorities and Literacy*. Berlin, New York, Amsterdam: Mouton, 77–98.

Altoma, S. 1974. Language Education in Arab Countries and the Role of the Academies. In Fishman, J. A. (ed.) *Advances in Language Planning*. The Hague: Mouton, 279–315.

Ammon, Ulrich. 1989. Zur Geschichte der Sprachverbreitungspolitik der Bundesrepublik Deutschland von den Anfängen bis 1985. *Deutsche Sprache 3*, 229–63.

Ammon, Ulrich. 1990. German as an International Language. *International Journal of the Sociology of Language 83*, 135–70.

Anderson, C. Arnold. 1966. Literacy and Schooling on the Development Threshold: Some Historical Cases. In Arnold, C. A. and Bowman, M. J. (eds) *Education and Economic Development*. London: Frank Cass.

Anderson, Edmund A. 1987. Indonesian Language Month 1986: Tempest at the Forum. *New Language Planning Newsletter* 1 (3), 1–3.

Apel, Karl-Otto. 1976. Sprechakttheorie und transzendentale Sprachpragmatik zur Frage ethischer Normen. In Apel, Karl-Otto (ed.) *Sprachpragmatik und Philosophie*. Frankfurt/M.: Suhrkamp, 10–173.

Asmah, Haji Omar. 1982. Language Spread and Recession in Malaysia and the Malay Archipelago. In Cooper, R. L. (ed.) *Language Spread: Studies in Diffusion and Social Change*. Bloomington: Indiana University Press, 198–213.

Aster, Ernst von. 1963. *Geschichte der Philosophie*. Stuttgart: Kröner.

Baetens Beardsmore, Hugo and Kohls, Jürgen. 1988. Immediate Pertinence in the Acquisition of Multilingual Proficiency: The European Schools. *Schola Europaea* 101, 66-79; 102, 4−12.

Baker, C. 1985. *Aspects of Bilingualism in Wales*. Clevedon: Multilingual Matters.

Baker, Philip and Mühlhäusler, Peter. 1990. From Business to Pidgin. *Journal of Asian Pacific Communication* 1 (1), 87−115.

Bank of Japan. 1988. *Comparative International Statistics 1988*. Tokyo.

Barkan, Mildred. 1980. Mind as Life and Form. In Rieber, R. W. (ed.) *Body and Mind Past, Present, and Future*. New York: Academic Press, 131−54.

Barlow, Joel. 1970 [1807]. The Columbiad. In Bottorff, W. K. and Ford, A. L. (eds) *The Works of Joel Barlow*. 2 vols. Gainsville, Fl.: Scholars' Facsimiles & Reprints.

Barrera i Vidal, Albert. 1991. Le catalan, une langue d' Europe. *Sociolinguistica* 5, 99−110.

Baum, Richard. 1987. *Hochsprache, Literatursprache, Schriftsprache: Materialien zur Charakteristik von Kultursprachen*. Darmstadt: Wissenschaftliche Buch gesellschaft.

Becker, G. 1975. *Human Capital*. New York: Columbia University Press.

Beneke, Jürgen. 1981. Foreign Languages on the Top Floor: European Executives Evaluate Their Foreign Language Needs. In Freudenstein, R., Beneke, J., Pönisch, H. (eds). *Language Incorporated*. Oxford/Munich: Pergamon Press/Max Hueber Verlag, 23−41.

Ben-Rafael, Eliezer and Brosh, Hezi. 1991. A Sociological Study of Second Language Diffusion: The Obstacles to Arabic Teaching in the Israeli School. *Language Problems and Language Planning* 15 (1), 1−24.

Bentahila, A. 1983. *Language Attitudes among Arabic French Bilinguals in Morocco*. Clevedon: Multilingual Matters.

Benton, Lauren and Noyelle, Thierry. 1991. *Adult Illiteracy and Economic Performance*. Paris: OECD Publication Service.

Berg, Thomas. 1988. *Die Abbildung des Sprachproduktionsprozesses in einem Aktivationsflußmodell: Untersuchungen an deutschen und englischen Versprechern*. Tübingen: Narr.

Bever, T. G., Carroll, J. M., and Hurtig, R. 1977. Analogy or Ungrammatical Sequences that are Utterable and Comprehensible are the Origins of New Grammars in Language Acquisition and Linguistic Evolution. In Bever, T. G., Katz, J. J., and Langendoen, D. T. (eds) *An Integrated Theory of Linguistic Ability*. Sussex: The Harvester Press, 149−82.

Bhola, H. S. 1982. *Campaigning for Literacy*. Berlin: Deutsche Stiftung für internationale Entwicklung and International Coucil for Adult Education.

Bickerton, Derek. 1981. *Roots of Language*. Ann Arbor: Karoma.

Biggs, Robert D. 1980. The Ebla Tablets: An Interim Perspective. *Biblical Archeologist* 43, 76−87.

Bikales, Gerda. 1986. Comment: The Other Side. In Language Rights and the

English Language Amendment. *International Journal of the Sociology of Language* 60, 77–85.

Bikales, Gerda and Imhoff, Gary. 1985. *A Kind of Discordant Harmony: Issues in Assimilation.* Washington, DC: US English.

Billmeier, G. 1969. *Worthäufigkeitsverteilung vom Zipfschen Typ überprüft an deutschem Textmaterial.* Hamburg: Buske.

Bloomfield, Leonard. 1933. *Language.* New York: Holt.

Boeglin, Bruce. 1987. Nature and Cost of Interpretation Services at the United Nations. In Tonkin, H. and Johnson-Weiner, K. M. (eds) *The Economics of Language Use.* New York: Center for Research and Documentation on World Language Problems, 17–24.

Bolinger, Dwight. 1980. *Language: The Loaded Weapon.* London, New York: Longman.

Born, Joachim and Dickgießer, Sylvia. n. d. *Deutschsprachige Minderheiten: Ein Überblick über den Stand der Forschung für 27 Länder.* Mannheim: Institut für deutsche Sprache im Auftrag des Auswärtigen Amtes. (October 1989).

Bottéro, Jean. 1987. The Culinary Tablets at Yale. *Journal of the American Oriental Society* 107 (1), 11–19.

Bourdieu, Pierre. 1977. The Economics of Linguistic Exchange. *Social Science Information* 6, 645–68.

Bourdieu, Pierre. 1982. *Ce que parler veut dire: L'économie des changes linguistique.* Paris: Fayard.

Bowen, David. 1980. Death of a Monoglot Salesman. *Marketing* July 16, 28f.

Bowen, Margareta. 1987. Changes in Free-Lance Interpreter Remuneration Over Time. In Tonkin, H. and Johnson-Weiner, K. M. (eds) *The Economics of Language Use.* New York: Center for Research and Documentation on World Language Problems, 141–51.

Braun, Peter. 1989. Internationalisms: Identical Vocabularies in European Languages. In Coulmas, F. (ed.) *Language Adaptation.* Cambridge, London: Cambridge University Press, 158–67.

Breasted, James H. 1926. *The Conquest of Civilization.* New York, London: Harper.

Breton, Albert. 1978. Nationalism and Language Policies. *Canadian Journal of Economics* 11 (4), 656–68.

Brook, M. 1980. The "Mother-tongue" Issue in Britain: Cultural Diversity or Control? *British Journal of Sociology of Education* 1 (3), 237–55.

Budget of the United States Government 1982, 1985, 1990. Washington, DC: Government Printing Office.

Bühler, Karl. 1934. *Sprachtheorie: Die Darstellungsfunktion der Sprache.* Berlin: Fischer. [*Theory of Language. The Representational Function of Language.* Translated by Donald Fraser Goodwin. Amsterdam: John Benjamins, 1990.]

Bühler, Karl. 1976 [1933]. *Die Axiomatik der Sprachwissenschaft.* Edited by Elisabeth Ströker. Frankfurt/M.: Klostermann.

Bungarten, Theo (ed.). 1988. *Sprache und Information in Wirtschaft und Gesellschaft: Referate eines internationalen Kongresses.* Tostedt: Attikon.

Burchfield, Robert. 1985. *The English Language.* Oxford, New York: Oxford University Press.

Calvet, Louis-Jean. 1974. *Linguistique et colonialisme: petit traitè de glottophagie.* Paris: Payot.

Calvet, Louis-Jean. 1984. Troc, marché et échange linguistique. *Langage et Société* 27, 55-81.

Calvet, Louis-Jean. 1987. *La guerre des langues et les politiques linguistiques.* Paris: Payot.

Campbell, Hugo W. 1983. De Nederlandse taal als luxe-waar op de Surinaamse markt? In Charry, E., Koefoed, G., and Muysken, P. (eds) *De talen van Suriname.* Muiderberg: Coutinho, 188-200.

Campe, Joachim Heinrich. 1807. *Wörterbuch der Deutschen Sprache.* Braunschweig: Schulbuchhandlung.

Carnap, Rudolf. 1934. *Logische Syntax der Sprache.* Vienna: Springer.

Cassirer, Ernst. 1925. *Philosophie der symbolischen Formen.* 3 vols. Darmstadt: Wissenschaftliche Buchgesellschaft.

Castles, S. and Kosach, G. 1973. *Immigrant Workers and Class Structure in Western Europe.* Oxford, London: Oxford University Press.

Cavanagh, Kim L. 1988. Igirisu [England]. *Gekkan Nihongo* 3, 8f.

Channels. 1982. No. 1 (1), June. [Newsletter of Translators' and Interpreters' Educational Society, Stanford].

Chaudenson, R. 1987. Industries de la langue, éducation et développement. In *Langue et Economie: Colloque International.* CNRS, Université de Provence, 45–84.

Cheng, Chin-Chuan. 1982. Chinese Varieties of English. In Kachru, B. B. (ed.) *The Other Tongue: English Across Cultures.* Oxford, New York: Pergamon, 125–40.

Cheng, Helen N. L. and Zi, R. N. C. 1987. In-house English Language Training: A Survey of Fifteen Organizations. In Lord, R. and Cheng, H. (eds) *Language Education in Hong Kong.* Hong Kong: The Chinese University Press, 173–85.

Chiera, Edward. 1938. *They Wrote on Clay.* Chicago and London: The University of Chicago Press.

Childe, Gordon. 1982 [1942]. *What Happened in History.* Harmondsworth: Penguin.

Chomsky, Noam. 1965. *Aspects of the Theory of Syntax.* Cambridge, Mass.: The MIT Press.

Christ, Herbert. 1987. Deutsch als Fremdsprache: Bedarf und Nachfrage in sprachenpolitischer Betrachtungsweise. In Sturm, D. (ed.) *Deutsch als Fremdsprache weltweit.* Munich: Hueber, 207–15.

Cipolla, Carlo M. 1991. *Between History and Economics: An Introduction to*

Economic History. Oxford: Blackwell.

Claes, F. 1980. *A Bibliography of Netherlandic Dictionaries*. Munich: Kraus International.

Clark, Herbert H. and Wilkes-Gibbs, Deanna. 1986. Referring as a Collaborative Process. *Cognition* 22, 1–39.

Clyne, Michael G. 1968. Zum Pidgin-Deutsch der Gastarbeiter. *Zeitschrift für Mundartforschung* 35, 130–9.

Clyne, Michael G. 1972. *Perspectives on Language Contact*. Melbourne: Centre for Migrant Studies.

Clyne, Michael G. 1975. German and English Working Pidgins. *Linguistic Communications* 13, 1–20.

Coleman, Hywel. 1985. Talking Shop: Language and Work. *International Journal of the Sociology of Language* 51, 105–29.

Commins, Patrick. 1988. Socioeconomic Development and Language Development in the Gaeltacht. *International Journal of the Sociology of Language* 70, 1–28.

Conniff, Richard. 1988. In Chattanooga: How not to Sound like a Southerner. *Time*, March 7, 12f.

Conrad, Andrew W. and Fishman, Joshua A. 1977. English as a World Language: The Evidence. In Fishman, J. A., Cooper, R. L., and Conrad, A. W., (eds) *The Spread of English*. Rowley, Mass.: Newbury House, 3–76.

Cooper, Robert L. 1986. Selling Language Reform. In Tannen, D. and Alatis, J. E. (eds) *Georgetown University Roundtable on Languages and Linguistics 1985*. Washington, DC: Georgetown University Press, 275–81.

Cooper, Robert L. 1989. *Language Planning and Social Change*. Cambridge, New York: Cambridge University Press.

Cooper, Robert L. and Carpenter, S. 1969. Linguistic Diversity in the Ethiopian Market. *Journal of African Languages* 8, 160–8.

Cooper, Robert L. and Seckbach, F. 1977. Economic Incentives for the Learning of a Language of Wider Communication: A Case Study. In Fishman, J. A., Cooper, R. L., and Conrad, A. W. (eds) *The Spread of English*. Rowley, Mass.: Newbury House, 212–19.

Coseriu, Eugenio. 1974. *Synchronie, Diachronie und Geschichte: Das Problem des Sprachwandels*. Munich: Fink.

Coulmas, Florian. 1981. *Über Schrift*. Frankfurt: Suhrkamp.

Coulmas, Florian. 1985. *Sprache und Staat. Studien zur Sprachplanung und Sprachpolitik*. Berlin: de Gruyter.

Coulmas, Florian. 1987. What Writing Can Do to Language: Some Preliminary Remarks. In Battestini, S. P. X. (ed.) *Georgetown University Round Table on Languages and Linguistics 1986*. Washington, DC: Georgetown University Press, 107–29.

Coulmas, Florian. 1988. Overcoming Diglossia: The Rapprochement of Written and Spoken Japanese in the 19th Century. In Catach, Nina (ed.)

Vers une théorie de la langue écrite. Paris: CNRS, 191–201.

Coulmas, Florian. 1989a. *The Writing Systems of the World.* Oxford: Blackwell.

Coulmas, Florian. 1989b. The Surge of Japanese. *International Journal of the Sociology of Language* 80, 115–31.

Coulmas, Florian. 1989c. Language Adaptation. In Coulmas, F. (ed.) *Language Adaptation.* Cambridge, New York: Cambridge University Press, 1–25.

Coulmas, Florian. 1990. The Status of German. *International Journal of the Sociology of Language* 83, 171–85.

Coulmas, Florian. 1991a. European Integration and the Idea of the National Language: Ideological Roots and Economic Consequences. In Coulmas, F. (ed.) *A Language Policy for the European Community: Prospects and Quandaries.* Berlin, New York: Mouton de Gruyter, 1–43.

Coulmas, Florian. 1991b. The Future of Chinese Characters. In Cooper, R. L. and Spolsky, B. (eds) *The Influence of Language on Culture and Thought: Essays in Honor of Joshua A. Fishman's Sixty-Fifth Birthday.* Berlin, New York: Mouton de Gruyter, 227–43.

Coulmas, Florian, Thümmel, Wolf, and Wunderlich, Dieter. 1981. Sprachwissenschaft in China: Bericht über eine Informationsreise im September 1980. Teil 2, *Linguistische Berichte* 74, 45–81.

Couttenier, Ivan. 1989. Belgian Politics in 1988. *Res Publica* 302–30.

Dante, Alighieri. 1890. *De vulgari eloquentia.* English translation by A. Ferres Howell. London: Kegan Paul. [Written 1305 in Latin, first published 1577 in Paris.]

Daoust, Denise. 1987. Une décennie de planification linguistique au Québec: Un premier bilan sociolinguistique. Conférence préparée pour le colloque "Language Planning and Political Development," Bad Homburg, Reimers-Stiftung. Shorter English version in Weinstein, B. (ed.). 1990. *Language Planning and Political Development.* Norwood, NJ: Ablex, 108–30.

Daswani, C. J. 1989. Aspects of Modernization in Indian Languages. In Coulmas, F. (ed.) *Language Adaptation.* Cambridge, New York: Cambridge University Press, 79–89.

Daswani, C. J. 1991. Literacy and Development in South-East Asia. Paper presented at the *International Conference "Attaining Functional Literacy: A Cross-Cultural Perspective"* Tilburg University, October 10–12, 1991.

Day, Richard R. 1985. The Ultimate Inequality: Linguistic Genocide. In Wolfson, N. and Manes, J. (eds) *Language of Inequality.* Berlin, New York, Amsterdam: Mouton, 163–81.

de Certeau, M., Julia, D., and Revel, J. 1975. *Une politique de la langue: La Révolution française et les patois, l'enquête de Grégoire.* Paris: Gallimard.

Décsy, G. 1973. *Die linguistische Struktur Europas.* Wiesbaden: Harrassowitz.

DeFrancis, John. 1950. *Nationalism and Language Reform in China.* Princeton: Princeton University Press.

DeFrancis, John. 1984. *The Chinese Language: Fact and Fantasy.* Honolulu: The

University of Hawaii Press.

DeFrancis, John. 1989. *Visible Speech: The Diverse Oneness of Writing Systems.* Honolulu: University of Hawaii Press.

Deniau, Xavier. 1983. *La Francophonie.* Paris: Presses Universitaires de France.

Denison, Norman. 1977. Language Death or Language Suicide? *International Journal of the Sociology of Language* 12, 13–22.

Denison, Norman. 1982. A Linguistic Ecology for Europe? *Folia Linguistica* 16, 5–16.

de Rooij, Jaap and Verhoeven, Gerard. 1988. Orthography Reform and Language Planning for Dutch. *International Journal of the Sociology of Language* 73, 65–84.

Deroy, Louis. 1980. *L'emprunt linguistique.* Paris: Les Belles Lettres.

Derrida, Jacques. 1967. *De la grammatologie.* Paris: Les Editions de Minuit.

Desheriev, Y. D. 1973. Language Policy and Principles of Definition of Relative Language Utility. In *Anthropology and Language Science in Educational Development.* Educational Studies and Documents. New Series No. 11. Paris: UNESCO, 47–9.

Deutscher Bundestag (ed.). 1986. *Die Deutsche Sprache in der Welt.* Bonn: Deutscher Bundestag: Referat Öffentlichkeitsarbeit.

De Volkskrant. 1989. Kamer ontstemd over Engels als voertaal. December 14.

De Vries, J. W. 1988. Dutch Loan Words in Indonesian. *International Journal of the Sociology of Language*, 73, 121–36.

Diamond, Stanley. 1990. English, the Official Language of California 1983–88. In Adams, K. L. and Brink, D. T. (eds) *Perspectives on Official English: The Campaign for English as the Official Language of the USA.* Berlin, New York: Mouton de Gruyter, 111–19.

Die Welt. 1989. Deutsch, please! September 6.

Dillard, J. L. 1972. *Black English.* New York: Random House.

Diringer, David. 1948. *The Alphabet: A Key to the History of Mankind.* London: Hutchinson.

Djité, Paulin G. 1987. Francophonie in Africa: Some Obstacles. *Journal of the Washington Academy of Sciences* 77 (1), 40–6.

Djité, Paulin G. 1990. The Place of African Languages in the Revival of the Francophonie Movement. *International Journal of the Sociology of Language* 86, 87–102.

Djité, Paulin G. (forthcoming). Language and Development in Africa. *International Journal of the Sociology of Language* 100.

Documents COM(88) 841. 1989. Proposals for Council Decisions: Establishing the Lingua Programme to Promote Training in Foreign Languages in the European Community. *Documents of the Commission of the European Community*, January 6.

Dorian, Nancy. 1973. Grammatical Change in a Dying Dialect. *Language* 49, 431–8.

Dorian, Nancy. 1977. The Problem of the Semi-Speaker in Language Death. *International Journal of the Sociology of Language* 12, 23–32.

Dorian, Nancy. 1981. *Language Death: The Life Cycle of a Scottish Gaelic Dialect.* Philadelphia: University of Pennsylvania Press.

Dorian, Nancy (ed.). 1989. *Investigating Obsolescence.* London: Cambridge University Press.

Dressler, Wolfgang. 1972. On the Phonology of Language death. *Papers of the Chicago Linguistic Society* 8: 448–57.

Dressler, Wolfgang and Ruth Wodak-Leodolter (eds). 1977. Language Death. *International Journal of the Sociology of Language* 12.

Dressler, Wolfgang and Ruth Wodak-Leodolter. 1977. Language Preserveration and Language Death in Brittany. *International Journal of the Sociology of Language* 12, 33–44.

Drosdowski, Günther. 1984. Die Dudenredaktion. In Wimmer, R. (ed.) *Sprachkultur: Jahrbuch 1984 des Instituts für deutsche Sprache.* Düsseldorf: Schwann, 85-92.

Drozd, L. 1981 [1964]. Grundfragen der Terminologie in der Landwirtschaft. In von Hahn, W. (ed.) *Fachsprachen.* Darmstadt: Wissenschaftliche Buchgesellschaft, 114–71.

Drozd, L. and Seibicke, W. 1973. *Deutsche Fach- und Wissenschaftssprache: Bestandsaufnahme, Theorie, Geschichte.* Wiesbaden: Brandstetter.

Durkacz, Victor E. 1983. *The Decline of the Celtic Languages.* Edinburgh: The University of Edinburgh Press.

Eastman, Carol. 1990. Dissociation: A Unified Language Policy Outcome for Kenya. *International Journal of the Sociology of Language* 86, 69–86.

EC Council of Ministers. 1977. Directive 486 on the Education of Children of Migrant Workers. July 25, 1977. *Official Journal of the European Communities,* August 6, 77.

EC Document 1-306/82. 1982. Opinion of the Committee on Youth, Culture, Education, Information and Sport on the Motion for a resolution on the multilingualism of the European Community. Brussels: EC.

Eckermann, Johann Peter. 1955. *Gespräche mit Goethe in den letzten Jahren seines Lebens.* Wiesbaden: Insel-Verlag.

Eco, Umberto. 1973. *Zeichen: Einführung in einen Begriff und seine Geschichte.* Frankfurt: Suhrkamp.

Eco, Umberto. 1979. *A Theory of Semiotics.* Bloomington, Ind.: Indiana University Press.

Economist. 1987. Two Tongues for Europe: English und Französisch über alles. July 18, 16.

Eggers, Hans. 1969. *Deutsche Sprachgeschichte,* vol. 3. Reinbek: Rowohlt.

Eisenstadt, S. N. 1964. Social Change, Differentiation and Evolution. *American Sociological Review* 29, 3, 375–86.

Eisenstein, Elizabeth. 1979. *The Printing Press as an Agent of Change.* London:

Cambridge University Press.

Emmert, Hans-Dieter. 1987. Deutsch als Fremdsprache und Germanistik in der Türkei. In Sturm, D. (ed.) *Deutsch als Fremdsprache in der Welt: Situationen und Tendenzen.* Munich: Hueber, 61–73.

ENCRAGES. 1986. Les industries de la langue: Enjeux pour l'Europe. *Actes du colloque de Tours,* no. 16, Autumn 1986, Université de Paris VIII.

Erlinghagen, Helmut. 1975. *Japan: Ein deutscher Japaner über die Japaner.* Stuttgart: Deutsche Verlagsanstalt.

Esman, Milton J. 1985. The Politics of Official Bilingualism in Canada. In Beer, W. R. and Jacob, J. E. (eds) *Language Policy and National Unity.* Totowa, NJ: Rowman & Allanheld.

Estoup, J. B. 1916. *Gammes sténographiques,* 4th edition. Paris: Institut Sténographique.

Extra, Guus and Vallen, Ton. 1988. Language and Ethnic Minorities in the Netherlands. *International Journal of the Sociology of Language* 73, 85–110.

Falkenstein, Adam. 1936. *Archaische Texte aus Uruk: Ausgrabungen der Deutschen Forschungsgemeinschaft in Uruk-Warka.* Leipzig: O. Harrassowitz.

Falkenstein, Adam. 1953. Die babylonische Schule. *Saeculum* 4, 125–37.

Fasold, Ralph. 1984. *The Sociolinguistics of Society.* Oxford: Blackwell.

Felber, H. 1984. *Terminology Manual.* Paris: UNESCO.

Feldbusch, Elisabeth. 1985. *Geschriebene Sprache.* Berlin: de Gruyter.

Feng Zhiwei. 1988. The "FEL" Formula: An Economical Law for the Formation of Terms. *Social Sciences in China,* Winter 1988, 171–80.

Ferguson, Charles A. 1968. Language Development. In Fishman, J. A., Ferguson, C. A., and Das Gupta, J. (eds) *Language Problems of Developing Nations.* New York: John Wiley and Sons.

Filipović, Rudolf. 1982. *The English Element in European Languages. vol. 2: Reports and Studies.* Zagreb: Institute of Linguistics.

Finkenstaedt, Thomas and Schröder, Konrad. 1990. *Sprachenschranken statt Zollschranken? Grundlegung einer Fremdsprachenpolitik für das Europa von morgen.* Essen: Stifterverband für die Deutsche Wissenschaft (Materialien zur Bildungspolitik 11).

Fischer Weltalmanach 1990. Frankfurt: Fischer.

Fishman, Joshua A. 1964. Language Maintenance and Language Shift as a Field of Inquiry. *Linguistics* 9, 32-70.

Fishman, Joshua A. (ed.). 1966. *Language Loyalty in the United States.* The Hague: Mouton.

Fishman, Joshua A. 1972. *Language and Nationalism.* Rowley, Mass.: Newbury House.

Fishman, Joshua A. 1985a. Toward Multilingualism as an International Desideratum in Government, Business, and the Professions. *Annual Review of Applied Linguistics* 6, 2–9.

Fishman, Joshua A. 1985b. The Lively Life of a "Dead" Language. In Wolfson, N. and Manes, J. (eds) *Language of Inequality*. Berlin, New York, Amsterdam: Mouton, 207–22.

Fishman, Joshua A. 1988. "English Only": Its Ghosts, Myths, and Dangers. *International Journal of the Sociology of Language* 74, 125–40.

Fishman, J. A., Ferguson, C. A., and Das Gupta, J. (eds). 1968. *Language Problems of Developing Nations*. New York: John Wiley & Sons.

Fitouri, C. 1983. *Biculturalisme, bilinguisme et éducation*. Neuchâtel-Paris: Delachaux et Niestlé.

Floc'h, Guillaume. 1981. Emploi du breton et vente du poisson en Bretangne du sud. *International Journal of the Sociology of Language* 29, 29–50.

Foster, Philip J. 1972. Problems of Literacy in Sub-Saharan Africa. In Sebeok, T. A. (ed.) *Current Trends in Linguistics*, vol. 8. The Hague: Mouton, 587–617.

Français du Monde. 1982. Interview with M. Michel Jobert. No. 17 (October) 9, 13.

Fraser, Bruce. 1975. Hedged Performatives. In Cole, P. and Morgan, J. L. (eds) *Syntax and Semantics*, vol. 3. New York: Academic Press, 187–210.

Freyenhagen, J. 1981. Fast eine Million Bundesbürger kann weder lesen noch schreiben. *Süddeutsche Zeitung*, January 10, 11.

Frideres, J. S. 1988. Visible Minority Groups and Second-Language Programs: Language Adaptation. *International Journal of the Sociology of Language* 80, 83–98.

Friedland, Klaus. 1987. Wirtschaftsgemeinschaft und Staatshoheit als Problem der Hanse. In Ureland, P. S. (ed.) *Sprachkontakte in der Hanse: Aspekte des Sprachausgleichs im Ostsee- und Nordseeraum*. Tübingen: Niemeyer, 7–19.

Frumkina, R. M. 1970. Über das sogenannte "Zipfsche Gesetz." Mannheim: *Forschungsberichte des Instituts für deutsche Sprache* 4, 117–32.

Fry, Dennis. 1977. *Homo Loquens: Man as a Talking Animal*. London: Cambridge University Press.

Gabelentz, Georg von der. 1901. *Die Sprachwissenschaft: Ihre Aufgaben, Methoden und bisherigen Ergebnisse*. Leipzig. (Reprint 1969, Tübingen).

Gadamer, Hans-Georg. 1960. *Wahrheit und Methode*. Gesammelte Werke, vol. 1, 1986. Tübingen: J. C. B. Mohr.

Gage, William W. 1986. The World Balance of Languages. In Fishman, J. A., Tabouret-Keller, A., Clyne, M., Krishnamurti, B., and Abdulaziz, M. (eds) *The Fergusonian Impact: In Honor of Charles A. Ferguson on the occasion of his 65th Birthday*. Berlin, New York: Mouton de Gruyter, vol. 2, pp. 371–83.

Gakujutsu shingikai gakujutsu yôgo bunkakai [Subcommittee on Scientific Terms, Science Council, Japanese Ministry of Education]. 1983. *Gakujutsu yôgo shinsa kijun* [Criteria for Deliberation of Scientific Terms]. Tokyo:

Ministry of Education.

Galbraith, John Kenneth. 1976. *Money: Whence it Came, Where it Went.* London: Penguin.

Galbraith, John Kenneth. 1987. *A History of Economics: The Past as the Present.* Harmondsworth: Penguin.

Galinski, C. and Nedobity, W. 1989. *International and Regional Co-operation in Terminology.* Vienna: Infoterm.

Gandhi, Mohandes. 1954. *Sarvodaya (The Welfare of All).* Edited by B. Kumarappa. Ahmedabad: Navajivan Publishing House.

Gandhi, Mohandes. 1959. New Life for Khadi. *The Collected Works of Mahatma Gandhi*, vol. 59. New Delhi: Publications Division.

Gandhi, Mohandes. 1960. Its Meaning. *The Collected Works of Mahatma Gandhi*, vol. 60. New Delhi: Publications Division.

Gandhi, Mohandes. 1965. *Our Language Problem.* Bombay: Bharatiya Vidya Bhavan (Pocket Gandhi Series No. 13).

Gao Mingkai and Liu Zhengtan. 1958. *Xiandai hanyu wailaici yanjiu* [Investigation of loanwords in modern Chinese]. Beijing: Wenzi gaige chubanshe.

Gelb, I. J. 1963. *A Study of Writing.* Second revised edition. Chicago, London: The University of Chicago Press.

Gellner, Ernest. 1983. *Nations and Nationalism.* Oxford: Blackwell.

Giese, Heinz W. and Gläss, Bernhard. (eds). 1989. *Alphabetisierung und Elementarbildung in Europa.* Oldenburg: Zentrum für wissenschaftliche Weiterbildung der Universität Oldenburg.

Giesecke, Michael. 1979. Schriftspracherwerb und Erstlesedidaktik in der Zeit des "gemein teutsch": Eine sprachhistorische Untersuchung der Lehrbücher Valentin Ickelsamers. *Osnabrücker Beiträge zur Sprachtheorie* 11, 48–72.

Glück, Helmut. 1987. *Schrift und Schriftlichkeit: Eine sprach- und kulturwissenschaftliche Studie.* Stuttgart: Metzler.

Goethe, Johann Wolfgang von. 1986. *Faust: Der Tragödie erster und zweiter Teil. Urfaust.* Herausgegeben und kommentiert von Erich Trunz. Munich: Verlag C. H. Beck. [Translation by Philip Wayne. 1949. London: Penguin Books.]

Goethe-Institut. 1988. *Goethe-Institut Jahrbuch 1987/88.* Munich.

Gonzales, A. 1978. A Southeast Asian Perspective on the Role of Minority Languages as Languages of Education. In Yap, A. (ed.) *Language Education in Multilingual Societies.* Singapore: Singapore University Press, 135–44.

Goody, Jack. 1977. *The Domestication of the Savage Mind.* Cambridge: Cambridge University Press.

Goody, Jack. 1986. *The Logic of Writing and the Organization of Society.* London, New York: Cambridge University Press.

Goody, Jack and Watt, Ian. 1968. The Consequences of Literacy. In Goody, Jack (ed.) *Literacy in Traditional Societies.* Cambridge: Cambridge University Press, 27–68.

Gorter, Durk (ed.). 1987. The Sociology of Frisian. *International Journal of the Sociology of Language* 64.

Green, M. W. 1981. The Construction and Implementation of the Cuneiform Writing System. *Visible Language* 15, 4: 345–72.

Grice, H. P. 1975. Logic and Conversation. In Cole, P. and Morgan, J. L. (eds) *Syntax and Semantics*, vol. 3. New York: Academic Press, 41–58.

Grillo, R. D. 1989. *Dominant Languages: Language and Hierarchy in Britain and France.* Cambridge: Cambridge University Press.

Grimes, Barbara F. (ed.). 1988. *Ethnologue: Languages of the World.* Eleventh edition. Dallas, Tx.: Summer Institute of Linguistics, Inc.

Grimm, Jacob. 1822. *Deutsche Grammatik.* Second edition, vol. 1. Göttingen.

Große, Rudolf. 1980. Soziolinguistische Grundlagen des Meißnischen Deutsch. *Akten des VI. Internationalen Germanisten-Kongresses Basel 1980*, edited by Heinz Rupp and Hans-Gert Roloff. vol. 2. Bern, Frankfurt: Lang, 344–347.

Grundmann, Hilmar. 1985. 3 Millionen erwachsene deutschsprachige Analphabeten in unserem Lande: Versagt der Deutschunterricht in unseren Schulen? *Sprache und Beruf* 3, 53–5.

Guiraud, Pierre. 1959. *Problèmes et méthodes de la statistique linguistique.* Dordrecht: D. Reidel.

Gumperz, John J. and Cook-Gumperz, Jenny. 1981. Ethnic Differences in Communicative Style. In Ferguson, C. A. and Brice-Heath S. (eds) *Language in the USA.* London: Cambridge University Press, 430–45.

Haarmann, Harald. 1980. *Multilingualismus*, 2 vols. Tübingen: Narr.

Haarmann, Harald. 1990. "Basic" Vocabulary and Languages in Contact: The Disillusion of Glottochronology. *Indogermanische Forschungen* 95, 1–37.

Haberland, Hartmut. 1990. Whose English, Nobody's Business. *Journal of Pragmatics* 13, 927–38.

Habermas, Jürgen. 1976. Was heißt Universalpragmatik? In Apel, Karl-Otto (ed.). *Sprachpragmatik und Philosophie.* Frankfurt/M.: Suhrkamp, 174–272.

Häfele, Margot. 1977. Anforderungen der betrieblichen Wirklichkeit an die Sprache. *Muttersprache* 87 (2), 86–98.

Hagen, S. (ed.) 1988. *Languages in British Business: An Analysis of Current Needs.* London: Centre for Information on Language Teaching.

Håkausson, H. (ed.). 1982. *International Marketing and Purchasing of Industrial Goods: An Interaction Approach.* Chichester: John Wiley and Sons.

Hall, Robert A. Jr. 1966. *Pidgin and Creole Languages.* Ithaca: Cornell University Press.

Halliday, M. A. K. 1978. *Language as Social Semiotic: The Social Interpretation of Language and Meaning.* London: Edward Arnold.

Hamann, Johann Georg. 1761. Vermischte Anmerkungen über die Wortfügung in der französischen Sprache. In Hamann, J. G. *Schriften zur Sprache.* Edited by Josef Simon. Frankfurt/M.: Suhrkamp 1967, 95–104.

Hammink, Kees. 1987. *Alfabetiseren: Tien jaar vechten tegen ongelijkheid*. Amersfoort.

Hancock, I. F. 1972. A Domestic Origin for the English Derived Atlantic Creoles. *The Florida Foreign Language Reporter* 7 (8), 52.

Hancock, I. F. 1976. Nautical Sources of Krio Vocabulary. *International Journal of the Sociology of Language* 7, 23–36.

Hanley, Charles J. 1981. Frenchifying Quebec: Don't Say Bread, Say Pain. *The Daily Yomiuri*, May 7.

Harris, Roy. 1980. *The Language Makers*. Ithaca, NY: Cornell University Press.

Harris, Roy. 1986. *The Origin of Writing*. London: Duckworth.

Hartig, Matthias. 1990. Deutsch als Standardsprache. *International Journal of the Sociology of Language* 83, 121–33.

Hartmann, Nicolai. 1926. *Ethik*. Berlin: de Gruyter.

Haugen, Einar. 1950. The Analysis of Linguistic Borrowing. *Language* 26 (2), 210–31.

Haugen, Einar. 1953. *The Norwegian Language in America: A Study in Bilingual Behavior*. 2 vols. Philadelphia: University of Pennsylvania Press.

Haugen, Einar. 1966. Language, Dialect, Nation. *American Anthropologist* 68, 922–35.

Hausmann, Franz Josef. 1985. Lexikographie. In Schwarze, C. and Wunderlich, D. (eds) *Handbuch der Lexikologie*. Königstein/Ts.: Athenäum, 367–411.

Havelock, Eric A. 1963. *Preface to Plato*. Cambridge, Mass.: Harvard University Press.

Hawkes, Jaquetta and Wooley, Leonard. 1963. *Prehistory and the Beginnings of Civilization*. New York: Harper and Row.

Hayashi Shuji. 1988. *Culture and Management in Japan*. Tokyo: University of Tokyo Press.

Hegel, Georg Wilhelm Friedrich. 1854. *Grundlinien der Philosophie des Rechts: oder, Naturrecht und Staatswissenschaft im Grundrisse*. 3rd ed. Berlin: Duncker and Humbolt. Trans. T. M. Knox *Hegel's Philosophy of Law*. 1953. Oxford: Clarendon.

Heidegger, Martin. 1951. *Erläuterungen zu Hölderlins Dichtung*, 2nd edition. Frankfurt/M.: Klostermann.

Heidegger, Martin. 1959. *Unterwegs zur Sprache*. Pfullingen: Verlag Günther Neske.

Heidelberger Forschungsprojekt "Pidgin-Deutsch". 1975. *Sprache und Kommunikation ausländischer Arbeitnehmer*. Kronberg: Scriptor Verlag.

Heller, Klaus. 1970. Der Wortschatz unter dem Aspekt des Fachwortes: Versuch einer Systematik. *Wissenschaftliche Zeitschrift der Karl-Marx-Universität Leipzig. Gesellschafts- und Sprachwissenschaftliche Reihe* 19, 531–44.

Herder, J. G. [1767] Über die neuere deutsche Literatur. Erste Sammlung von Fragmenten. In: *Frühe Schriften 1764–1772*. Edited by Ulrich Gaier.

Frankfurt: Deutscher Klassiker Verlag, 161–259.

Herder, J. G. [1771]. Über den Ursprung der Sprache. In *Herders Werke, Dritter Teil*. Berlin, Leipzig, Vienna: Deutsches Verlagshaus Bong & Co., 137–229.

Heyd, Uriel. 1954. Language Reform in Modern Turkey. *Oriental Notes and Studies* 5. Jerusalem: Israel Oriental Society.

Hildebrandt, Herbert W. and Jinyun Liu. 1991. Communication through Foreign Languages: An Economic Force in Chinese Enterprises. In Coulmas, Florian (ed.) *The Economics of Language in the Asian Pacific. Journal of Asian Pacific Communication*, vol. 2, 45–67.

Hill, K. C. (ed.). 1979. *The Genesis of Language*. Ann Arbor: Karoma.

Hirsch, Donald. 1991. Overcoming Adult Illiteracy. *OECD Observer* 171, Aug/Sept 1991, 21–4.

Hobbes, Thomas. 1973. *Leviathan*. London, New York: Academic Press.

Hockett, Charles F. 1960. The Origin of Speech. *Scientific American* 203, 88–96.

Hodge, Carlton T. 1975. Ritual and Writing: An Inquiry into the Origin of Egyptian Script. In Kinkade, M. D., Hale, K. L., and Werner, O. (eds) *Linguistics and Anthropology: in Honor of C. F. Voegelin*. Lisse: Peter de Ridder, 331–50.

Hodgkin, Thomas. 1957. *Nationalism in Colonial Africa*. New York: New York University Press.

Hoenigswald, Henry M. 1989. Language Obsolescence and Language History: Matters of Linearity, Leveling, Loss, and the Like. In Dorian, N. (ed.) *Investigating Obsolescence: Studies in Language Contraction and Death*. Cambridge, New York: Cambridge University Press, 347–54.

Hoffmann, Fernand. 1979. *Sprachen in Luxemburg: Sprachwissenschaftliche und literarhistorische Beschreibung einer Triglossie-Situation*. Luxembourg: Institut Grand-Ducal. Wiesbaden: Steiner.

Holden, Nigel J. 1987. Language Barriers as Differential Constraints on the International Behavior of Firms. In Tonkin, H. and Johnson-Weiner, K. M. (eds) *The Economics of Language Use*. New York: Center for Research and Documentation on World Language Problems, 119–39.

Hoogvelt, A. M. M. 1978. *The Sociology of Developing Societies*. London: Macmillan.

Hörisch, Jochen. 1990. Poesie des Geldes. *Universitas* 4, 334–44.

Hudson, Richard. 1990. Review of "Investigating Obsolescence" edited by Nancy Dorian. *Language* 66 (4), 831–4.

Huebner, T. 1989. Language and Schooling in Western and American Samoa. *World Englishes* 8 (1), 59–72.

Hüllen, Werner. 1981. Teaching English for Special Purposes. In Freudenstein, R., Beneke, R., and Pönisch, H. (eds) *Language Incorporated: Teaching Foreign Languages in Industry*. Oxford, New York: Pergamon Press.

Humboldt, Wilhelm von. 1963a [1830]. Über die Verschiedenheit des menschlichen Sprachbaus und ihren Einfluß auf die geistige Entwicklung des Menschengeschlechts. *Werke in fünf Bänden*, vol. 3. Stuttgart: Cotta, 368–756.

Humboldt, Wilhelm von. 1963b [1822]. Über den Nationalcharakter der Sprachen. *Werke in fünf Bänden*, vol. 3. Stuttgart: Cotta, 64–81.

Humboldt, Wilhelm von. 1963c [1827]. Über die Verschiedenheiten des menschlichen Sprachbaues. *Werke in fünf Bänden*, vol. 3. Stuttgart: Cotta, 144–367.

Hume, David. 1964. Of the Origin of Justice and Property. In *A Treatise of Human Nature*. Book 3, 258–273 (reprint of second edition). Aalen: Scientia Verlag.

Husserl, Edmund. 1913. *Ideen zu einer reinen phänomenologischen Philosophie*. Halle.

Hutchins, W. J. 1986. *Machine Translation: Past, Present, Future*. Chichester: Ellis Horwood Ltd.

Ibrahim, Muhammad H. 1989. Communicating in Arabic: Problems and Prospects. In Coulmas, F. (ed.) *Language Adaptation*. Cambridge, New York: Cambridge University Press, 39–59.

Ickelsamer, Valentin. 1972. [1527] *Ein teutsch Grammatica: Die rechte weis aufs kürzist lesen zu lernen*. Edited by H. Fechner (Documenta linguistica. Deutsche Grammatiken des 16. bis 18. Jahrhunderts). Hildesheim.

Illich, Ivan and Sanders, Barry. 1988. *ABC: The Alphabetization of the Popular Mind*. San Francisco: North Point Press.

Instituto della Enciclopedia Italiana. 1986. *Linguistic Minorities in Countries Belonging to the European Community*. Luxemburg: Office of Official Publication of the European Communities.

International Monetary Fund. 1988. *Annual Report 1988*. Washington, DC.

Jacob, James E. 1990. Language Policy and Political Development in France. In Weinstein, Brian (ed.) *Language Policy and Political Development*. Norwood, NJ: Ablex, 43–65.

Jakobson, Roman. 1945. The Beginning of National Self-Determination in Europe. *The Review of Politics* 7, 29–42. Reprinted in: Fishman, J. A. (ed.) *Readings in the Sociology of Language*. The Hague, Paris: Mouton, 585–97.

Jalaluddin, A. K. 1983. Problems of Transition of Rural Indian Society from Oral to Written Tradition through Adult Education. *Journal of Pragmatics* 7 (5), 517–31.

Japan Foundation. 1988. *Wagakuni no nihongo kyôiku no shisaku ni tsuite* [Directions for teaching Japanese as a foreign language]. Tokyo.

Japan Times. 1988. Vive le français! December 28.

Jensen, Hans. 1969. *Die Schrift in Vergangenheit und Gegenwart*. Berlin: VEB

Deutscher Verlag der Wissenschaften (reprint of third edition). (*Sign, Symbol and Script.* New York: Putnam's, 1969)

Jernudd, Björn H. 1968. Is Self-Instructional Language Teaching Profitable? *IRAL* 6 (4), 349–60.

Jernudd, Björn H. and Shapiro, Michael J. (eds). 1989. *The Politics of Language Purism.* Berlin, New York: Mouton de Gruyter.

Jernudd, Björn and Sung-Hwan Jo. 1985. Bilingualism as a Resource in the United States. *Annual Review of Applied Linguistics* 6, 10–18.

Jespersen, Otto. 1924. *The Philosophy of Grammar.* London: George Allen and Unwin.

Jespersen, Otto. 1926. *Growth and Structure of the English Language.* Fifth edition. Leipzig: Teubner.

Jespersen, Otto. 1933. Nature and Art in Language. In *Selected Writings.* London: Allen and Unwin, 660–71.

Jespersen, Otto. 1964. *Language: Its Nature, Development and Origin.* New York: W. W. Norton and Co. [First edition 1921]

Jiten jiten sôgô mokuroku (General index of dictionaries and encyclopedias [Japanese]). Tokyo: Shuppan nyûsusha, 1989.

Johnson, Samuel. 1964 [1755]. *Samuel Johnson's Dictionary: A Modern Selection.* Edited by McAdam, E. L. Jr. and Milne, George. New York: Pantheon Books.

Joseph, John Earl. 1987. *Eloquence and Power: The Rise of Language Standards and Standard Languages.* London: Frances Pinter.

Jungraithmayr, H. and Möhlig, W. J. G. (eds). 1983. *Lexikon der Afrikanistik.* Berlin: Dietrich Reimer Verlag.

Kabashima Tadao. 1979. *Nihon no moji: Hyôki taikei-o kangaeru* [Japanese letters. About the writing system.] Tokyo: Iwanami.

Kandiah, Thiru. 1978. A Standard Language and Socio-Historical Parameters: Standard Lankan Tamil. *International Journal of the Sociology of Language* 16, 59–75.

Kasher, Asa. 1985. Philosophy and Discourse Analysis. In Van Dijk, T. A. (ed.) *Handbook of Discourse Analysis*, vol. 1. London, New York: Academic Press, 231–248.

Kasher, Asa. 1986. Politeness and Rationality. In Johansen, J. D. and Sonne, H. (eds) *Pragmatics and Linguistics: Festschrift for Jacob L. Mey.* Odense University Press, 103–14.

Kay, M. 1975. Automatic Translation of Natural Languages. In: Bloomfield, M. and Haugen, E. (eds) *Language as Human Problem.* Guildford: Lutterworth Press.

Kerr, A. N. 1984. Language and the Education of Immigrants' Children in Sweden. In Kennedy, C. (ed.) *Language Planning and Language Education.* London: Allen & Unwin, 172–185.

Keynes, John Maynard. 1932. *Essays in Persuasion.* New York: Harcourt, Brace and Co.

Khlief, B. B. 1980. *Language, Ethnicity and Education in Wales.* The Hague: Mouton.

Khubchandani, Lachman M. 1983. *Plural Languages, Plural Cultures: Communication, Identity, and Sociopolitical Change in Contemporary India.* Honolulu: University of Hawaii Press.

Kieffer, Charles. 1977. The Approaching End of the Relict Southeast Iranian Languages Ormuri and Parāči in Afghanistan. *International Journal of the Sociology of Language* 12, 72–100.

Kimura, Hiroko. 1987. Limited Language Skills Force Refugees into Blue-Collar Jobs. *Japan Times*, 12 (1), 1987, 1.

Kirkness, A. 1975. *Zur Sprachreinigung im Deutschen 1789–1871.* 2 vols. Tübingen: Niemeyer.

Klaverkämper, H. and Weinrich, H. (eds). 1986. *Deutsch als Wissenschaftssprache.* Forum für Fachsprachenforschung. Tübingen: Narr.

Kloss, Heinz. 1967. "Abstand Languages" and "Ausbau Languages." *Anthropological Linguistics* 9 (7), 29–41.

Kloss, Heinz. 1969. *Grundfragen der Ethnopolitik im 20. Jahrhundert: Die Sprachgemeinschaften zwischen Recht und Gewalt.* Wien, Stuttgart: Braunmüller Universitäts-Verlagsbuchhandlung.

Kloss, Heinz. 1974. Die den internationalen Rang einer Sprache bestimmenden Faktoren. Ein Versuch. In Kloss, H. (ed.) *Deutsch in der Begegnung mit anderen Sprachen: Im Fremdsprachen-Wettbewerb, als Muttersprache in Übersee, als Bildungsbarriere für Gastarbeiter.* Forschungsberichte des Instituts für Deutsche Sprache Bd. 20. Mannheim, 7–77.

Kloss, Heinz. 1978 [1952]. *Die Entwicklung neuer germanischer Kultursprachen von 1800 bis 1950.* 2nd. enlarged edition, Düsseldorf: Schwann.

Kloss, Heinz. 1984. Umriß eines Forschungsprogrammes zum Thema "Sprachentod." *International Journal of the Sociology of Language* 45, 65–76.

Koch, Harald. 1991. Legal Aspects of a Language Policy for the European Communities: Language Risks, Equal Opportunities, and Legislating a Language. In Coulmas, F. (ed.) *A Language Policy for the European Community. Prospects and Quandaries.* Berlin, New York: Mouton de Gruyter, 147–161.

Kocks, Andreas. 1988. *Untersuchung zum Fremdsprachenbedarf in der Duisburger Stahlindustrie.* Duisburg: LAUD C15.

Kocks, Andreas. 1989. *Frendsprachenbedarf in Handel und Industrie: Eine Untersuchung in Duisburg.* Duisburg: LAUD C18.

Kommission für Rechtschreibfragen des Instituts für Deutsche Sprache, Mannheim. 1988. *Vorschlag zur Neuregelung der deutschen Rechtschreibung.* Mannheim: Institut für Deutsche Sprache.

Kramer, Samuel Noah. 1963. *The Sumerians.* Chicago: Chicago University Press.

Krauss, R. M. and Glucksberg, S. 1977. Social and Non-Social Speech. *Scientific American* 236, 100–105.

Kühn, Peter. 1978. *Deutsche Wörterbücher: Eine systematische Bibliographie*. Tübingen: Niemeyer.

Kuo, Eddie C. Y. 1979. Measuring Communicativity in Multilingual Societies: The Case of Singapore and West Malaysia. *Anthropological Linguistics* 21 (7), 328–40.

Kusterer, Hermann. 1980. Das Sprachenproblem in den Europäischen Gemeinschaften: Ein Plädoyer für Pragmatik. *Europa-Archiv*, Folge 22, 693–8.

Kuter, Lois. 1989. Breton vs. French: Language and the Opposition of Political, Economic, Social, and Cultural Values. In Dorian, N. (ed.) *Investigating Obsolescence: Studies in Language Contraction and Death*. Cambridge, New York: Cambridge University Press, 75–89.

Kutsuwada O., Mishima K. and Ueda Kouji. 1987. Zur Situation des Deutschunterrichts in Japan. In Sturm, D. (ed.) *Deutsch als Fremdsprache weltweit*. Munich: Hueber, 75–82.

Kwan-Terry, Anna. 1991. The Economics of Language in Singapore: Students' Use of Extracurricular Language Lessons. In Coulmas, Florian (ed.) *The Economics of Language in the Asian Pacific, Journal of Asian Pacific Communication*, vol. 2, 69–89.

Labov, William. 1965. On the Mechanism of Linguistic Change. In Kreidler, C. W. (ed.) *Georgetown University Monograph Series on Languages and Linguistics*, no. 18. Washington, DC: Georgetown University Press, 91–114.

Lakoff, George and Johnson, Mark. 1980. *Metaphors We Live By*. Chicago and London: The University of Chicago Press.

Landry, Alain. 1987. Using New Technologies to Serve Language: An Investment. In Tonkin, H. and Johnson-Weiner, K. M. (eds) *The Economics of Language Use*. New York: Center for Research and Documentation on World Language Problems, 47–54.

Landsberg, Marge E. (ed.). 1988. *The Genesis of Language: A Different Judgment of Evidence*. Berlin, New York, Amsterdam: Mouton de Gruyter.

Language Planning Newsletter. 1983. "Monotony": New Greek Writing System Saves Millions. vol. 9 (2), 8.

Large, J. A. 1983. *The Foreign Language Barrier: Problems in Scientific Communication*. Oxford: Blackwell.

Large, J. A. 1985. *The Artificial Language Movement*. Oxford: Blackwell.

Lee McKay, S. and Wong, S. C. (eds). 1988. *Language Diversity: Problem or Resource? A Social and Educational Perspective on Language Minorities in the United States*. New York: Newbury House.

Leech, Geoffrey N. 1983. *Principles of Pragmatics*. London, New York: Longman.

Leibniz, Gottfried Wilhelm. 1983 [1717]. *Unvorgreifliche Gedanken, betreffend die Ausübung und Verbesserung der deutschen Sprache. Zwei Aufsätze.* Edited by Uwe Pörksen. Stuttgart: Reclam.

Leloux, Hermanus Johannes. 1987. Mittelniederdeutsch und Mittelniederländisch in Brügge. Soll und Haben einer Geschäftssprache. In Ureland, P. S. (ed.) *Sprachkontakte in der Hanse: Aspekte des Sprachausgleichs im Ostsee- und Nordseeraum.* Tübingen: Niemeyer, 123–33.

Le Monde. 1985. L'enseignement des langues vivantes. February 7, 13.

Lenin, W. I. 1961. Über das Selbstbestimmungsrecht der Nationen. *Werke,* Vol. 20. Berlin: Dietz Verlag, 395ff.

Leopold, Werner F. 1959. The Decline of German Dialects. *Word* 15, 130–53.

Le Page, R. B. 1964. *The National Language Question: Linguistic Problems of Newly Independent States.* London: Oxford University Press.

Le Page, R. B. 1981. *Caribbean Connections in the Classroom.* University of York.

Le Page, R. B. and Tabouret-Keller, A. 1985. *Acts of Identity.* Cambridge: Cambridge University Press.

Lévi-Strauss, Claude. 1955. *Tristes tropiques.* Paris: Plon.

Lévi-Strauss, Claude. 1958. *Anthropologie structurale.* Paris: Plon.

Lévi-Strauss, Claude. 1969. *The Elementary Structures of Kinship.* Revised edition, translated by J. H. Bell, J. R. von Sturmer and R. Needham. Boston: Beacon Press.

Lévy-Bruhl, L. 1918. *Les fonctions mentales dans les sociétés inférieures.* Paris: Presses universitaires de France.

Lewis, E. Glyn. 1977. Bilingualism in Education: Cross-National Research. *International Journal of the Sociology of Language* 14, 5–30.

Lewis, E. Glyn. 1987. Attitudes to the Planned Development of Welsh. *International Journal of the Sociology of Language* 66: 11–26.

Lewis, Glyn. 1972. *Multilingualism in the Soviet Union.* The Hague: Mouton.

L'Express. 1984. Les inquisiteurs du bon français. November 23.

Lieberman, S. J. 1977. Sumerian Loanwords in Old-Babylonian Akkadian. *Harvard Semitic Studies* 22.

Lieberman, S. J. 1980. Of Clay Tablets, Hollow Clay Balls, and Writing: A Sumerian View. *American Journal of Archeology* 84, 339–58.

Lieberson, Stanley. 1980. Procedures for Improving Sociolinguistic Surveys of Language Maintenance and Language Shift. *International Journal of the Sociology of Language* 25, 11–27.

Lindner, Renate. 1984. Fremdsprachen bei Schering: Das Kursangebot und seine Geschichte im Spiegel der Unternehmensentwicklung. In Schröder, Konrad (ed.) *Die Neueren Sprachen,* topic issue: Außerschulisches Fremdsprachenlernen und Frendsprachenbedarf. Frankfurt, 83 (1), 69–77.

Linguistic Minorities Project. 1985. *The Other Languages of England.* London: Routledge and Kegan Paul.

Lipfert, H. 1988. *Devisenhandel,* 3rd edition. Frankfurt: Georg Lingenbrink.

Locke, John. 1959 [1960]. *An Essay Concerning Human Understanding.* New

York: Dover Books.

Löffler, Heinrich. 1985. *Germanistische Soziolinguistik*. Berlin: Erich Schmidt Verlag.

Louven, E. 1983. Chinesische Wirtschaftsterminologie: Definitionen und Kompatibilitätsprobleme. *China Aktuell* 4, 235–42; 8, 503–8.

Lowe, Judy. 1982. Language in International Business: Some Training Implications. *Journal of European Industrial Training* 6 (1), 23–5.

Lowenberg, Peter H. 1988. Malay in Indonesia, Malaysia, and Singapore: Three Faces of a National Language. In Coulmas, F. (ed.) *With Forked Tongues: What are National Languages Good for?* Ann Arbor: Karoma, 146–79.

Luhmann, Niklas. 1988. *Die Wirtschaft der Gesellschaft*. Frankfurt/M.: Suhrkamp.

Luther, Martin. 1912–1921. *Tischreden*, 6 vols. Weimar: H. Böhlaus Nachfolger.

Mackey, William F. 1976. *Bilinguism et contact des langues*. Paris: Klincksieck.

Mackey, William F. 1984. Bilingual Education and its Social Implications. In Edwards, John (ed.) *Linguistic Minorities: Policies and Pluralism*. London: Academic Press, 151–177.

Mahmoud, Youssef. 1987. Cost-Benefit Analysis and Language Planning in the United Nations. In Tonkin, H. and Johnson-Weiner, K. M. (eds) *The Economics of Language Use*. New York: Center for Research and Documentation on World Language Problems, 33–44.

Mair, Lucy. 1963. *New Nations*. London: Weidenfeld & Nicolson.

Mandelbrot, Benoit. 1954. Structure formelle des textes et communication. *Word* 10 (1), 1–27.

Marina, S. J. 1987. Principles Adopted for the Enrichment of Kiswahili Language. *New Language Planning Newsletter* 2 (2).

Marschak, Jacob. 1965. Economics of Language. *Behavioral Science* 10, 135–40.

Marshall, David F. 1986. The Question of an Official Language: Language Rights and the English Language Amendment. *International Journal of the Sociology of Language* 60, 7–75.

Martinet, André. 1955. *Economie des changements phonétiques: Traité de phonologie diachronique*. Bern: A. Francke [Bibliotheca romanica].

Martinet, André. 1969. *Langue et fonction: Une théorie fonctionelle du langage*. Paris: Denoël.

Martinet, André. 1975. Phonetik und Sprachentwicklung. In Cherubim, D. (ed.) *Sprachwandel: Reader zur diachronischen Sprachwissenschaft*. Berlin: de Gruyter, 150–76.

Marx, Karl. 1953 [1857]. *Grundrisse der Kritik der politischen Ökonomie*. Berlin: Dietz Verlag.

Marx, Karl. 1964. *Das Kapital: Kritik der politischen Ökonomie*. Dritter Band. Berlin: Dietz Verlag.

Marx, Karl and Engels, Friedrich 1969 [1845]. *Die deutsche Ideologie: Kritik der neuesten deutschen Philosophie in ihren Repräsentanten Feuerbach, B. Bauer und Stirner, und des deutschen Sozialismus in seinen verschiedenen Propheten.* Berlin: Dietz Verlag.

Massamba, David P. B. 1989. An Assessment of the Development and Modernization of the Kiswahili Language in Tanzania. In Coulmas, F. (ed.) *Language Adaptation.* Cambridge: Cambridge University Press, 60–78.

Mattheier, Klaus J. 1990. Dialekt und Standardsprache: Über das Varietätensystem des Deutschen in der Bundesrepublik. *International Journal of the Sociology of Language* 83, 59–81.

Matthews, Niall and Nakamura Mami (eds). 1989. *Executive Training Programme in Japan.* Tokyo EC Delegation.

McBee, S. 1985. English out to Conquer the World. *US News and World Report,* February 18, 49–52.

McCallen, Brian. 1989. *English: A World Commodity.* London: The Economist Intelligence Unit Ltd.

McCord, William. 1991. *The Dawn of the Pacific Century.* New Brunswick and London: Transaction Publishers.

McLuhan, Marshall. 1962. *The Gutenberg Galaxy.* London: Routledge and Kegan Paul.

McLuhan, Marshall. 1964. *Understanding Media.* New York: McGraw Hill.

Mencken, H. L. 1945. *The American Language.* New York: Alfred A. Knopf.

Merritt, M. and M. H. Abdulaziz. 1988. Swahili as a National Language in East Africa. In Coulmas, F. (ed.) *With Forked Tongues: What are National Languages Good for?* Ann Arbor: Karoma, 48–67.

Miller, Roy A. 1982. *Japan's Modern Myth.* New York, Tokyo: Weatherhill.

Misra, B. G. 1982. Language Spread in a Multilingual Setting: The Spread of Hindi as a Case Study. In Cooper, R. L. (ed.) *Language Spread: Studies in Diffusion and Social Change.* Arlington, Va.: Center for Applied Linguistics, 148–57.

Möhn, Dieter. 1977. Ziele und Ergebnisse der Fachsprachenforschung und der Terminologiearbeit. *Muttersprache* 2, 67–76.

Möhn, Dieter. 1981. Fach- und Gemeinsprache: Zur Emanzipation und Isolation der Sprache. In von Hahn, W. (ed.) *Fachsprachen.* Darmstadt: Wissenschaftliche Buchgesellschaft, 172–217.

Moore, J. L. 1910. *Tudor–Stuart Views on the Growth, Status, and Design of the English Language.* Halle a. S.: M. Niemeyer.

Moore, Wilbert E. 1961. The Social Framework of Economic Development. In Braibanti, R. and Spengler, J. J. (eds) *Tradition, Values and Socio-Economic Development.* Durham, NC: Duke University Press.

Moser, Hugo. 1971. Typen sprachlicher Ökonomie im heutigen Deutsch. In *Sprache und Gesellschaft.* Schriften des Instituts für deutsche Sprache in Mannheim, Jahrbuch 1970. Düsseldorf: Schwann, 89–117.

Mühlhäusler, Peter. 1982. Language and Communicational Efficiency: The Case of Tok Pisin. *Language and Communication* 2 (2), 105–21.

Mühlhäusler, Peter. 1986. *Pidgin and Creole Linguistics*. Oxford: Blackwell.

Murasaki Kyoko. 1976. *Karafuto Ainugo* [The Ainu language in Sachalin]. Tokyo: Kokusho kankôkai.

Murray, K. M. Elisabeth. 1977. *Caught in the Web of Words: James A. H. Murray and the Oxford English Dictionary*. New Haven and London: Yale University Press.

Nelde, Peter H. (ed.). 1980. *Languages in Contact and in Conflict*. Wiesbaden: F. Steiner.

Nelde, Peter H., Extra, G., Hartig, M., and de Vriendt, M.-J. (eds). 1981. *Sprachprobleme bei Gastarbeiterkindern*. Tübingen: Narr.

Neumann, Günther. 1965. Russonorwegisch und Pidginenglisch. *Nachrichten der Giessener Hochschulgesellschaft* 34, 219–32.

Neumann, Günther. 1966. Zur Chinesisch-Russischen Behelfssprache von Kjachta. *Sprache* 12, 237–51.

Neustupný, J. V. 1987. *Communicating with the Japanese*. Tokyo: The Japan Times.

Neustupný, J. V. 1989. *Strategies for Asia and Japan Literacy*. Melbourne: Japanese Studies Centre.

New Language Planning Newsletter 4, 2. Language Institute of Australia. December 1989, 3–5.

Ngũgĩ, W. T. 1986. *Decolonising the Mind: The Politics of Language in African Literature*. London: James Currey.

Nichigai Associates. 1988. *Honyaku toshomokuroku*, 3 vols. [Index of translated books]. Tokyo.

Nissen, Hans J. 1985. The Emergence of Writing in the Ancient Near East. *Interdisciplinary Science Reviews* 10 (4), 349–61.

Nissen, Hans J., Damerow, Peter, and Englund, Robert K. 1990. *Frühe Schrift und Techniken der Wirtschaftsverwaltung im alten Vorderen Orient*. Berlin: Verlag franzbecker.

Nohlen, Dieter (ed.). 1984. *Lexikon Dritte Welt*. Reinbek: Rowohlt.

Nyikos, Julius. 1988. A Linguistic Perspective on Illiteracy. In Empleton, S. (ed.) *The Fourteenth LACUS Forum 1987*. Lake Bluff, Ill.: Linguistic Association of Canada and the United States, 146–63.

O'Brien, Terence. 1979. Economic Support for Minority Languages. In Alcock, A. E., Taylor, B. K., and Welton, J. M. (eds) *The Future of Cultural Minorities*. London: The MacMillan Press, 82–101.

Ohta, Hiroshi. 1979. Language Barriers in Japan: An Economist's View. *International Social Science Journal* 31 (1), 79–85.

Oliver, Roland and Fage, J. D. 1978. *A Short History of Africa*. London: Pelican.

Olson, David R. 1970. Language and Thought: Aspects of a Cognitive Theory of Semantics. *Psychological Review* 77, 257–73.

Ong, Walter J. 1982. *Orality and Literacy: The Technologizing of the Word.* London, New York: Methuen.

Oppenheim, A. L. 1957. A Bird's-Eye View of Mesopotamian Economic History. In Polanyi, K., Arensberg, C. M., and Pearson, H. W. (eds) *Trade and Market in the Early Empires.* New York: The Free Press, 27–37.

Oppenheim, A. L. 1964. *Ancient Mesopotamia: Portrait of a Dead Civilization.* Chicago: University of Chicago Press.

Ó Riagáin, Pádraig. 1991. National and International Dimensions of Language Policy when the Minority Language is a National Language: The Case of Irish in Ireland. In Coulmas, F. (ed.) *A Language Policy for the European Community: Prospects and Quandaries.* Berlin, New York: Mouton de Gruyter, 255–77.

Ornstein-Galicia, Jacob L. 1989. Regressed or "Downgraded Varieties" of Language: A First Approach. In Ammon, U. (ed.) *Status and Function of Language and Language Varieties.* Berlin, New York: de Gruyter, 291–323.

Orwig, Dafydd. 1988. The Determination of the Basques. *Contact Bulletin* (Le Bureau Européen pour les langues moins répandues) 5 (1), 1f.

Oud de Glas, M. 1979. Les besoins langagiers aux Pay-Bas: Compte-rendu d'un projet de recherches. *Etudes de Linguistique Appliquée* 3, 86–94.

Oud de Glas, M. 1983. Foreign Language Needs: A Survey of Needs. In van Els, T. and Oud de Glas, M. (eds) *Research into Foreign Language Needs.* Augsburg: Universität, 19–34.

Oxenham, John. 1980. *Literacy: Writing, Reading and Social Organization.* London: Routledge and Kegan Paul.

Paget, Richard. 1930. *Babel or the Past, Present and Future of Human Speech.* London: Kegan Paul, Trench, Trubner and Co.

Panikkar, K. M. 1969. *Asia and Western Dominance.* New York: Collier Books.

Parsons, Talcott. 1960. *Structure and Process in Modern Society.* Glencoe, Illinois.

Parsons, Talcott. 1964. Evolutionary Universals. *American Sociological Review* 29 (3), 339–57.

Parsons, Talcott. 1977. *Social Systems and the Evolution of Action Theory.* New York: The Free Press.

Pasierbsky, Fritz. 1989. Adaptation Processes in Chinese: Word Formation. In Coulmas, F. (ed.) *Language Adaptation.* Cambridge, New York: Cambridge University Press, 90–103.

Pattanayak, P. D. 1981. *Multilingualism and Mother Tongue Education.* New Delhi: Oxford University Press.

Paul, Hermann. 1909. *Prinzipien der Sprachgeschichte.* Fourth edition. Halle a. S.: Max Niemeyer.

Pelikan, Pavel. 1989. Evolution, Economic Competence, and the Market for Corporate Control. *Journal of Economic Behavior and Organization* 12, 279–303.

Perren, G. E. and Holloway, M. F. 1965. *Language and Communication in the*

Commonwealth. London: Her Majesty's Stationary Office.

Personal Report for the Executive. 1986. Plain English Pays. Research Institute of America, 2.

Peters, Robert. 1987. Das Mittelniederdeutsche als Sprache der Hanse. In Ureland, P. S. (ed.) *Sprachkontakte in der Hanse: Aspekte des Sprachausgleichs im Ostsee- und Nordseeraum*. Tübingen: Niemeyer, 65–88.

Polanyi, Karl. 1957. Marketless Trading in Hammurabi's Time. In Polanyi, K., Arensberg, C. M., and Pearson, H. W. (eds) *Trade and Market in the Early Empires*. New York: The Free Press, 12–26.

Polenz, Peter von. 1978. *Geschichte der deutschen Sprache*. Ninth edition. Berlin, New York: de Gruyter.

Polomé, Edgar C. 1986. A Few Notes of Dutch Terms of Indian Origin. In Johansen, J. D. and Sonne, H. (eds) *Pragmatics and Linguistics: Festschrift for Jacob L. Mey*. Odense University Press, 141–50.

Pons-Ridler, Suzanne and Ridler, Neil B. 1987. The Territorial Concept of Official Bilingualism: A Cheaper Alternative for Canada. In Tonkin, H. and Johnson-Weiner, K. M. (eds) *The Economics of Language Use*. New York: Center for Research and Documentation on World Language Problems, 95–105.

Pool, Jonathan. 1972. National Development and Language Diversity. In Fishman, J. A. (ed.) *Advances in the Sociology of Language*, vol. 2. Den Haag: Mouton: 213–30.

Pool, Jonathan. 1990. Language Regimes and Political Regimes. In Weinstein, Brian (ed.) *Language Policy and Political Development*. Norwood, NJ: Ablex, 241–61.

Pool, Jonathan. 1991. Two Languages for the Price of One? The Propaedeutic Puzzle. *Esperantic Studies* 1, 2f.

Pope, Maurice. 1966. The Origin of Writing in the Near East. *Antiquity* 40, 17–23.

Pörksen, Uwe. 1989. The Transition from Latin to German in the Natural Sciences and its Consequences. In Coulmas, F. (ed.) *Language Adaptation*. Cambridge, London: Cambridge University Press, 127–134.

Powell, Marvin A. 1981. Three Problems in the History of Cuneiform Writing: Origins, Direction of Script, Literacy. *Visible Language* 15 (4), 419–40

Prentice, D. J. 1990. Malay (Indonesian and Malaysian). In Comrie, B. (ed.) *The Major Languages of East and South-East Asia*. London: Routledge, 185–207.

President's Commission on Foreign Language and International Studies. 1979. *Strength through Wisdom: A Critique of US Capability*. Washington, DC: US Government Printing Office.

Price, Glanville. 1979. The Present Position and Viability of Minority Languages. In Alcock, A. E., Taylor, B. K., and Welton, J. M. (eds)

The Future of Cultural Minorities. London: The MacMillan Press, 30–43.

Pride, John B. and Liu Ru-Shan. 1988. Some Aspects of the Spread of English in China since 1949. *International Journal of the Sociology of Language* 74, 41–70.

Quine, Willard Van Orman. 1960. *Word and Object.* Cambridge, Mass.: The MIT Press.

Rabin, Chaim. 1986. Language Revival and Language Death. In Fishman, J. A., Tabouret-Keller, A., Clyne, M., Krishnamurti, B., and Abdulaziz, M. (eds) *The Fergusonian Impact: In Honor of Charles A. Ferguson on the Occasion of His 65th Birthday.* Berlin, New York, Amsterdam: Mouton de Gruyter, vol. 2, 543–54.

Rabin, Chaim. 1989. Terminology Development in the Revival of a Language: The Case of Contemporary Hebrew. In Coulmas, F. (ed.) *Language Adaptation.* London: Cambridge University Press, 26–38.

Rawkins, Philip M. 1987. The Politics of Benign Neglect: Education, Public Policy, and the Mediation of Linguistic Conflict in Wales. *International Journal of the Sociology of Language* 66, 27–48.

Raynauld, André and Marion, Gérard 1972. Une analyse économique de la disparité inter-ethnique des revenus. *Revue Economique* 23, 1–19.

Reagan, Ronald. 1981. *Public Papers of President Ronald Reagan.* Washington, DC: US Government Printing Office.

Reinecke, John E. 1937. *Marginal Languages.* Unpublished PhD thesis, Yale University.

Renfrew, Colin. 1989. *Archeology and Language: The Puzzle of the Indo-European Origins.* London: Penguin.

Renouvin, M. Bertrand. 1989. L'utilité économique et commerciale de la language française: Rapport du Conseil Economique et Social. *Journal Officiel de la République Française.*

Richard, C. 1984. La langue française, garante de la diversité culturelle du monde. *Dialogue et Cultures* 26, 31–5.

Richards, I. A. 1943. *Basic English and its Uses.* London: Kegan Paul, Trench, Trubner.

Ridler, N. and Pons-Ridler, S. 1986. An Economic Analysis of Canadian Language Policies: A Model and its Implementation. *Language Problems and Language Planning* 10 (1), 42–58.

Rivarol, Antoine de. 1906. *Oeuvres choisies de A. Rivarol . . . avec une préface par M. de Lescure.* Paris: E. Flammarion.

Roaetxe, Karmele. 1991. Politique linguistique et norme basque. Paper presented at the symposium "Standardisation Linguistique", Académie Suisse des Sciences Humaines, April 15–22.

Robillard, Didier de. 1987. Vers une approche globale des rapports entre langue et économie. In *Langue et Economie: Colloque International.* CNRS, Université de Provence, 9–36.

Rollins, Richard M. 1980. *The Long Journey of Noah Webster.* University of Pennsylvania Press.

Romaine, Suzanne. 1988. Contributions from Pidgin and Creole Studies to a Sociolinguistic Theory of Language Change. *International Journal of the Sociology of Language* 71, 59–66.

Rossi-Landi, Ferruccio. 1968. *Il linguaggio come lavoro e come mercato.* Milano: Bompiani.

Rossi-Landi, Ferruccio. 1974. *Linguistics and Economics.* The Hague: Mouton.

Rubin, Joan. 1979. *Directory of Language Planning Organizations.* Honolulu: University of Hawaii Press.

Russell, Bertrand. 1918. The Philosophy of Logical Atomism. In Russell, B. *Logic and Knowledge: Essays 1901–1950.* 1956. Edited by Marsh, R. C. London: Allen and Unwin.

Sack, Ronald H. 1981. The Temple Scribe in Chaldean Uruk. *Visible Language* 15 (4), 409–18.

Saitô Tsuyoshi. 1977. *Meiji no kotoba: Higashi kara nishi e no kakebashi* [Words of the Meiji period: A bridge from East to West]. Tokyo: Kodansha.

Sakaguchi, Alicja. 1989. Towards a Clarification of the Function and Status of International Planned Languages. In Ammon, U. (ed.) *Status and Function of Languages and Language Varieties.* Berlin, New York: de Gruyter, 399–440.

Samarin, William J. 1968. Lingua Francas of the World. In Fishman, J. A. (ed.) *Readings in the Sociology of Language.* The Hague, Paris: Mouton, 660–72.

Samhaber, Ernst. 1964. *Das Geld: Eine Kulturgeschichte.* Munich: Keyser.

Sankoff, Gillian. 1979. The Genesis of a Language. In: Hill, K. C. (ed.) *The Genesis of Language.* Ann Arbor: Karoma, 23–47.

Sapir, Edward. 1921. *Language: An Introduction to the Study of Speech.* New York: Harcourt, Brace and World.

Saussure, Ferdinand de. 1972 [1916]. *Cours de linguistique générale.* Edition preparée par Tullio de Mauro. Paris: Payot. [English translation by W. Baskin. 1974. *Course in General Linguistics.* Glasgow: Collins].

Schaling, Frits. 1988. Voeren staat weer geheel centraal. *NRC–Handelsblad* September 14.

Scharff, A. 1942. Archäologische Beiträge zur Frage der Entstehung der Hieroglüphenschrift. *Sitzungsberichte der Bayerischen Akademie der Wissenschaften, philologisch-historische Abteilung,* Heft 3.

Scheler, Max. 1921. *Der Formalismus in der Ethik und die materiale Wertethik.* Halle: M. Niemeyer.

Schenkel, Wolfgang. 1983. Wozu die Ägypter eine Schrift brauchten. In Assmann, A., Assmann, J., and Hardmeier, C. (eds) *Schrift und Gedächtnis: Beiträge zur Archäologie der literarischen Kommunikation.* Munich: Fink, 45–63.

Schiffman, Harold F. 1990. The Balance of Power in Multiglossic Languages: Implications for Language Shift. *University of Washington Language and Society*

Papers LD4.

Schirmer, Alfred. 1911. *Wörterbuch der deutschen Kaufmannssprache, auf geschichtlichen Grundlagen.* Strasbourg: Verlag von Karl J. Trübner.

Schleicher, August. 1873. *Die Darwinsche Theorie und die Sprachwissenschaft.* Weimar.

Schlick, Moritz. 1934. Über das Fundament der Erkenntnis. *Erkenntnis* 4: 79–99.

Schmandt-Besserat, Denise. 1978. The Earliest Precursors of Writing. *Scientific American* 238, 50–9.

Schmandt-Besserat, Denise. 1979. Reckoning before Writing. *Archeology* 32, 23–31.

Schmölders, Claudia (ed.). 1979. *Die Kunst des Gesprächs: Texte zur Geschichte der europäischen Konversationstheorie.* Munich: dtv.

Scotton, Carol Myers. 1982. Learning Lingua Francas and Socio-economic Integration: Evidence from Africa. In Cooper, Robert L. (ed.) *Language Spread.* Bloomington, In.: Indiana University Press, 63–94.

Searle, John. 1984. *Minds, Brains and Science.* Cambridge, Mass.: Harvard University Press.

Seckinger, Beverly. 1988. Implementing Morocco's Arabization Policy: Two Problems of Classification. In Coulmas, F. (ed.) *With Forked Tongues: What Are National Languages Good For?* Ann Arbor: Karoma, 68–90.

Seelow, Frank. 1990. Geldwandel und Welthandel. *Universitas* 4, 322–7.

Seibicke, Wilfried. 1959. Fachsprache und Gemeinsprache. *Muttersprache* 69, 70–84.

Siegel, J. 1989. English in Fiji. *World Englishes* 8 (1), 47–58.

Simmel, Georg. 1977 [1907]. *Philosophie des Geldes.* Berlin: Duncker & Humboldt. [*The Philosophy of Money.* English translation by T. Bottomore and D. Frisby. 1978. London: Routledge and Kegan Paul.]

Simon, Paul. 1980. *The Tongue-tied American: Confronting the Foreign Language Crisis.* New York: Continuum.

Simpson, David. 1986. *The Politics of American English, 1776–1850.* New York, Oxford: Oxford University Press.

Skudlik, Sabine. 1990. *Sprachen in der Wissenschaft: Die Stellung des Deutschen und die Anglophonie in der internationalen Kommunikation.* Tübingen: Narr.

Skutnabb-Kangas, T. and Phillipson, R. 1989. "Mother Tongue": The Theoretical and Sociopolitical Construction of a Concept. In Ammon, U. (ed.) *Status and Function of Languages and Language Varieties.* Berlin, New York: de Gruyter, 450–77.

Slaughter, M. M. 1985. Literacy and Society. *International Journal of the Sociology of Language* 56, 113–39.

Smith, Adam. 1759. Considerations Concerning the First Formation of Languages. Addendum to *The Theory of Moral Sentiments.* Third edition, London: Strahan and Cadell, vol. 2, 401–62.

Smith, Adam. 1904. *An Inquiry into the Nature and Causes of the Wealth of Nations*. London: Methuen.

Solèr, Clau. 1986. Ist das Domleschg zweisprachig? *Bündner Monatsblatt* 11–12, 283–300.

Solla Price, Derek J. de. 1963. *Little Science, Big Science*. New York: Columbia University Press.

Spencer, John. 1985. Language and Development: The Unequal Equation. In Wolfson, N. and Manes, J. (eds) *Language of Inequality*. Berlin, New York, Amsterdam: Mouton, 387–97.

Spengler, Oswald. 1922. *Der Untergang des Abendlandes*, vol. 2. Munich: C. H. Beck.

Srivastava, R. N. 1984a. Literacy Education for Minorities: A Case Study from India. In Coulmas, F. (ed.) *Linguistic Minorities and Literacy*. Berlin, New York: Mouton, 39–46.

Srivastava, R. N. 1984b. Consequences of Initiating Literacy in the Second Language. In Coulmas, F. (ed.) *Linguistic Minorities and Literacy*. Berlin, New York: Mouton, 29–37.

Stadermann, H. J. 1988. *Weltwirtschaft*. Tübingen: J. C. B. Mohr [UTB 1510].

Stalpers, Judith. 1992. *Progress in Discourse: The Impact of Foreign Language Use on Business Talk*. PhD Thesis, Tilburg University.

Starr, P. and Roberts, A. 1982. Community Structure and Vietnamese Refugee Adaptation: The Significance of Context. *International Migration Review* 16 (3), 595–619.

Steiner, George. 1975. *After Babel*. London: Oxford University Press.

Steinke, Klaus. 1979. Die sprachliche Situation der deutschen Minderheit in Rumänien. In Ureland, P. S. (ed.) *Standardsprache und Dialekt in mehrsprachigen Gebieten Europas*. Tübingen: Niemeyer (Linguistische Arbeiten 82), 183–203.

Strassner, Erich. 1986. Dialekt als Ware. *Zeitschrift für Dialektologie und Linguistik* 53 (3), 310–42.

Strevens, P. 1982. World English and the World's English: or, Whose Language is it anyway? *Journal of the Royal Society of the Arts* (June), 418–31.

Stubbs, Michael. 1991. Educational Language Planning in England and Wales: Multi-Cultural Rhetoric and Assimilationist Assumptions. In Coulmas, F. (ed.) *A Language Policy for the European Community: Prospects and Quandaries*. Berlin, New York: Mouton de Gruyter, 215–39.

Sturm, Dietrich. 1987. Deutsch als Fremdsprache im Ausland. In Sturm, D. (ed.) *Deutsch als Fremdsprache in der Welt: Situationen und Tendenzen*. Munich: Hueber, 11–25.

Tabouret-Keller, Andrée (ed.). 1981. Regional Languages in France. *International Journal of the Sociology of Language* 29.

Tabouret-Keller, Andrée. 1991a. Some Major Features of the Sociolinguistic

Situation in Europe and the European Charter on Regional and Minority Languages. In *Sociolinguistics Today: International Perspectives*. London: Routledge for University of Hong Kong.

Tabouret-Keller, Andrée. 1991b. Factors of Constraints and Freedom in Setting a Language Policy for the European Community: A Sociolinguistic Approach. In Coulmas, F. (ed.) *A Language Policy for the European Community: Prospects and Quandaries*. Berlin, New York: Mouton de Gruyter, 45–57.

Takakura, S. 1960. The Ainu of Northern Japan: A Study in Conquest and Acculturation. *Transactions of the Philosophical Society of Philadelphia* 50 (4).

Taylor, Douglas. 1968. New Languages for Old in the West Indies. In Fishman, J. A. (ed.) *Readings in the Sociology of Language*. The Hague, Paris: Mouton, 607–19.

Teeuw, A. 1959. The History of the Malay Language. *Bijdragen tot de Taal-, Land- en Volkenkunde* Bd. 115 (2), 138–56.

Thelen, Peter and Reinhold, Richard S. 1981. Language Training in Industry: The Case of Ford Werke Aktiengesellschaft (Germany). In Freudenstein, R., Beneke, J., and Pönisch, H. (eds) *Language Incorporated: Teaching Foreign Languages in Industry*. Oxford, New York: Pergamon Press, 143–50.

Thorburn, Thomas. 1971. Cost-Benefit Analysis in Language Planning. In Rubin, J. and Jernudd, B. H. (eds). 1971. *Can Language be Planned?* Honolulu: The University of Hawaii Press, 253–62.

Timm, Leonora A. 1980. Bilingualism, Diglossia and Language Shift in Brittany. *International Journal of the Sociology of Language* 25, 29–41.

Todd, Loreto. 1974. *Pidgins and Creoles*. London: Routledge & Kegan Paul.

Todd, Loreto. 1984. *Modern Englishes: Pidgins and Creoles*. Oxford: Blackwell.

Todorov, Tzvetan. 1982. *La conquête de l'amerique: La question de l'autre*. Paris: Editions du Seuil.

Tovey, Hilary. 1988. The State and the Irish Language: The Role of Bord na Gaeilge. *International Journal of the Sociology of Language* 70, 53–68.

Toynbee, Arnold J. 1965 [1946]. *A Study of History*. New York: Dell.

Trubetzkoy, N. S. 1958. *Grundzüge der Phonologie*. Göttingen: Vandenhoek & Ruprecht [sixth edition 1977].

Truchot, Claude. 1990. *L'anglais dans le monde contemporain*. Paris: Le Robert.

Trudgill, Peter. 1977. Creolization in Reverse: Reduction and Simplification in the Albanian Dialects of Greece. *Transactions of the Philological Society 1976/77*, 32–50.

Tsuda Aoi. 1984. *Sales Talk in Japan and the United States*. Washington, DC: Georgetown University Press.

Turnbull, P. W. and Cunningham, M. T. 1981. *International Marketing and Purchasing*. London: Macmillan Press.

Umiker-Sebeok, Jean (ed.) 1987. *Marketing and Semiotics: New Directions in the Study of Signs for Sale*. Berlin, New York: Mouton de Gruyter.

UNESCO. 1964. *World Literacy Programme*. Paris: UNESCO.

UNESCO. 1965. *Literacy as a Factor in Development*. Paris: UNESCO, Minedlit 3.

UNESCO. 1982. *Planning of Literacy Programmes*. Bangkok: UNESCO Regional Office for Education in Asia and the Pacific.

Ureland, P. S. (ed.). 1978. *Standardsprache und Dialekte in mehrsprachigen Gebieten Europas*. Tübingen: Niemeyer.

Ureland, P. S. 1987. Einleitung. In Ureland, P. S. (ed.) *Sprachkontakte in der Hanse: Aspekte des Sprachausgleichs im Ostsee- und Nordseeraum*. Tübingen: Niemeyer, vii–xxxiii.

Ureland, P. Sture (ed.). 1987. *Sprachkontakte in der Hanse: Aspekte des Sprachausgleichs im Ostsee- und Nordseeraum*. Tübingen: Niemeyer.

Vaillancourt, François. 1978. La charte de la langue française du Québec: Un essai d'analyse. *Canadian Public Policy/Analyse de politiques* 4, 284–308.

Vaillancourt, François. 1987. The Costs and Benefits of Language Policies in Québec, 1974–1984: Some Partial Estimates.In Tonkin, H. and Johnson-Weiner, K. M. (eds) *The Economics of Language Use*. New York: Center for Research and Documentation on World Language Problems, 71–93.

Vaillancourt, François. 1988. Le statut économique du français et des fracophones au Québec. *Interface* September/October, 23–27.

Vaillancourt, François. 1991. The Economics of Language: Theory, Empiricism and Application to the Asian Pacific. In Coulmas, Florian (ed.) *The Economics of Language in the Asian Pacific*. *Journal of Asian Pacific Communication*, vol. 2, 29–44.

Van de Craen, Pete and Willemyns, Roland. 1988. The Standardization of Dutch in Flanders. In Stalpers, J. and Coulmas, F. (eds) *The Sociolinguistics of Dutch: International Journal of the Sociology of Language* 73, 45–64.

Van Langendonck, Willy. 1988. Categories of Word-Order Iconicity. Paper presented at the 12th International Congress of Anthropological and Ethnological Sciences, Zagreb 1988.

Van Sommers, Peter. 1989. Where Writing Starts: The Analysis of Action Applied to the Historical Development of Writing. Paper presented at the Fourth International Graphonomics Society Conference, Trondheim, July 1989.

Vanstiphout, H. L. J. 1979. How Did They Learn Sumerian? *Journal of Cuneiform Studies* 21, 118–30.

Verdoodt, Albert. 1980. Maintien de la langue: Substitution de la langue et développement socio-économique. *Grazer Linguistische Studien* 11, 326–35.

Vestergaard, Torben and Schröder, Kim (1985). *The Language of Advertising*. Oxford: Blackwell.

Viereck, Wolfgang. 1988. The Political and Technological Impact of the United States in the 1950's and Early 1960's as Reflected in Several European Languages. *Folia Linguistica* 21 (1–2), 141–52.

Vollmer, Jürgen. 1989. Eurotra: Goals, Organization and Framework Design.

Terminologie et Traduction 1. Luxembourg: Office of Official Publications of the European Communities, 85–95.

Voloshinov, Valentin N. 1973. *Marxism and the Philosophy of Language.* New York: Seminar Press. (First Russian edition 1929.)

Voorhoeve, Jan. 1983. De oorsprong van het Surinaams. In Charry, E., Koefoed, G., and Muysken, P. (eds) *De talen van Suriname.* Muiderberg: Coutinho, 38–46.

Vos, F. 1963. Dutch Influences on the Japanese Language. *Lingua* 12, 341–88.

Vossler, Karl. 1925. *Geist und Kultur in der Sprache.* Heidelberg: Carl Winter's Universitätsbuchhandlung.

Ward, W. A. 1964. Relations between Egypt and Mesopotamia from Prehistoric Times to the End of the Middle Kingdom. *Journal of the Economics and Social History of the Orient* 7, 1–45, 121–135.

Wardhaugh, Ronald. 1987. *Languages in Competition.* Oxford: Blackwell.

Watanabe Osamu. 1989. Internationalisierung und die zweite Fremdsprache. In Bauer, H. L. (ed.) *Deutsch als zweite Fremdsprache in der gegenwärtigen japanischen Gesellschaft.* Munich: Iudicium Verlag, 44–55.

Wattenberg, Ulrich. 1985. Die fünfte Computergeneration. *Versicherungsbetrieb* 1, 17–22.

Weber, E. 1976. *Peasants into Frenchmen: The Modernization of Rural France 1870–1914.* Palo Alto: Stanford University Press.

Weber, Max. 1920. *Gesammelte Aufsätze zur Religionssoziologie.* Band 1. Tübingen: J. C. B. Mohr.

Weber, Max. 1924. *Wirtschaftsgeschichte: Abriss der universalen Sozial- und Wirtschaftsgeschichte.* Edited by S. Hellmann and M. Palyi. Munich and Leipzig: Duncker & Humbolt.

Weber, Max. 1930. *The Protestant Ethic and the Spirit of Capitalism.* Translated by Talcott Parsons. New York: Charles Scribner and Sons.

Weber, Max. 1956. *Wirtschaft und Gesellschaft: Grundriss der verstehenden Soziologie.* Fourth edition prepared by H. Winckelmann. Tübingen: J. C. B. Mohr. [*Economy and Society.* Edited by Guenther Roth and Claus Wittich, 2 vols. Berkeley, Los Angeles, London: University of California Press, 1978].

Webster, Noah. 1789. *Dissertations on the English Language, with an Essay on a Reformed Mode of Spelling.* Boston.

Webster, Noah 1802. *Miscellaneous Papers on Political and Commercial Subjects.* New York.

Webster, Noah. 1806. *Compendious Dictionary of the English Language, in which Five Thousand Words are Added to the Number Found in the Best English Compends.* Hartford and New Haven.

Weinreich, Uriel. 1966. *Languages in Contact: Findings and Problems.* London, The Hague: Mouton.

Weinrich, Harald. 1958. Münze und Wort: Untersuchungen an einem Bildfeld. *Romanica. Festschrift Rohlfs.* Halle, 508–21.

Weinrich, Harald. 1985. *Wege dere Sprachkultur*. Stuttgart: Deutsche Verlags-Anstalt.

Weinstein, Brian. 1983. *The Civic Tongue: Political Consequences of Language Choices*. New York: Longman.

Weinstein, Brian. 1990. Language Policy and Political Development: An Overview. In Weinstein, Brian (ed.) *Language Policy and Political Development*. Norwood, NJ: Ablex, 1–21.

Weisgerber, Leo. 1962. *Die sprachliche Gestaltung der Welt*. Düsseldorf: Schwann.

Wesseling, H. L. 1988. *Indië verloren, rampspoed geboren: En andere opstellen over de geschiedenis van de Europese expansie*. Amsterdam: Bert Bakker.

Whinnom, Keith. 1971. Linguistic Hybridization and the 'Special Case' of Pidgins and Creoles. In Hymes, Dell (ed.) *Pidginization and Creolization of Languages*. London: Cambridge University Press, 91–115.

Whinnom, Keith. 1977. The Context and Origin of Lingua Franca. In Meisel, J. (ed.) *Pidgins, Creoles, Languages in Contact*. Tübingen: Narr, 3–18.

Williams, Glyn. 1987. Bilingualism, Class Dialect, and Social Reproduction. *International Journal of the Sociology of Language* 66, 85–98.

Williamson, R. C. and van Eerde, J. A. (ed.). 1980. Language Maintenance and Language Shift. *International Journal of the Sociology of Language* 25.

Winter, Werner. 1983. Tradition and Innovation in Alphabet Making. In Coulmas, F. and Ehlich, K. (eds) *Writing in Focus*. Berlin, New York: Mouton, 227–38.

Witte, Barthold. 1987. Was ist los mit der deutschen Sprache? *Frankfurter Allgemeine Zeitung*, July 8, 7.

Witte, Barthold. 1989. "Ein Schlüssel zum Verständnis unseres Landes in der Welt." Bonn gibt jährlich rund 450 Millionen DM für die Sprachförderung aus. *Bildung und Wissenschaft* 9–10 Bonn: INTERNATIONES, 16–21.

Wittgenstein, Ludwig. 1960. *Philosophische Untersuchungen*. Frankfurt/M.: Suhrkamp.

Woll, Artur. 1981. *Allgemeine Volkswirtschaftslehre*, 7th edition. Munich: Beck.

World Almanac and Book of Facts 1987. New York: World Almanac.

Wurm, Stephen A. 1977. Pidgins, Creoles, Lingue Franche, and National Development. In Valdman, A. (ed.) *Pidgin and Creole Linguistics*. Bloomington: Indiana University Press, 333–357.

Wüster, Eugen. 1959. Die internationale Angleichung der Fachausdrücke. *Elektrotechnische Zeitschrift* 80 (16), 550–2.

Wüster, Eugen. 1979. *Einführung in die allgemeine Terminologie und terminologische Lexikographie*. 2 vols. Vienna, New York: Springer.

Wyler, Siegfried. 1987. On Definitions in LSP. In Sprissler, M. (ed.) *Standpunkte der Fachsprachenforschung*. Tübingen: Narr, 79–90.

Yanabu Akira. 1977. *Honyaku no shisô: "Shizen" to "nature"* [The Spirit of Translation. "Shizen" and "nature"]. Tokyo: Heibonsha.

Zeisberger, David. 1830. A Grammar of the Language of the Lenni Lenape or Delaware Indians. Translation of P. S. Du Ponceau. *Transactions of the American Philosophical Society*, 3, 65–251. Philadelphia.

Zentella Ana Celia. 1988. Language Politics in the USA. In: Craige, B. J. (ed.) *Literature, Language, and Politics*. Athens, GA: University of Georgia Press, 39–53.

Zgusta, L. 1971. *Manual of Lexicography*. The Hague: Mouton.

Zhu Wanjin and Chen Jianmin. 1991. Some Economic Aspects of the Language Situation in China. In: Coulmas, Florian (ed.) *The Economics of Language in the Asian Pacific. Journal of Asian Pacific Communication*, vol. 2, 91–101.

Zipf, George Kingsley. 1949. *Human Behavior and the Principle of Least Effort: An Introduction to Human Ecology*. New York: Hafner.

Index of Names

Index of Subjects